The Psychology of
Open Teaching and Learning

An Inquiry Approach

The Psychology of Open Teaching and Learning

An Inquiry Approach

Edited by

Melvin L. Silberman

Jerome S. Allender

Jay M. Yanoff

Temple University

Little, Brown and Company
Boston

372.13
S 582

Preface

Since the first news of the educational revolution in British schools, the desire for more open ways of teaching children has been rapidly increasing. In place of the closed and prescriptive structures found in our classrooms today, educators are seeking alternatives that would allow students to become personally involved in the learning process and to develop inquiry skills for dealing with constantly growing and changing bodies of knowledge.

Effective changes in our approach to teaching and learning will not come, however, without a careful examination of the psychology behind open education. Understanding the outlook of psychologists such as Jerome Bruner, Abraham Maslow, Jean Piaget, and Carl Rogers is important for anyone who wants to encourage student involvement and inquiry activity. Moreover, a sufficient grasp of their views cannot be attained by traditional modes of instruction. Just as our understanding of children suggests that they acquire knowledge by their own inquiries into the world around them, we must also recognize that an examination of the psychology of open teaching and learning has to be a process of personal exploration. Thus the book is designed to enable the reader to conduct this inquiry through his own questions and concerns.

This book is adaptable to the needs of various education courses and in-service programs. Although its most logical use may be as an educational psychology text, it should also be a helpful vehicle for inquiry in any course or workshop concerned with actively involving students in the learning process. At the same time, the book is suitable for a wide range of purposes—from independent study to a program for large groups. In contrast to the typical book of readings, it contains extensive activity suggestions and guidelines for inquiring into its contents. In addition, the readings cover a broader range of issues and views than do other books on open education.

The Psychology of Open Teaching and Learning is an out-growth of three years of experience in restructuring a course on the teaching-learning process. Our goal has been to create an opportunity for education students to investigate problems in teaching and learning in ways that demonstrate the value of student-directed inquiry. To enable us to develop and do research on our teaching program during this time, we have had generous support from the College of Education at Temple University and the Esso Education Foundation. Their assistance has also allowed us to create a Center for Student-Directed Learning that serves as a base for helping beginning course instructors as well as people working in open schools in the area.

Staff members of the Center and student volunteers have contributed significantly to the selection of readings and the creation and testing of inquiry materials that comprise this book. The work of the following people is greatly appreciated: Robert Allender, Charles Fischer, Rhoni Groff, Earle Knowlton, Joanna Mason, John Matter, Kathleen Murphy, Gail Stern, Barbara Tracer, Cecilia Tyler, and Patricia Wisch. The capable assistance of Susan Doroff, Janet Katz, John Matter, and Gail Stern in preparing the final manuscript should be acknowledged as well. We are also indebted to the authors and publishers who gave us permission to have their articles and book excerpts reproduced. Finally, to the hundreds of students who have experienced the materials in this book, we feel a deep sense of gratitude for their encouragement of our endeavors and for their invaluable feedback.

Contents

Part 2/Cognitive Functioning   97

Part 3/The Teaching Process 213

The Psychology of
Open Teaching and Learning

An Inquiry Approach

Orientation

To anyone preparing to be a teacher, studying the psychology of the teaching-learning process should be of utmost importance. Yet it is often a meaningless exercise, especially when a course of study does not directly attack the problems of classroom teaching. The aim of this book, therefore, is to facilitate a problem-oriented investigation of teaching and learning, to aid pre-service and in-service teachers in making personal decisions about their classrooms. The problems posed here represent the obstacles usually encountered by a teacher who seeks to guide optimal growth and real learning. The materials and activities included will enable a student of the teaching-learning process to personally resolve many of the questions and issues that underlie these problems.

Our purpose is not to examine every major problem in teaching and learning. We have chosen instead to help the reader inquire into topics of study that are relevant to the concept of open teaching and learning. An open approach to the teaching-learning process recognizes the valid wish of every student to be involved in some way in the direction of his own learning. It respects children's natural impulse to learn and understands the ways they gain and create knowledge. Of special concern, it changes the function of a teacher from "telling information" to one of providing choice and facilitating inquiry activity. However, to view open teaching and learning as a method in which a teacher may be trained is to oversimplify. Unless a teacher understands the psychological bases of this approach and develops his own conception of it, making classroom applications will be difficult. Furthermore, careful inquiry into the psychology of open teaching and learning requires general consideration of the environmental conditions and thinking skills necessary for learning and of how this knowledge might be applicable in many different circumstances. For these reasons we have chosen our particular bias; it includes a broad view of the teaching-learning process and at the same time is relevant to some of the most current educational ideas.

Our bias is not limited to the nature of the concepts in this book. We assume that learning is a meaningful experience only when the learner is personally involved in his own inquiry. Toward this end, we have included activity choices, which can be used to structure an inquiry into the resource material provided. This is a radical departure from the typical book of readings. Even though most teachers did not learn under open conditions when they were students, these activities and the book as a whole can be used to create such an experience, and the student of teaching can increase his ability to bring this approach to learning into his own classroom.

Subject Matter

Each of the three parts of the book is devoted to an important content area in the teaching-learning process. These areas are broadly defined in order to permit a wide range of exploration and to increase the possibility of integrating the materials with other, more detailed ways of organizing a course about teaching and learning. Although the order of the content areas may be altered, the sequence in which we have presented them is meant to structure the overall inquiry.

3

Part 1: The Learning Environment

The first content area is concerned with the psychological factors that allow and encourage student involvement in learning. The emphasis in this part is on the motivational drives and emotional needs of the learner and the classroom conditions that are responsive to them. Three issues are highlighted: how involvement in learning is stimulated and inhibited, how the interpersonal qualities of teachers affect the learner, and how much and what kind of direction students should give to the learning process.

Part 2: Cognitive Functioning

The second content area refers to the processes by which knowledge is gained and created, and it focuses on the cognitive factors that foster intellectual growth. The goal of this part is to enable the student to examine the ways the mind functions, in order to understand how principles of effective teaching can be developed. The major areas identified as starting points for inquiry are: how the brain processes information; how people solve problems, make discoveries, and create new ideas; and the skills needed in order for meaningful learning to occur.

Part 3: The Teaching Process

The third content area is concerned with approaching teaching in ways that are responsive to the emotional needs and cognitive functioning of the learner. The focus is on the role of the teacher in creating an open learning environment and stimulating inquiry activity. Issues treated in detail are: how to structure learning experiences, how to utilize innovative instructional materials and programs, and how to establish teacher-student dialogue.

It may be helpful to think about the inter-relationship between these three content areas. In general, the focus of the first two content areas is the emotional and cognitive characteristics of the learner. The last content area, in contrast, is concerned with the teaching processes that are responsive to these views of the learner.

Inquiry Materials

In each part of the book are materials to be used to guide an inquiry into a content area.

The Problem:

Each content area is introduced by a brief discussion of the area's meaning and relevance to teachers. These remarks include a statement of a major problem on the basis of which an inquiry into the content area can be focused. Each of the problems represents a basic issue that teachers must confront in their work: How does a learning environment stimulate growth without undermining students' need for security? How does a teacher help rather than interfere with the mental processes of the learner? How can a teacher guide his students without inhibiting their initiative and assumption of responsibility?

4

Initiating Activities:

The problem statement for each content area is followed by four initiating activities, the purpose of which is to enable the reader to experience and reflect upon aspects of the major problem and, as a result, become sensitive to personally felt questions related to the central issues. The activities accomplish this by eliciting thoughts about the problem and encouraging the identification of conflicting ideas, those that lack supporting evidence and those that seem to require further development. The initiating activities are designed for individual, small group, or whole class use, and they employ techniques such as role playing, simulated problem situations, rating scales, and speculative discussion. These choices are provided to show alternative ways of viewing the problem. The selection of initiating activities depends on particular circumstances. An instructor may also create his own activities on the basis of ideas generated by those provided.

Topics of Study:

The purpose of this section is to help students identify study topics relevant to the ideas and questions arising from the initiating experiences. Readings for each content area have been divided into three categories, each of which focuses on specific issues. Each topic is presented with comments about the problems it treats, a list of discussion questions, and an annotated list of the suggested readings.

Inquiry Activities:

Recommendations are given here for planning activities that facilitate a search into the readings for information and ideas relevant to the inquiry being conducted in a content area. The six inquiry activities can be used to structure group discussions or individual study related to the major ideas in the readings.

Readings:

The readings themselves have been chosen for their relevance to the specific problems of each content area and their general contribution to the concept of open teaching and learning. Within each part of the book, there is a balance between theoretical and descriptive material. An introductory article by one of the editors accompanies each group of readings. Its purpose is to provide a general discussion of problems and ideas concerning the content area. Overall, the readings emphasize ways of thinking about critical issues rather than convey basic information or research findings.

Additional Resources:

A list of resource material which supplements the readings in each content area is provided. It contains not only books and articles but also films and other instructional materials.

Resolution Activity:

At the end of each content area, a resolution activity calls for integration and application of the ideas generated in the inquiry by means of an analysis of a specific situation illustrating the major problem stated at the beginning of the content area.

Feedback:
The reader will find a short feedback form at the end of each part of the book which can be used by the instructor to appraise the needs and feelings of students, and which can be a basis for a class review of the inquiry undertaken for a particular content area.

Various uses of these materials are possible. Generally speaking, however, there are two basic alternatives, the choice depending on the purposes of the course in which this book is being utilized. Some instructors may decide to treat the book as a collection of readings supplementing regular class activities. This alternative is especially attractive when an instructor wishes to involve his students in independent study as part of their work outside of class. The problem statements and initiating activities can be examined to acquaint the student with the issues discussed in the readings as well as to help him discover the problems he wishes to explore. The topics of study will help guide his choice of readings. The grouping of readings into three categories allows for different options. One is to work with only one group, a plan that would be most suitable when time is unusually limited or when a student's interests are specific. Another option is to use two or three groups of readings and to determine in what sequence they should be explored. This plan is appropriate when there is a desire to cover most or all of the topics of study. Still another option is to create an original topic of study, using all the readings that are helpful and adding others as needed. This plan makes the most sense when the readings must be adapted to a particular line of investigation. Regardless of which option is chosen, the student should find among the inquiry and resolution activities tasks that help him evaluate and integrate ideas in the readings he has selected.

The second alternative is to consider the book as an inquiry guide for directing class activities. In this approach, the materials are used to guide a class inquiry into each content area. For example, the problem statement and initiating activities are employed to involve students in the inquiry by encouraging problem sensing and the discovery of interests. The topics of study and inquiry activities are utilized to aid the formulation of goals and the direction of the inquiry. The readings and the additional resources are approached as sources of information and ideas relevant to the inquiry. And, finally, the resolution activity and feedback form are viewed as ways to help bring together students' thinking in order to resolve the issues with which the class inquiry began.

When the inquiry materials are used in this manner, an effort should be made to create an inquiry experience having some focus and continuity. A deliberate process of determining goals, choosing resource materials, and planning activities is needed. Forming goals is important in establishing the direction of the inquiry; when goals are ignored, it is not possible to determine what questions and information are relevant. Choosing resource materials is necessary to facilitate a search for information likely to lead to the achievement of the inquiry's goals. Planning activities is critical for defining the procedures to be used in arriving at meaningful resolutions to the formulated problems.

To begin this process, each topic of study should be considered in an effort to find among the listed questions and readings those related to thoughts and interests sparked by the initiating activities. With these relationships in mind, it is then meaningful to ask what might be accomplished as a result of an inquiry. The answer might be issues that require better understanding, skills that need to be developed, or specific problems in teaching that must be resolved. With goals tentatively set, readings holding the most promise for contributing to the inquiry can be selected. Activity planning can begin by searching the selected readings for information and ideas that pertain to the goals that have been formed. Treating the readings as resource material is different from the typical practice of studying and discussing readings as an end in themselves, isolated from any central purpose. Searching for information does not imply, however, that a cursory look at the readings will be sufficient. On the contrary, when a reading is important to a particular inquiry, it may be necessary to analyze specific sections closely, even at the risk of ignoring other parts. Within an inquiry approach, it is also feasible to treat selected readings as background material. Activities would then be planned to gather information from sources such as lectures, tapes, films, classroom observations, simple experiments, standardized tests, and other instructional materials. Careful attention, though, has to be paid to how such resources will be used in an activity. The worth of a film, a lecture, or an experiment, for example, is greatly limited when there is little opportunity to relate the information gained to an ongoing inquiry.

Whenever possible, activities should be designed so that major ideas and concepts can be experienced and tested. Experiencing ideas is necessary for a fuller understanding of their meaning. For example, an intellectual grasp of the concepts of defense mechanisms and mental sets is not the same as experiencing one's own defensiveness when placed in a threatening situation and one's inability to solve what seems to be a simple problem. Testing ideas is important to establish their relevance. A theory may seem impressive on the surface, but it may not be helpful when used to explain a classroom event or to remedy a problem. Generally speaking, activities planned to experience or test ideas are very involving. They do require, however, careful and creative planning. To assist in carrying out such activities, the six activity plans provided for each content area are of special value. They explore many of the major ideas and concepts likely to arise during the search process. It should be possible to select a few of them for use in planning almost any inquiry that might be developed.

Having pursued a coordinated set of inquiry activities, a point is reached where it makes sense to bring together any insights acquired into some tangible form of resolution. This last step in the inquiry process should be addressed productively to the major problem with which study of the content area was initiated. Complete resolution of the problem may not be possible, but there will at least be a new level of understanding for anyone who has participated in the inquiry. The resolution activities can be used to achieve a productive resolution.

Direct class use of the inquiry materials necessitates active student involvement in directing the inquiry. However, student-directed activity can be organized and guided in different ways to meet the needs of a particular course. To orient both instructors and students to these possibilities, we now turn to a consideration of alternative ways of structuring a course based on the inquiry materials that have been provided.

Approaches to Student-Directed Learning

Since its beginning in 1969, the Center for Student-Directed Learning at Temple University (with which we are associated) has maintained a program to prepare teachers to involve their future students in the teaching-learning process. The plan of training and research that has been followed is intentionally quite broad and has not been limited to a single style of teaching. As a result, the generation of ideas about ways of structuring student-directed inquiry activities that are particularly applicable to education courses and in-service workshops has been continuous. Out of this experience have come three basic models of student direction. Each is described in terms of a college course, but modifications for in-service workshops and other settings should be easily managed.

Teacher-guided Student Direction:

This approach mainly involves inquiry activities undertaken by a class as a whole; small group activities and individual projects can be helpful at some points, but they are not critical. Reliance on large group activities ensures that the instructor has adequate opportunity to give direction, participate, criticize, and make suggestions. Initially, the instructor makes choices for the class from his position of expertise and from his early knowledge of class interests and needs. Midway through the course, deliberate attempts can be made to show students where they can easily contribute to the planning and direction of activities. Toward the end, students can be encouraged to do more of the planning. Throughout the course, however, students may expect the teacher to be responsible for providing direct guidance, when needed, at every point in an inquiry.

An instructor could begin a teacher-guided class by selecting for the first content area initiating activities suitable for a large group discussion. He would then integrate the students' ideas with his own and begin planning. For example, the instructor might ask his students to write him a note indicating ideas they felt are confusing, contradictory, and needing further development. On the basis of these notes and of his own interests and goals, the instructor could choose topics of study and readings as well as select inquiry activities for the class, or he might present alternative plans to the class for discussion and possible modification. Perhaps the first activity would consist of a lecture that provided some basic theory and information — as would be found in any typical course. Throughout the first content area, the instructor could invite student feedback to test whether his plans are responsive to students' needs. Thus the second content area could be based on the instructor's knowledge of the students' readiness and interests. After initiating the second content area, however, he could involve students more actively in planning. For example, after previewing topics of study, students could chose the questions and readings they wished to pursue and plan a few of the activities themselves. By the third content area, students could go through the entire planning, as a class, in small groups, or perhaps as individuals. Their plans would be subject to the advice and criticism of the instructor, but after some negotiation was completed, students might also take over the leadership of activities or engage in independent study. The instructor would have to intervene only when he felt his guidance was necessary or appropriate.

Group-planned Student Direction:

This approach utilizes small groups that plan their own inquiry in consultation with the instructor. Each group meets on a regular basis as if it were a class, only occasionally meeting with the other groups or working on independent projects. Although the instructor can still give direct guidance, he would have to divide his time according to the number of groups that are formed.

Group planning implies that students would have to expect to continue their work regardless of whether the instructor is present. For activities involving initiating experiences and searching for information, time for the instructor to help and for the group to work alone might be regularly scheduled. Such time could also include informal lectures, which can be requested by groups. To begin planning the inquiry, the instructor's actual direct involvement might be minimal; in contrast, his role in requiring a group to defend its choices of goals, resource material, and activity plans, as well as to evaluate its ongoing inquiry is critical and time consuming. One practical way of relating to several groups in this manner would be to form within each group a rotating planning committee, which could meet with the instructor between classes. Such committees could have the responsibility of taking the rough goals and plans of its group and transform them into activities that really allow for people to inquire together. They also might assume the leadership of these activities and thus have quasi-teaching experiences within the course. In addition, when the instructor is not available, guidance could be given by former students acting in the capacity of student consultants or group facilitators.

Imagine a model four-week schedule; with at least twelve weeks of classes per semester, for a single content area. In the first week, having read the problem statement, groups work on the initiating activities of their choice. At the end, they record ideas that need further development. Having divided up the previewing of the topics of study, each group begins the planning process. Time in the second week is devoted to arriving at common goals, formulating questions, and selecting readings. Tentative plans are negotiated and are followed by written plans to which the instructor and each group of students have agreed. In the third week, group-planned activities are carried out, and in the fourth week, more group-planned activities and a resolution activity are conducted.

Of course, many variations of this schedule are possible. For example, if two weeks of activities planned in advance seem excessive, a group could plan for one at first and plan for the remaining week at the end of the third week in any sequence. Another schedule that has proven effective is to plan one activity at a time, evaluating and planning after each what the group should do next.

Individually Oriented Student Direction:

This approach employs a great deal of self-directed, independent study. Students are responsible to a group or class for general planning and reporting of ideas and findings, but the majority of their energy is concentrated in furthering a personal inquiry.

In a course using this approach, students might begin each content area by discussing the major problem statement and working with some initiating activities, either as a class or in small groups. On the basis of this experience, each student can develop personal goals derived from the major problem and negotiate them with the instructor, the rest of the class, or a small group. This negotiation is necessary so that the student considers the relevance of the goals he is choosing. Once the focus of an inquiry is established, however, the student would be relatively free to develop it in his own way.

Except that he is required to check his plans with the instructor, a student's planning could chiefly be the result of his own individual efforts, unless he wished to work with students who have similar interests. Although group activities (a lecture, a film, etc.) might be made available periodically, searching for information would typically lead to independent study. Choosing to participate in group activities would be done on the basis of whether they are helpful to an individual's inquiry. The resolution phase of the inquiry might bring students together to exchange information and insights, or it might remain focused on helping students to complete individual projects and come to personal conclusions. The most active tasks for the instructor are providing individual consultation and keeping the overall structure of the environment sufficiently organized to minimize the interference that many activities can cause for each other.

Additional viable approaches can be created by interweaving the ones just presented. For example, a model can be devised in which different stages of the inquiry would have a teacher-guided, group, or individual orientation. Another possibility would be to gradually change the approach over the course of the semester. For instance, the first content area could be teacher guided, followed by a group planning approach for the second and an individual orientation for the third. Offering two or three approaches at the same time is also feasible, with some modifications. Students could choose the mode of student direction that best meets their needs. Regardless of the model that is chosen, it should support and facilitate the instructor's goals. It is therefore important for an instructor to weigh the models carefully when deciding how to facilitate student direction.

Part 1
The Learning Environment

The Problem: What Should a Learning Environment Provide? The Conflict of Safety and Growth

An inquiry into the teaching-learning process appropriately begins with an examination of psychological conditions conducive to learning. Mainly, this refers to the importance of helping students to become involved. Without involvement, the teaching-learning process tends to be lifeless and meaningless. Of course, other issues and problems could serve as starting points, but we have chosen this problem because it is all-encompassing. Delving into it can clarify and challenge basic assumptions about children's abilities and needs, and thus it serves well as a basis for the content areas that follow.

Teachers continually face the task of creating and maintaining a classroom environment that stimulates involvement in learning. No single condition establishes such a climate, and yet only one critical, missing ingredient may produce disinterest among students. Furthermore, regardless of what a teacher objectively thinks he is doing, how each student perceives his classroom environment greatly determines the degree of involvement he will be willing to seek. Clearly, a teacher's decisions about the learning environment he wants in his classroom necessitates an active inquiry. It is not enough to resolve that a "relaxed," "warm," or "student-centered" climate is important. These labels are descriptions of a constellation of values, attitudes, and concrete behaviors which are meaningless unless their theoretical dynamics and their practical implications are carefully understood.

A concern for what a learning environment should provide to involve students is very much intertwined with the problem of meeting emotional needs. Whenever a person is faced with new and perhaps risky situations, he usually attempts to protect himself psychologically. If he feels that his ability to protect himself is threatened, he tends to be particularly reluctant to take on challenging experiences and often tries to remove himself from the situation. Abraham H. Maslow theorizes in "Defense and Growth" that with regard to safety and growth, "Every human being has *both* sets of forces within him. One set clings to safety and defensiveness out of fear, tending to regress backward, hanging on to the past . . . *afraid* to take chances, afraid to jeopardize what he already has, *afraid* of independence, freedom and separateness. The other set of forces impels him forward toward wholeness of Self and uniqueness of Self, toward full functioning of all his capacities." He also argues that "in the choice between giving up safety or giving up growth, safety will ordinarily win out." The question we as teachers face is how to minimize the dangers and how to maximize the attractions of learning and personal growth so that students, rather than being defensive and self-protective, will choose to be involved. Learning is, after all, a way of experiencing new and different phenomena. Probably any learning situation is naturally anxiety provoking. How then can a teacher honor a student's need to be assured of his safety and at the same time fulfill his own responsibility to provide a challenging environment?

Initiating Activities

Each of the following activities can help you to begin your inquiry. They are designed to draw out your ideas and thoughts about what a learning environment should provide to maximize growth. After engaging in one or more of these activities, list the ideas that emerged during this experience and place them in these categories:

1. ideas that contradict each other
2. ideas that lack evidence or philosophical support
3. ideas that seem incomplete

Doing this should enable you to select relevant and helpful topics and readings.

1/Hiding Weaknesses

You have probably been in a situation where you know that a student is seeking the "easy way out." When this occurs, teachers should ask themselves what makes the person act this way. In this activity you are encouraged to think about the behavior of students trying to hide their weaknesses and then analyze the conditions that might have led to such behavior.

Imagine that you are visiting a friend who is a teacher, and in the ensuing conversation he begins talking about his classes. He complains that many of his students have been avoiding challenging work. He likes to give them choices, but they seem to seek the easy way out. When they work at the blackboard, they hide, erase, cover up, or correct their mistakes so that he won't see them. At other times, when the students are correcting their work at their seats, they change their incorrect answers even though they know that the work will not be graded. The teacher suspects that the students who behave in this way are those who fail to question him about things they do not understand in class. He often finds out about their confusion only in their subsequent work. He has asked you if you have any ideas about why his students are hiding their weaknesses.

Group Activity

Although you do not have any more information about the teacher's class than that which is provided, you can speculate about why the students are acting as they are. Each person in a group or class should develop as many hypotheses as possible about why students' weaknesses are being concealed. The hypotheses can be combined into a list, which a group or class can examine together. The most promising ideas can be discussed.

Individual Activity

Try to develop a short general theory to explain why students hide weaknesses. Consider the aspects of a learning environment that minimize the need for such behavior as well as those that encourage it. Keep track of ideas you may want to explore further.

2/Freedom in the Classroom

You have probably heard of people who have advocated greater freedom in the classroom and believe in making choices available to students. This is a controversial issue. The following task allows you to examine and comment on a teacher who is thinking about these ideas:

Assume that you have been teaching for a year or two and that you feel comfortable in the school in which you work. As part of a program initiated by the faculty to share ideas and to stimulate dialogue, teachers have been encouraged to send notes to each other. You have just received the following note, which was distributed by a fellow faculty member:

Recently, it has become clear to me that one of the important aspects of an educational environment is that it should provide choice. Probably, one of the things students hate most about classrooms is their sameness. Usually students are given the same books, the same assignments, and the same activities. This means that students have to wait a lot. They have to wait for the teacher to tell them what to do next, wait for other students to find the right page or finish their work, and wait for teachers to acknowledge their waving hands. If students are really going to learn, they must have a sense that the classroom is a place in which they have some autonomy and self-control. Otherwise it becomes a kind of tight box from which they cannot escape.

Group Activity

It is important to react to the letter-writer's views and in some way to carry on a dialogue with him. Try to avoid arguing with his motives. Either as a class or in small groups, a discussion can be held in which different students play the roles of the teachers who might actually be involved in the school where it was written. One person can be the teacher who has written the note, and others can be fellow teachers. You might imagine that you have met one another in the faculty lounge and are interested in discussing the note.

Individual Activity

Outline a note to the teacher who wrote the original one. What would it say? It might be helpful for you to actually write a note to this teacher and exchange it with other students in your class.

3/Remembering Teachers

Students have many different encounters with teachers during their school experience. Some are remembered with excitement and fondness, others with resentment and hate. In this activity you are to look back at encounters you have had with teachers and examine the qualities they had that encouraged or limited students.

To help you think back on your schooling, a list of some experiences you may have had is provided. Try to remember if the following ever happened to you:

1. A teacher discussed a weakness of yours in front of other students.
2. You needed some help in solving a difficult problem, and the teacher encouraged and helped you to think out the problem yourself.
3. You overheard your teacher say something about you to another teacher.
4. A teacher told you he understood what you were feeling.
5. You were excited about a project, but no one gave you encouragement.
6. A teacher told you something personal about himself that made you respect him.
7. You were asked to think for yourself and then were criticized for your thoughts.
8. A teacher told you that he would trust a decision you were to make for the class.
9. You needed time to finish an assignment, but the teacher claimed that it was necessary to move on.
10. After you openly expressed your dislike for a class activity, the teacher eagerly asked you to recommend some changes.

Group Activity

Either in a small group or with the whole class, try to describe the qualities you saw in your teachers that explain why they acted as they did. Identify the qualities helpful to students and those that limit them. Take enough time to share and compare your ideas with those of other students.

Individual Activity

Try to think of personal experiences similar to those listed. See if you can remember the qualities of the teachers associated with them. You can separate the list into positive and negative behaviors and attempt to suggest the qualities of teachers that lead to each.

4/Motivation and Learning

All teachers need to understand the motivating drives and emotional needs of their students. In this activity you are to examine some of your perceptions of what fosters or discourages these drives and needs of children.

Read the following statements and decide if you tend to agree or disagree with each of them. If you want, you may check the appropriate space so that you can remember your response. There are no absolutely right or wrong responses, but try to have some reason for your decision.

	Tend to agree	Tend to disagree	Not sure
1. A person needs to feel some pressure to be motivated to learn.	____	____	____
2. When students are actively involved in the planning and direction of their education, they learn more.	____	____	____
3. Younger children need more structure than older children.	____	____	____
4. When a teacher provides choices, students are less negative about school work.	____	____	____
5. Children have a natural desire to learn.	____	____	____
6. It is unforgivable for a teacher to label a child lazy.	____	____	____
7. Students need to be reminded that "work" is an important value in school.	____	____	____
8. A teacher's empathy for a student can get in the way of the educating process.	____	____	____
9. Childen benefit from classroom routines.	____	____	____
10. Praising students is crucial to the development of their self concept.	____	____	____

Group Activity

After students have completed the checklist, it may be helpful for the whole class or small groups to tally the results. Try discussing items that provoke the most disagreement among the participants in your group. Also check to see if different reasons exist when most students have given the same responses.

Individual Activity

Think about your reasons for choosing your responses. Then take each statement that you disagreed with and try to change the wording so that you can agree with it. Make a list of statements that you feel deserve further examination.

17

Topics of Study

Here are three topics that provide a range of choices for examining issues and problems relevant to the study of the learning environment:

1. The Stimulation of Learning. This topic is concerned with the nature of human motivation and how a student's intrinsic drive to learn is generally encouraged and inhibited.
2. The Teacher's Relationship to Students. This topic focuses on the ways in which a teacher's personal relationship with students can enhance their natural learning tendencies and decrease the need for self-protective strategies.
3. The Direction of Learning. This topic explores the forms of self-control and active participation that students should have in the learning process if a teacher wants to allow for maximum growth.

The three topics should be considered as not unrelated but rather as different points of emphasis. "The Stimulation of Learning" is probably the most general; the others cover more specific questions and concerns. In addition to the readings suggested in the elaboration of these topics of study, Melvin L. Silberman's "What Schooling Does to Children" (pp. 27–32) should be read as an introduction to the content area. Silberman discusses, in general terms, the problematic aspects of school environments. This article can be integrated into other activities where it seems appropriate and helpful.

A good way to begin thinking about how to direct the inquiry is to read the Silberman article and explore all three topics of study. Find among the questions and readings those corresponding to interests that were stimulated by the initiating experiences of this content area.

1/The Stimulation of Learning

The stimulation of learning is basic to the study of the teaching-learning process. Without knowledge of how and under what conditions a learner becomes involved in educative activities, planning a learning environment is difficult. Some worthwhile questions about the stimulation of learning are:

1. How much does involvement in learning depend upon prodding and external rewards?
2. What are some of the intrinsic motives of students upon which the teacher can depend for the stimulation of learning?
3. What is the role of fear in the learning process?
4. Under what conditions do children become defensive and self-protective?

Readings

Jerome S. Bruner, "The Will to Learn" (pp. 33–40)

This chapter from Bruner's book *Toward a Theory of Instruction* is of great value when one is considering the psychological conditions that stimulate learning. Bruner's view is that human beings possess internal motives that can be channeled effectively into educational activities. He discusses in some detail intrinsic sources of motivation such as curiosity, competence, identification, and reciprocity. You may find it helpful, as you read this article, to reflect upon past learning experiences, in school and in other circumstances, in which you felt very involved. Do the factors Bruner describes adequately explain your involvement?

John Holt, "Excerpts from How Children Fail" (pp. 41–42)

The two excerpts from *How Children Fail* compare the learning behavior of a pre-school child to that of students in a school in which Holt observed and taught. The description of the pre-school child is helpful for understanding in simple terms the theory that human organisms are naturally curious, exploratory, and willing to risk failure. The older students are portrayed as defensive and self-protective in the face of potential failure. After reading these excerpts, you might find it helpful to consider the sources of fear in schools.

Abraham H. Maslow, "Defense and Growth" (pp. 43–51)

In this chapter from *Toward a Psychology of Being*, Maslow presents the view that human beings have within them two sets of forces or needs — one that strives for growth and one that clings to safety. Although not written specifically for educators, this chapter is useful for examining the emotional needs that any learning environment must fulfill. In a long footnote Maslow provides a good illustration of how a child naturally approaches a new experience and how an overly directive adult can inhibit curiosity. Maslow's theory has important implications about the role of choice in the learning process.

George Dennison, "Excerpt from Lives of Children" (pp. 52–56)

This chapter from Dennison's book can be useful as the basis for a general discussion of the environmental conditions that stimulate learning. Using John Dewey as his theoretical frame of reference, Dennison contrasts the learning environment in the home of a pre-school child to that in most schools and maintains that many positive qualities of the former are totally missing or reversed in the classroom. He briefly describes how the First Street School (a free school for urban, poor children) tried to provide optimal conditions for growth. Comparing Dennison's ideas with the contrasting selections from *How Children Fail* by Holt and with Bruner's discussion of reciprocity might be useful.

2/The Teacher's Relationship to Students

One of the most influential aspects of any learning environment, regardless of the philosophy that guided its design, is the quality of the interpersonal relationships a teacher establishes. Teachers are aware of this when they express concern about how they should present themselves to their students and how they prefer to be regarded by their students. Thus an examination of the ways in which teachers can relate to their students is an important part of an inquiry into the conditions necessary for learning. Some questions about the teacher's relationship to students that may help to organize an inquiry are:

1. What interpersonal qualities in teachers promote nondefensiveness and learning?
2. How do teachers' judgments and expectations affect their students?
3. How can a teacher serve as a model to his students?
4. In what ways should a teacher express his personal feelings and attitudes toward his students?

Readings

Carl R. Rogers, "The Interpersonal Relationship in the Facilitation of Learning" (pp. 57–62)

Rogers describes in teachers three interpersonal qualities that help learners: realness, acceptance, and empathic understanding. He gives examples of how teachers with whom he has been associated have exhibited these qualities. It might be interesting to explore how they foster the conditions of safety and growth described by Maslow. For example, do they affect the way students think of themselves and subsequently act in response to the teacher? It might also be helpful to consider what behavior of teachers reflects their personal attitudes toward students.

Herbert Kohl, "Excerpt from *The Open Classroom*" (pp. 63–65)

Kohl describes the preconceived notions and expectations about students that teachers develop from school records and from students' behavior early in the school year. He discusses the theory that such expectations become self-fulfilling and suggests ways teachers can deal with their perceptions of students; he shows how an open classroom environment can be used to gain respect for individual differences in children. After reading this chapter from *The Open Classroom*, you might try to recall personal experiences in which you were a victim of your teacher's preconceptions.

Sidney M. Jourard, "Fascination: A Phenomenological Perspective on Independent Learning" (pp. 66–75)

Jourard's article is a description of man's capacity for fascination and its inhibition by certain modes of social training. Jourard provides a useful view of the problem of how to reconcile the contradictions between social pressure and independent learning. Two types of teachers, gurus and commissars, are contrasted in terms of their interpersonal qualities and their effect on the learner. Jourard's list of teachers' positive qualities has some similarities to Rogers' list but includes important additions.

Jerome S. Bruner, "The Will to Learn" (pp. 33–40)

Bruner describes children's natural desire to identify and be in a reciprocal relationship with adults who are significant in their environment. There is also a useful discussion of how teachers are "competence models" to their students. From a psychodynamic point of view, these factors are considered to be of great importance in the development of interpersonal relationships. (See also page 19.)

3/The Direction of Learning

When asking what a learning environment should provide, we must consider who should control the learning process. To what degree, for example, should students decide what they are going to learn, what materials they are going to use, and what experiences will best enhance their learning? Consideration of the kind of freedom to create in a learning environment is important for any teacher who wants to promote growth in learning as well as emotional security. These questions about the direction of learning are worth examining:

1. What contributes to a student's sense of control and autonomy in a learning environment?
2. How does student direction in a learning situation help children to meet their safety needs?
3. What need does a child have for structure and guidance?
4. Under what conditions do children make wise choices?

Readings

Abraham H. Maslow, "Defense and Growth" (pp. 43–51)

Maslow discusses the necessity for choice in a child's environment so that a child has control over how his emotional needs are met. This article is especially relevant to education because Maslow views choice from a perspective that differs from the typical debate about authoritarian versus democratic classrooms. The author's long footnote is particularly helpful in a discussion of structure and guidance. You will find it useful after reading Maslow to reflect on his assertion that a child's choices are usually wise. What kind of choices would you allow your students to make? (See also p. 19.)

Philip W. Jackson, "The Student's World" (pp. 76–84)

Jackson's article describes what life in classrooms is usually like for students. He finds the classrooms in which he has observed to be pervaded by institutional rules and regulations which restrict individuality and foster conformity and docility. He discusses how the typical classroom environment inhibits freedom of movement and activity. The article is valuable as a basis for discussing the kinds of restrictions that arise in classrooms unless special attention is given to how they are designed and organized.

Joseph Featherstone, "Excerpt from *Schools Where Children Learn*" (pp. 85–90)

This chapter from Featherstone's book is a discussion of British infant schools. In many of these schools a student is free to explore for himself, choose what he wants to do, speak to his classmates, work independently, and take time to complete tasks. Featherstone compares what happens in these British classrooms with what happens in American classrooms. This selection is useful for stimulating discussion on the relationship of educational goals and learning environments.

George Dennison, "Excerpt from *Lives of Children*" (pp. 52–56)

Beyond its general significance, described on page 19, this reading is particularly helpful for developing a fuller conception of the dimensions of freedom and their meaning for a child. Dennison has an unusual and provocative way of writing about the kinds of freedom that facilitate involvement in learning and the restrictions that inhibit it.

Inquiry Activities

With the selection of topics of study and resource material in mind, you are ready to plan activities. In general, they should be geared toward searching the readings for relevant information and ideas. Such a search should include examining major concepts and looking at their educational implications. Some of the central concepts are:

competence motivation   continuum of experience
reciprocity   confirmation
realness   self-fulfilling expectations
the hidden curriculum   defense mechanisms

It is also helpful to compare points of similarity and difference among the authors' views and ideas. A particularly effective means of searching for information is to divide the readings among students in a group and to plan discussions in which many different ideas are brought to bear. In addition to the usual kinds of discussion, be sure to plan activities that provide a way of testing and experiencing major ideas and concepts. Usually such activities require careful and creative planning, but the involvement they stimulate makes the effort worthwhile. The following inquiry activity plans are for actual use and as a source for generating other creative plans.

1/Intrinsic Motivation

In his article "The Will to Learn," Bruner maintains that all children have the capacity for intrinsic response to stimulating learning activities. This point of view deserves serious consideration because it affects a teacher's decisions about how to involve students.

The following remarks contain a teacher's thoughts about the value of intrinsic motivation. After reading the comments, test their content against your own experiences and against the readings suggested in this part. To prepare for discussion, reading the teacher's remarks before exploring the readings might be a good idea.

I have read a great deal about the value of involving children by appealing to intrinsic motives. It sounds intriguing, but I cannot help but feel that it is in conflict with some of my experiences as a teacher.

I teach a heterogeneous class; that is, a few students have a high level of interest, a few are academically disinterested, and the rest are somewhere in the middle. In addition, I have found that students respond to a system of rewards — including grades, competitive games, and helpful comments and criticisms. It is not that I am unaware of some faults of such a system, but it seems to be true that students become rather dependent on their teachers and it is difficult to rely on internal motivation.

2/Safety and Growth

Maslow's article has been viewed, in previous remarks about the learning environment, as seminal reading, and therefore its implications for education deserve special study. One interesting activity to serve this purpose involves an examination of the second diagram on page 44. Maslow suggests that growth is most likely to occur "when the delights of growth and anxieties of safety are greater than the anxieties of growth and the delights of safety." This activity is designed to test the meaning of these factors: the delights and anxieties of growth and the delights and anxieties of safety.

Imagine under what conditions each event listed below would encourage students to (1) take risks and seek new experience and (2) avoid risks and be closed to new experience.

1. coming into a class for the first time
2. standing up to make a speech in a class
3. discussing one's ideas with classmates
4. sensing a problem in the classroom and wanting to talk to the teacher about it
5. wanting to ask a question in class
6. taking a test

3/Relating to Students

In this edited version of a third-grade teacher's description of one of her students, the teacher discusses not only her perceptions of the students but also some of their behavior toward each other in the classroom:

Gloria is what I might term an average student. She works very hard to improve whatever she does. She has very little self-confidence. She needs lots and lots of teacher-approval. For everything she does, she has to have a very quick reply back, you know, "Right." She'll come up to the desk and ask whether she's doing it the right way when she probably knows full well that she is, but she seems to need a lot of the teacher's time. She's had a history of this sort of thing, where she demands quite a bit of the teacher — as if there were one teacher for each child and this of course would be the kind of relationship that she likes. I do try to give her as much attention as I can, but sometimes she'll manufacture reasons to get the teacher's attention. For instance, if there's a question on how to do something that we've done day after day, she'll insist that I explain it again to her. She did sit very close to me at first, and the social worker and myself, after talking the problem over, thought it might be best if she weren't quite so close. It makes it very easy for her to come to the desk. She still seems to need a great deal of love and affection. I get love-letters from her constantly which is — oh, somewhat normal for a third grader. They still love their teacher dearly, but with her it's a love-letter every day. She has a need for a feeling of belonging to somebody, a very great need. She's even turned to bothering the boys, which at this age, too, isn't as normal as it would be if she were a year or two older.

Think about the teacher's attitudes and behavior toward this child in terms of these pairs of concepts of Rogers and Jourard:

prizing   realness
confirmation   disclosure

What should the teacher's relationship be toward Gloria from both Rogers' and Jourard's points of view?

4/Teacher Evaluation

In the excerpt from *The Open Classroom*, Kohl makes the point that teachers' expectations or pre-judgments about students "influence behavior in subtle ways." He finds that often they cause defensiveness and resistance in students or they become self-fulfilling — that is, the student conforms to rather than resists the label placed upon him. Even after a teacher gets to know his students, however, his judgments or evaluations can have these consequences. The problem of teacher evaluation, therefore, also deserves careful consideration, and the following questions might help to organize a discussion of it:

1. In what ways can a teacher praise or criticize his students without causing embarrassment, guilt, resentment, and defensiveness?
2. How can a teacher get his students to view his evaluations as helpful information rather than as indications of reward and punishment?
3. To what extent should a teacher's relationship to his students be based on evaluation of performance and behavior?
4. What functions should classroom evaluation perform?

An interesting way to explore these questions is to think of them in relation to your own courses and instructors. By now, there should have been numerous instances in which your instructors have evaluated students in some way. It is likely that you have some thoughts, at this point in the semester, about your instructors' role in evaluating classroom performance. Drawing upon these events and ideas, you should be able to bring relevant personal knowledge to bear on the preceding questions. Along with these considerations, ask yourself whether you would respond to the questions differently if your frame of reference was an elementary or high school classroom rather than a college setting.

5/Experiencing Student-Directed Learning

Our learning experiences in school have mainly been directed and supervised by teachers. This fact may make it difficult for us to understand what Maslow and

Dennison are saying about students' needs to feel some control over the learning process. It may be useful, therefore, to create an experience in which the student's direction of learning is personally felt.

Find out some of the special skills and areas of knowledge possessed by students in your class. Some possibilities you could investigate are:

analyzing art	photography	folk dancing
computer programming	first aid	polling techniques
automobile mechanics	cooking	electronics

Divide the class into groups of four and have each group select the person whose topic or skill is of greatest interest. Instead of having that person teach his interest in a directive fashion, have the members of the group use him solely as a resource person. He should encourage them to determine the aspects of the topic they want to explore and the skills they want to develop. In doing this, the "students" ought to ask questions of their own choosing and seek advice from the "teacher" when it makes sense to do so. Time should be set aside to evaluate this experience from the point of view of the "teacher" and of the "students." Feelings about one's need for safety or desire for growth could serve as the basis for a productive discussion.

6/Problems in Student-Directed Classrooms

In "The Student's World," Philip W. Jackson describes painful features of classroom life, such as delay, denial, and interruptions, and the demands for patience and feelings of resignation they engender. The British classroom described by Joseph Featherstone, on the other hand, appears to avoid many of the negative aspects identified by Jackson. Because the students he observed directed their own learning to a considerable degree, it was unnecessary for them to fake involvement and conform to classroom rituals to impress the teacher.

Despite their ability to solve such problems, however, classrooms that encourage student-directed learning tend to create new problems demanding careful attention and imaginative solutions. How might a teacher deal with these events without destroying the learner's sense of control over his own actions?

1. A student wanders aimlessly around the classroom day after day without being able to become involved in the activity choices available.
2. A student typically chooses to read books that are below his reading level.
3. A student plans a project infeasible to carry out.
4. A student develops a clumsy method for solving math problems.
5. A student stays almost exclusively with one subject.
6. A student seems to be satisfied with simplified ways of understanding good literature.

Readings

Melvin L. Silberman

What Schooling Does to Children

School is the setting for a major portion of children's lives. For well over a thousand hours a year, children are influenced by what happens there. It is important, therefore, to examine what the school environment is generally like for them and what aspects of it require change.

The most pervasive but often overlooked aspect of school life is its institutional quality. While it is commonly believed that the main concern of schools is instruction, schooling is a much broader experience than being taught what is contained in textbooks. Students learn not only facts, skills, and concepts but also rules of membership in a social institution. Often this learning experience may have greater impact on students' ultimate well-being than do those experiences we commonly identify with the academic curriculum. The school's rules, routines, and procedures form what has been called a "hidden curriculum" (Jackson, 1968) designed to mold individual behavior to the requirements of institutional living. This curriculum is made necessary by the fact that personal interests can rarely be accommodated in schools. Students must often yield when their own wishes and plans inconvenience other people or interfere in other ways with the efficient operation of the school. A group of students, for example, may want to finish a chemistry experiment but the school schedule calls for them to proceed to their next class. Or a request by students to rearrange their desks may have to be

denied because, among other considerations, it would make it difficult for the janitor to sweep the floor.

Acquiescing to these procedural rules, however, is a painful process for most students, especially when the rules are numerous and rigidly applied. Jackson (1968) finds, for example, that whether students want to be called on in class discussion, or request the teacher's help, or use materials in short supply, they usually must wait their turn. They must also wait for each other to be quiet or get to the right page before the teacher will proceed. In addition, countless instructions and directions must be endured, even though a good number of them, according to Brenner, Hofmann, and Weddington (1964), do not refer to the academic activity at hand. Finally, spontaneous desires must often be held in abeyance until the proper time and place. Mastering the hidden curriculum is also made difficult by confusion as to what is expected when institutional requirements conflict with educational demands. It is common for students to be expected to be passive and conforming in school and yet, at the same time, intellectually curious and aggressive.

Whenever school personnel do not fully grapple with the problems of institutional living, they risk solving them in unsatisfactory ways. For example, students may be asked to line up before leaving or entering school even though less regimented ways of avoiding pushing and shoving are possible. One reason that alternative solutions are not explored is that current procedures appear to be necessary. Without giving the matter much thought, administrators cannot conceive how to manage students without recourse to the means they have instituted. To compound the problem, classroom teachers may place an even greater value on the procedures the school principal expects them to enforce. For instance, besides dismissing students by rows, teachers might choose the quietest row first. Thus, obedience to rules of dismissal becomes a virtue in itself, quite apart from its functional necessity. When this happens, students learn to view conformity as morally right and nonconformity as morally wrong. They learn little about why rules and regulations are necessary nor how to determine when they are unnecessary. In this regard, many teachers who have allowed brief experiments in classroom government report that their students create extremely stringent and inflexible rules for themselves. One of the implications of their remarks is that children are not mature enough to handle self-government. Quite possibly, however, the students are merely exaggerating what they have been taught about classroom procedures. Their efforts to control themselves reflect the same unquestioning stance toward rule making that the school adopts. Little attention is given to understanding when classroom conditions require institutionalized procedures and how they can be planned to avoid unpleasant consequences for individual people.

Beyond the learning of rules and procedures which govern personal action, membership in school requires a set of psychological adjustments. One of these adaptations is learning to live in school without the assurance of the adult acceptance that children take for granted at home. Teachers, after all, cannot be as intimate and patient with their students as parents can be with their children. Their energies are severely taxed by the several roles they perform for many students simultaneously.

These limitations, unfortunately, often lead to a kind of teacher favoritism. This occurs when teachers develop certain perceptions, preferences, and expectations concerning their students in order to simplify the task of relating to many children. For example, Kohl (1967) found from personal experience that by perceiving some students as defiant, unmanageable, or disturbed, he could reject their claim on his attention and still preserve his self-image as a responsive teacher. In this regard, a study by Feshbach (1969) suggests that student teachers attempt to ease the problems of classroom management by showing preference to children who are conforming and orderly over those who are independent and active. Moreover, research by Rosenthal and Jacobson (1968) supports the notion that teachers come to expect greater academic improvement in some students than in others. Such differential expectations, it could be argued, allow a teacher to channel his efforts when his energies are at a premium. As a result of this favoritism, some students are lucky enough to have teachers who believe in them, care for them, and help them learn. The students who are the victims of teachers' biased vision, however, often receive less attention and concern. What makes their neglect particularly problematic is that children often react to it in ways which confirm and perpetuate their teacher's negative perceptions and expectations.

The problem of changing how teachers perceive their students is exacerbated by the categories used in schools to describe children. When students are viewed in terms of their I.Q., achievement test scores, social class background, and conformity to classroom rules and procedures, the possibility that they will be stereotyped rather than seen as individuals is increased. All too frequently, these categories are merely used by teachers to make quick predictions about a child. If the predictions are negative, the temptation to ignore or reject him is great. Occasionally, teachers reveal instances in which they regretted the fast impression they formed of a child. After getting to know him, they had a richer view of the student as a person and were able to respond more warmly to him. Unfortunately, some children do not get a "second look" and even if they did, they may already have begun to act in ways which fulfill the teacher's initial expectations. What we need are conceptions of the teaching-learning process in which teachers would not have to depend so greatly on tight categories of perceiving children. Without this dependence, teachers might be less threatened by these traditional indices of what to expect from students and thus more open to who they really are.

A second demand made in schools is that students manage their lives in a highly congested social environment. Approximately thirty people inhabit a room which has far less space than a family enjoys in a house. We confine students to quarters in which their ability to stretch their feet, walk around, and spread out their possessions is limited. Furthermore, the ratio of students to teacher and to materials is quite high, even in the least crowded classrooms.

Because classrooms are crowded places, students are usually required to do things together most of the time. Individually, they have little opportunity for private action. Personal pursuits sooner or later conflict with the teacher's rules or the wishes of classmates. Even where the chance to be alone arises, it has been found that a student's ability to go about his business without being interrupted or distracted is virtually impossible (Jackson and Wolfson, 1968). As a result of these crowded conditions, a sense of privacy and individuality is difficult to achieve. In an environment which is essentially unresponsive to individual differences, according to Adams and Biddle (1970), one student is practically indistinguishable from another.

Paradoxically, students' failure to find psychological privacy in the classroom is frequently accompanied by an inability to interact meaningfully with each other. Because of the crowded social environment in the classroom, children are often beseeched to keep to themselves, to desist from talking with classmates, and above all, to avoid showing their work to each other. For children to ignore each other is, of course, as impossible as finding privacy.

The impact on children of spending five hours a day in crowded classrooms cannot be easily studied. Adults, moreover, cannot fully comprehend the experience because the conditions under which they work are rarely as congested. By comparison, classrooms provide less freedom of movement, less personalized facilities, and more distraction than do most adult work settings. Despite our distance from classroom life, however, we might logically deduce that children have very little incentive to develop their own interests and plans in school. To have such incentive would require that individual students experience the classroom as a place for their own use. What is needed are ways of designing classrooms so that space can be used flexibly to create several types of physical settings in which students can learn. With greater choice as to how any activity can be organized, a classroom could accommodate a variety of purposes and thereby make it a less depersonalizing climate in which to live and work.

Schooling is, thirdly, an experience in withstanding continual evaluation of one's words and actions. Probably in no other setting is one so often judged as a person. To make matters worse, these judgments are typically voiced before an audience of peers. As Dreeben (1968) suggests, classroom praise and criticism, although intended to help the learner, may threaten him instead.

To cope with this threat to their self-respect, many students find it necessary to devote their mental energies to strategize how to avoid failure and shame. The strategies they use depend on the intensity of that threat. Those whose position in the class pecking order is secure maintain the teacher's favor by zealously complying with the academic and social expectations of the school. Others stay on the teacher's "good side" by feigning involvement, hiding misdeeds, and misinforming the teacher. The less secure the student, the more likely is he to be forced to engage in this "cheating." For students to whom classroom evaluation is an especially threatening experience, however, active attempts to impress the teacher are often too risky. So, these students, as Holt (1964) has described, actually choose failure. Saving face becomes more important to them than learning and thinking.

When we witness students in school laughing, daydreaming, or complaining, it is hard to believe that many of them are apprehensive. The problem of observing the apprehension created by classroom evaluation is that children respond to it in ways which disguise their real fears. Nonetheless, it is visible if one looks

29

closely enough. It is reflected best in the choices apprehensive students make in the classroom. If the teacher's judgments did not threaten them, they would choose to use their mental energies to tackle new ideas rather than scheme how to hide their shortcomings.

School is a place where children are not accepted at their present stage of development. Growth is expected. But children grow only after they feel safe; that is, they will seek out new knowledge most fully when they are convinced that penalties will not be invoked if they fail. Failure itself is not anxiety producing. The persistence which infants show in their attempts to master the environment suggests that human beings are not naturally afraid of failure. It becomes problematic, though, when a person believes he will lose something of value to him (e.g., approval, good grades, a special privilege) if he does not succeed. The only way to relieve a child's anxiety about the teacher's evaluations is to assure him that they will not be held against him. The problem is how students can be evaluated so that their successes and failures are viewed as helpful information rather than as indications of reward and punishment.

A fourth condition to which students must adjust in school is the pervasive authority of school personnel. While it is true that students can make some choices for themselves, Friedenberg (1963) argues that teachers and principals have broad discretionary jurisdiction over students. They can decide what content will be in the curriculum as well as what disciplinary action to take when students do not follow rules and regulations. Even in schools where students have a voice in those matters, the privilege to do so can be withdrawn at any time. If students are dissatisfied with the school's decisions, they have no official power to press their grievances. In short, the school authorities are very much in control.

Basically, schools ask their students to conduct meaningful lives with few rights, privileges, and opportunities for responsibility and choice. Most administrators and teachers, of course, do not consciously try to be autocratic but few know how to avoid it. They rely on their authority to demand and restrict in order to carry out their educational functions. In response, students give up any sense of autonomy. They come to feel that their education is largely out of their hands. More importantly, they come to believe in the school's definition of their capacity for freedom and responsible decision-making.

One of the common fears in giving students greater control in school is that they will not act responsibly. There are many experiments in classroom freedom, however, which demonstrate that this fear is unfounded. In Kallet's experience (1966), children who attend schools in which restrictions are placed on moving and talking, activities are closely supervised, and decisions are rarely left to students, are far less self-reliant than their counterparts in freer schools.

The concern that children make wise choices may be partly invalid to begin with. It suggests that children are prone to make personally irresponsible decisions. Yet, Maslow (1968) finds that people generally make wise choices if they are truly free to do so. Only when they are frightened into making self-protective decisions, he believes, are their choices irrational. The real problem may not be whether children can be trusted with freedom but whether it is possible in schools to allow each student to be fully free to make his own choices.

In recent years, increased attention has been given to questions concerning the school's authority over its students. Attempts have been made to lessen the distance between teachers and students, to relax regulations concerning physical appearance and other personal matters, and to reduce the number of academic requirements to which a student must adhere. But, as welcome as these liberalizing efforts may be, they have not changed the basic powerlessness of students. It is questionable whether a school can be run like a political democracy. On the other hand, by assuming the right to be autocratic, school personnel deny students the opportunity to achieve some meaningful direction over their own lives.

One of the major effects of these psychological demands of school life is to make students overly concerned about their personal well-being and thus insensitive to their relations with each other. To make matters worse, peer tensions and antagonisms are directly encouraged in many classrooms. For example, Henry (1957) has observed that it is common for teachers to ask students to evaluate each other and thus magnify the threat which classroom evaluation poses for students. According to Minuchin (1965), they also invite destructive competition among students by dominating social interaction and thereby becoming the sole source of recognition in the classroom. Furthermore, studies by Lippitt and Gold (1959) and Hawkes (1968) show that teachers influence the formation of peer cliques by their expression of differential attitudes and expectations for different children. In most cases, the antagonism, competition, and social exclusion engendered in classrooms are unintended. Hence, the tension among classmates in schools often goes unrecognized and untreated.

Even though teachers do not intend to facilitate negative relations among their students, they cannot dismiss them, as they sometimes do, by appealing to the myth that children are naturally cruel to each other. Actually, the most serious vice of children is their imitation of significant adults around them. Their identification with adult behavior patterns is evidenced by extensive modeling of their teachers. For example, students are quick to attach evaluative labels to each other. They also tend to select friends and reject others on the basis of traditional academic indices without much regard for personal qualities.

When we think of a man with character and personal strength, we think, in part, of a person who recognizes desirable qualities in others, who is loyal to those he befriends, and who is able to give help as well as receive it. We frown on a man who exploits the weaknesses of others, who submits too readily to those more powerful than he, or who envies his peers. The social attributes which students are encouraged, intentionally or not, to adopt in schools are more likely to create the latter man. If we want schools to help children learn how to build human relationships as well as develop academic skills, we must be careful not to put students in a position which makes it difficult for them to respect and cooperate with each other.

From these remarks, one can readily sense that schooling presents challenging problems to children. They must contend with a morass of institutional rules and regulations, the personal preferences and biases of their teachers, and the crowded social conditions of the classroom. They must also learn to live with frequent public evaluation, limited rights and privileges, and tensions among peers. What children experience when confronted with these demands is difficult to pinpoint and doubtlessly varies from student to student. The testimony presented in several books and articles suggests, however, that students' feelings fall into such negative categories as uncertainty, fear, and resentment.

How concerned we are about the psychological conditions under which children live in schools depends, perhaps, on how necessary we feel are unpleasant experiences to a child's growth and development. Our concern might also depend on the extent to which we tolerate these conditions in our adult lives, in our responsibilities at work and in our relations with the major institutions of society. It might be more helpful, though, to assess the psychological quality of schooling by asking what kind of images of themselves children develop as a result of going to school. Does their schooling help them to believe in themselves, that is, to see themselves as competent, resourceful, capable of altering some parts of their environment? If we are to compel children to live at least ten years of their lives in schools, we owe it to them to explore seriously the answer to this question. If children do not form positive views of themselves as a result of their schooling, we are obligated to rethink how schools can be organized so that children will view them as a valuable resource in their lives.

References

Adams, Raymond S., and Bruce J. Biddle. *Realities of Teaching: Explorations with Video Tape*. New York: Holt, Rinehart and Winston, 1970.
Brenner, Anton, Helmut Hofmann, and Rachel Wed-

dington. "School Demands." *Elementary School Journal* 64 (1964): 261–264.

Dreeben, Robert. *On What Is Learned in School.* Reading, Mass.: Addison-Wesley, 1968.

Feshbach, Norma D. "Student Teacher Preferences for Elementary School Pupils Varying in Personality Characteristics." *Journal of Educational Psychology* 60 (1969): 126–132.

Friedenberg, Edgar Z. "The Modern High School: A Profile." *Commentary* 36 (1963): 373–380.

Hawkes, Thomas H. "Structural Constraints Upon Interpersonal Communication in the Classroom: A Study of Reciprocal Sociometric Choice Dyads." Paper presented at the American Educational Research Association, February 1968.

Henry, Jules. "Attitude Organization in Elementary School Classrooms." *American Journal of Orthopsychiatry* 27 (1957): 117–133.

Holt, John. *How Children Fail.* New York: Pitman, 1964.

Jackson, Philip W. *Life in Classrooms.* New York: Holt, Rinehart and Winston, 1968.

Jackson, Philip W., and Bernice J. Wolfson. "Varieties of Constraint in a Nursery School." *Young Children* 23 (September 1968): 358–367.

Kallet, Anthony. "Two Classrooms." *This Magazine Is About Schools* 1 (1966): 45–59.

Kohl, Herbert. *36 Children.* New York: New American Library, 1967.

Lippitt, Ronald, and Martin Gold. "Classroom Social Structure as a Mental Health Problem." *Journal of Social Issues* 15 (1959): 40–49.

Maslow, Abraham H. *Toward a Psychology of Being.* 2d ed. New York: Van Nostrand Reinhold, 1968.

Minuchin, Patricia. "Solving Problems Cooperatively: A Comparison of Three Classroom Groups." *Childhood Education* 41 (1965): 480–484.

Rosenthal, Robert, and Lenore Jacobson. *Pygmalion in the Classroom.* New York: Holt, Rinehart and Winston, 1968.

Jerome S. Bruner

The Will to Learn

The single most characteristic thing about human beings is that they learn. Learning is so deeply ingrained in man that it is almost involuntary, and thoughtful students of human behavior have even speculated that our specialization as a species is a specialization for learning. For, by comparison with organisms lower in the animal kingdom, we are ill equipped with prepared reflex mechanisms. As William James put it decades ago, even our instinctive behavior occurs only once, thereafter being modified by experience. With a half century's perspective on the discoveries of Pavlov, we know that man not only is conditioned by his environment, but may be so conditioned even against his will.

Why then invoke the idea of a "will to learn"? The answer derives from the idea of education, a human invention that takes a learner beyond "mere" learning. Other species begin their learning afresh each generation, but man is born into a culture that has as one of its principal functions the conservation and transmission of past learning. Given man's physical characteristics, indeed, it would be not only wasteful but probably fatal for him to reinvent even the limited range of technique and knowledge required for such a species to survive in the temperate zone. This means that man cannot depend upon a casual process of learning; he must be "educated." The young human must regulate his learning and his attention by reference to external requirements. He must eschew what is vividly right under his nose for

Reprinted by permission of the publishers from Jerome S. Bruner, *Toward a Theory of Instruction*. Cambridge, Mass.: Harvard University Press, Copyright © 1966, by the President and Fellows of Harvard College.

what is dimly in a future that is often incomprehensible to him. And he must do so in a strange setting where words and diagrams and other abstractions suddenly become very important. School demands an orderliness and neatness beyond what the child has known before; it requires restraint and immobility never asked of him before; and often it puts him in a spot where he does not *know* whether he knows and can get no indication from anybody for minutes at a time as to whether he is on the right track. Perhaps most important of all, school is away from home with all that fact implies in anxiety, or challenge, or relief.

In consequence of all this the problem of "the will to learn" becomes important, indeed exaggerated. Let us not delude ourselves: it is a problem that cannot be avoided, though it can be made manageable, I think. We shall explore what kinds of factors lead to satisfaction in "educated" learning, to pleasure in the practice of learning as it exists in the necessarily artificial atmosphere of the school. Almost all children possess what have come to be called "intrinsic" motives for learning. An intrinsic motive is one that does not depend upon reward that lies outside the activity it impels. Reward inheres in the successful termination of that activity or even in the activity itself.

Curiosity is almost a prototype of the intrinsic motive. Our attention is attracted to something that is unclear, unfinished, or uncertain. We sustain our attention until the matter in hand becomes clear, finished, or certain. The achievement of clarity or merely the search for it is what satisfies. We would think it preposterous if somebody thought to reward us with praise or profit for having satisfied our curiosity.

33

However pleasant such external reward might be, and however much we might come to depend upon it, the external reward is something added. What activates and satisfies curiosity is something inherent in the cycle of activity by which we express curiosity. Surely such activity is biologically relevant, for curiosity is essential to the survival not only of the individual but of the species. There is considerable research that indicates the extent to which even nonhuman primates will put forth effort for a chance to encounter something novel on which to exercise curiosity. But it is clear that unbridled curiosity is little more than unlimited distractibility. To be interested in everything that comes along is to be interested in nothing for long. Studies of the behavior of three-year-olds, for example, indicate the degree to which they are dominated from the outside by the parade of vivid impressions that pass their way. They turn to this bright color, that sharp sound, that new shiny surface. Many ends are beyond their reach, for they cannot sustain a steady course when the winds shift. If anything, they are "too curious." They live by what psychologists have long called the laws of primary attention: attention dominated by vividness and change in the environment. There has been much speculation about the function of this early and exhausting tempo of curiosity. One neuropsychologist, Donald Hebb, has suggested that the child is drinking in the world, better to construct his neural "models" of the environment. And, it is plain that a stunted organism is produced by depriving an infant of the rich diet of impressions on which his curiosity normally feeds with such extravagance. Animals raised in homogenized environments show crippling deficits in their later ability to learn and to transfer what they have learned. Children "kept in the attic" by misguided or psychotic parents show the same striking backwardness. Indeed, even the children who have suffered the dull, aseptic environment of backward foundling homes often show a decline in intelligence that can be compensated only by vigorous measures of enrichment. So surely, then, an important early function is served by the child's omnivorous

capacity for new impressions. He is sorting the world, storing those things that have some recurrent regularity and require "knowing," discriminating them from the parade of random impressions.[1]

But if attention is to be sustained, directed to some task and held there in spite of temptations that come along, then obviously constraints must be established. The voluntary deployment of curiosity, so slowly and painfully mastered, seems to be supported in part by the young child's new-found capacity to "instruct himself," literally to talk to himself through a sustained sequence. And in part the steadying force seems to be the momentum of concrete overt acts that have a way of sustaining the attention required for their completion by shutting off irrelevant impressions. In time, and with the development of habitual activities, and of language, there emerges more self-directed attention, sometimes called derived primary attention. The child is held steady not so much by vividness as by the habitual round of activity that now demands his attention. Little enough is known about how to help a child become master of his own attention, to sustain it over a long, connected sequence. But while young children are notoriously wandering in their attention, they can be kept in a state of rapt and prolonged attentiveness by being told compelling stories. There may be something to be learned from this observation. What makes the internal sequence of a story even more compelling than the distractions that lie outside it? Are there comparable properties inherent in other activities? Can these be used to train a child to sustain his curiosity beyond the moment's vividness?

Observe a child or group of children building a pile of blocks as high as they can get them. Their attention will be sustained to the flashing point until they reach the climax when the pile comes crashing down. They will return to build

[1] For a further account of the functions of early curiosity, see J. S. Bruner, "The Cognitive Consequences of Early Sensory Deprivation," *Psychosomatic Medicine*, 21.2:89–95 (1959).

still higher. The drama of the task is only its minor virtue. More important is the energizing lure of uncertainty made personal by one's own effort to control it. It is almost the antithesis of the passive attraction of shininess and the vivid. To channel curiosity into more powerful intellectual pursuits requires precisely that there be this transition from the passive, receptive, episodic form of curiosity to the sustained and active form. There are games not only with objects, but with ideas and questions — like Twenty Questions — that provide such a disciplining of the channeling of curiosity. Insofar as one may count on this important human motive — and it seems among the most reliable of the motives — then it seems obvious that our artifical education can in fact be made less artificial from a motivational standpoint by relating it initially to the more surfacy forms of curiosity and attention, and then cultivating curiosity to more subtle and active expression. I think it is fair to say that most of the success in contemporary curriculum building has been achieved by this route. When success comes, it takes the form of recognition that beyond the few things we know there lies a domain of inference: that putting together the two and two that we have yields astonishing results. But this raises the issue of competence, to which we must turn next.

For curiosity is only one of the intrinsic motives for learning. The drive to achieve competence is another. Professor Robert White puts the issue well:

> According to Webster, competence means fitness or ability, and the suggested synonyms include capability, capacity, efficiency, proficiency, and skill. It is therefore a suitable word to describe such things as grasping and exploring, crawling and walking, attention and perception, all of which promote an effective — a competent — interaction with the environment. It is true, of course, that maturation plays a part in all these developments, but this part is heavily overshadowed by learning in all the more complex accomplishments like speech or skilled manipulation. I shall argue that it is necessary to make competence a motivational concept; there is *competence motivation* as well as competence in its more familiar sense of achieved capacity. The behavior that leads to the building

up of effective grasping, handling, and letting go of objects, to take one example, is not random behavior that is produced by an overflow of energy. It is directed, selective, and persistent, and it continues not because it serves primary drives, which indeed it cannot serve until it is almost perfect, but because it satisfies an intrinsic need to deal with the environment. [2]

Observations of young children and of the young of other species suggest that a good deal of their play must be understood as practice in coping with the environment. Primatologists describe, for example, how young female baboons cradle infant baboons in their arms long before they produce their own offspring. In fact, baboon play can be seen almost entirely as the practice of interpersonal skills. Unlike human children, baboons never play with objects, and this, the anthropologists believe, is connected with their inability to use tools when they grow up. And there is evidence that early language mastery, too, depends on such early preparation. One linguist recently has shown how a two-year-old goes on exploring the limits of language use even after the lights are out, parents removed, communication stopped, and sleep imminent.[3]

The child's metalinguistic play is hard to interpret as anything other than pleasure in practicing and developing a new skill. Although competence may not "naturally" be directed toward school learning, it is certainly possible that the great access of energy that children experience when they "get into a subject they like" is made of the same stuff.

We get interested in what we get good at. In general, it is difficult to sustain interest in an activity unless one achieves some degree of competence. Athletics is the activity par excellence where the young need no prodding to gain pleasure from an increase in skill, save where prematurely adult standards are imposed on little leagues formed too soon to ape the big

[2] R. W. White, "Motivation Reconsidered: The Concept of Competence," *Psychological Review*, 66:297–333 (1959).

[3] Ruth H. Weir, *Language in the Crib* (The Hague: Mouton, 1962).

ones. A custom introduced some years ago at the Gordonstoun School in Scotland has become legendary. In addition to conventionally competitive track and field events within the school, there was established a novel competition in which boys pitted themselves against their own best prior record in the events. Several American schools have picked up the idea and, while there has been no "proper evaluation," it is said that the system creates great excitement and enormous effort on the part of the boys.

To achieve the sense of accomplishment requires a task that has some beginning and some terminus. Perhaps an experiment can serve again as a parable. There is a well-known phenomenon known to psychologists by the forbidding name of the Zeigarnik Effect. In brief, tasks that are interrupted are much more likely to be returned to and completed, and much more likely to be remembered, than comparable tasks that one has completed without interruption. But that puts the matter superficially, for it leaves out of account one factor that is crucial. The effect holds only if the tasks that the subject has been set are ones that have a structure — a beginning, a plan, and a terminus. If the tasks are "silly" in the sense of being meaningless, arbitrary, and without visible means for checking progress, the drive to completion is not stimulated by interruption.

It seems likely that the desire to achieve competence follows the same rule. Unless there is some meaningful unity in what we are doing and some way of telling how we are doing, we are not very likely to strive to excel ourselves. Yet surely this too is only a small part of the story, for everybody does not want to be competent in the same activities, and some competencies might even be a source of embarrassment to their possessors. Boys do not thrill to the challenge of sewing a fine seam (again, in our culture), nor girls to becoming competent street fighters. There are competencies that are appropriate and activating for different ages, the two sexes, different social classes. But there are some things about competence motives that transcend these particulars. One is that an activity (given that it is "approved"), must have some meaningful structure to it if it requires skill that is a little bit beyond that now possessed by the person — that it be learned by the exercise of effort. It is probably the combination of the two that is critical.

Experienced teachers who work with the newer curricula in science and mathematics report that they are surprised at the eagerness of students to push ahead to next steps in the course. Several of the teachers have suggested that the eagerness comes from increased confidence in one's ability to understand the material. Some of the students were having their first experience of understanding a topic in some depth, of going somewhere in a subject. It is this that is at the heart of competence motives, and surely our schools have not begun to tap this enormous reservoir of zest.

While we do not know the limits within which competence drives can be shaped and channeled by external reward, it seems quite likely that they are strongly open to external influence. But channelization aside, how can education keep alive and nourish a drive to competence — whether expressed in farming, football, or mathematics? What sustains a sense of pleasure and achievement in mastering things for their own sake — what Thorstein Veblen referred to as an instinct for workmanship? Do competence motives strengthen mainly on their exercise, in whatever context they may be exercised, or do they depend also upon being linked to drives for status, wealth, security, or fame?

There are, to begin with, striking differences among cultures and between strata within any particular society with respect to the encouragement given to competence drives. David McClelland, for example, in writing about the "achieving society," comments upon the fact that in certain times and places one finds a flowering of achievement motivation strongly supported by the society and its institutions and myths alike.[4] Emphasis upon individual respon-

[4] David C. McClelland, *The Achieving Society* (Princeton, N.J.: Van Nostrand, 1961).

sibility and initiative, upon independence in decision and action, upon perfectibility of the self — all of these things serve to perpetuate more basic competency motives past childhood.

But cultures vary in their evaluation of *intellectual* mastery as a vehicle for the expression of competence. Freed Bales, for example, in comparing Irish and Jewish immigrant groups in Boston, remarks that the Jewish, much more than the Irish, treat school success and intellectuality as virtues in their own right as well as ways of upward mobility.[5] The reasons can be found in history. Herzog and Zborowski, in their book on eastern European Jewish communities, suggest that the barrier erected against Jews' entering other professions may have helped foster the cultivation of intellectual excellence as a prized expression of competence.[6]

A culture does not "manage" these matters consciously by the applications of rewards and reproofs alone. The son of the rabbi in the eastern European *stetl* was not punished if he wished to become a merchant rather than a Talmudic scholar, and, indeed, if he chose to become the latter he typically went through long, extrinsically unrewarding, and arduous training to do so. More subtle forces are at work, all of them fairly familiar but too often overlooked in discussing education. One of them is "approval." The professional man is more "respected" than the manual worker. But that scarcely exhausts the matter. Respected by whom? Contemporary sociologists speak of the approval of one's "reference group" — those to whom one looks for guides to action, for the definition of the possible, for ultimate approbation. But what leads *this* individual to look to *that* particular reference group?

What appears to be operative is a process we cavalierly call identification. The fact of identification is more easily described than explained. It refers to the strong human tendency to model one's "self" and one's aspirations upon some other person. When we feel we have succeeded in "being like" an identification figure, we derive pleasure from the achievement and, conversely, we suffer when we have "let him down." Insofar as the identification figure is also "a certain kind of person" — belongs to some group or category — we extend our loyalties from an individual to a reference group. In effect, then, identification relates one not only to individuals, but to one's society as well.

While this account is oversimplified, it serves to underline one important feature of identification as a process — its self-sustaining nature. For what it accomplishes is to pass over to the learner the control of punishment and reward. Insofar as we now carry our standards with us, we achieve a certain independence from the immediate rewards and punishments meted out by others.

It has been remarked by psychologists that identification figures are most often those who control the scarce psychological resources that we most desire — love, approval, sustenance. Let me skip this issue for a moment and return to it later.

The term identification is usually reserved for those strong attachments where there is a considerable amount of emotional investment. But there are "milder" forms of identification that are also important during the years of childhood and after. Perhaps we should call those who serve in these milder relationships "competence models." They are the "on the job" heroes, the reliable ones with whom we can interact in some way. Indeed, they control a rare resource, some desired competence, but what is important is that the resource is attainable by interaction. The "on the job" model is nowhere better illustrated than in the manner in which the child learns language from a parent. The tryout-correction-revision process continues until the child comes to learn the rules whereby sentences are generated and transformed ap-

[5] R. Freed Bales, "The 'Fixation Factor' in Alcohol Addiction: A Hypothesis Derived from a Comparative Study of Irish and Jewish Social Norms," unpublished doctoral dissertation, Harvard University, 1944.
[6] Mark Zborowski and Elizabeth Herzog, *Life Is with People: The Jewish Little-Town of Eastern Europe* (New York: International Universities Press, 1952).

propriately. Finally he develops a set of productive habits that enable him to be his own sentence maker and his own corrector. He "learns the rules of the language." The parent is the model who, by interaction, teaches the skill of language.

In the process of teaching a skill the parent or teacher passes on much more. The teacher imparts attitudes toward a subject and, indeed, attitudes toward learning itself. What results may be quite inadvertent. Often, in our schools, for example, this first lesson is that learning has to do with remembering things when asked, with maintaining a certain undefined tidiness in what one does, with following a train of thought that comes from outside rather than from within and with honoring right answers. Observant anthropologists have suggested that the basic values of the early grades are a stylized version of the feminine role in the society, cautious rather than daring, governed by a ladylike politeness.

One recent study by Pauline Sears underlines the point.[7] It suggests that girls in the early grades, who learn to control their fidgeting earlier and better than boys, are rewarded for excelling in their "feminine" values. The reward can be almost too successful, so that in later years it is difficult to move girls beyond the orderly virtues they learned in their first school encounters. The boys, more fidgety in the first grade, get no such reward and as a consequence may be freer in their approach to learning in later grades. Far more would have to be known about the other conditions present in the lives of these children to draw a firm conclusion from the findings, but it is nonetheless suggestive. There are surely many ways to expand the range of competence models available to children. One is the use of a challenging master teacher, particularly in the early grades. And there is film or closed-circuit television, opening up enormously the range of teachers to whom

the student can be exposed. Filmed teaching has, to be sure, marked limits, for the student cannot interact with an image. But a kind of pseudo interaction can be attained by including in the television lesson a group of students who are being taught right on the screen, and with whom the student can take common cause. Team teaching provides still another approach to the exemplification of a range of competences, particularly if one of the teachers is charged specially with the role of gadfly. None of the above is yet a tried practice, but pedagogy, like economics and engineering, often must try techniques to find not only whether they work, but how they may be made to work.

I would like to suggest that what the teacher must be, to be an effective competence model, is a day-to-day working model with whom to interact. It is not so much that the teacher provides a model to *imitate*. Rather, it is that the teacher can become a part of the student's internal dialogue — somebody whose respect he wants, someone whose standards he wishes to make his own. It is like becoming a speaker of a language one shares with somebody. The language of that interaction becomes a part of oneself, and the standards of style and clarity that one adopts for that interaction become a part of one's own standards.

Finally, a word about one last intrinsic motive that bears closely upon the will to learn. Perhaps it should be called reciprocity. For it involves a deep human need to respond to others and to operate jointly with them toward an objective. One of the important insights of modern zoology is the importance of this intraspecies reciprocity for the survival of individual members of the species. The psychologist Roger Barker[8] has commented that the best way he has found to predict the behavior of the children whom he has been studying in great detail in the midst of their everyday activities is to know their situations. A child in a baseball game behaves baseball; in the drugstore the

[7] Pauline Sears, "Attitudinal and Affective Factors Affecting Children's Approaches to Problem Solving," in J. S. Bruner, ed., *Learning About Learning* (Washington, D.C.: U.S. Office of Education, 1963).

[8] Roger Barker, "On the Nature of the Environment," *Journal of Social Issues*, 19.4:17–38 (1963).

same child behaves drugstore. Situations have a demand value that appears to have very little to do with the motives that are operative. Surely it is not simply a "motive to conform"; this is too great an abstraction. The man who is regulating his pressure on the back of a car, along with three or four others, trying to "rock it out," is not so much conforming as "fitting his efforts into an enterprise." It is about as primitive an aspect of human behavior as we know.

Like the other activities we have been discussing, its exercise seems to be its sole reward. Probably it is the basis of human society, this response through reciprocity to other members of one's species. Where joint action is needed, where reciprocity is required for the group to attain an objective, then there seem to be processes that carry the individual along into learning, sweep him into a competence that is required in the setting of the group. We know precious little about this primitive motive to reciprocate, but what we do know is that it can furnish a driving force to learn as well. Human beings (and other species as well) fall into a pattern that is required by the goals and activities of the social group in which they find themselves. "Imitation" is not the word for it, since it is usually not plain in most cases what is to be imitated. A much more interesting way of looking at what is involved is provided by the phenomenon of a young child learning to use the pronouns "I" and "you" correctly. The parent says to the child, "You go to bed now." The child says, "No, you no go to bed." We are amused. "Not *me* but *you*," we say. In time, and after a surprisingly brief period of confusion, the child learns that "you" refers to himself when another uses it, and to another person when he uses it — and the reverse with "I." It is a prime example of reciprocal learning. It is by much the same process that children learn the beautifully complicated games they play (adult and child games alike), that they learn their role in the family and in school, and finally that they come to take their role in the greater society.

The corpus of learning, using the word now as synonymous with knowledge, is reciprocal. A culture in its very nature is a set of values, skills, and ways of life that no one member of the society masters. Knowledge in this sense is like a rope, each strand of which extends no more than a few inches along its length, all being intertwined to give a solidity to the whole. The conduct of our educational system has been curiously blind to this interdependent nature of knowledge. We have "teachers" and "pupils," "experts" and "laymen." But the community of learning is somehow overlooked.

What can most certainly be encouraged — and what is now being developed in the better high schools — is something approximating the give and take of a seminar in which discussion is the vehicle of instruction. This is reciprocity. But it requires recognition of one critically important matter: you cannot have both reciprocity and the demand that everybody learn the same thing or be "completely well rounded in the same way all the time. If reciprocally operative groups are to give support to learning by stimulating each person to join his efforts to a group, then we shall need tolerance for the specialized roles that develop — the critic, the innovator, the second helper, the cautionary. For it is from the cultivation of these interlocking roles that the participants get the sense of operating reciprocally in a group. Never mind that this pupil for this term in this seminar has a rather specialized task to perform. It will change. Meanwhile, if he can see how he contributes to the effectiveness of the group's operations on history or geometry or whatnot, he is likely to be the more activated. And surely one of the roles that will emerge is that of auxiliary teacher — let it, encourage it. It can only help in relieving the tedium of a classroom with one expert up here and the rest down there.

At the risk of being repetitious, let me restate the argument. It is this. The will to learn is an intrinsic motive, one that finds both its source and its reward in its own exercise. The will to learn becomes a "problem" only under specialized circumstances like those of a school, where a curriculum is set, students confined, and a path fixed. The problem exists not so much in learning itself, but in the fact that what the school imposes often fails to enlist the natural energies that sustain spontaneous learing — curiosity, a desire for competence, aspiration to emulate a model, and a deep-sensed commitment to the web of social reciprocity. Our concern has been with how these energies may be cultivated in support of school learning. If we know little firmly, at least we are not without reasonable hypotheses about how to proceed. The practice of education does, at least, produce interesting hypotheses. After all, the Great Age of Discovery was made possible by men whose hypotheses were formed before they had developed a decent technique for measuring longitude.

You will have noted by now a considerable de-emphasis of "extrinsic" rewards and punishments as factors in school learning. There has been in these pages a rather intentional neglect of the so-called Law of Effect, which holds that a reaction is more likely to be repeated if it has previously been followed by a "satisfying state of affairs." I am not unmindful of the notion of reinforcement. It is doubtful, only, that "satisfying states of affairs" are *reliably* to be found outside learning itself — in kind or harsh words from the teacher, in grades and gold stars, in the absurdly abstract assurance to the high school student that his lifetime earnings will be better by 80 percent if he graduates. External reinforcement may indeed get a particular act going and may even lead to its repetition, but it does not nourish, reliably, the long course of learning by which man slowly builds in his own way a serviceable model of what the world is and what it can be.

John Holt

Excerpts from How Children Fail

June 16, 1959

A year ago I was wondering how a child's fears might influence his strategies. This year's work has told me. The strategies of most of these kids have been consistently self-centered, self-protective, aimed above all else at avoiding trouble, embarrassment, punishment, disapproval, or loss of status. This is particularly true of the ones who have had a tough time in school. When they get a problem, I can read their thoughts on their faces, I can almost hear them, "Am I going to get this right? Probably not; what'll happen to me when I get it wrong? Will the teacher get mad? Will the other kids laugh at me? Will my mother and father hear about it? Will they keep me back this year? Why am I so dumb?" And so on.

Even in the room periods, where I did all I could to make the work non-threatening, I was continually amazed and appalled to see the children hedging their bets, covering their losses in advance, trying to fix things so that whatever happened they could feel they had been right, or if wrong, no more wrong than anyone else. "I think it will sort of balance." They are fence-straddlers, afraid ever to commit themselves — and at the age of ten. Playing games like Twenty Questions, which one might have expected them to play for fun, many of them were concerned only to put up a good front, to look as if they knew what they were doing, whether they did or not.

These self-limiting and self-defeating strategies are dictated, above all else, by fear. For

many years I have been asking myself why intelligent children act unintelligently at school. The simple answer is, "Because they're scared." I used to suspect that children's defeatism had something to do with their bad work in school, but I thought I could clear it away with hearty cries of "Onward! You can do it!" What I now see for the first time is the mechanism by which fear destroys intelligence, the way it affects a child's whole way of looking at, thinking about, and dealing with life. So we have two problems, not one: to stop children from being afraid, and then to break them of the bad thinking habits into which their fears have driven them.

What is most surprising of all is how much fear there is in school. Why is so little said about it? Perhaps most people do not recognize fear in children when they see it. They can read the grossest signs of fear; they know what the trouble is when a child clings howling to his mother; but the subtler signs of fear escape them. It is these signs, in children's faces, voices, and gestures, in their movements and ways of working, that tell me plainly that most children in school are scared most of the time, many of them very scared. Like good soldiers, they control their fears, live with them, and adjust themselves to them. But the trouble is, and here is a vital difference between school and war, that the adjustments children make to their fears are almost wholly bad, destructive of their intelligence and capacity. The scared fighter may be the best fighter, but the scared learner is always a poor learner.

July 20, 1960

My seventeen-month-old niece caught sight of my ball point pen the other day, and reached out for it. It has a plastic cap that fits over the point. She took hold of it, and after some pushing and pulling, got the cap off. After looking it over, she put it back on. Then off again; then on again. A good game! Now, if I want to be able to use my pen, I have to keep it out of sight, for when she sees it, she wants to play with it. She is so deft in putting it back on that it makes me wonder about all I've read about the lack of coordination in infants and the imprecision of their movements. Under the right circumstances — when they are interested — they may be much more skillful than we think.

These quiet summer days I spend many hours watching this baby. What comes across most vividly is that she is a kind of scientist. She is always observing and experimenting. She is hardly ever idle. Most of her waking time she is intensely and purposefully active, soaking up experience and trying to make sense out of it, trying to find how things around her behave, and trying to make them behave as she wants them to.

In the face of what looks like unbroken failure, she is so persistent. Most of her experiments, her efforts to predict and control her en-vironment, don't work. But she goes right on, not the least daunted. Perhaps this is because there are no penalties attached to failure, except nature's — usually, if you try to step on a ball, you fall down. A baby does not react to failure as an adult does, or even a five-year-old, because she has not yet been made to feel that failure is shame, disgrace, a crime. Unlike her elders, she is not concerned with protecting herself against everything that is not easy and familiar; she reaches out to experience, she embraces life.

Watching this baby, it is hard to credit the popular notion that without outside rewards and penalties children will not learn. There are some rewards and penalties in her life; the adults approve of some things she does, and disapprove of others. But most of the time she lives beyond praise or blame, if only because most of her learning experiments are unobserved. After all, who thinks about the meaning of what a baby is doing, so long as she is quiet and contented? But watch a while and think about it, and you see that she has a strong desire to make sense of the world around her. Her learning gives her great satisfaction, whether anyone else notices it or not.

Abraham H. Maslow

Defense and Growth

This chapter is an effort to be a little more systematic in the area of growth theory. For once we accept the notion of growth, many questions of detail arise. Just how does growth take place? Why do children grow or not grow? How do they know in which direction to grow? How do they get off in the direction of pathology?

After all, the concepts of self-actualization, growth and self are all high-level abstractions. We need to get closer to actual processes, to raw data, to concrete, living happenings.

These are far goals. Healthily growing infants and children don't live for the sake of far goals or for the distant future; they are too busy enjoying themselves and spontaneously living for the moment. They are *living*, not *preparing* to live. How can they manage, just being, spontaneously, not *trying* to grow, seeking only to enjoy the present activity, nevertheless to move forward step by step? i.e., to grow in a healthy way? to discover their real selves? How can we reconcile the facts of Being with the facts of Becoming? Growth is not in the pure case a goal out ahead, nor is self-actualization, nor is the discovery of Self. In the child, it is not specifically purposed; rather it just happens. He doesn't so much search as find. The laws of deficiency-motivation and of purposeful coping do not hold for growth, for spontaneity, for creativeness.

The danger with a pure Being-psychology is that it may tend to be static, not accounting for the facts of movement, direction and growth. We tend to describe states of Being, of self-ac-

tualization as if they were Nirvana states of perfection. Once you're there, you're there, and it seems as if all you could do is to rest content in perfection.

The answer I find satisfactory is a simple one, namely, that growth takes place when the next step forward is subjectively more delightful, more joyous, more intrinsically satisfying than the previous gratification with which we have become familiar and even bored; that the only way we can ever know what is right for us is that it feels better subjectively than any alternative. The new experience validates *itself* rather than by any outside criterion. It is self-justifying, self-validating.

We don't do it because it is good for us, or because psychologists approve, or because somebody told us to, or because it will make us live longer, or because it is good for the species, or because it will bring external rewards, or because it is logical. We do it for the same reason that we choose one dessert over another. I have already described this as a basic mechanism for falling in love, or for choosing a friend, i.e., kissing one person gives more delight than kissing the other, being friends with *a* is more satisfying subjectively than being friends with *b*.

In this way, we learn what we are good at, what we really like or dislike, what our tastes and judgments and capacities are. In a word, this is the way in which we discover the Self and answer the ultimate questions Who am I? What am I?

The steps and the choices are taken out of pure spontaneity, from within outward. The healthy infant or child, just Being, as *part* of his Being, is randomly, and spontaneously curious, exploratory, wondering, interested. Even when he is non-purposeful, non-coping, expressive, spontaneous, not motivated by any deficiency of the ordinary sort, he tends to try out his powers, to reach out, to be absorbed, fascinated, interested, to play, to wonder, to manipulate the world. *Exploring, manipulating, experiencing*, being interested, choosing, delighting, *enjoying* can all be seen as attributes of pure Being, and yet lead to Becoming, though in a serendipitous way, fortuitously, unplanned, unanticipated. Spontaneous, creative experience can and does happen without expectations, plans, foresight, purpose, or goal.[1] It is only when the child sates himself, becomes bored, that he is ready to turn to other, perhaps "higher," delights.

Then arise the inevitable questions. What holds him back? What prevents growth? Wherein lies the conflict? What is the alternative to growth forward? Why is it so hard and painful for some to grow forward? Here we must become more fully aware of the fixative and regressive power of ungratified deficiency-needs, of the attractions of safety and security, of the functions of defense and protection against pain, fear, loss, and threat, of the need for courage in order to grow ahead.

Every human being has *both* sets of forces within him. One set clings to safety and defensiveness out of fear, tending to regress backward, hanging on to the past, *afraid* to grow away from the primitive communication with the mother's uterus and breast, *afraid* to take chances, afraid to jeopardize what he already has, *afraid* of independence, freedom and separateness. The other set of forces impels him forward toward wholeness to Self and uniqueness of Self, toward full functioning of all his

capacities, toward confidence in the face of the external world at the same time that he can accept his deepest, real, unconscious Self.

I can put all this together in a schema, which though very simple, is also very powerful, both heuristically and theoretically. This basic dilemma or conflict between the defensive forces and the growth trends I conceive to be existential, imbedded in the deepest nature of the human being, now and forever into the future. If it is diagrammed like this:

Safety ←——————⟨ PERSON ⟩——————→ Growth

then we can very easily classify the various mechanisms of growth in an uncomplicated way as

a. Enhancing the growthward vectors, e.g., making growth more attractive and delight producing.
b. Minimizing the fears of growth,
c. Minimizing the safetyward vectors, i.e., making it less attractive.
d. Maximizing the fears of safety, defensiveness, pathology and regression.

We can then add to our basic schema these four sets of valences:

Enhance the dangers   *Enhance the attractions*

Safety ←——————⟨ PERSON ⟩——————→ Growth

Minimize the attractions   *Minimize the dangers*

Therefore we can consider the process of healthy growth to be a never ending series of free choice situations, confronting each individual at every point throughout his life, in which he must choose between the delights of safety and growth, dependence and inde-

---

[1] "But paradoxically, the art experience cannot be effectively *used* for this purpose or any other. It must be a purposeless activity, as far as we understand 'purpose.' It can only be an experience in *being* — being a human organism doing what it must and what it is privileged to do — experiencing life keenly and wholly, expending energy and creating beauty in its own style — and the increased sensitivity, integrity, efficiency, and feeling of well-being are by-products" (1).

pendence, regression and progression, immaturity and maturity. Safety has both anxieties and delights; growth has both anxieties and delights. We grow forward when the delights of growth and anxieties of safety are greater than the anxieties of growth and the delights of safety.

So far it sounds like a truism. But it isn't to psychologists who are mostly trying to be objective, public, behavioristic. And it has taken many experiments with animals and much theorizing to convince the students of animal motivation that they must invoke what P. T. Young (2) called a hedonic factor, over and above need-reduction, in order to explain the results so far obtained in free-choice experimentation. For example, saccharin is not need-reducing in any way and yet white rats will choose it over plain water. Its (useless) taste *must* have something to do with it.

Furthermore, observe that subjective delight in the experience is something that we can attribute to *any* organism, e.g., it applies to the infant as well as the adult, to the animal as well as to the human.

The possibility that then opens for us is very enticing for the theorist. Perhaps all these high-level concepts of Self, Growth, Self-realization, and Psychological Health can fall into the same system of explanation with appetite experiments in animals, free choice observations in infant feeding and in occupational choice, and the rich studies of homeostasis (3).

Of course this formulation of growth-through-delight also commits us to the necessary postulation that what tastes good is also, in the growth sense, "better" for us. We rest here on the faith that if free choice is *really* free and if the chooser is not too sick or frightened to choose, he will choose wisely, in a healthy and growthward direction, more often than not.

For this postulation there is already much experimental support, but it is mostly at the animal level, and much more detailed research is necessary with free choice in humans. We must know much more than we do about the reasons for bad and unwise choices, at the constitutional level and at the level of psychodynamics.

There is another reason why my systematizing side likes this notion of growth-through-delight. It is that then I find it possible to tie it in nicely with dynamic theory, with *all* the dynamic theories of Freud, Adler, Jung, Schachtel, Horney, Fromm, Burrow, Reich, and Rank, as well as the theories of Rogers, Buhler, Combs, Angyal, Allport, Goldstein, Murray, Moustakas, Perls, Bugental, Assagioli, Frankl, Jourard, May, White and others.

I criticize the classical Freudians for tending (in the extreme instance) to pathologize everything and for not seeing clearly enough the healthward possibilities in the human being, for seeing everything through brown-colored glasses. But the growth school (in the extreme instance) is equally vulnerable, for they tend to see through rose-colored glasses and generally slide over the problems of pathology, of weakness, of *failure* to grow. One is like a theology of evil and sin exclusively; the other is like a theology without any evil at all, and is therefore equally incorrect and unrealistic.

One additional relationship between safety and growth must be specially mentioned. Apparently growth forward customarily takes place in little steps, and each step forward is made possible by the feeling of being safe, of operating out into the unknown from a safe home port, of daring because retreat is possible. We may use as a paradigm the toddler venturing away from his mother's knee into strange surroundings. Characteristically, he first clings to his mother as he explores the room with his eyes. Then he dares a little excursion, continually reassuring himself that the mother-security is intact. These excursions get more and more extensive. In this way, the child can explore a dangerous and unknown world. If suddenly the mother were to disappear, he would be thrown into anxiety, would cease to be interested in exploring the world, would wish only the return of safety, and might even lose his abilities, e.g., instead of daring to walk, he might creep.

I think we may safely generalize this example. Assured safety permits higher needs and impulses to emerge and to grow towards mastery. To endanger safety, means regression backward to the more basic foundation. What this means is that in the choice between giving up safety or giving up growth, safety will ordinarily win out. Safety needs are prepotent over growth needs. This means an expansion of our basic formula. In general, only a child who feels safe dares to grow forward healthily. His safety needs must be gratified. He can't be *pushed* ahead, because the ungratified safety needs will remain forever underground, always calling for satisfaction. The more safety needs are gratified, the less valence they have for the child, the less they will beckon, and lower his courage.

Now, how can we know when the child feels safe enough to dare to choose the new step ahead? Ultimately, the only way in which we can know is by *his* choices, which is to say only *he* can ever really know the right moment when the beckoning forces ahead overbalance the beckoning forces behind, and courage outweighs fear.

Ultimately the person, even the child, must choose for himself. Nobody can choose for him too often, for this itself enfeebles him, cutting his self-trust, and confusing his *ability* to perceive his own internal delight in the experience, his *own* impulses, judgments, and feelings, and to differentiate them from the interiorized standards of others.[2]

[2] "From the moment the package is in his hands, he feels free to do what he wants with it. He opens it, speculates on what it is, recognizes what it is, expresses happiness or disappointment, notices the arrangement of the contents, finds a book of directions, feels the touch of the steel, the different weights of the parts, and their number, and so on. He does all this before he has attempted to do a thing with the set. Then comes the thrill of doing something with it. It may be only matching one single part with another. Thereby alone he gets a feeling of having done something, that he can do something, and that he is not helpless with that particular article. Whatever pattern is subsequently followed, whether his interest extends to the full utilization of the set and therefore toward further gaining a feeling of greater and greater accomplishment, or whether he completely discards it, his initial contact with the erector set has been meaningful.

"The results of active experiencing can be summarized approximately in the following way. There is physical, emotional, and intellectual self-involvement;

If this is all so, if the child himself must finally make the choice by which he grows forward, since only he can know his subjective delight experience, then how can we reconcile this ultimate necessity for trust in the inner individual with the necessity for help from the environment? For he does need help. Without help he will be too frightened to dare. How can we help him to grow? Equally important, how can we endanger his growth?

The opposite of the subjective experience of

there is a recognition and further exploration of one's abilities; there is initiation of activity or creativeness; there is finding out one's own pace and rhythm and the assumption of enough of a task for one's abilities at that particular time, which would include the avoidance of taking on too much; there is gain in skill which one can apply to other enterprises, and there is an opportunity each time that one has an active part in something, no matter how small, to find out more and more what one is interested in.

"The above situation may be contrasted with another in which the person who brings home the erector set says to the child, 'Here is an erector set, let me open it for you.' He does so and then points out all the things in the box, the book of directions, the various parts, etc., and, to top it off, he sets about building one of the complicated models, let us say, a crane. The child may be much interested in what he has seen being done, but let us focus on one aspect of what has really been happening. The child has had no opportunity to get himself involved with the erector set, with his body, his intelligence, or his feelings, he has had no opportunity to match himself up with something that is new for him, to find out what he is capable of or to gain further direction for his interests. The building of the crane for him may have brought in another factor. It may have left the child with an implied demand that he do likewise without his having had an opportunity to prepare himself for any such complicated task. The end becomes the object instead of the experience involved in the process of attaining the objective. Also whatever he may subsequently do by himself will look small and mean compared to what had been made for him by someone else. He has not added to his total experience for coming up against something new for the next time. In other words, he has not grown from within but has had something superimposed from the outside. . . . Each bit of active experiencing is an opportunity toward finding out what he likes or dislikes, and more and more what he wants to make out of himself. It is an essential part of his progress toward the stage of maturity and self-direction" (4).

delight (trusting himself), so far as the child is concerned, is the opinion of other people (love, respect, approval, admiration, reward from others, trusting others rather than himself). Since others are so important and vital for the helpless baby and child, fear of losing them (as providers of safety, food, love, respect, etc.) is a primal, terrifying danger. Therefore, the child, faced with a difficult choice between his own delight experiences and the experience of approval from others, must generally choose approval from others, and then handle his delight by repression or letting it die, or not noticing it or controlling it by willpower. In general, along with this will develop a disapproval of the delight experience, or shame and embarrassment and secretiveness about it, with finally, the inability even to experience it.[3]

[3] "How is it possible to lose a self? The treachery, unknown and unthinkable, begins with our secret psychic death in childhood — if and when we are not loved and are cut off from our spontaneous wishes. (Think: what is left?) But wait — victim might even "outgrow" it — but it is a perfect double crime in which he him-it is not just this simple murder of a psyche. That might be written off, the tiny self also gradually and unwittingly takes part. He has not been accepted for himself, *as he is.* "Oh, they 'love' him, but they want him or force him or expect him to be different! Therefore he *must be unacceptable.* He himself learns to believe it and at last even takes it for granted. He has truly given himself up. No matter now whether he obeys them, whether he clings, rebels or withdraws — his behavior, his performance is all that matters. His center of gravity is in 'them,' not in himself — yet if he so much as noticed it he'd think it natural enough. And the whole thing is entirely plausible; all invisible, automatic, and anonymous!

"This is the perfect paradox. Everything looks normal; no crime was intended; there is no corpse, no guilt. All we can see is the sun rising and setting as usual. But what has happened? He has been rejected, not only by them, but by himself. (He is actually without a self.) What has he lost? Just the one true and vital part of himself: his own yes-feeling, which is his very capacity for growth, his root system. But alas, he is not dead. 'Life' goes on, and so must he. From the moment he gives himself up, and to the extent that he does so, all unknowingly he sets about to create and maintain a pseudo-self. But this is an expediency — a 'self' without wishes. This one shall be loved (or feared) where he is despised, strong

The primal choice, the fork in the road, then, is between others' and one's own self. If the only way to maintain the self is to lose others, then the ordinary child will give up the self. This is true for the reason already mentioned, that safety is a most basic and prepotent need for children, more primarily necessary by far than independence and self-actualization. If adults force this choice upon him, of choosing between the loss of one (lower and stronger) vital necessity or another (higher and weaker) vital necessity, the child must choose safety even at the cost of giving up self and growth.

(In principle there is no need for forcing the child to make such a choice. People just *do* it often, out of their own sicknesses and out of ignorance. We know that it is not necessary because we have examples enough of children who are offered all these goods simultaneously, at no vital cost, who can have safety and love *and* respect too.)

Here we can learn important lessons from the therapy situation, the creative educative situation, creative art education and I believe also creative dance education. Here where the situation is set up variously as permissive, admiring, praising, accepting, safe, gratifying, reassuring, supporting, unthreatening, non-valuing, non-comparing, that is, where the person can feel completely safe and unthreatened, then it becomes possible for him to work out and express all sorts of lesser delights, e.g., hostility, neurotic dependency. Once these are sufficiently catharted, he then tends spontaneously to go to other delights which outsiders perceive

where he is weak; it shall go through the motions (oh, but they are caricatures!) not for fun or joy but for survival; not simply because it wants to move but because it has to obey. This necessity is not life — not his life — it is a defense mechanism against death. It is also the machine of death. From now on he will be torn apart by compulsive (unconscious) *needs* or ground by (unconscious) conflicts into paralysis, every motion and every instant canceling out his being, his integrity; and all the while he is disguised as a normal person and expected to behave like one!

"In a word, I saw that we *become* neurotic seeking or defending a pseudo-self, a self-system; and we *are* neurotic to the extent that we are self-less (5).

to be "higher" or growthward, e.g., love, creativeness, and which he himself will prefer to the previous delights, once he has experienced them both. (It often makes little difference what kind of explicit theory is held by the therapist, teacher, helper, etc. The really good therapist who may espouse a pessimistic Freudian theory, *acts* as if growth were possible. The really good teacher who espouses verbally a completely rosy and optimistic picture of human nature, will *imply* in actual teaching, a complete understanding and respect for regressive and defensive forces. It is also possible to have a wonderfully realistic and comprehensive philosophy and belie it in practice, in therapy, or teaching or parenthood. Only the one who respects fear and defense can teach; only the one who respects health can do therapy.)

Part of the paradox in this situation is that in a very real way, even the "bad" choice is "good for" the neurotic chooser, or at least understandable and even necessary in terms of his own dynamics. We know that tearing away a functional neurotic symptom by force, or by too direct a confrontation or interpretation, or by a stress situation which cracks the person's defenses against too painful an insight, can shatter the person altogether. This involves us in the question of *pace* of growth. And again the good parent, or therapist or educator *practices* as if he understood that gentleness, sweetness, respect for fear, understanding of the naturalness of defensive and regressive forces, are necessary if growth is not to look like an overwhelming danger instead of a delightful prospect. He implies that he understands that growth can emerge only from safety. He *feels* that if a person's defenses are very rigid this is for a good reason and he is willing to be patient and understanding even though knowing the path in which the child "should" go.

Seen from the dynamic point of view, ultimately *all* choices are in fact wise, if only we grant two kinds of wisdom, defensive-wisdom and growth-wisdom. Defensiveness can be as wise as daring; it depends on the particular person, his particular status and the particular situation in which he has to choose. The choice of safety is wise when it avoids pain that may be more than the person can bear at the moment. If we wish to help him grow (because we know that consistent safety-choices will bring him to catastrophe in the long run, and will cut him off from possibilities that he himself would enjoy if only he could savor them), then all we can do is help him if he asks for help out of suffering, or else simultaneously allow him to feel safe and beckon him onward to *try* the new experience like the mother whose open arms invite the baby to try to walk. We can't *force* him to grow, we can only *coax* him to, make it more possible for him, in the trust that simply experiencing the new experience will make him prefer it. *Only* he can prefer it; no one can prefer it for him. If it is to become part of him, *he* must like it. If he doesn't, we must gracefully concede that it is not for him at this moment.

This means that the sick child must be respected as much as the healthy one, so far as the growth process is concerned. Only when his fears are accepted respectfully, can he dare to be bold. We must understand that the dark forces are as "normal" as the growth forces.

This is a ticklish task, for it implies simultaneously that we know what is best for him (since we *do* beckon him on in a direction we choose), and also that only he knows what is best for himself in the long run. This means that we must *offer* only, and rarely force. We must be quite ready, not only to beckon forward, but to respect retreat to lick wounds, to recover strength, to look over the situation from a safe vantage point, or even to regress to a previous mastery or a "lower" delight, so that courage for growth can be regained.

And this again is where the helper comes in. He is needed, not only for making possible growth forward in the healthy child (by being "available" as the child desires) and getting out of his way at other times, but much more urgently, by the person who is "stuck" in fixation, in rigid defenses, in safety measures which cut off the possibilities of growth. Neurosis is self-perpetuating; so is character struc-

48

ture. We can either wait for life to prove to such a person that his system doesn't work, i.e., by letting him eventually collapse into neurotic suffering, or else by understanding him and helping him to grow by respecting and understanding both his deficiency needs and his growth needs.

This amounts to a revision of Taoistic "let-be," which often hasn't worked because the growing child needs help. It can be formulated as "helpful let-be." It is a *loving* and *respecting* Taoism. It recognizes not only growth and the specific mechanism which makes it move in the right direction, but it also recognizes and respects the fear of growth, the slow pace of growth, the blocks, the pathology, the reasons for not growing. It recognizes the place, the necessity and the helpfulness of the outer environment without yet giving it control. It implements inner growth by knowing its mechanisms and by being willing to help *it* instead of merely being hopeful or passively optimistic about it.

All the foregoing may now be related to the general motivation theory, set forth in my *Motivation and Personality*, particularly the theory of need gratification, which seems to me to be the most important single principle underlying all healthy human development. The single holistic principle that binds together the multiplicity of human motives is the tendency for a new and higher need to emerge as the lower need fulfills itself by being sufficiently gratified. The child who is fortunate enough to grow normally and well gets satiated and *bored* with the delights that he has savored sufficiently, and *eagerly* (without pushing) goes on to higher more complex, delights as they become available to him without danger or threat.

This principle can be seen exemplified not only in the deeper motivational dynamics of the child but also in microcosm in the development of any of his more modest activities, e.g., in learning to read, or skate, or paint, or dance. The child who masters simple words enjoys them intensely but doesn't stay there. In the proper atmosphere he spontaneously shows ea-

gerness to go on to more and more new words, longer words, more complex sentences, etc. If he is forced to stay at the simple level he gets bored and restless with what formerly delighted him. He *wants* to go on, to move, to grow. Only if frustration, failure, disapproval, ridicule come at the next step does he fixate or regress, and we are then faced with the intricacies of pathological dynamics and of neurotic compromises, in which the impulses remain alive but unfulfilled, or even of loss of impulse and of capacity.[4]

What we wind up with then is a subjective device to add to the principle of the hierarchical arrangement of our various needs, a

[4] I think it is possible to apply this general principle to Freudian theory of the progression of libidinal stages. The infant in the oral stage, gets most of his delights through the mouth. And one in particular which has been neglected is that of mastery. We should remember that the *only* thing an infant can do well and efficiently is to suckle. In all else he is inefficient, incapable and if, as I think, this is the earliest precursor of self-esteem (feeling of mastery), then this is the *only* way in which the infant can experience the delight of mastery (efficiency, control, self expression, volition).

But soon he develops other capacities for mastery and control. I mean here not only anal control which though correct, has, in my opinion, been overplayed. Motility and sensory capacities also develop enough during the so-called "anal" stage to give feelings of delight and mastery. But what is important for us here is that the oral infant tends to play out his oral mastery and to become bored with it, just as he becomes bored with milk alone. In a free choice situation, he tends to give up the breast and milk in favor of the more complex activities and tastes, or anyway, to add to the breast these other "higher" developments. Given sufficient gratification, free choice and lack of threat, he "grows" out of the oral stage and renounces it himself. He doesn't have to be "kicked upstairs," or forced on to maturity as is so often implied. He *chooses* to grow on to higher delights, to become bored with older ones. Only under the impact of danger, threat, failure, frustration, or stress does he tend to regress or fixate; only then does he prefer safety to growth. Certainly renunciation, delay in gratification and the ability to withstand frustration are also necessary for strength, and we know that unbridled gratification is dangerous. And yet it remains true that these qualifications are *subsidiary* to the principle that sufficient gratification of basic needs is *sine qua non*.

device which guides and directs the individual in the direction of "healthy" growth. The principle holds true at any age. Recovering the ability to perceive one's own delights is the best way of rediscovering the sacrificed self even in adulthood. The process of therapy helps the adult to discover that the childish (repressed) necessity for the approval of others no longer needs exist in the childish form and degree, and that the terror of losing these others with the accompanying fear of being weak, helpless and abandoned is no longer realistic and justified as it was for the child. For the adult, others can be and should be less important than for the child.

Our final formula then has the following elements:

1. The healthily spontaneous child, in his spontaneity, from within out, in response to his own inner Being, reaches out to the environment in wonder and interest, and expresses whatever skills he has,

2. To the extent that he is not crippled by fear, to the extent that he feels safe enough to dare.

3. In this process, that which gives him the delight-experience is fortuitously encountered, or is offered to him by helpers.

4. He must be safe and self-accepting enough to be able to choose and prefer these delights, instead of being frightened by them.

5. If he *can* choose these experiences which are validated by the experience of delight, then he can return to the experience, repeat it, savor it to the point of repletion, satiation or boredom.

6. At this point, he shows the tendency to go on to more complex, richer experiences and accomplishments in the same sector (again, if he feels safe enough to dare).

7. Such experiences not only mean moving on, but have a feedback effect on the Self, in the feeling of certainty ("This I like; that I don't for *sure*"); of capability, mastery, self-trust, self-esteem.

8. In this never ending series of choices of which life consists, the choice may generally be schematized as between safety (or, more broadly, defensiveness) and growth, and since only that child doesn't need safety who already has it, we may expect the growth choice to be made by the safety-need gratified child. Only he can afford to be bold.

9. In order to be able to choose in accord with his own nature and to develop it, the child must be permitted to retain the subjective experiences of delight and boredom, as *the* criteria of the correct choice for him. The alternative criterion is making the choice in terms of the wish of another person. The Self is lost when this happens. Also this constitutes restricting the choice to safety alone, since the child will give up trust in his own delight-criterion out of fear (of losing protection, love, etc.).

10. If the choice is really a free one, and if the child is not crippled, then we may expect him ordinarily to choose progression forward.[5]

11. The evidence indicates that what delights the healthy child, what tastes good for him, is also, more frequently than not, "best" for him in terms of far goals as perceivable by the spectator.

12. In this process the environment (parents, therapists, teachers) is important in various ways, even though the ultimate choice must be made by the child:

    a. it can gratify his basic needs for safety, belongingness, love and respect, so that he can feel unthreatened, au-

---

[5] A kind of pseudo-growth takes place very commonly when the person tries (by repression, denial, reaction-formation, etc.) to convince himself that an ungratified basic need has really been gratified, or doesn't exist. He then permits himself to grow on to higher-need-levels, which of course, forever after, rest on a very shaky foundation. I call this "pseudo-growth by bypassing the ungratified need." Such a need perseverates forever as an unconscious force (repetition compulsion).

tonomous, interested and spontaneous and thus dare to choose the unknown;

  b. it can help by making the growth choice positively attractive and less dangerous, and by making the regressive choice less attractive and more costly.

13. In this way the psychology of Being and the psychology of Becoming can be reconciled, and the child, simply being himself, can yet move forward and grow.

References

1. F. Wilson, "Human Nature and Esthetic Growth," p. 213 in C. Moustakas (ed.), *The Self* (New York: Harper, 1956).
2. P. T. Young, *Motivation and Emotion* (New York: Wiley, 1961).
3. W. B. Cannon, *Wisdom of the Body* (New York: Norton, 1932).
4. B. Zuger, "Growth of the Individual's Concept of Self," *AMA American Journal on Diseased Children*, 83 (1952), p. 179.
5. Anonymous, "Finding the Real Self," a letter with a foreword by Karen Horney, *American Journal of Psychoanalysis*, 9 (1949), p. 7. [Excerpt reprinted by permission.]

George Dennison

Excerpt from The Lives of Children

Alfred North Whitehead, in his *Aims of Education*, tells us that one of the greatest of intellectual tasks is routinely performed by infants under the aegis of mother and father.

> The first intellectual task which confronts an infant is the acquirement of spoken language. What an appalling task, the correlation of meanings with sounds. It requires an analysis of ideas and an analysis of sounds. We all know that an infant does it, and that the miracle of his achievement is explicable. But so are all miracles, and yet to the wise they remain miracles.

All parents have observed this process. All know that they have contributed to it. Few indeed, however, will insist that it was they who *taught* their children to talk. Here again we find evidence that instruction, of itself, is not the highroad to learning.

What is it about the environment of the home that so marvelously supports this great intellectual task of infancy? I would like to pursue this for a moment, and then raise the question of transposing these environmental qualities into the overall structure of school.

Crying is the earliest "speech." Though it is wordless, it possesses in prototype many of the attributes of true speech: it is both expressive and practical, it effects immediate environmental change, it is directed to someone, and it is accompanied by facial expressions and "gestures." All these will be regularized, mastered by the infant long before the advent of words.

Two features of the growth of this mastery are striking:

1. The infant's use of gestures, facial expressions, and sounds is at every stage of his progress the true medium of his being-with-others. There is no point at which parents or other children fail to respond because the infant's mastery is incomplete. Nor do they respond as if it *were* complete. The infant, quite simply, is one of us, is of the world precisely as the person he already is. His ability to change and structure his own environment is minimal, but it is real: we take his needs and wishes seriously, and we take seriously his effect upon us. This is not a process of intuition, but transpires in the medium he is learning and in which we have already learned, the medium of sounds, facial expressions, and gestures.

2. His experimental and self-delighting play with sounds — as when he is sitting alone on the floor, handling toys and babbling to himself — is never supervised and is rarely interfered with. Parents who have listened to this babbling never fail to notice the gradual advent of new families of sounds, but though this pleases them, they do not on this account reward the infant. The play goes on as before, absolutely freely.

The infant, in short, is born into an already existing continuum of experience. The continuum is the medium within which his learning occurs. In the ordinary home the continuum is one of maximum relation. From the infant's point of view — even though he be often frustrated — the ratio of effort and effect is high indeed. There are no breaks in the continuum in the sense that important demands meet no response. (When this does occur, we read of it in case histories of autism and schizophrenia.) Volition, too, is maximized: nor does being alone, inventing, playing, following mere whim, in any way threaten the security of the continuum.

The role of imitation in all this is essential to any theory of learning. The extent and nature of it are often misunderstood. An infant of, say, fourteen months, not yet in possession of many words, will often enter vivaciously into the conversation of his parents, will look from face to face, join in the laughter, and "speak up" in sounds which are far from being words, but which are spoken with very definite facial expressions and in rising and falling tones. These will often be accompanied by hand gestures obviously copied from the parents. The infant seems to be imitating grown-up speech. But *is* this what he is doing? Parents are perhaps deceived because the sight is inevitably so charming, all that display of participation, with so little content. They forget that among their own motives the desire to charm, to enliven, to make a merry noise, is not insignificant. And they overestimate the content of what they themselves have said, for the truth is that the music of our ordinary conversations is of equal importance with the words. It is a kind of touching: our eyes "touch," our facial expressions play back and forth, tones answer tones. We experience even the silences in a physical, structural way; they, too, are a species of contact. In short, the physical part of everyday speech is just as important as the "mental" . . . and precisely this physical part has already, to an impressive extent, been mastered by the fourteen-month-old child. Too, when we raise the question of imitation, we tend to forget that the whole forms of our own speech consist actually of a great many parts, all of them very intricate: sounds, rhythms, accents, tones, breathing patterns, facial expressions, gestures. When even a small number of these are present in an infant's "speech," we are already far beyond the stage of mere imitation.

But in truth there never was such a stage. The infant is surrounded by the life of the home, not by instructors or persons posing as models. Everything that he observes, every gesture, every word, is observed not only as action but as a truly instrumental form. And this indeed, this whole life of the form, is what he seeks to master. It is what he learns. No parent has ever heard an infant abstracting the separate parts of speech and practicing them. It simply does not happen. Even in those moments that we might think of as instruction — when, for example, we are bending over the baby, saying "wa-ter" to correct his saying "waddah" — our inevitable élan is that of a game; and in any event, as every parent knows, the moment this élan vanishes and mere instruction takes over, the infant will abruptly cease to cooperate. It is not only that he is unable to conceptualize, but that we have removed the instrumentality he has all along been studying. He no longer recognizes the sounds as a *word*; and indeed, at this moment, they are not a word in the true sense, but a conceptual device of pedagogy.

When we see the infant in action, then, it is impossible to say that any given expression or gesture is an imitation. What we mean is that we recognize its source. The fact that we observe it at all indicates that it has already been assimilated, or is well on the way. We are observing it in use.

A true description of an infant "talking" with its parents, then, must make clear that he is actually taking part. It is not make-believe or imitation, but true social sharing in the degree to which he is capable. We need only reduce this complex actuality to the relative simplicity of imitation to see at once what sort of loss he would suffer. The vivacity, the keen interest, the immediate sharing in the on-going intercourse of others, and above all, the environmental effect — all these would vanish. His experience would be reduced to the dimensions of a chore, like that of an actor preparing a part. But in fact we cannot conceive of experience reduced to such dimensions. The infant, in short, is not imitating but doing. The doing is for real. It advances him into the world. It brings its own rewards in pleasure, attention, approval, and endless practical benefits.

This very distinction between imitating and doing lies at the heart of John Dewey's thoughts on education. It is the root meaning of "learning by doing," words which for many years now have been little more than a catch-phrase signifying the filling-in of blanks in prepackaged experiments. Dewey's strength lies in his profound understanding of the whole forms of experience: the unity, in growth, of *self*, *world*, and *mind*. It was because of his perception of this unity that he insisted that school be based in the community and not in the Board of Education. (Another of the disastrous myths of the educationists is that we have already availed ourselves of the thought of Dewey. Nothing could be further from the truth.)

These things, then, for the growing child, are maximized in the environment of the home: relationship, participation, freedom of movement, and freedom of volition with respect to the objects of attention. Knowledge is gained in immediately instrumental forms. The gain is accompanied by use and pleasure. The parents do not pose as models, but are living their lives, so that from the point of view of the infant the model is life itself.

Before comparing this optimum environment with the usual environment of school, I would like to give another example from the home, one more deliberately educative, and one again with which most parents are familiar.

Let us imagine a mother reading a bedtime story to a child of five. And let us apply Dewey's wholistic terms, bearing in mind that normal learning is not a function merely of intelligence, or of the growth of the self, but that self, mind, and world belong together as one fact. In Dewey's formulation, mind *is* the on-going, significant organization of self and world

We can judge the expansion of self and world by the rapt expression on the face of the child, the partly open mouth and the eyes which seem to be dreaming, but which dart upward at any error or omission, for the story has been read before a dozen times. Where does the story take place? Where does it happen in the present? Obviously in the mind of the child, characterized at this moment by imagination, feeling, discernment, wonderment, and delight. And in the voice of the mother, for all the unfolding events are events of her voice, characteristic inflections of description and surprise. And in the literary form itself, which might be described with some justice as the voice of the author.

The continuum of persons is obvious and close. The child is expanding into the world quite literally through the mother. But here the increment of *world*, so to speak, is another voice, that of the author, made durable in its subservience to literary form. Because of the form itself, there hover in the distance, as it were, still other forms and paradigms of life, intuitions of persons and events, of places in the world, of estrangement and companionship. The whole is supported by security and love.

There is no need to stress the fact that from the point of view of learning, these are optimum conditions. I would like to dwell on just two aspects of these conditions, and they might be described, not too fancifully, as *possession* and *freedom of passage*. The former refers to the child's relation to ideas and objects of perception, the latter to his relations with persons already associated with such forms.

Both the mother, in reading the story, and the author, in achieving it, are *giving* without any proprietory consciousness. The child has an unquestioned right to all that transpires; it is of his world in the way that all apprehendable forms are of it. We can hardly distinguish between his delight in the new forms and his appropriation of them. Nothing interferes with his taking them into himself, and vice versa, expanding into them. His apprehension of the new forms, their consolidation in his thoughts and feelings, is his growth . . . and these movements of his whole being are unimpeded by the actions of the adults. Certainly there is effort on his part, but it is experienced as fulfilling action. The effort does not include self-defense against the environment. Nor is it accidental that he is blessedly unaware of himself. This follows from the fact that he is already accepted, already included, by his mother's act of giving and by the absolute offer inherent in the literary form.

If we wished to retard his learning and complicate his growth, we could do it by the following steps: (1) turn his attention back upon himself by letting him know that he is being observed, measured, and compared with others; (2) destroy his innate sense of his own peerage among sensible forms by insisting that they are to be apprehended in standardized ways and that their uses are effectively controlled by others; (3) make his passage among persons dependent upon the measurements to which he has been subjected; (4) apply physical coercion to his freedom to move, to express his feelings, to act upon his doubts, to give or refuse his attention — all of which will convince him that learning is an act of disembodied will or of passive attention, neither of which he can find within himself; (5) present him with new forms in a rigidly preordained order and quantity, so that he will give up utterly the hope of the organic structure which proceeds outward from his own great attraction to the world.

We need not extend this list. It is obvious that I am describing the ordinary school. The results of such methods, *in extremis,* can be seen in the behavior of José as he sits beside me for a lesson. His attention is so centered in himself — in his fear of failure, his resentment, his self-contempt — that quite literally he cannot see what is under his nose. The words on the paper, the words of the teachers, books, pictures, events of the past — all these belong to school, not to the world at large, and certainly not, by prior right, to himself. His passage among persons — among teachers and schoolmates both, and among the human voices of books, films, etc. — is blocked and made painful by his sense of his "place," that is, by the mea-surements through which he must identify himself: that he has failed all subjects, is last in the class, is older than his classmates, and has a reading problem. He is under coercion of all kinds and no longer knows what it means to express his own wishes simply and hopefully, or to *give* his attention, or to take seriously his doubts and special needs. As for the organic unity of self, mind, and world, he is so fragmented, so invaded by an environment too much for his feeble defenses, that by any serious standard he must be described in terms of crisis.

I've been using the words "reality of encounter," "continuum of persons," and "relation." All these are vital aspects of environment. When a teacher conceives of his task as mere instruction, the accomplishment of a lesson, and when he addresses himself to his pupils as to containers of varying capacities into which the information must be poured, he is creating conditions which are fatal to growth. Testing, grading, seating arrangements according to the teacher's convenience, predigested textbooks, public address systems, guarded corridors and closed rooms, attendance records, punishments, truant officers — all this belongs to an environment of coercion and control. Such an environment has not consulted the needs of normal growth, or the special needs of those whose growth has already been impaired.

If the environment of the home is optimal for the great tasks of learning that belong to the early years, it is no longer so by the age of four or five. A larger community is essential, a larger body of peers, and perhaps persons of special talents. Yet in order to obtain these, it is not necessary to abandon utterly the environmental qualities that proved so marvelously supportive to the first tasks of learning, those remarkable feats which, in Whitehead's words, "to the wise remain miracles." Obviously we cannot make our schools into "second homes." Nor would it be desirable, for children are not born into families alone, but into nature and civilization as well. It would be crippling to delay the child's progress into the whole. We can, however, pay attention to the salient features of our only known excellent environment; and by experimentation we can discover which of its aspects can be carried over into the environment of school. This was precisely our opportunity at First Street. We made much of freedom of choice and freedom of movement; and of reality of encounter between teachers and students; and of the continuum of persons, by which we understood that parents, teachers, friends, neighbors, the life of the streets, form all one substance in the experience of the child. We abolished tests and grades and Lesson Plans. We abolished Superiors, too — all that petty and disgusting pecking order of the school bureaucracy which contributes nothing to the wisdom of teachers and still less to the growth of the child. We abolished homework (unless asked for); we abolished the category of truant. We abolished, in short, all of the things which constitute a merely external order; and in doing this, we laid bare the deeper motivations and powers which contribute to what might be called "internal order," i.e., a structuring of activities based upon the child's innate desire to learn, and upon such things as I have already described: the needs of children, the natural authority of adults, the power of moral suasion (the foundations of which are laid in the home), and the deep attachment and interest which adults inevitably feel toward the lives of children. This last — the motivation of teachers — tends to be lost sight of in the present low-grade careerism of the teaching profession. Yet many adults do find themselves and expend their love in precisely this function. Their own motivation is one of the most reliable sources of organic order.

Carl R. Rogers

The Interpersonal Relationship in the Facilitation of Learning

... It is in fact nothing short of a miracle that the modern methods of instruction have not yet entirely strangled the holy curiosity of inquiry; for this delicate little plant, aside from stimulation, stands mainly in need of freedom; without this it goes to wrack and ruin without fail. — ALBERT EINSTEIN

I wish to begin this paper with a statement which may seem surprising to some and perhaps offensive to others. It is simply this: Teaching, in my estimation, is a vastly overrated function.

Having made such a statement, I scurry to the dictionary to see if I really mean what I say. Teaching means "to instruct." Personally I am not much interested in instructing another. "To impart knowledge or skill." My reaction is, why not be more efficient, using a book or programmed learning? "To make to know." Here my hackles rise. I have no wish to *make* anyone know something. "To show, guide, direct." As I see it, too many people have been shown, guided, directed. So I come to the conclusion that I *do* mean what I said. Teaching is, for me, a relatively unimportant and vastly overvalued activity.

But there is more in my attitude than this. I have a negative reaction to teaching. Why? I think it is because it raises all the wrong questions. As soon as we focus on teaching, the question arises, what shall we teach? What, from our superior vantage point, does the other per-

Abridged version of an article appearing in *Humanizing Education: The Person in the Process*. Washington, D.C.: Association for Supervision and Curriculum Development, 1967. Reprinted with permission of the Association for Supervision and Curriculum Development and Carl R. Rogers. Copyright © 1967 by the Association for Supervision and Curriculum Development.

son need to know? This raises the ridiculous question of coverage. What shall the course cover? (Here I am acutely aware of the fact that "to cover" means both "to take in" and "to conceal from view," and I believe that most courses admirably achieve both these aims.) This notion of coverage is based on the assumption that what is taught is what is learned; what is presented is what is assimilated. I know of no assumption so obviously untrue. One does not need research to provide evidence that this is false. One needs only to talk with a few students.

But I ask myself, "Am I so prejudiced against teaching that I find no situation in which it is worthwhile?" I immediately think of my experience in Australia only a few months ago. I became much interested in the Australian aborigine. Here is a group which for more than 20,000 years has managed to live and exist in a desolate environment in which a modern man would perish within a few days. The secret of his survival has been teaching. He has passed on to the young every shred of knowledge about how to find water, about how to track game, about how to kill the kangaroo, about how to find his way through the trackless desert. Such knowledge is conveyed to the young as being *the* way to behave, and any innovation is frowned upon. It is clear that teaching has provided him the way to survive in a hostile and relatively unchanging environment.

Now I am closer to the nub of the question which excites me. Teaching and the imparting of knowledge make sense in an unchanging environment. This is why it has been an unquestioned function for centuries. But if there is one truth about modern man, it is that he lives in an environment which is *continually changing*. The one thing I can be sure of is that the physics which is taught to the present day student will be outdated in a decade. The teaching in psychology will certainly be out of date in 20 years. The so-called "facts of history" depend very largely upon the current mood and temper of the culture. Chemistry, biology, genetics, sociology, are in such flux that a firm statement made today will almost certainly be modified by the time the student gets around to using the knowledge.

We are, in my view, faced with an entirely new situation in education where the goal of education, if we are to survive, is the *facilitation of change and learning*. The only man who is educated is the man who has learned how to learn; the man who has learned how to adapt and change; the man who has realized that no knowledge is secure, that only the process of *seeking* knowledge gives a basis for security. Changingness, a reliance on *process* rather than upon static knowledge, is the only thing that makes any sense as a goal for education in the modern world.

So now with some relief I turn to an activity, a purpose, which really warms me — the *facilitation of learning*. When I have been able to transform a group — and here I mean all the members of a group, myself included — into a community of *learners*, then the excitement has been almost beyond belief. To free curiosity; to permit individuals to go charging off in new directions dictated by their own interests; to unleash curiosity; to open everything to questioning and exploration; to recognize that everything is in process of change — here is an experience I can never forget. I cannot always achieve it in groups with which I am associated but when it is partially or largely achieved then it becomes a never-to-be-forgotten group experience. Out of such a context arise true students, real learners, creative scientists and scholars and practitioners, the kind of individuals who can live in a delicate but ever-changing balance between what is presently known and the flowing, moving, altering, problems and facts of the future.

Here then is a goal to which I can give myself wholeheartedly. I see the facilitation of learning as the aim of education, the way in which we might develop the learning man, the way in which we can learn to live as individuals in process. I see the facilitation of learning as the function which may hold constructive, tentative, changing, process answers to some of the deepest perplexities which beset man today.

But do we know how to achieve this new goal in education, or is it a will-of-the-wisp which sometimes occurs, sometimes fails to occur, and thus offers little real hope? My answer is that we possess a very considerable knowledge of the conditions which encourage self-initiated, significant, experiential, "gut-level" learning by the whole person. We do not frequently see these conditions put into effect because they mean a real revolution in our approach to education and revolutions are not for the timid. But we do find examples of this revolution in action.

We know — and I will briefly describe some of the evidence — that the initiation of such learning rests not upon the teaching skills of the leader, not upon his scholarly knowledge of the field, not upon his curricular planning, not upon his use of audio-visual aids, not upon the programmed learning he utilizes, not upon his lectures and presentations, not upon an abundance of books, though each of these might at one time or another be utilized as an important resource. No, the facilitation of significant learning rests upon certain attitudinal qualities which exist in the personal *relationship* between the facilitator and the learner.

We came upon such findings first in the field of psychotherapy, but increasingly there is evidence which shows that these findings apply in the classroom as well. We find it easier to think that the intensive relationship between therapist and client might possess these qualities, but we are also finding that they may exist in the countless interpersonal interactions (as many as 1,000 per day, as Jackson [1966] has shown) between the teacher and his pupils.

What are these qualities, these attitudes, which facilitate learning? Let me describe them very briefly, drawing illustrations from the teaching field.

Realness in the Facilitator of Learning

Perhaps the most basic of these essential attitudes is realness or genuineness. When the facilitator is a real person, being what he is, entering into a relationship with the learner without presenting a front or a facade, he is much more likely to be effective. This means that the feelings which he is experiencing are available to him, available to his awareness, that he is able to live these feelings, be them, and able to communicate them if appropriate. It means that he comes into a direct personal encounter with the learner, meeting him on a person-to-person basis. It means that he is *being* himself, not denying himself.

Seen from this point of view it is suggested that the teacher can be a real person in his relationship with his students. He can be enthusiastic, he can be bored, he can be interested in students, he can be angry, he can be sensitive and sympathetic. Because he accepts these feelings as his own he has no need to impose them on his students. He can like or dislike a student product without implying that it is objectively good or bad or that the student is good or bad. He is simply expressing a feeling for the product, a feeling which exists within himself. Thus, he is a person to his students, not a faceless embodiment of a curricular requirement nor a sterile tube through which knowledge is passed from one generation to the next.

It is obvious that this attitudinal set, found to be effective in psychotherapy, is sharply in contrast with the tendency of most teachers to show themselves to their pupils simply as roles. It is quite customary for teachers rather consciously to put on the mask, the role, the facade, of being a teacher, and to wear this facade all day removing it only when they have left the school at night.

But not all teachers are like this. Take Sylvia Ashton-Warner, who took resistant, supposedly slow-learning primary school Maori children in New Zealand, and let them develop their own reading vocabulary. Each child could request one word — whatever word he wished — each day, and she would print it on a card and give it to him. "Kiss," "ghost," "bomb," "tiger," "fight," "love," "daddy" — these are samples. Soon they were building sentences, which they could also keep. "He'll get a licking." "Pussy's frightened." The children simply never forgot these self-initiated learnings. Yet it is not my purpose to tell you of her methods. I want instead to give you a glimpse of her attitude, of the passionate realness which must have been as evident to her tiny pupils as to her readers. An editor asked her some questions and she responded: " 'A few cool facts' you asked me for. . . . I don't know that there's a cool fact in me, or anything else cool for that matter, on this particular subject. I've got only hot long facts on the matter of Creative Teaching, scorching both the page and me" (Ashton-Warner, 163, p. 26).

Here is no sterile facade. Here is a vital *person*, with convictions, with feelings. It is her transparent realness which was, I am sure, one of the elements that made her an exciting facilitator of learning. She does not fit into some neat educational formula. She *is*, and students grow by being in contact with someone who really *is*.

Take another very different person, Barbara Shiel, also doing exciting work facilitating learning in sixth graders.[1] She gave them a great deal of responsible freedom, and I will mention some of the reactions of her students later. But here is an example of the way she shared herself with her pupils — not just sharing feelings of sweetness and light, but anger and frustration. She had made art materials freely available, and students often used these in creative ways, but the room frequently looked like a picture of chaos. Here is her report of her feelings and what she did with them.

> I find it (still) maddening to live with the mess — with a capital M! No one seems to care except me.

[1] For a more extended account of Miss Shiel's initial attempts, see Rogers, 1966. Her later experience is described in Shiel, 1966.

Finally, one day I told the children . . . that I am a neat, orderly person by nature and the mess was driving me to distraction. Did they have a solution? It was suggested they could have volunteers to clean up. . . . I said it didn't seem fair to me to have the same people clean up all the time for others — but it *would* solve it for me. "Well, some people *like* to clean," they replied. So that's the way it is (Shiel, 1966).

I hope this example puts some lively meaning into the phrases I used earlier, that the facilitator "is able to live these feelings, be them, and able to communicate them if appropriate." I have chosen an example of negative feelings, because I think it is more difficult for most of us to visualize what this would mean. In this instance, Miss Shiel is taking the risk of being transparent in her angry frustrations about the mess. And what happens? The same thing which, in my experience, nearly always happens. These young people accept and respect her feelings, take them into account, and work out a novel solution which none of us, I believe, would have suggested in advance. Miss Shiel wisely comments, "I used to get upset and feel guilty when I became angry — I finally realized the children could accept *my* feelings, too. And it is important for them to know when they've 'pushed me.' I have limits too" (Shiel, 1966).

Just to show that positive feelings, when they are real, are equally effective, let me quote briefly a college student's reaction, in a different course. " . . . Your sense of humor in the class was cheering; we all felt relaxed because you showed us your human self, not a mechanical teacher image. I feel as if I have more understanding and faith in my teachers now. . . . I feel closer to the students too." Another says, ". . . You conducted the class on a personal level and therefore in my mind I was able to formulate a picture of you as a person and not as merely a walking textbook." Or another student in the same course,

> . . . It wasn't as if there was a teacher in the class, but rather someone whom we could trust and identify as a "sharer." You were so perceptive and sensitive to our thoughts, and this made it all the more "authentic" for me. It was an "authentic" *experience*, not just a class (Bull, 1966).

I trust I am making it clear that to be real is not always easy, nor is it achieved all at once, but it is basic to the person who wants to become that revolutionary individual, a facilitator of learning.

Prizing, Acceptance, Trust

There is another attitude which stands out in those who are successful in facilitating learning. I have observed this attitude. I have experienced it. Yet, it is hard to know what term to put to it so I shall use several. I think of it as prizing the learner, prizing his feelings, his opinions, his person. It is a caring for the learner, but a non-possessive caring. It is an acceptance of this other individual as a separate person, having worth in his own right. It is a basic trust — a belief that this other person is somehow fundamentally trustworthy.

Whether we call it prizing, acceptance, trust, or by some other term, it shows up in a variety of observable ways. The facilitator who has a considerable degree of this attitude can be fully acceptant of the fear and hesitation of the student as he approaches a new problem as well as acceptant of the pupil's satisfaction in achievement. Such a teacher can accept the student's occasional apathy, his erratic desires to explore byroads of knowledge, as well as his disciplined efforts to achieve major goals. He can accept personal feelings which both disturb and promote learning — rivalry with a sibling, hatred of authority, concern about personal adequacy. What we are describing is a prizing of the learner as an imperfect human being with many feelings, many potentialities. The facilitator's prizing or acceptance of the learner is an operational expression of his essential confidence and trust in the capacity of the human organism.

I would like to give some examples of this attitude from the classroom situation. Here any teacher statements would be properly suspect, since many of us would like to feel we hold such attitudes, and might have a biased perception of our qualities. But let me indicate how this attitude of prizing, of accepting, of trusting, appears to the student who is fortunate enough to experience it.

Here is a statement from a college student in a class with Morey Appell.

Your way of being with us is a revelation to me. In your class I feel important, mature, and capable of doing things on my own. I want to think for myself and this need cannot be accomplished through textbooks and lectures alone, but through living. I think you see me as a person with real feelings and needs, an individual. What I say and do are significant expressions from me, and you recognize this (Appell, 1959).

One of Miss Shiel's sixth graders expresses much more briefly her misspelled appreciation of this attitude, "You are a wounderful teacher period!!!"

College students in a class with Dr. Patricia Bull describe not only these prizing, trusting attitudes, but the effect these have had on their other interactions.

... I feel that I can say things to you that I can't say to other professors.... Never before have I been so aware of the other students or their personalities. I have never had so much interaction in a college classroom with my classmates. The climate of the classroom has had a very profound effect on me ... the free atmosphere for discussion affected me ... the general atmosphere of a particular session affected me. There have been many times when I have carried the discussion out of the class with me and thought about it for a long time.

... I still feel close to you, as though there were some tacit understanding between us, almost a conspiracy. This adds to the in-class participation on my part because I feel that at least one person in the group will react, even when I am not sure of the others. It does not matter really whether your reaction is positive or negative, it just *is*. Thank you.

... I appreciate the respect and concern you have for others, including myself.... As a result of my experience in class, plus the influence of my readings, I sincerely believe that the student-centered teaching method does provide an ideal framework for learning; not just for the accumulation of facts, but more important, for learning about ourselves in relation to others.... When I think back to my shallow awareness in September compared to the depth of my insights now, I know that this course has offered me a learning experience of great value which I couldn't have acquired any other way.

... Very few teachers would attempt this method because they would feel that they would lose the students' respect. On the contrary. You gained our respect, through your ability to speak to us on our level, instead of ten miles above us. With the complete lack of communication we see in this school, it was a wonderful experience to see people listening to each other and really communicating on an adult, intelligent level. More classes should afford us this experience (Bull, (1966).

As you might expect, college students are often suspicious that these seeming attitudes are phony. One of Dr. Bull's students writes:

... Rather than observe my classmates for the first few weeks, I concentrated my observations on you, Dr. Bull. I tried to figure out your motivations and purposes. I was convinced that you were a hypocrite.... I did change my opinion, however. You are not a hypocrite, by any means.... I do wish the course could continue. "Let each become all he is capable of being." ... Perhaps my most disturbing question, which relates to this course is: When will we stop hiding things from ourselves and our contemporaries? (Bull, 1966).

I am sure these examples are more than enough to show that the facilitator who cares, who prizes, who trusts the learner, creates a climate for learning so different from the ordinary classroom that any resemblance is, as they say, "purely coincidental."

Empathic Understanding

A further element which establishes a climate for self-initiated, experiential learning is empathic understanding. When the teacher has the ability to understand the student's reactions from the inside, has a sensitive awareness of the way the process of education and learning seems *to the student*, then again the likelihood of significant learning is increased.

This kind of understanding is sharply different from the usual evaluative understanding, which follows the pattern of, "I understand what is wrong with you." When there is a sensitive empathy, however, the reaction in the learner follows something of this pattern, "At last someone understands how it feels and seems to be *me* without wanting to analyze me or judge me. Now I can blossom and grow and learn."

This attitude of standing in the other's shoes, of viewing the world through the student's eyes,

61

is almost unheard of in the classroom. One could listen to thousands of ordinary classroom interactions without coming across one instance of clearly communicated, sensitively accurate, empathic undrstanding. But it has a tremendously releasing effect when it occurs.

Let me take an illustration from Virginia Axline, dealing with a second grade boy. Jay, age 7, has been aggressive, a trouble maker, slow of speech and learning. Because of his "cussing" he was taken to the principal, who paddled him, unknown to Miss Axline. During a free work period, he fashioned a man of clay, very carefully, down to a hat and a handkerchief in his pocket. "Who is that?" asked Miss Axline. "Dunno," replied Jay. "Maybe it is the principal. He has a handkerchief in his pocket like that." Jay glared at the clay figure. "Yes," he said. Then he began to tear the head off and looked up and smiled. Miss Axline said, "You sometimes feel like twisting his head off, don't you? You get so mad at him." Jay tore off one arm, another, then beat the figure to a pulp with his fists. Another boy, with the perception of the young, explained, "Jay is mad at Mr. X because he licked him this noon." "Then you must feel lots better now," Miss Axline commented. Jay grinned and began to rebuild Mr. X. (Adapted from Axline, 1944.)

The other examples I have cited also indicate how deeply appreciative students feel when they are simply *understood* — not evaluated, not judged, simply understood from their *own* point of view, not the teacher's. If any teacher set herself the task of endeavoring to make one non-evaluative, acceptant, empathic response

per day to a pupil's demonstrated or verbalized feeling, I believe he would discover the potency of this currently almost nonexistent kind of understanding.

Let me wind up this portion of my remarks by saying that when a facilitator creates, even to a modest degree, a classroom climate characterized by such realness, prizing, and empathy, he discovers that he has inaugurated an educational revolution. Learning of a different quality, proceeding at a different pace, with a greater degree of pervasiveness, occurs. Feelings — positive and negative, confused — become a part of the classroom experience. Learning becomes life, and a very vital life at that. The student is on his way, sometimes excitedly, sometimes reluctantly, to becoming a learning, changing being.

References

M. L. Appell. "Selected Student Reactions to Student-centered Courses." Mimeographed manuscript, 1959.

S. Ashton-Warner. *Teacher.* New York: Simon and Schuster, 1963.

Virginia M. Axline. "Morale on the School Front." *Journal of Educational Research* 38: 521–33; 1944.

Patricia Bull. Student reactions, Fall 1965. State University College, Courtland, New York. Mimeographed manuscripts, 1966.

P. W. Jackson. "The Student's World." University of Chicago. Mimeographed, 1966.

C. R. Rogers. "To Facilitate Learning." In Malcolm Provus, editor, NEA Handbook for Teachers, *Innovations for Time to Teach*. Washington, D.C.: Department of Classroom Teachers, NEA, 1966.

Barbara J. Shiel. "Evaluation: A Self-directed Curriculum, 1965." Mimeographed, 1966.

Herbert Kohl

Excerpt from The Open Classroom

Teachers begin the school year burdened with expectations and preconceptions that often interfere with the development of open classrooms. Classes are "tracked" and students are placed together according to academic achievement. Reading achievement or I.Q. scores are usually used to decide which track a student "belongs" in, though sometimes teachers' judgments about their students' potential count too. There are top, middle, and bottom classes; A, B, C, and D "streams." No matter how schools try to conceal this grouping, the pupils know where they are placed. Bottom classes, the C and D streams, often tell their teachers at the beginning of the school year, "You can't expect much from us. We're dumb."

Teachers know the type of class they are expected to be teaching.[1] Before the teacher has even met his students his expectations of bright, mediocre, or dull individuals are set.

Even in schools which have abandoned tracking, the teacher is given a set of record cards by his supervisor which document the child's school life as perceived by his previous teachers. These cards usually contain achievement and I.Q. scores, personality evaluations, descriptions of conferences with the students' parents, judgments about his behavior in class and "study habits." Difficult pupils are identified as well as good (i.e., conforming and performing) ones.

Reprinted with permission from *The New York Review of Books.* Copyright © 1967 by Herbert Kohl.

[1] In some Union contracts there are even provisions for rotation of teachers from top to bottom, through the middle to the top again.

The record cards are probably designed not only as analyses of their pupils' careers at school, but as warnings to teachers on what to expect.

When the teacher meets his class on the first day of the school year, he is armed with all of this "professional" knowledge. Anticipating a dull class, for example, a teacher may have spent several weeks preparing simple exercises to keep his students busy. On the other hand, faced with the prospect of teaching a bright class, he may have found a new and challenging textbook or devised some ingenious scientific experiments.

If the record cards indicate that several pupils are particularly troublesome or, what is more threatening, "disturbed," the teacher will single them out as soon as they enter the room and treat them differently from the other pupils. He may do the same with bright students or ones rumored to be wise, funny, lazy, violent, scheming, deceitful.... The students will sense this and act in the manner expected of them. Thus the teacher traps both himself and his pupils into repeating patterns that have been set for years.

Expectations influence behavior in subtle ways: a successful though nervous and unhappy student may try to relax. His teacher says, "What's the matter? You're not yourself this week." This may produce feelings of guilt in the student, who then drives himself to succeed in spite of feeling that the price he is paying for academic achievement may be excessive.

A "difficult" student tries to make a new start and is quiet and obedient. His teacher responds to this behavior by saying, "You're off to a good start this year," and so informs the student that a bad start was expected of him. The student becomes angry and defiant.

A supposedly dull student gives a correct answer in class and is praised excessively. He is embarrassed and becomes withdrawn.

Even in kindergarten a teacher will have expectations. Some children are "disadvantaged," others have language problems. The teacher anticipates that they may not do well. Others come from intellectual or privileged homes and if they don't perform well something must be wrong.

Teachers' expectations have a tendency to become self-fulfilling.[2] "Bad" classes tend to act badly, and "gifted" classes tend to respond to the special consideration that they expect to be given to them if they perform in a "superior" way.

All of this is inimical to an open classroom, where the role of the teacher is not to control his pupils but rather to enable them to make choices and pursue what interests them. In an open classroom a pupil functions according to his sense of himself rather than what he is expected to be. It is not that the teacher should expect the same of all his pupils. On the contrary, the teacher must learn to perceive differences, but these should emerge from what actually happens in the classroom during the school year, and not from preconceptions.

I remember an incident where the effect of a teacher's expectations in one of my classes was pernicious. I have always been unable to avoid having favorites in my classes. I like defiant, independent, and humorous people, and my preferences naturally come out in my teaching. One year, several students were puzzled by my choice of favorites. The class had been together for three years and each year teachers chose the same four children as their favorite students. However, I had chosen different students and it

upset most of the class, especially the ones who had been favorites in the past. All the students were black. It took me several months to realize that the former favorites were all the lightest-skinned pupils in the class — in other words, the whitest were (by their white teachers) expected to be the nicest and most intelligent.

A teacher in an open classroom needs to cultivate a state of *suspended expectations*. It is not easy. It is easy to believe that a dull class is dull, or a bright class is bright. The words "emotionally disturbed" conjure up frightening images. And it is sometimes a relief to discover that there are good pupils in the class that is waiting for you. Not reading the record cards or ignoring the standing of the class is an act of self-denial; it involves casting aside a crutch when one still believes one can't walk without it. Yet if one wants to develop an open classroom within the context of a school which is essentially totalitarian, such acts of will are necessary.

What does it mean to suspend expectations when one is told that the class one will be teaching is slow, or bright, or ordinary? At the least it means not preparing to teach in any special way or deciding beforehand on the complexity of the materials to be used during a school year. It means that planning does not consist of finding the class's achievement level according to the record cards and tailoring the material to those levels, but rather preparing diverse materials and subjects and discovering from the students as the year unfolds what is relevant to them and what isn't.

Particularly it means not reading I.Q. scores or achievement scores, not discovering who may be a source of trouble and who a solace or even a joy. It means giving your pupils a fresh chance to develop in new ways in your classroom, freed from the roles they may have adopted during their previous school careers. It means allowing children to become who they care to become, and freeing the teacher from the standards by which new pupils had been measured in the past.

There are no simple ways to give up deeply

---

[2] For a study of self-fulfilling prophecies, see *Pygmalion in the Classroom: Teacher Expectation and the Pupil's Intellectual Ability*, by Robert Rosenthal and Lenore Jacobson, Holt, Rinehart & Winston, 1968.

64

rooted expectations. There are some suggestions, however:

    talk to students outside class
    watch them play and watch them live with other
        young people
    play with them — joking games and serious games

talk to them about yourself, what you care about
listen

In these situations the kids may surprise you
and reveal rather than conceal, as is usual in the
classroom, their feelings, playfulness, and intelligence.

Sidney M. Jourard

Fascination: A Phenomenological Perspective on Independent Learning

Learning for Others, and Learning for Myself

The announcement for this conference stated, "Recent insights from the behavioral sciences have expanded the perception of human potential, through a re-casting of the image of man from a passive, reactive recipient, to an active, seeking, autonomous, and reflective being. What are the implications of this impelling new image for our concern with man, the learner? Educators are giving increased attention to implementing in practice, the recognition that the learner has both the capacity and the need to assume responsibility for his continuing learning."

How did man ever come to be conceived as a passive, reactive recipient? By whom was he so conceived and why? And who recast the image? The peculiar thing about man is that he is *no thing*; no image can ever do full justice to his being. His being is a question to him. He lives his answers. He can be a passive, reactive recipient, and he can also be an active, seeking, autonomous and reflective being. Each way is a project, a choice, a decision.

Another peculiarity of man is that he can let others answer the question of his being for him. If he appears to others, and experiences himself as a passive, reactive recipient it is because he has let himself be persuaded to be that way by and for somebody. A man may live and show only his passive, reactive possibilities to his teacher, and to a researcher; in solitude, or with

Abridged version of Chapter 6 from *The Theory and Nature of Independent Learning*. Reprinted by permission of Intext Educational Publishers and the author. This article also appears in Jourard, S. M., *Disclosing Man to Himself*. New York: Van Nostrand Reinhold, 1968

some trusted other, he may experience and show his active, creative, or other unforeseen possibilities.

Social intercourse resembles a contest between definers of my being. If I experience myself as a passive and reactive, rather than as active, seeking, autonomous, and reflective; and if everyone sees me in this light, we may presume that such a conception is the outcome of a superb job of propaganda, brainwashing or persuasion. I have yielded to others' definition of me and thus I define and experience myself. If the authorities, the behavioral scientists, are beginning to say, "You know, we have been wrong, man seems to have the capacity to act, choose, and speak autonomously," it is perhaps because some authority has suspended his preconception of man, and let some men disclose their experience of themselves to the authority, who then listens. Other images of me are at least in part a reflection of what I have been invited or permitted to disclose of my experiences to the other who is forming an image.

We might well wonder why it is taking men so long to disclose their active and creative potentials to the image-makers, and why have image-makers been for so long blind and deaf to these possibilities that were always there? If you don't like the word image, you can replace it with "model." I suspect that the passive, reactive image or model has lasted so long because it serves a useful purpose to somebody and hence was imposed on man who then showed it back to the image-makers (the model makers.) Indeed passive, reactive men are predictable, manipulatable, and controllable, the very way they should be if they are to serve the interests of someone who can profit from the predicting, manipulating and controlling.

Independent learning is now a problem and hence this conference. I believe it is a "pedagogenic" problem. We produced it as physicians sometimes unintentionally produce the iatrogenic illnesses.

That independent learning is problematic is most peculiar, because man always and only learns by himself. The real question here is *what* does he learn, and for *whom*? Learning is not a task or problem; it is a way to be in the world. Man learns as he pursues goals and projects that have meaning for him. He is always learning something. Perhaps the key to the problem of independent learning lies in the phrase "the learner has the need and the capacity to assume responsibility for his own continuing learning." It may well be that those who train young people in the ways of their group, which is a most necessary task, have over-reached the mark. They have trained youngsters to believe that they cannot, dare not, learn anything without a teacher being close at hand. Or they may have persuaded them to believe that once they have learned this, they don't have to learn over again, they will "have it made."

Most youngsters, being human, independently learn something meaningful to them; namely, that it is dangerous or futile to become interested in something, to learn for oneself. It is only safe to learn for the teacher or for society's approval. One set of image molders or model implementers, the teachers (and I would rather call them the trainers) have been commissioned by social leaders to shape youngsters to an acquiescent mold. They implement their commission by invalidating a child's experience of spontaneous curiosity and fascination with respect to the world. They insist he learn only when and what he is taught. He must learn for others. The teachers and parents have robbed the children of their autonomy, their capacity to experience amazement, wonder, and fascination by invalidating it whenever it appears. Then they look at their product and find it wanting. They have produced a *Golem*, a humanoid, a dependent learner. Now, we here are asked to breathe life into it. We are caught on the horns of a dilemma. Children must be shown the ways of their groups. They must be trained, but they must also be able to transcend this training and learn for themselves if they are to experience their lives as meaningful and if the society in which they live is to grow and change.

The question is how to reconcile the contradictions between teaching children for society and letting them learn for themselves, such that children can serve their society without loss of freedom and capacity to go beyond what they have been taught. This is the same problem, writ large, that every serious teacher of piano, art, psychotherapy or even teacher of teaching faces: How to teach a pupil in the fundamental techniques of this art without producing a mere technician. In any of these arts we wish the learner to commit himself to objectives beyond mastery of exercises and techniques. Incidentally, it is here, possibly, that programed instruction seems useful. Although it seems to me to just postpone the inevitable encounter between a man and sheer effort, it seems to be a case of the elimination of struggle by the expert. It reminds me of air-conditioning. What happens when a person encounters hard, brute obstacles to the fulfillment of projects that are meaningful to him, when he has been sheltered from this encounter by "air conditioning" the experience?

In any of the arts I mentioned, we wish the learner to commit himself to objectives beyond the mastery of exercises and techniques, which is actually learning experienced by the learner as learning for the teacher. We wish the learner to commit himself to objectives even beyond current goals. We hope and, I think the teachers hope, that the pupil will seek to make actual his own image of beautiful music, or of pictures, or of healthy personality, or of independent learning. If the teacher has been effective, he will have shown his pupil that techniques are no more than a beginner's set of tools to be used up to the point that some impasse is reached. Then the true artist, the involved therapist, the committed teacher, committed to his own image of ultimate goals, not committed to means, will grope and leap into the unknown, exercising that courage that is not devoid of "fear and trembling." They will grope and leap into the unknown to invent, improvise, or discover new means to further the project of actualizing the image; and if the old version of ultimate goals has lost meaning, the pupil will envision a new embodiment of them.

Citizenship in society is no different from what I have just mentioned. Each society is nominally committed to certain ultimate goals — truth, justice, beauty; but its leaders tend to get fixed on some current version of these goals, and then commit the whole society to perpetuating itself in its present form, in its present power structure. They offer inertia, resistance to change. Newcomers to the society must be shaped if they are to be granted entry. The language and ideology of the group is to be inculcated into new members and the rewards promised for conformity to their teachers is a share in the goods available in that society. But if the goods turn out to be meaningless to a person, then the meaning and value of his conformity is lost.

The techniques of citizenship embodied in roles and rules has reached its impasse. New ways of being a citizen have to be invented. These are not likely to come into being unless they are evoked by new goals, new images. These new goals must originate in someone's experience as images of possibilities. I will return to this point a little bit later.

The Guru and the Commissar

Every man must learn to speak, move, even experience the world in the ways deemed right and sane where he lives. It is not easy. It takes a long time. The temptation to stray is strong. Commissars stand close to insure that each conforms to his prescribed position and role. Once a man masters the rules of the social game, what then? He plays the games so long as they yield meaningful rewards and the reward of meaning. Ultimately, the game becomes con-

fining, boring, even strangling. The man may then wish to opt out, but he cannot; there are no other games to play. So he may become sick. He will then be patched up by doctors who will pronounce him cured and then send him back into the game. If he seeks new realms of experience, he threatens the sleep of the unawakened. They condemn and invalidate him, so he gives up and becomes "normal." Or else, he seeks a richer experience in private while impersonating a typical person.

Since time immemorial, each society has secretly harbored some *gurus*. These wise men were sought by the sick, sufferers who may have been rich in goods, but poor in spirit. The *guru* taught the seeker to let go his attachments in this world, the better to concentrate on spiritual purification. The ultimate rewards were not wealth, fame, nor power, but rather enlightenment, and liberation, and an enriched, more meaningful experience of oneself and one's world. The *gurus* helped the seekers obtain liberation from entrapment in their culture. Now the society that would not fall must locate and treasure its *gurus*. It must protect them, and not deny seekers access to them. The *gurus* and their ways are not for everyone. *Gurus* cannot be hired, nor bought; they can only be deserved. A society without *gurus* is stagnant and it will perish, as did the dinosaurs, who were unable to change ways to cope with changing conditions.

In America, I think we are experiencing an absence in our midst, an absence of *gurus*. We have many commissars, but no one to lead beyond their ways. The commissars insure that everyone conforms to existing ways, to the image or model of man that is current, that is synonomous with goodness and sanity. Commissars use bribery, guile, and threats of force to get people to follow the prescribed ways — the ways which keep the society and its existing power structure intact. Who are the commissars? Most of our teachers are commissars. So are our parents, our policemen, our psychiatrists, our psychologists, even our neighbors. The radio, T.V., and the press function as commissars. All commissars collude to keep us wanting what we are supposed to want, and doing what we are supposed to do. Conform and be rewarded. Dissent and be damned, or unpopular, which is our current synonym for damnation.

If someone begins to depart from the way of being sane or good, he meets a graduated barrage of pressure aiming to bring him back in line. First the person will experience twinges or onslaughts of guilt and anxiety, if he even thinks of stepping out of line. If this built-in regulation fails, then there is the threat of graduated punishment from without. If the person will not yield to parental or family criticism, rejection or threat, the solid wall of community invalidation will confront him, to threaten exile or imprisonment. If the dissenter (who embodies a protest against ways to live that he cannot live) persists in his dissent, he may finally be condemned as mad, and be banished to a mental hospital where he is shocked, drugged, tranquilized, frozen, or operated upon to get him in line or out of the way.

Valeriy Tarsis, a Russian writer, published a novel this year called *Ward Seven* (New York: Dutton, 1965). He describes the contemporary situation dissenting intellectuals face in the Soviet Union. Instead of being shot or transported to Siberia, they are regarded as *insane* if they protest against the current regime. They are hospitalized, and then "treated" until they see the folly or the insanity of their ways. And so, the majority of people, young and old, stay in the role in which they have been trained. The commissars win out. In the ultimate victory of the commissars, each man becomes the unchallenged commissar over himself and I think this time is close at hand.

Behavioral scientists help commissars at their tasks. They say "You define your objectives, and we will show you the way, the most efficient way, to implement them." Teachers, parents, and psychiatrists are all informed of those ever new, more effortless, and automatic ways to bring people into line. School curricula are scientifically broken down into units; these are administered in palatable doses by scientifically informed trainers who employ the latest form of programing. Counseling centers, audio-visual aid depots, and a barrage of books and pamphlets are all available to help commissars carry out their assigned tasks of turning pupils off themselves and onto the ways they are supposed to follow. The result is we turn out more graduates from our training institutes than has ever been true before in our history, possibly in the history of mankind.

But we are discovering, those of us who graduated from such institutions, that something is missing. The something is *ourselves*. Somewhere along the line, we lost ourselves — our capacity to experience in new models and qualities. If we are at all sensitive, we notice the absence and we become concerned, and we start to seek ourselves and our lost capacity for experiencing. This conference is, in a sense, a quest for ourselves. I hope we find us, but I wouldn't be too sure we will.

Beyond the Tether

We created the problem of independent learning by the way we trained people for the social roles awaiting them in a social structure that resists change. Pedagogues, parents, people in general, invalidated the experiences of learners and shut down their capacity to entertain and pursue wonder and fascination. We created the problem and it haunts us, (I quote from the announcement of the conference) not because "behavioral sciences have expanded our conception of the human potential by recasting the image of man." No, the problem haunts us, I believe, because we find ourselves at the end of our tether. We are running in circles at its limit. The tether is firmly fixed to a peculiar debasement of a once magnificent image, the American way of life. Originally revolutionary and dynamic in conception, the American way of life is now a design for living in which more and more Americans cannot live without the aid of tranquilizers, and the threat from the ubiquitous commissar. Yet all the time we advertise this way of life abroad, and try to sell it

69

as we sell toilet paper and Buicks with "Hidden Persuaders." Our conference is only one manifestation, I believe, of a many faceted concern that sentient people are expressing, to seek ways of ameliorating a life that is becoming increasingly meaningless for many people.

What is independent learning? That is a good question for this conference, isn't it? No authoritative definition which I am aware of has been available, so I invented one to serve the purpose of my exposition. I will look at this phenomenon from the standpoint of the learner. What an observer might call independent learning, learning for oneself, the learner experiences as fascination with some aspect of the world which is envisioned in the mode of possibility. That is to say, in imagination. Independent learning is the embodiment and implementation of imaginative fascination. Some aspect of the world discloses itself to a person. He "flips" from the experiential mode of perception (just looking at the world as it discloses itself to him), to an imaginative consciousness. In that mode, he experiences himself as beckoned, challenged, invited or fascinated by this aspect of the world. The transmutation of this imagined possibility into an actuality then becomes the dominant project of his life. He lives it and he lives for it. The person, in whom fascination has been turned on or awakened, suffers a divine discontent, a magnificent obsession. He will wallow in his obsession, if others leave him alone. He will forget to eat, sleep, play games, socialize, or do anything else until he has brought his image of possibility into actuality or else lie nurturing the wounds from fumbling as he pursues his plan.

Once he has actualized his image of the possible, he may then again show an interest in other kinds of doing and being. But in the midst of his independent learning rampage, he is far from being well-rounded or socially adjusted. In fact, he may depart hugely from current images of how people should be. Indeed, the "turned on" learner needs to be protected from other people. He needs to be protected from self-consciousness, from the need to con-

form to images, and from distraction. He needs to be protected from serious self-destruction as he contemplates and absorbs himself in the encounter with his fetish. In this case, the fetish is the mystery or the missing skill. When he is thus turned on, no badly written text, no stuttering, boring teacher can be an obstacle or deterrent so long as they embody some of the knowledge that has become the life quest, just then. "The book or the teacher holds something I want just now. I will get it out of him somehow." That seems to express the spirit of what I am saying.

Independent learning defined as I attempted to define it, arises when our present existence has reached an impasse; when our experience has gone stale, when the project of staying the same has lost its meaning, and the person seeks a new interest in life. If he finds one, and he lets himself be addressed by it, he becomes possessed of the divine madness. The burden and dilemma that were his existence have now been thrown off; his existence is now the quest. He is turned on; he will not be diverted; he may appear ruthless if he pursues his quest. He cannot be bored by it, though he may bore others by his talk of it. This state of being, of being involved, of experiencing new possibilities of meaning for one's life, and then being engaged in their fulfillment, this is what I am construing as independent learning. It entails transcending the past, past involvements and interests, transcending social pressures; in short it is a matter of detachment and liberation from the momentum and inertia of previous ways of being, behaving, and experiencing.

Now the fascinated questing of which I speak, can be evoked in a number of ways. It may occur of itself in someone who is desperate enough; it seems to occur spontaneously in young children before they have been socialized. More commonly, when it does occur, it happens through a relationship between an entrapped person and some other who functions as his *guru* and exemplar. Someone who releases one's imagination, who expands one's consciousness, is someone who offers a "psychedelic" encounter. Indeed, the one functioning as a *guru* may aid the process of liberation from previous attachments by helping the person experience more keenly the degree to which he is trapped. The capacity to become fascinated may be repressed in an overly-trained person. The capacity to re-experience fascination may be impossible until some level of disengagement from usual concerns, ways, and commitments has been reached. Or the one who is to be the *guru* may function as a tempter and seducer. His way of life may evoke envy and/or admiration. His serenity, or his enthusiasm may evoke our curiosity. He may appear to be having more fun, living more fully, experiencing more, or he may disclose images of possibility that attract the attention of the bored, unfulfilled seeker who then becomes fascinated and subsequently experiences his previous involvement as obstacles to his pursuit of new meaning and experience.

Whatever the occasion for being thus turned on, it is this fascinating engagement with an image of possibility that I define as independent learning. We might call it awakening or inspiration, but it is always *intentional*; that is, it is always related to something in the world, it is always awakening to *something*, being inspirited by or for *something*, fascinated with *something*. And it is always embodied; that is, the person lives and acts his experience of awakening. The person who is in this turned on state, which he experiences as different from his usual repetitive experience, should appear different to an observer. In principle, then, we have the possibility of a psychology, a physiology, even an epidemiology and sociology of being turned on. I don't know what we would call it, a "turnology," or something.

Some Factors Which Facilitate Independent Learning

I think that the capacity to become fascinated anew after old fascinations have worn out is abetted by numerous factors, but it is the inter-personal factor that I want to focus upon here. Since each of us is an other to somebody, we can perhaps do something to foster independent learning in the others for whom we are the other. The basic factors in fostering independent learning, including the processes that underly it and make it emerge as a response to invitation and challenge, are the human responses: challenge, invitation, stimulation of imagination, confirmation, letting be, honest disclosure, and willingness to enter into dialogue. At least these factors seem to me to be relevant.

Confirmation: Martin Buber has said that each man wishes to be confirmed by his fellow and each has the capacity to confirm his fellow. To confirm the other in his being means to stand back and let his being "happen" to you. I invite him to tell me who he is, and I confirm him at each instant of his disclosure as being the one he is: As John, John in despair, John emerged with new goals and values. I view his disclosure with respect; I acknowledge its reality and authenticity.

Confirmation does not mean wishy-washy, insincere "permissiveness," because often the most direct confirmation is to take a stand in opposition to the disclosure of the other. The confrontation, the meeting, even in opposition confirms for the other that he is the one that he is. It lets him know that he exists. Confirmation means that I recognize the other person as the author of his acts and his utterances. He is the author. *He* is writing and living his own autobiography. It has not been programed for him. I attribute his acts and utterances to him and to his freedom. I confirm him as a free agent. He chooses his existence and is responsible for it.

The opposite of confirmation is invalidation and disconfirmation. There are many ways to invalidate another person and they all have the net effect of weakening his sense of his own identity and worth, his sense of being a source of experience and action. One can ignore the other. One can pretend he does not exist except as a doll, a thing, a nobody or as just another body. We hear people speaking in this way, "I want fifteen bodies for this job (experiment, class)." One can attribute his actions and utterances to some source other than his free intentionality. One can disconfirm all actions and utterances save those that are compatible with one's concept of the other. For instance, a mother might say, "That wasn't you when you did that. You weren't being yourself." Anything the child says or does which does not fit his mother's expectation of him is "not him." Under a regime of such disconfirmation a person will indeed come to doubt his own existence. He will lose his identity for himself and try to confine his experience and conduct only to that range consistent with his identity for the other. Confirmation is in a sense an act of love. One is acknowledging that other as one who exists in his own peculiar form, with the right to do so.

One recognizes that a concept of someone's being is only that: a concept, and not his being. One recognizes that it is for a person to reveal and define himself for us in *his* way, at *his* pace, thus reinforming and altering our experience and concept of him. It is not only *not* our duty, it is an outright sin to define another's being. Our concept of each other is always out of date. Yet, if another person has a weak sense of his identity for himself, if he is ontologically insecure, he may let us do this, define him, or even ask us to define him. "Tell me who I am, or, how I should be?" When I let the other person be, and confirm him in his being as he discloses it to me, I am creating an ambience in which he can dare to let go of his previous concepts and presentations of himself. They are not binding on him. My suspension of my preconception of his being, invites him to let go while he is in my presence. He can drop these self presentations, commitments, interests and goals, and explore the possibilities of new ones. Because he said he was interested in something yesterday, doesn't mean that he is committed to it today. He can weaken, regress, enter into himself while with me and feel assured that I am awaiting, perhaps with a hand holding his until he emerges to tell me who he now is. Inci-

dentally, about holding hands: last year I did a study of body contact, of who touches who, where, what are the correlates and so on. Americans are not a very touching people. "Don't touch me. I can't stand being touched." In a research at the University of Florida where there were something like 300 hours of time sampled observations of an elementary school teacher in a classroom with first grade children. Not once did a teacher's hand or part of her body come into contact with any part of the body of any of the children in the classroom. The probabilities against this are fantastic. There is a selective factor at work.

Disclosure: Another factor in the promotion of independent learning is disclosure. Earlier, I said that after a person has abandoned his previous incarnation, his way of presenting himself, after he entered his experiencing and then emerged, *he experiences the world as disclosing new possibilities*. The world is always there, but his way of experiencing it changes. You and I are part of his world, and we have the capacity to disclose ourselves to him even while he is embodied in his usual fixed roles and self-definitions. This is a fascinating thing. A tree, a lamp, a sky, the animal kingdom is always disclosing itself, but we don't always pay attention. People are part of the world and they can disclose their being more vigorously and insistently than a tree can. I can disclose my being with a shout and a roar and a pinch, if it takes that to capture a habit-ridden person's attention. When I am with him I can disclose to him how I experience myself and him. I can enter into dialogue with him. And with each of his utterances or acts, I can respond out of my experience and disclose to him what it is that I am experiencing. If I remain in contact with him consistently in dialogue, I may actually lead him to the edge of going out of his mind and habits, thus clearing the way for the emergence of a new self, new fascination, new experiencing. I ask you to consider dialogue; you say something from your being. Let's use jazz combo to illustrate. I blow a phrase on my trumpet and you respond with a passage on your saxophone.

Your response is a reply to me, a question and a challenge. And so I reply again and so it goes until the one of us loses his nerve and dares not let spontaneous true disclosure out. Dialogue has ended for a time.

Now switch to dialogue in psychotherapy. The patient says something to me. I reply in honesty. My reply (which is a disclosure of part of his world to him) evokes experiencing in him, so he utters this. This evokes a reply from me. We continue in this way until one of us has tripped off panic in the other and at this point insincerity, role playing and dissemblance begin. Truth and dialogue has ceased. One of the participants does not wish to be known and he holds back. In dialogue at its best, the participants remain in contact and let their reciprocal disclosures affect one another. If the dialogue occurs in the context of "letting be" and confirmation, then the weaker of the two may indeed flip into raw experiencing, find it safe if the other is authentically of good will and supporting, and emerge in an awakened turned on state. Authentic disclosure of self then, is a likely factor in the promotion of awakening, authentication and validation of the other, and in the emergence of independent learning.

More common than dialogue in interpersonal relations is semblance, role playing, impersonation of the "other" one wishes to seem to the other. Hence, the other person seldom truly encounters a *person in process*. Instead he meets the other as one who seems to have taken a pledge of consistency, as if the other one has pledged to be the same tomorrow as he was today. He meets a world of people who do not invite him into new possibilities. If I am in your world and I don't grow and change, then you are in a world that can obstruct and impede your growth. Now teacher-trainers are part of a world for somebody: children. In true encounter, there is a collapse of roles and self concepts. No one emerges from an encounter the same as he entered. My willingness to disclose myself to you, to drop my mask, is a factor in your trusting me and daring, then, to disclose yourself to me. This disclosure of yourself to me aids the

process of disengaging you from your previous ways of being. When I disclose myself to you, *I am your world*, and this world discloses new possibilities to you. It evokes new challenges and invitations that may stir you and revivify your imagination.

Challenging the other's imagination: This is another factor in independent learning. If independent learning is the implementation of fascination with imagined possibilities, then we must concern ourselves with ways to evoke the imaginative mode of experiencing. We already know a great deal about perception, the perceptual mode of experiencing, but imagining, the imaginative conscious, is less fully understood. To imagine means to transcend the here and now, to shut off one's perception for the time, and invent new possibilities that thus far cannot be perceived by anybody. The possibilities exist in the imaginative consciousness of the experiencer and it is for him to "real-ize" these, to make them real, to make them perceptible, to make it possible for him and others to perceive in actuality what before existed only as his image. The free imagination, like freedom itself, is a threat to all status quo. The free imagination appears to make intentional learning, independent learning possible.

The learner, even in a school room, is animated by the image of a future possible being that is not yet attained. The good pedagogue will seek to vivify and intensify this image of what it will be like when one can read, count, or play the piano. Even advertisements in comic books capitalize on this when they say "Can you see yourself as the life of the party? Would you like to be? Then enroll now." The dull child, the one who resists the teacher's efforts to teach, is often the one whose imagination has been turned off because the possible being it could disclose is frightening. Or his world is so threatening he must stay in the mode of perception lest a danger appear and he may not notice it. Imagining is dangerous because it means a cessation of vigilant scanning.

This makes me think of the "intellectual paranoids" in our universities who don't dare turn their imagining loose, who rivet their attention on their last set of words, lest an enemy be near to challenge them. The teacher who turns on the dull pupil, the coach who elicits the magnificent performance from someone of whom it could not have been expected, are people who themselves have an image of the pupils' possibilities, and they are effective in realizing their image. Good leaders who have a vivid image of possibility produce followers in whom this image is awakened, and the followers achieve remarkable feats on their own. The art of challenge needs to be better understood, but it does seem from this sketchy analysis to entail the ability to awaken a sleeping imagination so it can envision fascinating new possibilities of being. It also seems to involve the possibility of becoming fascinated. Good pornographers are able to awaken images of sexual possibilities, even in neurotics who ordinarily repress their sexual imagination. I think teachers who would like to turn students on might learn something from them. A good *guru* is able to awaken the imagination of possibilities in the experience of the seeker. Beyond the awakening of possibility, however, the good *guru* is effective at challenging a person to commit himself to realize the possibility.

Encouragement: It is often a long and discouraging voyage to make an envisioned possibility actual. A friend, parent, teacher, or *guru*, may help the independent learner make his way by offering courage, encouragement, and support in the face of blind alleys, setbacks, and temporary failures. Many people have the capacity to imagine possibilities, even fascinating possibilities, but they stop their pursuit after a failure or two. The helper will offer the support which keeps the seeker seeking and trying. The seeking is what is applauded, not solely the successful attainment. Kazantzakis puts these words into the mouth of Odysseus in *The Odyssey, a modern sequel.* Odysseus says, "Your voyages, O my soul, are my native land." Not the harbor, the *voyaging.* The seeking is what is applauded not solely the successful attainment. This also reminds me of the slogan in

Canada when I went to school. We were always told, we had it drummed into us, "It doesn't matter who wins the game, it is how hard and well you play that counts." And we believed it. I believe it to this day. It is an English import. Many people will neither imagine or try because they cannot be guaranteed visible success.

Conclusion

I am going to conclude now. Where are the *gurus*? People who relate to others in a confirming, authentic, challenging and encouraging way seem to be agents in fostering independent learning in others. Likely, too, they are fascinated people themselves, animated by images of possibility that they are in the process of actualizing. The imitation of admired role models — hero worship, identification — is certainly an influential factor in everyone's development. We should not underrate the importance of this in our deliberations here. Indeed, how admirable, how heroic, how growing, how seeking in fascination are the available *Others* in society just now? Who wants to be like his father, or his mother, or his school teacher?

If the young people of today are any illustration, they seem to be hell-bent on pursuing an image of a possible being that is portrayed for them by the mass media. The image of men who play with Bunnies, and of Bunnies who are playmates to Playboys, seem more to inspire fascination and the desire to learn how to look like one and behave like one than do professors of Introductory Psychology or the teachers of third-grade Social Studies. Now granted those who promote these models are corrupt *gurus.* They do it for cash, but they turn people on and we might well learn something from them. Hitler turned people on, and so did Jesus. I wonder if the "establishment" in society can tolerate *gurus*, or people who function like *gurus.* I wonder if schools, homes, industry, politics, and business will permit people to be turned on to projects of their own choosing.

Independent learners rock the boat. True education, as opposed to training, is by definition *subversive,* and it is at this point that I want to

74

comment about a statement that appears in a booklet entitled *A Guide to Preparation of Programs for Programed Instruction*. In this book it says, "Failure to define the purposes and specific goals is a little like setting out on a long journey without deciding on a destination. It might prove to be an interesting trip, but the traveler could wander for a long time, without getting far from his starting point and without ever reaching the distant places he wanted to visit." Now I rather think that education, as I am defining the term here, and which I am calling subversive, is indeed a failure to define the purpose and specific goals. Training, by contrast, deliberately reduces variance, diminishes freedom in a sense, and lessens autonomy. We cannot ignore the fact that education, as I have defined it, is a political act, or better it is the embodiment of the political stance of the loyal opposition, and sometimes the anarchist or revolutionary. Every society needs its anarchists, its *gurus*, its true educators and teachers, or it will shatter from its own rigidity. Do we have any, do we have enough, and are they honest?

Philip W. Jackson

The Student's World

When you were a child, how many times did you find yourself cornered by an adult, usually a strange aunt or uncle, who opened the conversation with that oldest of all gambits: "Well, how do you like school?" As an adult how often have you been left alone with someone else's child and, not knowing what else to say, found yourself falling back on some variant of the standard query: "How's school?" If you have not had both of these experiences, and each of them several times, you must be something of a recluse, for talk about school, when the dialogue is between an adult and a child, is almost as popular a social maneuver as talk about one's health or the weather.

Yet such talk, despite its popularity, rarely yields much information about what life in school is really like or how that life is experienced by the student to whom we are speaking. There seem to be two major reasons why this is so. First, in most instances neither the child nor the adult takes the query seriously. Both know that questions about school, like questions about personal health, are polite social gestures and usually are not intended to be answered fully or honestly. Thus, when asked about his classroom experiences, the fourth-grader who is having a miserable time with long division and who hates his teacher with a deep and abiding passion knows that he is expected to respond in much the same way as the victim of a migraine headache whose health is inquired into. Custom requires both sufferers to grin and say, "Fine, thank you."

Reprinted from *The Elementary School Journal* (April 1966), pp. 345–57, by permission of The University of Chicago Press and the author. Copyright © 1966.

A second limit to what we can learn about school life by talking to students arises from the fact that students may themselves not be acutely aware of what is happening to them in the classroom. Or, more precisely, they may never have tried to express the vague feelings and intuitive knowledge engendered by that experience. School life, like life in the military service, is not easy to describe to outsiders. You have to have been there.

But even being there is not enough, for when fellow students, or army veterans, discuss their common experience they often overlook or fail to mention some of the obvious and pervasive aspects of that experience. And often it is these familiar and seemingly trivial features of life that are the most revealing when it comes to capturing the flavor or unique quality of membership in a social institution. Accordingly, the remainder of this essay will focus on some aspects of school life that students rarely talk about in the presence of adults or even, in all probability, in the presence of other students.

The subjects to be discussed are not dramatic, or even intrinsically interesting, though I shall do my best to keep them from becoming deathly dull. What is more important, they concern things we all know, even though we do not think about them too much. My only justification for asking you to attend to such mundane matters is my hope that a consideration of these trivial but neglected events will deepen our insight into the character of the student's world and, hence, might lead us to ask new questions about our responsibility for establishing and maintaining that world.

Two warnings are necessary. First, I do not bring words of uplift and inspiration. In fact, some of the things I am going to say about schools and schooling will not be pleasant. They may even sound harsh. But I am convinced that educators are ready for such talk, provided it stems from good intentions, and that they prefer frankness, even though it may hurt, to the sticky sentiment and clichés that have come to characterize educational discussions from college courses to inservice workshops. Second, I am not going to present a plan of action for your consideration. Indeed, I am going to raise many more questions than I shall answer. Here again, I believe that more and more teachers are becoming tired of hearing experts, whether from the university or the central office, hand out the latest panacea for eliminating our educational woes. For a change, therefore, I will ask you to do nothing but think. If there are practical implications that follow from what I have to say, it is up to you to find them.

The Social Traffic of the Classroom

Anyone who has ever taught knows that the classroom is a busy place, even though it may not always appear so to the casual visitor. Indeed, recent attempts to describe that busyness have yielded data that have proved surprising even to experienced teachers. For example, we have found in our studies of elementary-school classrooms that the teacher engages in as many as a thousand interpersonal interchanges each day. No comparable data are available for high-school teachers, but there is reason to believe that the interpersonal demands are equally severe at that level. A look at these and other demands is instructive as we try to understand what life in the classroom is really like.

First, consider the rapidity of the teacher's actions. What keeps her hopping from Jane to Billy to Sam, and back again, in the space of a few seconds? Clearly much of this activity is done in the interest of instruction. In most classrooms the teacher acts as a gatekeeper who manages the flow of interaction. When more than one person wishes to say something (a common condition in educational gatherings), it is the teacher who decides who will speak and when. Or we might turn our observation around and say that it is the teacher who determines who will not speak, for usually the number of students who want to say something exceeds the number who are granted the privilege.

Supply Sergeant

Another time-consuming task for the teacher, at least in the elementary school, is that of serving as a supply sergeant. Classroom space and material resources are limited, and the teacher must allocate these resources judiciously. Not every student can use the big scissors at once; only one child at a time can look through the microscope or drink from the drinking fountain or use the pencil sharpener. Again, it is important to recognize that the number of students who want to use these resources at any given moment is often greater than the number that can use them.

Closely related to the job of doling out material resources is that of granting special privileges to deserving students. The teacher frequently must decide whether a student is to be allowed to hand in his homework paper late or make up a quiz that he missed or have an extra day to finish his laboratory assignment. In elementary-school classrooms it is usually the teacher who assigns coveted duties, such as serving on the safety patrol, running the movie projector, or clapping the erasers. Students soon learn that in school, as in life in general, many are called, but few are chosen.

Official Timekeeper

A fourth responsibility of the teacher, and one that calls our attention to another important aspect of classroom life, is that of serving as an official timekeeper. The teacher sees to it that things begin and end on time, more or less. He determines the proper moment for switching from discussion to workbooks, or from spelling to arithmetic. He decides whether a student has spent too long in the washroom or whether those who take the bus may be dismissed. In many schools the teacher is assisted in this job by elaborate systems of bells and buzzers, but even when the school day is mechanically punctuated by clangs and hums, the teacher is not relieved of his responsibility for watching the clock. School is a place where things often take place not because people want them to, but because it is time for them to happen.

Our concern here is with the student and the quality of his life in the classroom. Therefore, the frenetic activity of the teacher, as she goes about calling on people, handing out supplies, granting privileges, and turning activities on and off, is of interest to us only insofar as the student experiences that behavior. We are interested, in other words, in what it is like to be on the receiving end of the teacher's action.

To begin, it is safe to say that for most students, some of the time, and for some students, most of the time, the classroom is a great place to be. When new insights are formed and mastery is achieved, when the teacher's queries can be answered with confidence, when privileges are granted and praise bestowed, when natural interests and desires coincide with institutional expectations — at such moments (and such moments do occur more or less regularly for many students) life at school must be extremely satisfying. A sufficient number of such experiences might well create the desire for further education and could set the stage for a lifetime of scholarship and academic pursuits.

But it is probably also true that for most students, some of the time, and for some students, most of the time, the classroom comes close to resembling a cage from which there is no escape. When activities are dull and repetitious, when the student is not called on even though he has signalled the desire to be heard, when privileges are not granted and blame, rather than praise, is bestowed, when natural interests and desires are antithetical to the demands of the institution — at such moments (and such moments probably occur more or less regularly for many students) life in school must be extremely irksome.

The important point is that these unpleasant aspects of school life are experienced not only by those who are failing in their schoolwork (although students with low achievement might receive more than their share of these discom-

forts). Nor are they simply a function of the cantankerousness or maladroitness of particular classroom teachers (although poor professional preparation and psychological disorders of teachers may well add to the student's burden). It would seem, in other words, that much of the pain of school life is a natural outgrowth of the problems of institutional living and the management of social traffic. Given the arrangement in which one person is chiefly responsible for serving the educational needs of thirty or thirty-five others and for articulating the demands of this group with those of several other groups in the same building, three of the most salient features of school life — delay, denial, and interruption — are almost inevitable.

Delay

Consider for a moment the frequency of delay. When we examine the details of classroom life carefully, it is surprising to see how much of the student's time is spent in waiting. In the elementary school, the students often line up for recess, for lunch, and for dismissal, and they frequently have to wait for the lines to be straight before they move. During individual seatwork they wait for the teacher to come around to their desk to inspect their work. When the whole class is working together, there is the waiting for the slower pupil to finish the work that the faster ones have completed. During discussion there is the waiting for fellow students to answer the teacher's query. When motion pictures or slides are shown, there is usually a delay as the room and the equipment are made ready. As time for the bell approaches, students are waiting for it to ring, even though they may still have their eyes on the teacher.

No one knows for sure how much of the student's time is spent in neutral, as it were, but it is certainly a memorable portion. How many of us who have lived thousands of days in schools can remember waiting anxiously for the minutes to tick away until the dismissal bell freed us? How many of us whose lungs are lined with chalk dust can recall the hours spent looking out the classroom window as we waited for the group in which we were imbedded to move

78

sluggishly along? How many of us respond sympathetically to the following image of school life presented by George Santayana, as he describes his student days at Boston's Boys Latin School: "No blackboard was black; all were indelibly clouded with ingrained layers of old chalk; the more you rubbed it out, the more you rubbed it in. Every desk was stained with generations of inkspots cut deeply with initials and scratched drawings. What idle thoughts had been wandering for years through all those empty heads in all those tedious school hours! In the best schools almost all schooltime is wasted."[1]

Idleness, unfortunately, is only part of the picture, and perhaps not even the most important part. Waiting is not so bad and may even be beneficial when the things we are anticipating ultimately happen. Indeed, Longfellow was probably speaking with the voice of wisdom when, in his *Psalm of Life*, he advises us to "Learn to labour and to wait." But he was just a shade too optimistic when, in another poem (the title of which ironically is *The Student's Tale*), he promises his reader that "All things come round to him who will but wait." At least it is doubtful that Longfellow was referring to things that go on in classrooms, for there the waiting is sometimes in vain.

Denial

The denial of desire is commonplace in school, and likely it has to be. Not everyone who wants to speak can be heard, not all the student's queries can be answered to their satisfaction, not all their requests can be granted. It is true that, considered individually, most of these denials are psychologically trivial; but considered cumulatively, their significance increases. Part of learning how to live in school involves learning how to give up desire as well as waiting for its fulfillment.

Typically, things happen on time in school,

[1] From George Santayana, "The Latin School" in *Unseen Harvests*, edited by Claude M. Fuess and Emory S. Basford (New York: Macmillan, 1947), p. 487.

and, as a result, activities are often begun before interest is aroused and terminated before interest wanes. Once again, there is probably no alternative to this unnatural state of affairs. If we were to wait until students requested a history class on their own, as an instance, we would have a long wait. Similarly, if we allowed students to remain in their physical education classes until they grew tired of the game, there likely would not be time for other things. There seems to be no alternative, therefore, but to stop and start things on time, even though it means constantly interrupting the natural flow of interest and desire for at least some students.

Interruptions

But interruptions in the classroom are not confined to the beginning and ending of subject-matter periods. There are also more subtle ways in which activities are broken into. The irrelevant comment during class discussion, as an instance, often breaks the spell created by the relevant remarks that have preceded it. When the teacher is working individually with a student while others are present — a common arrangement in elementary-school classrooms — petty interruptions, in the form of minor misbehavior or students coming to the teacher for advice, are the rule rather than the exception. In countless small ways the bubble of reality created during the teaching session is punctured, and much of the teacher's energy is spent in patching up the holes, just as much of the student's energy is spent in attempting to ignore them. Students are constantly "turning back" to their studies after their attention has been momentarily drawn elsewhere.

Here, then, are three of the unpublicized features of school life: delay, denial, and interruption. As educators what do we make of them? Or better, what should we make of them? Let's dispense with extreme reactions first.

On the one hand, there is the temptation to ignore these aspects of classroom experience. After all, delay, denial, and interruption are features of life in several other settings. Why pay particular attention to these petty annoyances when they occur in school? Students themselves do not seem to be too upset by these occurrences, the argument continues; therefore, it is probably safe to ignore them, with perhaps a passing cluck of disapproval, and move to more pressing educational problems.

On the other hand, there is the temptation to magnify these undesirable events until they become all that can be seen of school life. This alternative, which might be called the school-is-hell approach, seems to be dominant on many of our college campuses these days. It is the credo of the new undergraduate religion: anti-establishmentarianism.

The trouble with these extreme positions, as with most, is that they can be maintained only by choosing to ignore certain salient features of our educational scene. Defenders of the optimistic leave-well-enough-alone point of view preserve their calm by remaining blind to the fact of widespread discontent in our schools. Defenders of the school-is-hell point of view must keep the edge on their fury by failing to acknowledge that there is massive satisfaction as well as massive dissatisfaction in our classrooms.

A more dispassionate point of view, although one that is unlikely to capture newspaper headlines, might lead us to examine the strategies that students develop to adapt to these mundane features of school life. What must be done, in other words, if the student is to live a large portion of his life in an environment in which delay, denial, and interruption are inevitable? Further, how do the strategies for adapting to these demands combine with, complement, or contradict the strategies for acquiring knowledge and developing intellectual mastery?

Patience and Resignation

The quintessence of virtue in an institutional setting is contained in the single word: *patience*. Without that quality life can be miserable for those who must spend time in our prisons, our hospitals, our corporation offices, and our schools. But virtue can become soured if tested too severely. And the conditions that lead to the development of patience can also, if carried too far, set the stage for the development of resignation — a much less virtuous condition. Indeed, the distinction between the patient person and the resigned person is not always easy to make on the basis of surface appearances, even though there is a world of difference in the psychological strength of the two.

While the patient person maintains a firm grasp on his own plans for the future and, hence, retains a sense of integrity, the resigned person does not. Resignation involves an act of psychological surrender in which one's own desires, plans, and interests are abandoned and action is taken on the basis of the desires, plans, and interests of others. The resigned person has not only given up hope, he has given up many other linkages between his motives and his actions. Resignation involves, in other words, a loss of feeling and a sense of no longer caring about what happens.

Returning to the situation in our schools, we can see that if students are to face the demands of classroom life with equanimity — rather than with disappointment, anger, and rebellion — they must learn to be patient. This means that they must be able to disengage, at least temporarily, their feelings from their actions. The hope is that the disengagement will not become permanent, that patience will not fade imperceptively into resignation. Yet in expressing this hope we acknowledge a real danger, for the one condition lies just beyond the other, along the same path. The problem for the teacher is to help students become uninvolved when conditions demand it, but not too uninvolved. We want students to be calm in the face of some of the frustrations caused by collective life in an institution, but we do not want them, in the jargon of adolescence, to "cool it."

Masquerade

The second-grader who groans with disappointment when an enjoyable classroom activity is terminated, and the fourth-grader who zestfully waves his hand while his classmate is struggling to answer the teacher's question, both will likely be transformed by the time they reach high school or college into the jaded "professionals" of the classroom — those living ink-blots whose enigmatic silence and languid slouch effectively mask both the presence and the absence of enthusiasm for educational affairs. Which ones are merely being patient, and which resigned? It is sometimes hard to tell.

Students also know that teachers like to see evidence of enthusiasm and involvement, and this knowledge causes alertness and other signs of interest to be worn as masks in much the same way as signs of indifference. Classroom courtesy demands that you keep your eye on the teachers and frown intensely at appropriate times even though your mind may be miles away. Again the teacher is faced with the problem of deciding which students are really with her as she goes about her work and which ones just appear to be with her.

The business of faking involvement and of masking withdrawal is not limited to the simple procedure of showing signs of attention when class is in session. These are not the only strategies by which students adapt to classroom demands. Nor are delay, denial, and interruption the only unpleasant aspects of school life with which the student must cope. The classroom, it must be remembered, is an evaluative setting in which the student must learn not just to comply with commands, but to comply in a way that yields a positive evaluation.

Thus arises the common practice of giving the teacher what she wants on written assignments and test questions, even though the assignments seem meaningless and the questions inane. Along with this practice goes the technique of disguising ignorance, of responding to the teacher's queries with sufficient ambiguity or with only thinly veiled flattery so that she will not discover and no longer care whether the student knows anything or not. (When I was a high-school student, this ploy was known as giving the teacher a "snow job." I do not know what name it goes under these days, but I am fairly confident that it is still being practiced.)

These forms of student behavior may be laughed off as harmless pranks, and sometimes they are nothing more than that. But all these acts of detachment and deception, each of which might be considered harmless, or even "cute," when used in moderation, grow out of attempts to deal with institutional constraints. When used excessively and in combination, they are the marks of the educational con-man, the student who has learned to size up teachers and give them what they want with all the shrewdness and feigned sincerity of a dishonest secondhand car dealer.

The Two Curriculums

Much that has been said up to this point can be summarized by suggesting that every school and every classroom really has two curriculums that the students are expected to master. The one that educators traditionally have paid the most attention to might be called the official curriculum. Its core is the three R's, and it contains all of the school subjects for which we produce study guides and workbooks and teaching materials. It is the curriculum that all the curriculum reform groups are shouting about these days.

The other curriculum might be described as unofficial or perhaps even hidden, because to date it has received scant attention from educators. This hidden curriculum can also be represented by three R's, but not the familiar one of reading, 'riting, and 'rithmetic. It is, instead, the curriculum of rules, regulations, and routines, of things teachers and students must learn if they are to make their way with minimum pain in the social institution called *the school*.

The Reward System

Two or three important observations might be made about the relationship between these two curriculums. One is that the reward system of the school is tied to both. Indeed, many of the rewards and punishments that sound as if they are being dispensed on the basis of academic success and failure are really more closely related to the mastery of the hidden curriculum. Consider, as an instance, the common teaching practice of giving a student credit for trying. What do teachers mean when they say a student tries to do his work? They mean, in essence, that he complies with the procedural expectations of the institution. He does his homework (though incorrectly), he raises his hand during class discussion (though he usually comes up with the wrong answer), he keeps his nose in his book during free study period (though he does not turn the page very often). He is, in other words, a "model" student, though not necessarily a good one.

It is hard to imagine any of today's elementary-school teachers failing a student who tries, even though his mastery of course content is slight. And elementary-school teachers are not alone in this respect. At higher levels of education as well rewards go to the solid citizen as well as to the budding scholar. Surely many of our valedictorians and presidents of our honor societies owe their success as much to institutional conformity as to intellectual prowess. No doubt that bright-eyed little girl stands trembling before the principal on graduation day arrived there at least partly because she typed her weekly themes neatly and handed her homework in on time.

This manner of talking about educational affairs may sound cynical and may be taken as a criticism of teachers or as an attempt to subvert the virtues of neatness, punctuality, and courteous conduct in general. But nothing of that kind is intended. The point is simply that in schools, as in prisons, good behavior pays off.

Just as conformity to institutional expectations can lead to praise, so can the lack of it lead to trouble. As a matter of fact, the relationship of the hidden curriculum to student difficulties is even more striking than is its relationship to student success. Consider, as an instance, the conditions that lead to disciplinary action in the classroom. Why do teachers scold students? Because the student has given the wrong answer? Or because, try as he may, he fails to grasp the intricacies of long division? Not usually. A student is more likely to be scolded for coming into the room late or for making too much noise or for not listening to the teacher's directions or for pushing while in line. The teacher's wrath, in other words, is commonly triggered by violations of institutional regulations and routines rather than by the student's intellectual deficiencies.

Even with the more serious difficulties that clearly entail academic failure, the demands of the hidden curriculum lurk in the shadows. When Johnny's parents are summoned to school because their son is not doing too well in arithmetic, what explanation will be given for their son's poor performance? More than likely blame will be placed on motivational deficiencies in Johnny rather than on his intellectual shortcomings. The teacher may even go so far as to say that Johnny is *unmotivated* during arithmetic period. But what does this mean? It means, in essence, that Johnny does not even try. And not trying, as we have seen, often boils down to a failure to comply with institutional expectations, a failure to master the hidden curriculum.

There is a further question that must be asked about the relationship between the official and the unofficial curriculums in our schools: To what extent does the mastery of one interfere with the mastery of the other? In other words, how do the demands of intellectual achievement relate to the demands of institutional conformity? Are they complementary or contradictory?

We have already seen that many features of classroom life call for patience, at best, and resignation, at worst. As the student learns to live in school, he learns to subjugate his own desires to the will of the teacher and to subdue his own actions in the interest of the common good. He learns to be passive and to acquiesce to the network of rules, regulations, and routines in which he is imbedded. He learns to tolerate petty frustrations and to accept the plans and the policies of higher authorities, even when their rationale is unexplained and their meaning unclear. Like the inhabitants of other institutional settings he learns that he must frequently shrug and say, "That's the way the ball bounces."

But the personal qualities that play a role in intellectual mastery are of a very different order from those that characterize the Company

Man. Curiosity, as an instance, that most fundamental of all scholarly traits, calls forth the kind of probing, poking, and exploring that is almost antithetical to the attitude of passivity that has just been described. The productive scholar must develop the habit of challenging authority and of questioning the value of tradition. He must insist on explanations for things that are unclear. The scholar must certainly be a disciplined man, but his discipline is developed in the service of his scholarship, rather than in the service of other people's wishes and desires. In short, intellectual mastery calls for sublimated forms of aggression rather than submission to constraints.

Docile Scholars

These brief descriptions exaggerate the real differences between the demands of institutional conformity and the demands of scholarship, but they do serve to call our attention to points of possible conflict between the two sets of demands. Can both sets be mastered by the same person? Apparently so. Certainly not all our student council presidents and valedictorians are academic Uriah Heeps. Some have clearly managed to retain their intellectual aggressiveness while at the same time acquiescing to the laws that govern the social traffic of our schools. Apparently it is possible, under certain conditions at least, to breed docile scholars, even though the expression might appear at first glance to be a contradiction in terms. But how are these successes achieved? At what cost? And how many fail to achieve the synthesis of the so-called well-rounded student?

A Social Price

The cost of scholastic success must be measured not only in terms of the intellectual energy expended or the non-academic gratifications denied. For many students there is also a social cost. The students who accede willingly and sincerely to both the intellectual and the institutional demands of the school run the risk of being perceived as defectors by their peers. At the lower levels of education these students are likely to be called *goody-goodies, tattletales,* and *teacher's pets;* at the upper levels they are called *greasy grinds, eager beavers,* and *squares.* In the eyes of many of their classmates the students who receive the highest praise from the authorities of the school are the ones who have sold out to the system. For many students this kind of name-calling, which is often correctly perceived as reflecting envy, is not difficult to endure and is a small price to pay for the admiration of adults whom they respect. For other students it is more important to appear to be a "regular guy." Many would rather be seen as a "buddy" than as a "brain."

The number of failures in our schools is much larger than the number of students who do not come up to snuff on our achievement tests or final exams. The failures include an untold number who seemingly succeed but who turn off their intellectual motors when the dismissal bell rings. These children have learned how to give the teacher what she wants all right, but in the process they have forgotten how to use their mental powers to give themselves what they want when the teacher is not around. This group includes the students who make the honor rolls and the dean's lists during the school year but who do not know what to do with themselves during the summer vacation. It includes the thousands who, after their formal schooling is finished and diploma hung on their wall, will never again be stirred by the quest for knowledge. It includes the millions for whom a childhood of teacher-watching is followed by an adulthood of television-viewing, with hardly a change of postures or facial expression to mark the transition. One almost expects them to raise their hands and ask Johnny Carson if they can go to the bathroom. Adequate as students? Yes. Adequate as adults? No.

Two Worlds

And who is to blame for these failures? The schools? The society? The individual? All three share the responsibility, I suppose, but it is the school's role with which we are particularly concerned at present. The school, it would seem, asks the student for a commitment to two worlds — the world of the institution and the world of scholarship. Unfortunately, it often succeeds in obtaining only a feigned commitment to either one.

What about our own commitment to these two worlds? How have we partialled out our own loyalty? How much have we ourselves become Company Men, more interested in an up-to-date register than an up-to-date idea, more concerned with straight lines than with straight thinking? After all, we too, like our students, are rewarded for doing things neatly, and on time, with a minimum of fuss and bother. How often have we received compliments from our principals for the surface show of scholarship, for the attractiveness of our bulletin boards rather than for the vigor and imaginativeness of the ideas we present to our pupils? Nor are our administrators the villains of the piece, for they, in their turn, are caught in the same bind. The public wants its institutions to be run quietly, efficiently, and economically. The best-attended school-board meeting is almost always the one at which the budget is discussed. And who is this elusive public but the very people we educators had yesterday in our classrooms. So the circle is complete. No one is responsible, yet everyone is.

What, then, is life like in school? It would seem to be a life of contradictory demands and competing tendencies, a life in which discovery and disappointment go hand in hand, where the unpredictable and the routine are combined daily. These monotonous settings of desks and blackboards and books provide a stage for the cyclic enactment of a dull drama, a play that is at once boring and exciting. No wonder our young friend only says, "Fine!" when we ask him how things are going in the classroom. School is a puzzling place, and the puzzles are not all intellectual ones.

Joseph Featherstone

Excerpt from Schools Where Children Learn

My wife and I had been told about good things happening in British classrooms, but we were scarcely prepared for what we found; in recent decades there has been a profound and sweeping revolution in English primary education, involving new ways of thinking about how young children learn, classroom organization, the curriculum, and the role of the teacher. We saw schools in some good local educational authorities — Bristol, Nottingham, Leicestershire, Oxfordshire — and a few serving immigrant areas in cities like London.

In what follows, I'm going to be as specific as I can about how classes work, how the room is laid out, what sort of things are in it, how the teacher and the children spend the day, and, in some detail, how a child learns to read, as an example of the kind of learning that goes on. I know that American teachers, particularly good ones, are rightly suspicious of most talk on education, because so little of what they hear relates to actual classroom practice. I hope I can be concrete enough. The relevance of these British classrooms to American education is a difficult question which I'll leave for later.

Primary schools in Britain divide into "infant" and "junior" schools. The infant schools in England take the children from the age of five to seven, and in some authorities, eight. It is in the infant schools that people learn to read and write and to work with numbers. Junior schools take children from seven or eight to eleven, and in some places twelve; they then go on to secondary school. Infant and junior

schools sometimes occupy the same building, and some authorities — Oxfordshire, for example — have a policy of putting them together in one unit, like an American elementary school.

It is important to understand that what goes on in good infant schools is much the same. The approach is similar, though the quality of teaching and children's work varies greatly.

Westfield Infant School, for example, is a one-story structure, like any of a thousand American buildings, on a working-class housing estate in Leicestershire. If you arrive early, you find a number of children already inside, reading, writing, painting, playing music, tending to pets. Teachers sift in slowly and begin working with students. Apart from a religious assembly (required by law), it's hard to say just when school actually begins because there is very little organized activity for a whole class. The puzzled visitor sees some small group work in mathematics ("maths") or reading, but mostly children are on their own, moving about and talking quite freely. The teacher sometimes sits at her desk, and the children flock to her for consultations, but more often she moves about the room, advising on projects, listening to children read, asking questions, giving words, talking, sometimes prodding.

The hallways, which are about the size of those in American schools, are filled with busy children, displays of paintings and graphs, a grocery store where children use play money and learn to count, easels, tables for collections of shells and plants, workbenches on which to pound and hammer nails and boards, big wooden boxes full of building blocks.

Classrooms open out onto the playground, which is also much in use. A contingent of children is kneeling on the grass, clocking the speed of a tortoise, which they want to graph against the speeds of other pets, and of people. Nearby are five-year-olds, finishing an intricate, tall tower of blocks, triumphantly counting as they add the last one, "twenty three, twenty four." A solitary boy is mixing powders for paint; on a large piece of paper attached to an easel, with very big strokes, he makes an ominous, stylized building that seems largely to consist of black shutters framing deep red windows. "It's the hospital where my brother is," he explains and pulls the visitor over to the class-library corner where a picture book discusses hospitals. He can't read it yet (he's five) but says he is trying. And he is; he can make out a number of words, some pretty hard, on different pages, and it is clear that he has been *studying* the book, because he wants badly to know about hospitals. At another end of the hall there is a quieter library nook for the whole school. Here two small boys are reading aloud; the better reader is, with indifferent grace, correcting the grateful slower boy as he stumbles over words.

The rooms are fairly noisy — more noisy than many American teachers or principals would allow — because children can talk freely. Sometimes the teacher has to ask for quiet. With as many as forty in some classes, rooms are crowded and accidents happen. Paint spills, a tub overflows, there are recriminations. Usually the children mop up and work resumes.

The visitor is dazed by the amount and variety and fluency of free writing produced: stories, free-verse poems with intricate images, precise accounts of experiments in "maths" and, finally, looking over a tiny little girl's shoulder, he finds: "Today we had visitors from America. . . ."

After a time, you overcome your confusion at the sheer variety of it all, and you begin making more definite observations. The physical layout of the classrooms is markedly different. American teachers are coming to appreciate the importance of a flexible room, but even in good elementary schools in the United States this usually means having movable, rather than fixed, desks. In the Westfield School there are no individual desks and no assigned places. Around the room (which is about the size of one you would find in an average American school) there are different tables for different activities: art, water and sand play, number work. The number tables have all kinds of number lines — strips of paper with numbers marked on them in sequence; on these children learn to count and reason mathematically. There are beads, buttons and odd things to count; weights and balances; dry and liquid measures; and a rich variety of apparatus for learning basic mathematical concepts, some of it home-made, some ready-made. The best of the commercial materials are familiar: Cuisenaire rods, the Dienes multibase material, Stern rods, and attribute or logical blocks. This sort of thing is stressed much more than formal arithmetic.

Every class has a library alcove, separated off by a room divider that also serves as a display shelf for books. Some library corners have a patch of carpet and an old easy chair. Every room has a "Wendy House," a play corner with dolls and furniture for playing house. Often there is a dress-up corner, too, with different kinds of cast-off adult clothes. The small children love the Wendy houses and dress-up corners, but you see older ones using them as well. Some classes have puppet theaters for putting on improvised plays with homemade puppets — although many make do with the legs of one table turned upside down on top of another for a makeshift stage. Often, small children perform dance dramas involving a lot of motion and a minimum of words.

Gradually it becomes clear how the day proceeds in one of these rooms. In many infant and some junior schools the choice of the day's routine is left completely up to the teacher; the teacher, in turn, leaves options open to the children. Classes for young children are reaching a point in many schools where there is no real difference between one subject in the curriculum and another, or even between work and play. A school day run on these lines is called, variously, the "free day," the "integrated curriculum," or the "integrated day." The term scarcely matters.

In a school that operates on the integrated day, the teacher usually starts the morning by listing the different activities available. A good deal of material is needed, according to the teachers, but the best of it is often home-made; in any case, it isn't necessary to have thirty or forty sets of everything, because most activities are for a limited number of people. "Six Children Can Play in the Wendy House," says a sign in one classroom. The ground rules are that they must clean up when they finish and they mustn't bother others.

A child might spend the day on his first choice, or he might not. Many teachers confess they get nervous if everybody doesn't do some reading and writing every day; others are committed in principle to letting children choose freely. In practice, many teachers give work when they think it's needed. In this, as in any other way of doing things, teachers tailor their styles to their own temperaments and to those of the children. But the extent to which children really have a choice and really work purposefully is astonishing.

How they learn reading offers an example of the kind of individual learning and teaching going on in these classrooms, even in quite large ones. (The mathematics work shows this even better, but that will be described later.) Reading is not particularly emphasized, and my purpose in singling it out is purely illustrative, though the contrast between English classes and most American ones, where reading is a formidable matter, is vivid and depressing.

At first it is hard to say just how they do learn to read since there are no separate subjects. A part of the answer slowly becomes clear, and it surprises American visitors used to thinking of the teacher as the generating force of education: children learn from each other. They hang around the library corners long before they can read, handling the books, looking at pictures, trying to find words they do know, listening and watching as the teacher hears other children's reading. It is common to see nonreaders studying people as they read, and then

imitating them, monkey doing what monkey sees. Nobody makes fun of their grave parodies, and for good reasons.

A very small number of schools in two or three authorities have adopted what they call "family" or "vertical" grouping, which further promotes the idea of children teaching children. In these schools, each class is a cross section of the whole school's population, all ages mixed together. This seems particularly successful in the early school years, when newcomers are easily absorbed, and older children help teach the young ones to clean up and take first steps in reading. The older children, too, benefit from classroom environment where they can occasionally be babyish; they also learn a good deal from the role of teacher they adopt. Family grouping needs smaller classes, teachers say, because it requires close supervision to make sure small children don't get overshadowed and big ones are still challenged. Teachers using family grouping swear by the flexibility it provides.

A range of reading schemes is used: sight reading, phonics, and so forth, whatever seems to work with a child. (Only about five percent of British schools use the Initial Teaching Alphabet — an improved alphabet, not a method of reading — that has proved successful with poor readers and adults both in England and in this country; principals of good schools we visited thought that ITA was unnecessary with a truly flexible reading program, but that in a rigid scheme it gave the slow reader another chance, and thus a break.) Increasingly in the better infant schools, there are no textbooks and no class readers, just books, in profusion. Instead of spending their scanty book money on forty sets of everything, schools have purchased different sets of reading series, as well as a great many single books, at all levels of difficulty. Teachers arrange their classroom libraries so they can direct students of different abilities to appropriate books, but in most classes a child can tackle anything he wants. As a check, cautious teachers ask them to go on their own through a graded reading series — which one doesn't matter.

However a child picks up reading, it will involve learning to write at the same time, and some write before they can read; there is an attempt to break down the mental barrier between the spoken, the written, and the printed word. When a child starts school, he gets a large, unlined notebook; this is his book for free writing, and he can put what he wants in it. On his own, he may draw a picture in it with crayon or pencil, discuss the picture with the teacher, and dictate a caption to her, which she then writes down for him: "This is my Dad." He copies the caption, writing just underneath. In this way he learns to memorize the look and sound of his dictated words and phrases until he reaches a point where, with help, he can write sentences. Often his notebook serves as his own first reading book.

He also gets a smaller notebook, his private dictionary, in which he enters words as he learns them. "I got a new word," a five-year-old brags to the visitor. Children are always running to the teacher for words as they find they have more and more to write. Good teachers don't give in without a struggle: the children have to guess the first letter and sound the word out before they get it. Thus they pick up phonetic skills informally, although some teachers do use sight cards and some formal phonics work. Gradually as a child amasses a reading and writing vocabulary, he reaches a fluent stage and you see six-year-olds writing stories, free-verse poems, accounts of things done in class, for an audience that includes other children as well as the teacher.

As a rule, teachers don't pay much attention to accuracy or neatness until a child is well on in his writing. They introduce grammar and spelling after a time, but not as separate subjects or ends in themselves. They are simply ways to say what you want more efficiently. Under these methods, the children choose the content of their writing, more attention is paid to content than externals such as punctuation, spelling, and grammar. In good schools these are presented as what they are: living ways to get a meaning across, to be understood. Even unimaginative teachers, who quibble with children about other work, can learn to respect the content of the free writing books and take it seriously. This emphasis on self-chosen content has produced a flowering of young children's literature in schools working with many kinds of teachers and children. There is growing recognition that different people flourish on different kinds of writing; storytellers and poets are not necessarily the same as those who can do elegant and graceful writing about mathematics. Impressive examples of free writing and poetry similar to what we saw are contained in the West Riding Education Committee's anthology, *The Excitement of Writing*. Samples of "maths" writing are included in the Schools Council's *Mathematics in the Primary Schools*, a wonderfully instructive book on many accounts.[1] Books made and illustrated by the children are coming to be a regular part of the curriculum in some schools.

Informal Schools

Of course children spend their time doing things other than reading, and the teachers in the schools we saw would be annoyed at the manner in which I've singled out one academic subject. The very best often argue that art is the key. The head of Sea Mills School in Bristol believes firmly that if the art is good, all else follows. All else does follow, richly, at Sea Mills, where the infants sat us down and performed a concert of skillful poetry and songs they had made up.

But my purpose was to show not reading methods but the changed role of the teacher. Formal classroom teaching — the instructor standing up front, talking to the group, or even the first-grade room divided up into reading groups which the teacher listens to separately as she tries desperately to keep order — has disappeared because it imposes a single pattern of learning on a whole group of children (thus forcing the schools to "track," or to group classes by ability), because it ignores the extent

[1] Schools Council's Council Curriculum bulletin no. 1, *Mathematics in the Primary Schools*, Her Majesty's Stationery Office, 1966.

to which children teach each other, and because in many workaday schools other methods are proving to be better. Ordinary, formally trained teachers take to the new role when they can see with their own eyes that the result is not chaos.

These methods mean more work for the teacher, not less. In informal conditions, it is essential for the teacher to keep detailed and accurate accounts of what a child is learning, even though at any given moment she might not know what he's up to. Children help by keeping their own records: in some schools they have private shelves where they store writing books, accounts of experiments and work in "maths," lists of the books they've read, and dates when they checked in with the teacher to read aloud. If American parents could see some of the detailed folders of each child's work, including samples of his art work, they would feel, quite rightly, that a report card is a swindle.

When the class seldom meets as a unit, when children work independently, discipline is less of a problem. It does not disappear as a problem, but it becomes less paramount. The purposeful self-discipline of these children is, we were told, just as surprising to middle-aged Englishmen as it is to Americans. It is a recent development, and by no means the product of luck; much hard work and thought go into the arrangement of these classrooms and their materials. When they work at it, teachers find they can make time during the day for children who need it. "I can give all my attention to a child for five minutes, and that's worth more to him than being part of a sea of faces all day," said a teacher in an East London school overlooking the docks. Other teachers say they can watch children as they work and ask them questions; there is a better chance of finding out what children really understand.

What we saw is no statistical sample. The practices of the good schools we visited in different kinds of communities are not standard, but there are reasons for thinking they are no longer strikingly exceptional. For the most part, these schools are staffed by ordinary teachers from the same sort of background as American teachers; they are not isolated experiments run by cranks or geniuses. The Plowden Committee's massive, and to American eyes, radical report in 1967 indicated that about one-third of England's 23,000 primary schools had been deeply influenced by the new ideas and methods, that another third were stirring under their impact, and that the remaining third were still teaching along the formal lines of British schools in the thirties, and of American schools today.

The change is most widespread and impressive in the infant schools, and becomes more scattered on the junior level. Yet junior schools in some authorities are playing stunning variations on the free themes developed by the infant schools, and these I shall discuss later; but, in general, change in the junior schools is slower, more diffident and complex.

Many formal schools — English and American — are probably doing a more effective job, in conventional terms, than these schools. It doesn't do to dogmatize. For example, by and large, in terms of measurable achievement on conventional tests, children in traditional, formal classes in England do slightly better than children from the freer classes. In one survey cited in the Plowden Report the difference is greatest in mechanical arithmetic, the least in reading. These are facts, but there are reasons for discounting them apart from evidence that the differences disappear in later school years. Formal schools teach children to take conventional tests; that is their function, and it would be surprising if all their efforts didn't produce some results. In view of the lack of test training in the freer schools, the students' results seem to me surprisingly high. The mathematics taught in the informal schools (mathematical relationships in which process of thought counts for more than arithmetical skill) and the English (free writing, rather than grammar and so on) put their students at a disadvantage on achievement tests, whose authors would probably be the first to admit this. England and America badly need new kinds of tests. My own strong impression is that in areas easy to define and probably not hard to test — ability to write, for example, or understanding of the math they were doing — the children in the good schools I saw, including slum schools, were far ahead of students in good formal schools in the United States.

The external motions teachers go through in the schools matter less than what the teachers are and what they think. An organizational change — the free day, for example, or simply rearranging classroom space — is unlikely to make much difference unless teachers are really prepared to act on the belief that in a rich environment young children can learn a great deal by themselves and that most often their own choices reflect their needs. When you see schools where teachers are acting on these assumptions, it is easy to share the Plowden Report's enthusiasm for informal, individual learning in the early years. The infant schools are a historical accident — nobody years ago gave much thought to why children should begin school at five — but British teachers are now realizing their advantages. With kindergarten and the first few years of school fused, children have an extended time in which to learn to read and write and work with numbers. This is especially effective if the pattern of learning is largely individual, if the teacher is important but doesn't stand in the way or try to take over the whole job. Many of the difficulties that plague formal first-grade classes disappear; children aren't kept back from learning, nor are they branded as problems if they take their time.

Additional Resources

Books

Dennison, George. *Lives of Children*. New York: Random House, 1969.
The entire book might be read to learn about Dennison's experiences with twenty-three children he taught at the First Street School.

Holt, John. *How Children Fail*. New York: Pitman, 1964.
Part 1 on strategy and part 2 referring to fear and failure of students are particularly helpful toward an understanding of the conditions that interfere with children's learning.

Jackson, Philip W. *Life in Classrooms*. New York: Holt, Rinehart and Winston, 1968.
Chapter 1 is recommended for its discussion of the demands of classroom life and their effect on students.

Leacock, Eleanor Burke. *Teaching and Learning in City Schools*. New York: Basic Books, 1969.
Leacock discusses the results of a comprehensive study of the socializing aspects of four urban elementary schools.

Leonard, George. *Education and Ecstasy*. New York: Delacorte Press, 1968.
Chapter 7, "Schools — For What?" is a provocative discussion of educational goals.

Maslow, Abraham H. *Toward a Psychology of Being*. New York: Van Nostrand Reinhold, 1968.
The entire book provides an understanding of humanistic psychology and its relevance to fields such as education.

Minuchin, Patricia, Barbara Biber, Edna Shapiro, and Herbert Zimiles. *The Psychological Impact of School Experience*. New York: Basic Books, 1969.
This book presents a massive study on the effects of four school environments with different philosophies of education.

Rosenthal, Robert, and Lenore Jacobson. *Pygmalion in the Classroom*. New York: Holt, Rinehart and Winston, 1968.
This is a report of a widely publicized study on the impact of teacher expectations on students.

Silberman, Melvin L., ed. *The Experience of Schooling*. New York: Holt, Rinehart and Winston, 1971.
This anthology provides a wide range of readings concerned with the psychological quality of the school experience.

Thelen, Herbert A. *Education and the Human Quest*. New York: Harper and Row, 1960.
Chapter 2, "What Makes Johnny Tick?" is helpful in thinking about the limitations of natural inquiry in children.

Articles

Berlyne, D. E. "Curiosity and Education." In *Learning and the Educational Process*, edited by J. D. Krumboltz. Chicago: Rand McNally, 1965.

Berlyne discusses the value of using intrinsic motivation as the basis for learning.

Bettelheim, Bruno. "Autonomy and Inner Freedom: Skills of Emotional Management." In *Life Skills in School and Society*, edited by Louis J. Rubin. Washington, D.C.: ASCD, 1969.

Bettelheim describes some of the emotional skills that allow an individual to function successfully and the kinds of school experiences that nurture their development.

Getzels, Jacob W., and Herbert A. Thelen. "The Classroom Group as a Unique Social System." In *The Dynamics of Instructional Groups*, NSSE 59th Yearbook. Chicago: University of Chicago Press, 1960.

This article presents a useful model of the interpersonal dynamics of the teacher-student relationship.

Sears, Pauline S. "Implications of Motivation Theory for Independent Learning." In *The Theory and Nature of Independent Learning*. Scranton, Pa.: International Textbook Co., 1967.

Sears discusses three theories of the development of motivation in children and their relative implications to the classroom.

Silberman, Melvin L. "Behavioral Expression of Teachers' Attitudes Toward Elementary School Students." *Journal of Educational Psychology* 60 (1969): 402–407.

This is a study of how teachers' attitudes toward their students are revealed in teachers' classroom behavior.

White, Robert W. "Motivation Reconsidered: The Concept of Competence." *Psychological Review* 66 (1959): 297–333.

On the basis of the research literature, White argues that motivation is essentially a desire for mastery over the various aspects of one's environment.

Films

Children as People. Polymorph Films, 331 Newbury Street, Boston, Mass. 02115.

This film shows classroom activity at the Fayerweather School, which utilizes an open classroom approach.

Critical Moments in Teaching Series. Holt, Rinehart and Winston, 383 Madison Avenue, New York, N.Y. 10017.

This is a series of short films that terminate at a critical point in a problematic situation. Recommended for use as a stimulus for discussing the teacher's relationship to students is *Walls*. Recommended for discussing the stimulation of learning is *First and Fundamental R*.

Resolution Activity

We began this content area by considering the problem of how a learning environment allows for growth experiences at the same time that it respects the need for safety. Any of the materials you have explored has in some way provided a perspective on this problem. It would be valuable to bring your inquiry to some state of resolution with solutions to the question "What should a learning environment provide?" or at least with a reformulation of the problem of safety versus growth. Rather than tackle this task abstractly, you may find it helpful to integrate the outcomes of an inquiry through an analysis of a specific situation.

The following note from a teacher describes the plight of a high school history teacher who has failed to involve his students. After reading the note, ask yourself what conditions for safety and growth you think this teacher has either created or ignored. You might also imagine that this teacher has previously sought your help. How would you explain to him the results of your inquiry into the learning environment in ways relevant to his concerns, and how would you help him to engage in his own inquiry into the learning environment?

Dear Colleagues:

I have been thinking a lot about a school history class that I am scheduled to teach for the fall semester. This time I want things to be different, but how? In previous classes, the students seemed to be putting forth the least amount of effort possible. For example, every time I asked challenging questions, they would sit and stare. Rarely was anyone willing to take a stab at the answer. If a student was called on, he would often shrug his shoulders and pretend he hadn't the faintest idea how to answer. Another example of the students' lethargy involved the reading assignments. I began many classes by asking if anyone had questions about what he read. Was there anything that wasn't understood? Rarely did students volunteer questions and yet when I proceeded to ask my own questions about the assignment, I often found that key ideas in the reading were not properly understood. What was really puzzling was that these students, on the surface, are ideal to teach. They are college-bound and bright. They came from the highest ability track in the school. What's more, I had taken special pains to make the class relevant. The readings and the class activities revolved around topics that should have been of considerable interest to my students — racism, war, ecology, etc. I wonder what I can do this time to involve my students more effectively?

Feedback

This form is provided for evaluating your own learning thus far — based upon your expectations. Your suggestions and recommendations taken collectively may be helpful for directing the inquiry in the next content area.

Rate the general usefulness of the resources you have used in your inquiry into the learning environment. Leave blank the selections you did not read. Use the following ratings:

1 = not very useful
2 = moderately useful
3 = very useful

_____ Silberman, "What Schooling Does to Children"
_____ Bruner, "The Will to Learn"
_____ Holt, "Excerpts from *How Children Fail*"
_____ Maslow, "Defense and Growth"
_____ Dennison, "Excerpt from *Lives of Children*"
_____ Rogers, "The Interpersonal Relationship in the Facilitation of Learning"
_____ Kohl, "Excerpt from *The Open Classroom*"
_____ Jourard, "Fascination: A Phenomenological Perspective on Independent Learning"
_____ Jackson, "The Student's World"
_____ Featherstone, "Excerpt from *Schools Where Children Learn*"

Rate your general interest and involvement thus far.

1	2	3	4	5	6	7	8	9
Low								High

How much do you feel you have learned during this content area?

1	2	3	4	5	6	7	8	9
Little								A lot

Describe any insight you have gained as a result of your involvement in this content area.

What unanswered questions still remain for you?

What aspects of your inquiries do you think you will find helpful in setting up your own classroom environment?

Part 2
Cognitive Functioning

The Problem: How Does the Mind Work? Understanding the Ways We Gain and Create Knowledge

Although the applicability of learning theory to classroom teaching is sometimes questioned, the opportunity for teachers to reflect upon and develop some personal theory about the ways we gain and create knowledge is clearly relevant. Teaching should not be a matter of transmitting stored information, concepts, and patterns of thinking into another person's head; rather, it should be a way of working with students to facilitate their acquisition of information and their creation of meaningful ideas about the world. Without a model of cognitive functioning, which provides some conception of how students perceive and solve classroom learning problems, it is difficult to imagine how a teacher can develop principles to guide him in his work. By examining the ways in which the mind functions in the process of gaining and creating knowledge, though, one is in a better position to determine what instructional practices are likely to help or interfere with the cognitive processes of students.

One noteworthy but simple fact about mental functioning is that thinking is going on in our minds all the time. Everyone has had the experience of suddenly realizing that he has been thinking about something for a few minutes without being aware of doing so. Indeed, the brain is continually "processing" information. Students' minds do not function like tape recorders or telephone switchboards, simply accumulating information by some associative process. More accurately, incoming information is continually being tested, reformulated, and acted upon. The problem every teacher must face is how to take into account and work with the continual information processing that is going on in their students. For example, a teacher needs to reflect on what occurs when he floods students with his own thoughts, however insightful they are, or when he gives elaborate demonstrations and explanations. What happens to students when they are put into a position of sustained, passive listening and observation? A teacher must also consider how a student's past learning experiences influence the way he views new concepts and problems. If a teacher fails to understand his students' cognitive frame of reference, his teaching will hinder more than help learning.

Initiating Activities

The four initiating activities for this content area are designed to allow you to examine your own cognitive functioning and to speculate about factors that directly aid learning. Again we suggest that you list ideas that arise in the activities you consider and place them in the following categories:

1. ideas that contradict each other
2. ideas that lack evidence or philosophical support
3. ideas that seem incomplete

Engaging in this process should enable you to select topics and readings relevant and helpful to you.

1/Why the Mind Gets Stuck

Have you ever met a person whom you know well and want to call by name, but for some reason or another you just cannot remember his name? We all have had experiences where our minds seem to get stuck. In this activity, you will speculate about why this happens.

You have probably had one of the following experiences:

1. You are trying to think of something and cannot remember it. Later, when supposedly you are not thinking about it, the idea "pops" into your conscious mind.
2. You have a disagreement with someone, and afterward you realize that your arguments would have been much better if you had said what you are thinking now, after the fact.
3. You have been thinking very hard about a problem but cannot solve it. When you finally decide to give up trying, the solution comes to you.

Group Activity

Have each group member write down his hypotheses about why each of these experiences occurs. This listing can be done by subgroups as well. From the lists of hypotheses, create one large list. Discuss conflicting hypotheses and rank them in order of their effectiveness in explaining why the mind gets stuck.

Individual Activity

Reflect upon the listed experiences and attempt to recall specific instances in which they occurred for you. Ask yourself how these experiences happened. When doing this, make a list of the promising ideas you have as well as the major questions that remain for you.

2/A Brain Buster[1]

In going about our daily tasks, we are constantly facing situations that require us to solve problems, yet our awareness of the processes we engage in during problem solving is often quite minimal. This activity is designed to let you participate in an abstract problem-solving experience and asks you to interpret how you went about tackling it. While solving this problem, try to be conscious of what your mind is doing to help you.

You are to pretend that rupps and hipps represent a new way of measuring distance and that dars, tors, and mors represent a new way of measuring time. A man drives from Town A, through Town B and Town C, to get to Town D. Your task is to determine how many tors the entire trip took. It should take from twenty to thirty minutes to determine the answer.

Answers to the following questions are clues to help you solve the problem. Use as few of them as possible. When you see a question that may have an answer that will be helpful, turn to the next page for the answer. The clues are in random order so be sure to choose carefully.

1. What is a hipp?
2. How far is it from B to C?
3. What is a tor?
4. How many mors are there in an hour?
5. How fast does the man drive from C to D?
6. How fast does the man drive from A to B?
7. How many hipps are there in a mile?
8. What is a dar?
9. How far is it from A to B?
10. How far is it from C to D?
11. What is a rupp?
12. What is a mor?
13. How fast does the man drive from B to C?

Group Activity

Initially, each person in the group should do the task by himself. Afterward, compare how you did and hypothesize why some people were successful and others were not. One possibility to explore is whether different strategies of working on the task were employed.

[1] We wish to thank Horacio J. A. Rimoldi for permission to use this problem-solving task. From his book, *Training in Problem-Solving*, Publication No. 21, Loyola University Psychometrics Laboratory.

After doing the task, interpret the causes of your success or failure in arriving at the answer. Ask yourself what your strategy was in approaching it and how much it helped or got in your way. Also, reflect on what was going on in your mind when you sensed you were doing well and when you seemed to be having trouble.

1. A hipp is a way of measuring distance.
2. It is 8 rupps from B to C.
3. A tor is 5 mors.
4. There are 2 mors in an hour.
5. The man drives from C to D at the rate of 30 rupps per tor.
6. The man drives from A to B at the rate of 24 rupps per tor.
7. There are 2 hipps in a mile.
8. A dar is 10 tors.
9. It is 4 rupps from A to B.
10. It is 10 rupps from C to D.
11. A rupp is 10 hipps.
12. A mor is a way of measuring time.
13. The man drives from B to C at the rate of 30 rupps per tor.

The answer is: 23/30 tors.

3/Learning and Understanding

We learn many concepts and tasks well but then forget them. Often, they are easier to learn a second time. Some concepts and tasks are learned so well initially that they are never forgotten, yet others are never mastered. In this activity you are to examine some learning tasks that you probably have encountered before and rate your understanding of them.

Do you have to relearn the concepts or skills on the next page? Do you have partial understanding of them? Do you know them well? Check the appropriate space so that you will have a record of your initial response for a discussion.

Group Activity

Compare responses for each item. On items where there is complete agreement, ask yourselves why they require no, partial, or complete relearning, whichever is the case. For items on which responses differ, explore why some group members failed to master or retain this learning.

Individual Activity

Examine each of the tasks and ask yourself why some require no relearning while others do. For those in which your understanding was incomplete in the first place, think about what would be necessary for you to gain more complete mastery.

	I would have to relearn this completely	I retain some understanding of this	I know this well
1. Using a new base system in mathematics	_____	_____	_____
2. Telling time	_____	_____	_____
3. Playing a musical instrument	_____	_____	_____
4. Understanding the nature of a socialistic society	_____	_____	_____
5. Reading maps	_____	_____	_____
6. Speaking a foreign language	_____	_____	_____
7. Riding a bicycle	_____	_____	_____
8. Applying the Pythagorean theorem	_____	_____	_____

4/Teaching Concepts

We have all tried to get another person to understand an idea we have, and everyone has had difficulty understanding what another person is saying. The teacher has the constant problem of making his meaning congruent with the students' so that learning will be facilitated. This activity will allow you to examine how teaching practices might be fitted to the ways the mind works.

Try to think how you would teach some of the following concepts to one of your classmates or friends. (Add other concepts to the list if necessary.)

1. how inflation is related to recession
2. how longitude differs from latitude
3. how music can be transposed from one key to another
4. how the right to due process provides equal protection under the law
5. how the human body maintains a reserve supply of energy

Group Activity

A group member should be chosen to teach one of the concepts to another person in the class. Take about ten minutes to teach the concept. The "teacher" and the "student" should compare their views of the success of the lesson. The rest of the class and group should interpret any discrepancies in the evaluations. The process can be repeated with a new teacher-student pair.

Individual Activity

Make notes about how you would teach one of the concepts. Try to analyze your plan for inclusion of students' ideas, past experiences, and thinking patterns. Examine in what way you can allow the learner to achieve a personal understanding of the concept. If possible, try out your plan on another student.

Topics of Study

The three topics of study listed below are offered as ways of considering the issues and problems in this content area.

1. The Nature of Thinking. This topic provides for a basic examination of how the mind works.
2. Discovery, Inquiry, and Creativity. This topic focuses on the processes by which we make discoveries, solve problems, and create new ideas.
3. Skills in Learning. This topic is concerned with determining the cognitive skills needed for different kinds of learning.

Although these topics are interrelated, they differ from each other in certain respects. "The Nature of Thinking" allows for a general understanding of the mental processes we use to gain knowledge. "Discovery, Inquiry, and Creativity" relates to special procedures by which new knowledge can be acquired and created. "Skills in Learning," concerned with the outcomes of learning rather than with the process itself, is specifically oriented to educational applications of cognitive theory. In addition to the articles suggested under these topics of study, Jay M. Yanoff's "The Functions of the Mind in the Learning Process" (pp. 114–121) serves as introductory reading for the entire content area. It is useful for providing an overall understanding of cognitive functioning. This article can also be integrated into future activities where it seems to be most appropriate and helpful. Read it carefully and also examine all three topics before deciding upon the direction of your inquiry.

1/The Nature of Thinking

Many educational psychologists are turning away from the question of how to cause learning to take place and are instead asking how the mind works. The reason for this shift is that the search for external events that produce observable changes in behavior seems to be less important than understanding the mental actions in our brains when we are engaged in learning. A highly technical understanding of cognitive functioning is not necessary, but it is clearly relevant to inquire into the way the human organism thinks.

These questions about the nature of thinking are worth considering and may bring others to mind:

1. Under what conditions does thinking become blocked?
2. By what general process do we learn new concepts?
3. In what ways do children think differently from adults?
4. How does the ability to think develop?

Readings

John Holt, "The Mind at Work" (pp. 122–128)

In this excerpt from *How Children Learn*, Holt discusses what goes on in his mind when thinking through problems or listening to the explanations of others. He gives several vivid examples of how he grasped an insight or worked out a solution even though his mind resisted continued productive functioning. Holt is also very adept at putting himself in the role of a child learning new concepts and provides a likely explanation of how language and other new learning occurs. After reading this excerpt, it would be helpful for you to restate in your own words the factors that, according to Holt, contribute to effective thinking.

Read D. Tuddenham, "Jean Piaget and the World of the Child" (pp. 129–136)

Tuddenham offers an overview of Jean Piaget's theory of cognitive development. Of particular importance are the processes of the mind that Piaget uses to explain learning: assimilation and accommodation. There is also a useful discussion of the cognitive functioning of children at different stages of development. It should prove beneficial to relate Piaget's theoretical ideas to Holt's experiences.

George A. Miller, Eugene Galanter, and Karl H. Pribram, "Excerpt from *Plans and the Structure of Behavior*" (pp. 137–146)

Miller, Galanter, and Pribram discuss the function of thinking as more than simply a reflex. In this excerpt from *Plans and the Structure of Behavior*, they explain how the mind processes incoming information by testing data against what is already known. The way the mind deals with incoming information involves (1) a test of readiness of the brain to accept the input, (2) an operation that seeks to match the test with prior experience, (3) a retest to see whether a match between incoming information and prior experience has been accomplished, before (4) the brain exits from control of that data.

J. Richard Suchman, "The Child and the Inquiry Process" (pp. 147–159)

Although this selection is concerned primarily with the process of inquiry, it contains some useful sections on general cognitive processes. In particular, Suchman's discussion of Piaget's major concepts should help to elucidate the mental operations that occur during learning. There are some interesting remarks about the development of thinking ability and the varied styles of thinking among children. For additional information about this article, see page 106.

2/Discovery, Inquiry, and Creativity

There is a trend in education toward self-directed learning. In a time when the pool of already accumulated knowledge is huge and constantly changing, the need to place greater emphasis on learning how to learn is being recognized. Moreover, the limited number of concepts that are taught directly have to be chosen for their long-range value in helping students to understand the underlying ideas of broad fields of knowledge. Teaching aimed at these purposes is largely based on the processes of discovery, inquiry, and creativity.

You probably have heard of these processes and understand that they are ways of solving problems and creating knowledge. Any attempt to teach with these purposes in mind, though, requires further exploration. Reflection on these questions will help bring into focus issues and relevant concerns:

1. What seem to be the distinguishing critical characteristics of human inquiry, discovery, and creativity?
2. In what ways are inquiry and discovery learning similar to and different from other forms of learning?
3. What factors help or prevent students from being creative?
4. What is the role of information in these learning processes?

Readings

Jerome S. Bruner, "The Act of Discovery" (pp. 160–168)

In this article Bruner examines major issues involved in discovery learning. He defines discovery in this way: "a matter of rearranging or transforming evidence in such a way that one is enabled to go beyond the evidence so reassembled to additional new insights." Several activities built into the article are helpful for gaining an understanding and testing the ideas that are presented. It would be worthwhile to think about some of your successful discovery experiences and ask yourself if they were accompanied by the sense of intellectual potency, the kind of intrinsic motivation, the learning of heuristics, and the efficient storage of information, which Bruner discusses.

Lee S. Shulman, "Psychological Controversies in Teaching" (pp. 169–177)

Shulman examines the ideas of Bruner and compares them with Gagné's concepts of the learning process. Comparing these theorists allows you to see two contrasting views of the role of discovery in learning. This article also provides helpful illustrations of the kind of teaching-learning procedures each implies. It is important to become aware of why and when a teacher would select these different approaches. For additional information about this article, see page 107.

J. Richard Suchman, "The Child and the Inquiry Process" (pp. 147–159)

Suchman provides a thorough examination of inquiry as an educational process. In this article are useful ways of thinking about inquiry activity and comments on its importance as an educational goal. Of special value is Suchman's discussion of how focus and freedom are necessary for inquiry activity to occur; these two concepts are usually considered contradictory. Suchman indicates how inquiry skills can be acquired in the classroom.

J. P. Guilford, "Factors That Aid and Hinder Creativity" (pp. 178–188)

Guilford discusses traits that he thinks promote creativity and cites studies illustrating his theories. Of particular interest are studies concerning the relationship of creativity and intelligence. He also suggests ways to implement his ideas in the classroom. While reading this article, notice the ways in which Guilford is oriented toward looking for the full potential of the human brain rather than its limitations.

3/Skills in Learning

A different way of approaching an inquiry into cognitive functioning is to examine the kinds of competence that contribute to effective thinking and learning. Such an approach is extremely important for teachers because they have an important influence, through the materials, experiences, and activities they provide, over the skills their students will develop. Focusing on skills also helps teachers to identify significant changes in their students. These questions about skills in learning are worth examining:

1. What does it mean to learn something really well?
2. What are the advantages and disadvantages of learning by discovery?
3. What are the skills of creative, inquiring people?
4. What skills do our schools overemphasize or ignore?

Readings

Richard S. Crutchfield, "Nurturing the Cognitive Skills of Productive Thinking" (pp. 189–196)
Crutchfield's article is useful for examining skills the learner needs for problem solving. Of special value are the steps in problem solving or discovery that he enumerates. There is also a helpful discussion of how schools neglect these skills. When reading this article, think about ways in which a school can promote systematic thinking skills while attempting to develop students' ability to solve problems in "real life" situations.

John Holt, "Excerpt from *How Children Fail*" (pp. 197–199)
John Holt asks, "How can we tell whether children understand something or not?" With his unique ability to express himself succinctly and meaningfully, Holt describes seven ways he can tell when he understands something. He suggests that understanding is "real learning" and that parroting or memorizing is "apparent learning." The critical difference between the two is explained through an example from mathematics.

Lee S. Shulman, "Psychological Controversies in Teaching" (pp. 169–177)
Shulman contrasts Bruner with Gagné to highlight two contrasting positions in discovery learning and the skills that each approach offers to the learner. The utility of each for your own learning should be examined. You might ask yourself which strategy best fits what you think children ought to learn in school.

Caleb Gattegno, "The Powers of Children" (pp. 200–206)

In this chapter from *What We Owe Children* Gattegno criticizes reliance on memorizing in schools. After describing memory as one of the weakest mental powers, Gattegno discusses the powerful skills children bring to school that could serve as a better basis for present and future learning. Of particular interest is his description of "stressing" and "ignoring" skills. He proposes a model of instruction where teaching is subordinated to learning rather than the reverse.

Inquiry Activities

In a search of the readings for relevant information, you should find many help-ful explanatory concepts and ideas. Careful study and discussion of excerpts from the readings where terms like the following are described or defined might be very worthwhile:

assimilation and accommodation	mental templates
discovery	problem formulation
divergent thinking	schema
fixation	transfer value
information processing	transformation

It is especially meaningful to use personal experiences as a basis of inquiry into this content area. There are many times in our lives when someone fails to un-derstand how we were looking at a problem or when we are unsuccessful in "teaching" an idea or skill to another person. Careful reflection on such experi-ences can be most rewarding. For similar reasons, activities that involve learning and thinking experiments are valuable. A wide range of simple learning, problem solving, and creativity tasks are described in the readings in this content area. De-veloping and testing hypotheses empirically about conditions affecting perfor-mance on these tasks can be both fun and insightful.

In addition to these suggestions, it is also important to plan activities that pro-vide a way of testing and experiencing the major ideas of this content area. The inquiry activity plans that follow are provided for actual use and as a source for generating other creative plans.

1/Assimilation and Accommodation

In the selections by Suchman, Tuddenham, and Yanoff, there is a discussion of Piaget's concepts of assimilation and accommodation. Assimilation refers to cog-nitive processes in which new stimuli are integrated by the brain in terms of pre-existing information and concepts. Accommodation refers to alterations in pat-terns of thinking required when existing templates do not match the demands of new input.

In this activity you will apply your understanding of assimilation and accom-modation. For each of the activities listed below, determine the assimilative pro-cesses that might be involved when a student is first introduced to them as well as the accommodations that would be required for their attainment.

1. learning to use a dictionary
2. understanding the nature of feudalism
3. establishing the causes for seasonal changes during the year
4. mastering the concept of "percentage"

2/Explaining Ideas

John Holt speaks of a delusion some teachers have that they can communicate a structure or working model of something they have developed out of a great deal of experience by translating it into a string of words and transplanting it whole into the minds of their students. This misconception is related to an oversimplified view of the role of mental functioning in the learning process, for it assumes that the learner perceives something as the teacher does. Participation in an exaggerated form of this experience is worthwhile in order to achieve an understanding of its dynamics. This activity can be carried out with at least one other person, but it is best suited for a small group.

Have each member of the group draw an abstract figure that he knows no other person has seen before. When all drawings are finished, one person at a time should try to describe his drawing to the others, without showing it. After hearing the description, the listeners should try to draw what is being described. When all drawings are completed, a comparison can be made between the original and the others. The discussion can center around what each person was thinking while completing the task and the implications for the way we teach children. For example, consideration can be given to the way children are taught to read, to understand mathematical relationships, and to use cursive writing.

3/Discovery and Creativity

Bruner and Guilford describe factors that help and block discovery and creativity. This activity is meant to involve you in these processes, as opposed to merely discussing the authors' ideas.

Task A

For one of the following objects list as many uses as you can:

1. brick
2. pencil
3. paper clip
4. toothpick
5. piece of paper

Task B

Solve each of the following problems which might be faced by a classroom teacher:

1. think of several purposes for having students study animals
2. suggest alternative ideas for a student who is having difficulty memorizing his lines for a class play

3. develop different ways of explaining what is the concept of checks and balances in government

A way of reflecting on this experience is to relate it to definitions of discovery and creativity. For example, examine your ideas to see how they reflect mental shifts or new insights. What do you think prevented you from imagining some of the uses in Task A that others discovered? How do your solutions to Task B differ from those of other students?

4/The Process of Inquiry

Bruner, Shulman, and Suchman all assume that discovery and inquiry learning involve active information processing. The ways in which information is processed may differ, however, with the kinds of problems that are being attacked. To illustrate this difference, in this activity you are to compare your mental processes when you are trying to resolve a problem that has an answer to those that occur when a problem requires a personal resolution. You should compare your inquiry in Problem A with that in Problem B. For example, which inquiry was easier to organize? Which allowed for more shifts in the directions taken? You might also consider the different ways you would help students with tasks having known and unknown solutions.

Problem A

Using a collection of at least forty randomly selected buttons placed on a table, think of a characteristic common to more than one button. The other participants try to determine the common element by completing the following question: "Do the buttons you have in mind have . . . ?" In an attempt to find what you are considering, a student might ask you, for example, "Are you thinking of buttons with two holes in them?" The person who determines the answer thinks of the next characteristic for the group to determine.

Problem B

The following list contains statements describing learning difficulties of some students. One student is to select the statement closest to his personal experience. Other participants should try to determine the reasons for his difficulty by interviewing the student. (Preferably, the student himself should be somewhat perplexed about his problem.) They can ask him as many questions as they think are necessary to help them establish a cause. The process can be repeated with other students.

1. I have great difficulty understanding poetry.
2. Despite three years of studying a foreign language, I speak it very haltingly.
3. I am confused by the difference between reinforcement and information processing theories of learning.
4. I block completely when it comes to understanding modern mathematics.
5. I can never write anything creative.

5/Real Learning

John Holt describes seven ways that he knows that he understands (p. 197). This activity is designed to evaluate Holt's means of testing understanding by asking you to use them in relation to your own knowledge.

Below are several concepts that may be familiar to you. Choose the idea you think you understand best or supply one of your own and apply each of the tests that Holt describes.

1. a line infinitely long
2. the structure of a classical symphony
3. a proportional mixture of hydrogen and oxygen making water
4. $E = MC^2$
5. the difference between a bull market and a bear market
6. the Freudian theory of the psychosexual stages of development

Do you think you understand the concept you chose using Holt's criteria? Can you think of other ways of testing real learning? Can you think of concepts in educational psychology of which you and others in your class seem to have a complete understanding in Holt's terms? If so, try to test your grasp of them as well.

6/Comparing Learning Skills

This activity is designed to help you compare the differential skills that are likely to be developed by using the strategies of Gagné and Bruner, which are discussed in the Shulman selection. Choose either Problem A or Problem B.

Problem A
With at least one other student decide whether you want to teach a lesson, using Gagné's approach or Bruner's approach, to a small group of students or to the whole class. The lesson might be reading music, analyzing the meaning of a poem, using a slide rule, or understanding a proportional representation system of voting. You should plan together and, using different strategies, both teach the same concepts. Each lesson should take approximately fifteen minutes, and time should be allowed for the "teachers" to discuss the skills they wanted to develop and their success.

Problem B
Read the following list, and try to determine the skills you might learn in each of the experiences if you were being taught by Bruner's approach. Then for the

same experience determine the skills Gagné's strategy would be likely to produce.

1. learning what makes a telegraph work
2. learning how to add fractions
3. learning to give a speech
4. trying to find out why an athletic team is losing
5. learning how city government works

Readings

Jay M. Yanoff

The Functions of the Mind in the Learning Process

A teacher needs to understand the functions of the mind to facilitate learning. Intellectual skills can be taught best when they are based on a model of thinking. This article will present such a model and indicate its implications for educational practice.

Two popular ways that have been used to conceptualize the cognitive process are to compare it with a telephone switchboard and a computer. In the switchboard model, one person dials a number (the stimulus) and the message is sent to the receiving party who answers (the response). The contact is direct. The connection between the stimulus and the response does not alter the system between. The connection is specific and the line can be disconnected when the call is completed. No call can be made unless the wires are linked and there is no principle that making a call does anything fundamental to any of the wires except those involved in the call.

The switchboard model, however, is limited in several ways. It fails to recognize the brain as the primary organ of learning; rather it focuses on the stimulation and the response. We have all had experiences when learning has taken place even though we could not make a specific response. If this model is placed into educational practice, it serves to teach what is offered by the teacher or the materials he uses. There is no way that this model can account for creative or imaginative thinking. It is also limited by a

This article was written expressly for this book and is published here for the first time. Copyright © 1972 by Jay M. Yanoff.

teacher's means of reinforcing an answer (response). In this model, routine, conventional thinking tends to be reinforced and creative and inventive behavior is not.

The computer model allows for a more comprehensive examination of thinking in the learning process. In this model, information is fed into a computer. The computer stores the information in memory banks for later recall. When given the appropriate directions, the computer prints out information that it has stored. The programmer's final command to the computer is to stop. In this model the brain is viewed as a total, active system with memory drums and feedback. The more information that is stored, the more useful the computer becomes. But the computer model in some ways is also incomplete since it does not account for the ability of the brain to seek data, act on its own, and stop when finished (all of which a computer cannot do). What is needed, then, is a model that avoids some of the inadequacies of the switchboard or computer models, one that offers a more comprehensive analysis of cognition in the learning process.

A Model of Cognition

The model illustrated below is a basis for conceptualizing what takes place in the thinking-learning process. It is based on the practical experiences of the author as well as various theoretical foundations presented by Allender (in preparation), Getman (1962), Hebb (1949), Hill (1963), Kephart (1960), Osgood (1953), Penfield (1969), Piaget (1954, 1969),

Model of Cognition

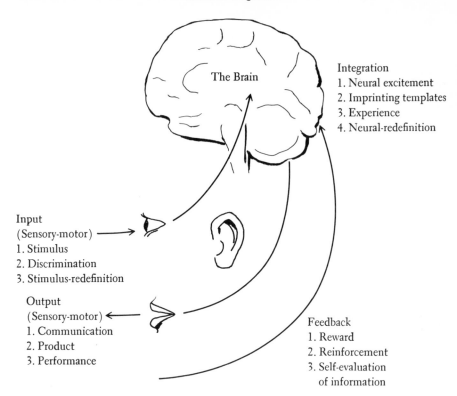

The Brain

Integration
1. Neural excitement
2. Imprinting templates
3. Experience
4. Neural-redefinition

Input
(Sensory-motor) →
1. Stimulus
2. Discrimination
3. Stimulus-redefinition

Output
(Sensory-motor) ←
1. Communication
2. Product
3. Performance

Feedback
1. Reward
2. Reinforcement
3. Self-evaluation
   of information

and Simpson (1968). The process is separated into the following major functions:

1. input — the stimulation of the sense organs for reception of information to be sent to the brain
2. integration — the process by which the brain receives information, acts upon it, and initiates some reaction
3. output — the sensory-motor application of messages sent from the brain for action in the environment
4. feedback — the realization by the brain that appropriate output has been given

Input

Perception and learning have been investigated by Bartley (1969), Getman (1962), Osgood (1953), Piaget (1969), and Simpson (1968). Their work supports the notion that the perceptual system provides the input for the cognitive processes. The sense organs feed the brain its information. Cognition begins here, with appropriate perception.

Look at the figures below.

•   •

Figure A   Figure B

Light energy travels from the paper and stimu-

115

lates the retina in your eye. Just as the optic nerve transforms light into electrical impulses and carries the information from your eye to the brain, the other sense organs take in data and transform it into language the brain can understand. The role of the sensory organs is to receive the stimuli: the eyes for seeing, the ears for hearing, the nose and mouth for smell and taste, the skin for touch, and the entire body for awareness in space or kinesthesia. When there is a stimulus available, the sense organs can be activated. They are then able to transform the information into messages for the brain. This is similar to the way data is fed into the computer. If no stimulus exists, however, there can be no perception. Sight begins when the eyes are stimulated by light rays. If there is no light, there can be no sight. If, on the other hand, the eye itself does not function properly, sight will be impaired. In each of the perceptual modes there are two essential elements: (1) a well functioning organ and (2) adequate stimulation.

The sensory organ itself has the ability to become a discriminating unit. When you compare Figures A and B, your eyes discriminate the difference in the degree of light stimulation between the two figures. The degree of discrimination is impaired in individuals with color blindness. There is a breakdown in the process which does not allow the brain to receive the color messages properly.

In the sensory system, wherever organs exist in pairs (eyes and ears), the pair must function together to allow for accurate perception. Try catching a ball with one eye closed. Your depth perception is impaired because you are receiving information with only one eye. When you use both eyes you receive information from three dimensions; one eye transmits only two dimensions. Getman (1962) has shown the necessity of activating both eyes for accurate visual input. When the perceptual system operates efficiently, the organs receive the stimuli, discriminate, and pass accurate messages to the brain. This process can be called *stimulus redefinition*.

116

Integration

Integration is the process by which the brain receives electrical impulses, the redefined stimuli, and acts upon them. The brain has the power to scan its memory bank to see if the incoming data is congruent with any prior experience. If the stimulus will fit into a previously formed category, the brain can act upon it. However, if the information is new, the impulses are newly imprinted. The mind seeks to find a likeness or a fit of information before it forms a new imprint.

Think about an *arfnif*. Does an *arfnif* fit into any previous categories you know? Is it a food? Animal? Fish? Emotion? Sport? Since *arfnif* does not fit into these categories, you might assume that it is a nonsense term. Your brain will make a new imprint of it. The next time you encounter *arfnif* you will not necessarily imprint, as it is a part of your prior experience.

When you imprinted *arfnif*, a new concept or idea took shape in your mind. Allender (in preparation) would maintain that you have found a new "mental template" in this imprinting process. A template is a pattern that allows one to reproduce a specified shape. In the case of the brain, a template allows one to record an idea or experience. In more concrete terms, templates form the structure of the mind. We can represent the brain as a series of unlimited, interrelated templates. As data bombards the mind, it (1) recalls previously formed templates, (2) connects previously formed templates, or (3) develops new templates.

Piaget (1954) uses the term "assimilation" to describe that process in which incoming data fits previously formed templates. When new templates are formed, he calls the process accommodation. Real learning takes place in accommodation. Studies by Hebb (1949), Miller, Galanter and Pribram (1960), and Penfield (1969) stress the inherent activity of the brain as well as its function as an information processing system. Different from the computer, which can only store data, templates allow the brain to test and evaluate all incoming stimuli. The brain accepts, acts upon, or in many cases, screens stimuli at a conscious and an unconscious level.

Stop reading for a moment and listen to the sounds around you. Your mind has screened out or filtered these distracting stimuli and allowed you to concentrate selectively upon your reading. If the mind accepted all stimuli equally, one would be overwhelmed with the chaos of input to the point of inaction. Unlike the videotape machine, which records all visual and auditory stimuli, the mind maintains order and sanity by selecting that data to which it wishes to attend.

The mind is not only a receptive mechanism but also a seeking instrument. In a totally dark room, your brain seeks light. In silence, your brain seeks noise. The brain has the need to reach out into the environment and experience stimuli.

Individuals seek to involve more than one sensory mode to conceptualize reality. Simpson (1968), Bush and Giles (1969), Kephart (1960), and Getman (1962) advocate multisensory approaches to learning. The more senses that are involved in each experience, the better able an individual is to develop reality templates. Visual input alone is unsatisfactory, so we ask to feel the fabric, to taste the candy, and to smell the flower. The young child learning to read finds more satisfaction from reading aloud than from merely following the words with his eyes. Think how many senses are employed when you consider buying a new car!

The brain also has the ability to initiate action and to stop action by its own will. The mind is able to rearrange the templates that have been assimilated and accommodated to initiate its own new templates. What is truly unique is the ability of the mind to *stop* thinking of one idea and make a shift to a completely new one. By its own choice, the mind can direct itself to start or stop particular processing. This ability differentiates it from the computer, which must be directed by the programmer who tells it what to do and how to do it. Man's thinking must always be an input to the computer. The integration process in a computer cannot reach the potential of the mind. There has never been a creative computer because it cannot reorder or change its action without being directed to do so.

Creative individuals are those who have developed skills for making the mind initiate. For a man to think creatively and develop new ideas, he must take existing templates and restructure them. One must "break mental sets" — think beyond reality to be truly creative. Penfield (1969) proposes that the mind and the individual are one and the same. The child is able to reach out with his mind and condition his own cortex. These complex functions of the integrative process differentiate man from all other animals, as well as from the computer.

Output

To date, there is no known way to accurately measure the cognitive process. Output gives us some indication. Output is the expression of ideas or templates from the brain that have been redefined as electrical impulses. These impulses have been carried to the neuro-muscular system, where they are redefined and exhibited in three ways: (1) communication, (2) product, and (3) performance. Communication may be any form of language-based interaction. Products are typically the construction of an idea. A student's answer on a written test or his art project are forms of output expressed as products. Performance is an exhibition of an ability, such as singing a song and giving a speech. Combinations of more than one of these modes of output are used to express sophisticated thinking. Generally speaking, we judge an individual by his output.

Everyone has more in his mind than can possibly be demonstrated by his output. We have ideas in our heads, but because our output is always somewhat limited, we have all experienced frustration. There have been times when we felt that we were judged unfairly by our output — when we could not adequately express what we were really thinking. One may have heard a comical story, but when trying to retell it to another person, it does not sound funny. Perhaps you have tried to draw a picture of something, but you find that the product is not an accurate representation of what you see. One cannot fully explain love, and yet he knows that it is very real to him. Poets find they must say less in order to say more.

From the time the brain triggers a response, there is no way the output system can increase the expression of that response before it is expressed. Concepts are lost through an inability to express an idea in oral language. Muscular coordination keeps one from drawing what he has visualized or from running as fast as he wishes. Inability to transfer sounds heard into sounds reproduced keeps one from singing as he would like. Output can never fully represent what has occurred in the integrative process.

An individual can improve the expression of his thinking. Simpson (1968) and Getman (1962) contend that the more a person exercises and trains the sensory-motor mechanisms of expression, the more closely he is able to match his output with his thinking. Individuals have a basic need for expression, to facilitate their mental processes, to identify self, and to test reality.

Feedback

Feedback is the recycling of an individual's thinking. Hill (1963) suggests that the feedback system operates like a thermostat. When the temperature falls, the thermostat turns on the furnace to make the temperature rise. When the temperature rises to a certain point, the thermostat turns the furnace off. The temperature in the room is the input of the system and the activity of the furnace is the output. The effect of the output is fed back into the system as input.

Feedback involves adjustments in the cognitive process. The action is often so quick and automatic that the individual is unaware of it. When a person sings, hearing is his feedback. He can adjust his singing according to what he hears.

When an individual produces some output, feedback fixes the template. Reward and reinforcement are examples of feedback similar to that of the thermostat. They can be defined as whatever strengthens the tendency for a particular response to follow a specific stimulus. Programmed materials have been developed to give students a bit of information immediately followed by reinforcement. We have even seen the advent of behavior modification with its emphasis on output and reward feedback.

The major feedback agent, however, is the individual's self-evaluation of information. This process allows the individual to continually test ideas and deal with higher cognitive processes. Pribram (1964), in challenging the need for external feedback, contends that within the brain, feedback involves (1) a test of readiness with regard to input, (2) an operation that seeks to match the test, (3) a retest to see whether a match was made, and then (4) an exit from control. Real learning, memory, and recall are increased when the learner can evaluate himself and is sensitive to his own needs for input or stimulation.

Through active engagement with his environment, an individual is able to learn a wide range of concepts and develops a complex cognitive structure. Man will, when he has not been made apathetic by deprivation, aroused by threat or frustration, or damaged in any way, naturally seek to understand his world.

Some Implications for Teaching

Since information is fed to the brain through the senses, a learning environment should provide multisensory stimulation. It should allow a student to explore and manipulate. By providing such multisensory experiences in the classroom, the teacher allows the student to learn through his strongest perceptual mode. If a child shows auditory strength, a phonetic approach may be best for teaching reading. The whole-word approach may be best for teaching the visually oriented child. An environment that is responsive to the child's individual input and processing styles allows him to seek the means by which he can deal most effectively with his environment. Some children learn best through listening, others through seeing, and still others through physical manipulation. It is important then that each experience in school involve as many of the senses as possible. Through a wide range of experiences, man will develop the templates that will give order to a complex world.

Just as the teacher must provide multisensory stimulation, too much distracting input can hinder learning. Some students find it hard to function in the classroom with its mass of stimuli. The teacher should provide places where a student can work quietly and at his own rate. The teacher and the student together can determine the optimal levels of stimulation and what levels are distracting. Intense noise levels and visual distractions keep children from being able to concentrate. The use of divided sections in the classroom, carpeting, and elimination of interruptions by intercoms and bells cut down distractions. The teacher, the biggest distraction in the classroom, should temper the extent of his verbal bombardment. Even the teacher's desk should be moved from the front of the room so that it is not distracting. The teacher should be a facilitator not a distractor.

It is important that teachers be aware of the degree of perceptual input in their classrooms to be able to provide optimal stimulation while minimizing distractions. When the teacher provides an environment that is flexible for himself and his students, it can be adapted to an individual child's cognitive style.

The difference between seeing and visualizing provides a good example of the significance of integration to the thinking process. Of importance is not only that the child can see but also that he can utilize and interpret the information being fed to his brain. Seeing is only input, while visualization combines input with integration. In schools, most of a student's information is received through vision and audition. Persons should use extreme care when evaluating a child's vision or audition so that acuity is not mistaken for understanding.

Teachers often complain about a child's short attention span and his inability to concentrate. One must agree that most lessons in school are just too long. One way to view a child's attention span is to consider the concept of time. A short wait in a doctor's office may seem like hours, while at a sporting event or in a lively discussion, hours seem to pass like minutes. When students can choose areas they wish to study, when they are actively involved in the planning process, when they are able to make decisions concerning areas which effect them, and when they are able to implement their decisions, their attention span increases.

Creativity involves the most advanced integrative processes. Teachers need to provide experiences where children can sense problems, formulate strategies, review resources, and seek resolutions. This discovery or inquiry approach provides the individual with problem-solving skills which help develop his potential for creative thinking. He must utilize previously formed resources to develop new ideas. A new and creative idea is greater than the sum of the mental templates from which the idea has been drawn. A major concern of teachers should be ways to enhance the thinking of children. Experience in problem-solving situations provides a student with the necessary skills to think about his changing environment. After a problem is sensed, the person must formulate an attack for the solution. He must determine what he is seeking and how he will find resolution.

The more formulation activities that a teacher can present to students the better able they will be to attack future problems. These problem-solving activities encourage students to use their minds to the fullest.

One consideration in development of thinking skills is the process of coming to resolution. The brain has the capacity to make decisions quickly — sometimes, too quickly. The teacher is often faced with the problem of slowing down the process. Instead of asking for recall which necessitates quick responses, the teacher should ask students to consider alternative ways of thinking. This forces students to use more templates and thus develops the process of creative thinking. The teacher can facilitate this process by letting students brainstorm or hypothesize as many alternative answers as they can.

Products have short lives, while process skills allow the individual to adapt to many varied situations. One of the teachers' main functions should be to allow for, encourage, and facilitate creative thinking. Schools for thinking will produce students who think.

As the aim of education turns more toward creative thinking, new modes of evaluation must be developed and implemented. Testing situations should encourage a student to utilize his thinking processes rather than to repeat specific answers. Measuring the degree of impact may be an effective way to evaluate the relationship between classroom experience and learning. As the classroom becomes more open, new alternatives for expression of output become available. Instead of the traditional recall of ideas, teachers can provide exciting challenges for students to pursue. These experiences should be designed so that each student can have some self-measure of success.

A teacher certainly can evaluate and be helpful to students, but the testing experience should provide for each individual to work at his best. He should not be compared to others. Examples of testing that utilize this concept are: (1) The teacher asks students what problems they sense and encourages them to pursue some conclusions, as opposed to, students solving the teacher's problems. (2) The student develops his own workbooks, which he uses instead of the standardized ones. (3) The student is asked to hypothesize and theorize about real situations. For example, What would the world be like if the Spanish Armada had not been defeated? Activities such as these only begin to open the minds of students. The teacher should continually search for better ways to explore the workings of the thinking process. Teachers should use caution to avoid the pitfalls of classrooms where recall and recitation are the foremost means of student expression. Joint planning and evaluation by student and teacher can help to promote potential output.

If the classroom is to become a place where students can exhibit many forms of expression or output of ideas, the teacher must provide an environment that eliminates repression and encourages expression. The classroom should be supplied with varied media, perceptual-motor games, manipulative devices, nonrestricting materials, and problem-solving tasks. The classroom should be a forum for expressing ideas, feelings, and insights.

If the teacher is to play the role of a helping person, he must provide means by which students can express what is in their heads. A piece of art work can be seen as having as much expression of self as a dialogue. Each mode of output should be seen as an attempted exposure of oneself to the world. When this exposure is received with acceptance, reassurance, and support, the student is more willing to risk further display of self.

Self-evaluation is the most valuable form of feedback. When an individual can critically evaluate his own thinking, greater growth is achieved. Emphasis should then be taken off reward and reinforcement and directed toward a student's own evaluation.

Students gain confidence and are willing to risk more when they have experienced success. The teacher should help students to have successful experiences and build upon them to develop a positive self-image. A confident person is willing to take more risks, which in turn provide more experiences and allow him to develop more templates. Positive feedback builds templates which encourage more templates to be built, while negative feedback deters templates from being formed. A teacher must encourage the positive, constructive forms of feedback that allow for more cognitive growth. Such feedback may include asking students to consider how much they think they learned, asking them what is still confusing to them, asking at what point they got stuck in thinking, asking how they feel about the class, and asking what would make learning better for them. The teacher is then able to respond to individual or group needs.

The feedback system is not merely a collection of stimulus-response units but is a continually ongoing process returning to the integration level. It makes the learner examine for himself, whether he senses his learning is on the right track or gone astray, and allows him to make the decision to change.

Summary

Man's brain is a powerful instrument. It not only receives data but is also able to reach into the environment for sensory feeding. Man's senses are not as keen as other animals. Birds see better, dogs have better hearing, and deer are able to detect odors more easily. Man is not the strongest animal, nor is he the fastest. The ability of his mind differentiates man from all other animals. He uses language, creates and initiates — all from within the functionings of his mind. He cannot store information at the rate of the computer, but he can think. And thinking gives him power.

Schools must be oriented to help children learn the skills of thinking so that they can either intelligently adapt themselves to the environment or change it. To be able to make the changes necessary for better learning, teachers must consider how information is received by the senses, the way the mind uses data, and the means of expression that people have. Then, and only then, can the teacher provide a learning environment that is responsive to each child's cognitive functioning.

References

Allender, Jerome S. A *Radical Psychology of Learning*. Manuscript in preparation.

Bartley, S. Howard. *Principles of Perception*. New York: Harper and Row, 1969.

Bush, Wilma Jo, and Marian Taylor Giles. *Aids to Psycholinguistic Teaching*. Columbus, Ohio: Merrill, 1969.

Getman, G. N. *How to Develop Your Child's Intelligence*. Luverne, Minn.: Author, 1962.

Hebb, D. O. *The Organization of Behavior*. New York: Wiley, 1949.

Hill, Winfred F. *Learning: A Survey of Psychological Interpretations*. San Francisco: Chandler, 1963.

Kephart, Newell C. *The Slow Learner in the Classroom*. Columbus, Ohio: Merrill, 1960.

Miller, G. A., E. Galanter, and Karl Pribram. *Plans and the Structure of Behavior*. New York: Holt, Rinehart and Winston, 1960.

Osgood, Charles E. *Method and Theory in Experimental Psychology*. New York: Oxford University Press, 1953.

Penfield, Wilder. "Consciousness, Memory and Man's Conditioned Reflexes." In *On the Biology of Learning*, edited by Karl Pribram. New York: Harcourt, Brace, Jovanovich, 1969.

Piaget, Jean. *The Mechanisms of Perception*. New York: Basic Books, 1969.

———. *The Construction of Reality in the Child*. New York: Basic Books, 1954.

Pribram, Karl. "Neurological Notes on the Art of Educating." In *Theories of Learning and Instruction*, NSSE 63rd Yearbook, Part 1, edited by Ernest Hilgard. Chicago: University of Chicago Press, 1964.

Simpson, Dorothy M. *Learning to Learn*. Columbus, Ohio: Merrill, 1968.

John Holt

The Mind at Work

One of the puzzles we had in my fifth-grade class was a geometrical puzzle called *Hako*. You began with a number of thin, flat, rectangular plastic pieces arranged a certain way in a shallow box. The aim was to slide them around, without turning them or lifting them out of the box, so as to finish with the largest piece, a square, at the opposite end of the box from which it started. Though I spent many hours on it, I was never able to do it. This exasperated me. What exasperated me even more was that I seemed to be able to prove that the puzzle was impossible — though I knew it was not. Like most people, I began by moving the pieces around in a kind of blind, haphazard way. Before long, and unwisely, I grew impatient with this. There were too many possible moves, this could go on forever. The thing to do was use the brain and figure it out. So, moving the pieces very carefully, and analyzing each move, I deduced that in order to get the large piece from the top to the bottom, certain other things had to happen along the way. There had to be a point at which certain of the pieces were going up past the big piece while it was going down. Then, still carefully analyzing, I showed that this could only happen if certain other pieces moved in certain ways. Finally, I proved that they could not be moved in those ways. Therefore the problem was impossible.

The trouble was, I knew it wasn't impossible. Companies don't sell impossible puzzles; they would be sued, or worse. Besides, the puzzle

had been mentioned in the *Scientific American*. Besides that, and worst of all, some students had done it. With all my heart I wanted to believe that they had lied or cheated, but I couldn't convince myself; they weren't the type. I remember thinking furiously, "I suppose anyone could do this puzzle if he were willing to sit in front of it like a nitwit, moving the pieces around blindly, until just by dumb luck he happened to get it. I haven't got time for that sort of thing." More to the point, I felt above that sort of thing.

I went back to the puzzle many times, hoping that I would find some fresh approach to it; but my mind kept moving back into the little groove it had made for itself. I tried to make myself forget my supposed proof that the problem was impossible. No use. Before long I would be back at the business of trying to find the flaw in my reasoning. I never found it. Like many other people, in many other situations, I had reasoned myself into a box. Looking back at the problem, and with the words of Professor Hawkins in my ears, I saw my great mistake. I had begun to reason too soon, before I had allowed myself enough "Messing About," before I had built a good enough mental model of the ways in which those pieces moved, before I had given myself enough time to explore all the possible ways in which they could move. The reason some of the children were able to do the puzzle was not that they did it blindly, but that they did not try to solve it by reason until they had found by experience what the pieces could do. Because their mental model of the puzzle was complete, it served them; because mine was incomplete, it failed me.

In one of the classes I previously shared with

Bill Hull, we worked a good deal with a three-dimensional puzzle named *Soma*, also described and discussed in the *Scientific American*. In this, twenty-seven cubes of wood were glued together to make six four-cube pieces and one three-cube piece. The aim was to use these seven pieces to make various other shapes, beginning with a cube and other simple shapes, and going on to more complicated and difficult shapes such as the Tunnel, the Bathtub, the Castle, etc. It was a splendid puzzle, one of the very best I have ever seen, among other reasons because children can work on it at many different degrees of difficulty.

My first meeting with this puzzle was embarrassing. A person familiar with it can make the cube in less than half-a-minute in any one of several different ways. By the time I started trying to make the cube, a number of the children were able to do it in about fifteen seconds. My first effort took me about fifty minutes. I tried to keep my struggles out of the sight of the children, but there were some pointed questions. Fortunately I was able to avoid falling into the trap of analyzing too soon, perhaps only because I could not see how to. Unable to think of any "sensible" way to proceed, I fiddled with the pieces, trying to fit them this way and that, making mistakes, working myself into dead ends, going back and starting again. One of the frustrating things about this particular puzzle is that if you have it almost right, you know you have it entirely wrong. When you find yourself saying, "If this piece just looked like that piece, I could do it," you have to start almost from the beginning. By many such trials and errors, retrials and corrections, I was finally able, like many of the children, to build up a good mental model of the way these pieces worked. With this model I could tell, without having to try it out, that a certain piece, or even combination of pieces, would not go in a certain spot, and could see several pieces in advance when I was going wrong. Before long I became one of the class experts.

Such experiences suggest a reason why so much that seems to me trivial, misleading, or downright false, has been written about child psychology. The psychologists, on the whole, have not done enough of Professor Hawkins' "Messing About." They have not seen enough children in their native habitat — homes, schools, playgrounds, streets, stores, anywhere. They haven't talked or played with enough of them, or helped them, or comforted them, or coerced them, or made them pleased, or excited, or rebellious, or angry. Unless he is very fortunate, a young psychologist is very likely to have his head stuffed full of theories of children before he has had a chance to look at any. When he does start looking at them, it is likely to be in very special laboratory or testing situations. Like many teachers, he may not recognize the many ways in which children betray anxiety, because he has never seen them in a situation in which they were not anxious. Also, like me trying to do the puzzle, he may be so much a prisoner of his theories that he cannot see anything that does not fit into them.

For such reasons I would like to stress again what I said very early in this book. My aim in writing it is not primarily to persuade educators and psychologists to swap new doctrines for old, but to persuade them to *look* at children, patiently, repeatedly, respectfully, and to hold off making theories and judgments about them until they have in their minds what most of them do not now have — a reasonably accurate model of what children are like.

I should add, too, that I am not trying to deny the importance of close, deductive, analytical, logical reasoning. In its proper place, it is a useful, powerful, often essential tool. I am only trying to say that out of its place, it is likely to be not only useless but harmful, and that its place is not everywhere. It works when we have a very limited amount of evidence, all we are going to get, and from it have to reconstruct the past — find out who committed a crime, or how and why an accident took place, or what is ailing in a particular man, or machine. It works when we can limit and isolate, one by one, the variables we have to deal with. Thus the skilled repairman, trying to find out why a machine is working badly, checks its various elements, one by one, until he finds the one that is causing the trouble. Thus the scientist, meeting a new phenomenon in the lab, changes, one by one, the conditions of the experiment until he finds the one that seems to affect the phenomenon. And we use this kind of reasoning to check our hypotheses, our theories or hunches about why things work as they do. We say, "If this theory is true, then certain other things ought to happen," and then we find out whether in fact they do happen. If they do, the theory is confirmed, temporarily, at least. The story is told of Einstein that, after the observations of some astronomers seemed to have confirmed his Theory of Relativity, a woman congratulated him on his theory having been proved right. He said, "Madam, a thousand experiments can never prove me right; a single experiment can prove me wrong." Even when the facts seem to support our reasoning, we must, like Einstein, not assume that we have found the final truth.

But if there are times and places and conditions where this kind of reasoning is useful, there are others where it does not work at all. If the experience before us is completely new and strange; if there is much new material to be observed, material that doesn't seem to fall into any recognizable pattern or order; if we cannot tell what are the variables that influence the situation, much less isolate them, we will be unwise to try to think like a detective, or a scientist in a laboratory.

Some years ago, some sociologists were trying to draw analogies between the behavior of molecules in a gas and the behavior of human beings in society, and from there between the laws that describe or explain the behavior of gasses and comparable laws that would supposedly describe and explain the behavior of human beings in society. This is a very good example of how not to use the scientific method. In such situations, we must use our minds very differently. We must clear them of preconceived notions, we must suspend judgment, we must open ourselves to the situation, take in as much data as we can, and wait patiently for some kind of order to appear out of the chaos. In short, we must think like a little child.

It may be useful to describe a few situations

in which I had to, and was able to, make myself think this way. One bright summer day some friends took me to the Haystack School of Arts and Crafts in Maine. There, for the first time, I saw a hand loom. One of the teachers had it out in the sunshine, on one of the many broad, wooden terraces that look down a hill and over the sea. She was setting it up for some weaving, and my hosts gathered around to talk about what she was doing and was planning to do.

After looking at the machine a while, and listening to this informed talk, I felt the faint beginnings of anxiety. A hand loom is a very open machine; all the parts of it can be clearly seen. It seemed to me that after some careful looking and reasoning I ought to be able to figure out how this machine worked. But I couldn't. It looked like nothing but a jumble and confusion of little parts, wires, and scraps of wood. None of it made any sense at all. Nor could I think how to make sense of it. Where to begin?

In such situations we tend to have a defensive reaction, which I began to sense in myself. Confronted with what it cannot grasp, the mind tends to turn away, to shut it out. We say to ourselves, "Oh, well, who cares about looms and weaving, anyway?" We seek the relief of thinking about something that we can grasp and understand. Having learned to recognize this protective and cowardly strategy, I would not allow myself to use it. I thought, "Come on, now, quit acting like a scared kid." I examined the loom more carefully, and began to ask myself intelligent questions. What's this for? Where does this lead? But no use. It remained as much a mystery as ever. The anxiety grew, with a little shame added. Some of this was caused by not being able to make sense of the loom. Some was caused by my feeling that as a supposedly fairly intelligent man I ought to be able to make sense out of it. Like children in school, I was worried by the fear of not being able to live up to my own concept of myself. Finally, I knew that everyone else around me knew how that loom worked, and knew that I didn't. I could almost hear them thinking, "Funny about John, he's usually pretty smart about most things, yet that simple loom, that you would think anyone could understand, is too much for him." Then, to make matters worse, they began to try to help by giving explanations. They spoke with that infuriating mixture of indulgence and impatience with which the expert always explains things to the non-expert. It is always gratifying to be able to understand what someone else cannot; and more gratifying yet to make yourself his benefactor, by explaining it to him; and still more gratifying — unless you are required to make him understand — if in spite of your explanation he continues not to understand. In this spirit my friends began to say, "It's really very simple; this piece here . . ."

After a certain amount of this I said, rather sharply, "Please stop talking about it, and just let me look at it." I thought to myself, "Remember what you have learned about learning. Be like a child. Use your eyes. Gag that teacher's mouth inside your head, asking all those questions. Don't try to analyze this thing, look at it, take it in." And shutting out of mind the knowing conversation of the others, I did so. Now and then the voice inside would begin to ask questions. I silenced it, and for sometime went on looking.

There were many other things to see: potters, print makers, and most exciting of all, glass blowers. After seeing them all, we started home. And as we drove a most extraordinary thing began to happen. I was not thinking about the loom; as my host was a potter, we were talking mostly about the pottery. But as we talked, a loom began slowly to put itself together in my mind. There is no other way to describe it. Suddenly, for no reason, the image of a particular part would suddenly appear in my consciousness, but in such a way that I understood what that part was for. When I say "understood," I don't mean that some kind of verbal explanation went along with it. I mean that I could see what the part was for and what it did, I could almost see it doing its work. If I had been building a loom and had had that part in my hand, I would have known where to put it.

This loom-building process was very slow. It would be interesting to have a record of the order in which the parts of this loom appeared and assembled themselves, but I have none. Sensing that something important was happening in the non-verbal, non-conscious part of my mind, I did not want to look too hard at the process, lest I bring it to a stop. Also, I had no way of knowing, at any time, how much further it would go. When the first part of the loom appeared in my surprised consciousness, I had no reason to believe that other parts would later appear in the same way. However, they did, some during our trip home, others during the rest of the day, some even the following day. By the end of that day, a loom had made itself in my mind. There was a working model of a loom in there. If I had had to build a loom, I would have known at least roughly what parts were needed and where they went. There was much about the loom that I didn't know, but I now knew where knowledge left off and ignorance began; knew the questions I needed to ask; knew enough to be able to make sense of the answers. Some of what people had told me, trying to explain the loom, came back to me, and now I could see what their words meant.

Explanations. We teachers — perhaps all human beings — are in the grip of an astonishing delusion. We think that we can take a picture, a structure, a working model of something, constructed in our minds out of long experience and familiarity, and by turning that model into a string of words, transplant it whole into the mind of someone else. Perhaps once in a thousand times, when the explanation is extraordinarily good, and the listener extraordinarily experienced and skillful at turning word strings into non-verbal reality, and when explainer and listener share in common many of the experiences being talked about, the process may work, and some real meaning may be communicated. Most of the time, explaining does not increase understanding, and may even lessen it.

A few years ago I spent an evening, at Bill Hull's house, in the company of a number of people who were all interested in teaching mathematics to children. For most of the evening we talked about things we had done in classes, or were thinking of doing. As the party began to break up, one of the group, a most distinguished visitor from abroad, confessed that although most of the materials he had developed for children dealt with numbers and numerals, or with algebra, his own real love was geometry. Not the old-fashioned plane geometry that most people have met in school, but a much more advanced and exotic geometry. Memory tells me that he called it projective geometry, though it didn't sound like the only projective geometry I had ever read about. I asked him what he liked so much about this branch of mathematics. He replied that it was the beauty and simplicity of the theorems. "Such as what?" I asked. It was a mistake. His eyes flashed with enthusiasm. Such as the proof that intersection of two quartics is a twisted cubic. Seeing a glazed look in my eyes, he began to sketch the proof. I held up a hand, laughing, and said, "Whoa, wait a minute, I've never even heard of these things, I don't know what a quartic or a cubic is, much less a twisted cubic." Too late. The teaching fit was on him. He began to "explain." As he saw that I still did not understand, he began to grow exasperated — like most teachers when their "explanations" are not being understood. "It's really very simple!" he said, as his hands sketched complicated shapes in the air. I was amused, but appalled. Here was a really great teacher, who for years had been working with young children trying to find ways to have them experience and discover, with hands and eyes, the relationships of mathematics. Yet in spite of his long experience, he believed so strongly in the magic power of explanations that he thought he could drop me into the middle of an advanced and complex branch of mathematics, in which I had absolutely no knowledge or experience, and with a few words and waves of the hand make the whole thing clear.

Jerome Bruner has said that one thing that happens in school is that children are led to believe they don't know or can't do something that they knew, or could do, before they got to school. I have seen this demonstrated many times, but never as vividly as in the following

example, quoted from the prospectus of the Green Valley School, in which George von Hilsheimer writes:

> One of our art associates once conducted an experiment in her art resources classroom. As the children entered the classroom they found construction paper on the desks. The teacher held up a folded fan — like those you and I have made many times — "Know what this is?"
> "Oh, yes!"
> "Can you make one?"
> "Yes! Yes!"
> Every child quickly made the little fan. The teacher then read from the book the instructions on how to make the fan. She read slowly, with proper emphasis and phrasing. The instructions were well designed to be clear to the fifth grade mind. After reading, the teacher asked the children to make the fans again. Not one child could make a fan. The teacher sat at each desk and tried to get the children to go back to the first way they had made the fan (with the fan still lying on the desk). They could not.
> There have been many such experiments in educational psychology. Unfortunately, few teachers and even fewer school systems take such evidence seriously. We do.

Such stories make many defenders of the system angry. They say, "But human knowledge is stored and transmitted in symbols. We have to teach children to use them." True enough. But the only way children can learn to get meaning out of symbols, to turn other people's symbols into a kind of reality or a mental model of reality, is by learning first to turn their own reality into symbols. They have to make the journey from reality to symbol many times, before they are ready to go the other way. We must begin with what children see, do, and know, and have them talk and write about such things, before trying to talk to them much about things they don't know. Thus, given children who knew how to make a paper fan, it might not be a bad idea at all to ask them to try to tell someone else how to make one, without using any gestures, as if they were talking over a phone. I used to ask fifth-graders how they would explain over the phone the difference between right and left, to someone who could speak English but did not happen to know those words. Such games are exciting and use-

126

ful. But when we do what we do most of the time in school — begin with meaningless symbols and statements, and try to fill them with meaning by way of explanations, we only convince most children either that all symbols are meaningless or that they are too stupid to get meaning from them.

Perhaps the greatest dangers of becoming too bound up with symbols, too symbol-minded, if I may be allowed the phrase, is that we don't know how to give them up, get them out of the way, when they are of no use to us. We become addicts. There are times when words, symbols, only get between us and reality. At such times, we must be ready to let them go, and use our minds in more appropriate ways — more child-like ways.

Such an experience took place not long ago when I was visiting A. S. Neill at Summerhill School in England. The weather was terrible, the public rooms of the school were deserted, the students were all in their rooms, so there was nothing much to see around the school. Neill himself was laid up in his room with a painful attack of sciatica, and was eager for company. So we had a long and very interesting talk. More than once, thinking I had taken enough of his time, I got up to go, but he waved me back in my chair, where I was more than glad to stay.

At about three o'clock his brother-in-law came in, and asked if he could use the TV to watch the England-Scotland rugby match. Neill asked me if I knew anything about rugby. I said I didn't; he said he didn't either. We decided to watch the game. Before it had gone on two minutes, I found myself in the same panicky confusion that had gripped me when I looked at the loom. Rugby is a hard game for a novice to understand. It is like a crazy combination of soccer and football, just enough like either one to be misleading. As I watched, the teacher-voice in my head began to ask, "Why did he do that? Why did he put the ball there? Why is he running that way?" And so on. But there were no answers.

After a few futile minutes of this, I saw that this was the loom situation again. I didn't know

enough about the game to be able to reason about it. No use to ask questions. Neill couldn't answer them. His brother-in-law — a taciturn man — wouldn't. Anyway, I didn't know enough to know what questions to ask. The only thing to do was to turn off the questions and watch — like a child. Take it all in. See everything, worry about nothing. This is what I did. When the voice inside began to yammer, I silenced it. At half-time I seemed to know no more than at the start. Everything that happened on that field surprised me. During the half the announcers, as in every land, talked learnedly about the play during the first half. Not a word they said made any sense. I listened, like a child listening to adult conversation, taking in the words without knowing or caring what they might mean. Soon the second half started, as puzzling as the first. Then, suddenly, about ten minutes into the period, the patterns of the game all fell into place. Like the loom, the game put itself together in my mind. I suddenly found that I knew what the players were doing, what they were trying to do, what they might do next, why the plays the announcer called good were in fact good, why the mistakes he pointed out were in fact mistakes. There was still much I didn't know, details of the game, rules, penalties. But I knew enough to ask about them, and to make some sense out of the answers.

Not long afterwards, I had another chance to think like a child. Going south from London on a train, I found myself in a compartment — a small, closed-in section seating eight passengers — with a Scandinavian couple. They were talking rapidly in their native language, of which I understood nothing. For a while, I paid no attention, looking at England through the train window, and thinking my own thoughts. Then, after a while, it occurred to me that this was an interesting opportunity to listen to language as a baby listens to it. Still looking out the window, I began to pay close attention to what they were saying. It was very much like listening to a complicated piece of modern music. I have discovered, after hearing many concerts and records, that the best way to listen to

127

strange and unfamiliar music, to keep your attention focussed sharply on it, is to try to reproduce the music in your mind — instant imitation. In the same way, I was trying to reproduce in my mind, as soon as I heard them, the sounds made by these people as they talked. I didn't get them all, but I got many of them. Also, though I wasn't looking for patterns — there wasn't time for that — I was alert for them, so that when a sound or word came along that I had heard before, it made an extra impression. It was an interesting and absorbing exercise. By the time forty minutes had passed, and I had reached my stop, I had begun to feel, and almost recognize, a few of the sounds and words in their talk. Perhaps this kind of raw listening would be useful for students studying a foreign language. We might have a record, or a tape, of a voice reading a particular passage, first at rapid conversational speed, then more slowly, finally so slowly that each word could be heard separately. From listening to such tapes, students might become sensitive to the relation between the separate sounds of a language and the sound of the flow of the whole language.

Read D. Tuddenham

Jean Piaget and the World of the Child

Let us turn first to Piaget's theory of cognitive development. Here a confusing situation arises for the English-speaking student. Piaget's five important books of the early 1920's were translated fairly promptly into English in the first flurry of interest in his work. These volumes — *Language and Thought of the Child, Judgment and Reasoning in the Child, The Child's Conception of Physical Causality*, and *The Moral Judgment of the Child* — are widely available. It is their contents — the famous inquiries about what makes clouds move, the origins of dreams, the basis of rules for games, and a host of other such topics — which come to mind for many people when Piaget is mentioned.

Now these works were gradually superseded in Piaget's theoretical formulations, but the point has not been sufficiently appreciated. In this country, there was a decline of interest in Piaget during what Koch (1959) has called the "Age of Theory" in American psychology —

Abridged version of article by Read D. Tuddenham, "Jean Piaget and the World of the Child," *American Psychologist*, XXI, 1966, pp. 207–217. Copyright © 1966 by the American Psychological Association. Reproduced by permission of the APA and the author.

Public lecture given at Berkeley on May 23, 1964, as a part of the University of California fete celebrating the four hundredth anniversary of the founding of the University of Geneva.

The author wishes to acknowledge his indebtedness to earlier writers on Piaget, not all of whom could be mentioned in the lecture. However, special acknowledgement is owing to Flavell (1962) in connection with the biographical account and to Wolff (1960) for portions of the summary of theory.

roughly from the early '30s to the end of the war — a tough-minded period dominated by the rules of "hypothetico-deduction" and "operational definition" and animated by belief in the imminence of a precisely quantitative behavior theory. Piaget's work was not easily reconciled with the fashions of the period, and little was translated. Now the tide has turned, and at least a portion of Piaget's recent work is available in English, not to mention several excellent "explanations" of him by Wolff (1960), Wohlwill (1960), Hunt (1961), and especially Flavell's comprehensive volume of 1963. However, the essential continuity of development of Piaget's ideas is obscured by the discontinuity of translation. So different are the recent works from the old ones, that to read them one must master a new vocabulary and a new theoretical formulation, and this time the task is made more difficult by the heavy emphasis upon propositions of symbolic logic to explicate the developmental stages of reasoning.

To the early Piaget belonged the painstaking compilation of the forms of verbal expression according to age level from 3 years to 10 years: the demonstration that children's "explanations" of phenomena pass through *stages*, from early animistic, through magical and artificialist forms, to rational thought, and that at each level, the child constructs a systematic "cosmology" according to the modes of reasoning available to him at that stage. The empirical bases for these findings were the children's verbalizations as elicited by the *méthode clinique*, with its inherent risks of misinterpretation of what the child is trying to express. Piaget was severely and perhaps unjustly criticized on this account,

129

for he was sharply aware of the problem. As he put it (1929),

> It is so hard not to talk too much when questioning a child, especially for a pedagogue! It is so hard not to suggest! And above all, it is so hard to find the middle course between systematization due to preconceived ideas, and incoherence due to the absence of any directing hypothesis! . . . In short, it is no simple task, and the material it yields needs to be subjected to the strictest criticism [p. 8].

In retrospect, Piaget (1952a) recognizes that his method in those years was much too exclusively verbal.

> I well knew that thought proceeds from action, but believed then that language directly reflects the act, and that to understand the logic of the child one has to look for it in the domain of verbal interactions. It was only by studying the patterns of intelligent behavior of *the first two years* that I learned that for a complete understanding of the genesis of intellectual operations, manipulation and experience with objects had first to be considered [p. 247].

As Piaget notes, the shift from reliance on verbalization to observation and experiment is most important for genetic epistemology because it permits one to study infants as well as the later stages of growth, and by more or less comparable methods.

The cognitive theory starts from the central postulate that motor action is the source from which mental operations emerge. The *action* of the organism is central to the acquisitions of the operations (i.e., ideas, or strategies), which we acquire for coping with the world. In the Hegelian dialectical form which his lectures often assume, Piaget contrasts his emphasis upon the active interplay of organism and environment, both with the environmentalist view in which experience or conditioning is impressed upon a passive organism, and with the nativist view that intellectual capabilities exist preformed and merely unfold in the course of development.

Motor action is *adaptive*, and so are the cognitive activities which more and more replace overt motor behavior. Piaget's biological orientation is seen in his assertion that intelligence is an adaptation, and only one aspect of biological

adaptation. Intelligence is an organizing activity which extends the biological organization. With respect to intelligence, a subject to which Piaget has given much attention, it should be noted that his interest is in the typical, not in the range of variation. For him, the word "intelligence" lacks the mental-testing connotations with which it is usually invested in English, and corresponds rather to "intellect" or to intellectual activity or adaptation.

> Life is a continuous creation of increasingly complex forms, and a progressive balancing of these forms with the environment [Piaget, 1952b, p. 3].

> Intellectual adaptation is the progressive differentiation and integration of inborn reflex mechanisms under the impact of experience. The differentiation of inborn reflex structures and their functions give rise to the mental operations by which man conceives of objects, space, time, and causality, and of the logical relationships which constitute the basis of scientific thought [Wolff, 1960, p. 9].

Another central postulate is that intellectual operations acquired by interaction between organism and environment are acquired in a *lawful sequence*. It should be emphasized again that Piaget's concern is with elucidating the sequence, *not* with establishing exact age norms for its stages. It should also be noted that Piaget has set out to write the ontogenetic history of cognition — *not* a complete account of personality development. What lies outside the cognitive domain is rigorously excluded.

The innate equipment consists of reflexes present at birth. A few reflexes, e.g., yawning or sneezing, are relatively fixed and unmodifiable by experience, though some, like the Babinski, change with maturation. The majority of reflexes, for example, grasping, *require* stimulation for their stabilization, are modified as a result of experience, and constitute the basic behavioral units from which more complex forms of behavior emerge. Most important, the feedback from the activation of a reflex alters all subsequent performance of that reflex. Thus, behavior is simultaneously determined by: first, the inborn structure; second, past activations, i.e., experience; and third, the particular present situation.

Now corresponding to each innate reflex there is assumed to exist in the mind a reflex *schema*, which will not become a stable structure unless repeatedly activated by external stimulation. The concept of schema is difficult. It is described as a flexible mental structure, the primary unit of mental organization. It is too invested with motor connotations to translate as "idea"; and being initially innate, it can hardly be a memory trace. Yet it covers both, and when fully developed bears some resemblance to Tolman's sign Gestalt.

When a reflex responds to a suitable external stimulus, the total sensory perception *and* motor activity are incorporated into the schema of that reflex, and change it; so that when the reflex is again stimulated, the schema has been modified. The stimulus is never again experienced in quite the same way, nor is the response quite the same. Thus the schema is invoked to account for the modification of response, *and* for the alteration of perception in the course of learning. In other words, the organism experiences and reacts to the environment always in terms of an existing organization. All experiences of a particular kind are molded into the already present schema, and in turn alter it according to the reality conditions. Hence, experiences are not recorded as isolated stimulus-response connections, or engrams impressed on a passive brain field, but are integrated into a constantly changing structure.

For the dual aspects of learning, Piaget has used the terms *assimilation* and *accommodation*. He points out first that there exists a fundamental coordination or tuning of the organism to its environment. We have eyes and skin receptors preadapted for the photic and thermal radiation found on earth, ears for sensing rapid waves of pressure in earth's atmosphere, and so forth. There exists, moreover, a fundamental tendency of organisms to take in substances and stimulations for which there already exist the appropriate internal structures and organization. This taking in is called *assimilation*. At a biological level, it refers to the physical incorporation of suitable nutrients into organic structure. At a primitive psychological level, it refers

to the incorporation of the sensory and motor components of a behavioral act into the reflex schema they have activated. At more complex levels, assimilation refers to the tendency of the mental apparatus to incorporate ideas into a complex system of thought schemata.

Parallel to assimilation is the function of *accommodation*, i.e., the process by which a schema *changes* so as to adapt better to the assimilated reality. At the biological level, accommodation refers to modification of the organism in response to stimulation, e.g., skin tanning in response to sunlight, or muscle growth in response to exercise. At the lowest psychological level, it refers to the gradual adaptation of the reflexes to new stimulus conditions — what others have called conditioning or stimulus generalization. At higher levels it refers to the coordination of thought patterns to one another and to external reality.

While assimilation and accommodation seem not too far from conventional learning theory, the concept of *aliment* is more unfamiliar. Whatever can be assimilated to a schema is aliment for that schema. Now the aliment is not the *object* which seems from the point of view of the observer to activate behavior, but rather those properties of the object which are assimilated and accommodated to. For example, a nursing bottle filled with milk may be organic aliment for the metabolism, sucking aliment for the reflex sucking schema, and visual aliment for the visual schema. And if the idea strikes you as bizarre that a reflex requires to be fed, as it were, by appropriate stimulation, consider Riesen's (1947) report on the degeneration of the visual apparatus in chimpanzees reared in the dark — or the more familiar degeneration of unstimulated muscles when polio destroys the motor pathways.

Why the careful distinction between an object and its properties? Because for the infant the object does not exist! The idea of an object grows gradually out of the coordination of several schemata — that which is perceived by several sensorial avenues *becomes* the object. At first, the infant has not even awareness of the boundaries of his own body. Objects in the perceptual field — including his own hands and feet — are responded to according to the infant's limited reflexive repertoire. He sucks in response to oral stimulation, grasps in response to palmar stimulation, but makes no attempt to grasp the nursing bottle which he competently sucks; or to follow visually the bottle he can clutch if placed in his hand. Only gradually, by a process called generalizing assimilation, do stimuli which were initially specific aliment for one schema become aliment for other schemata. In parallel accommodation, a schema becomes attuned to more complex inputs, and tends to become coordinated with other schemata which are simultaneously activated. When this happens, things previously known tactilely by being grasped can be recognized by sight alone. Similarly, grasping attempts of increasing accuracy can be directed toward sources of visual stimulation. In such a fashion does the baby come to populate the world with objects, one of which is his own body, which supplies him at once with visual, tactile and kinesthetic stimuli — and when he cries, with auditory ones.

However, the infant still does not attach the concept of permanence to objects. "Out of sight" is quite literally "out of mind." One of Piaget's most interesting experiments — and one which can be repeated by any parent of an infant — concerns the growth of the idea of permanent objects. If you catch a young baby's attention with a small toy, and then hide it, he will make little response. When somewhat older, he will show diffuse motor behavior. If now he once happens to touch it, he will gradually learn to search more efficiently where the object is hidden. However, if the object is hidden in a different place, in full sight of the baby, he will search not where he saw it hidden, but where previously he had touched it. It is an intellectual achievement of some magnitude when the very young child learns to coordinate the space of things seen with the space of things touched, and seeks to touch an object where hitherto he has only seen it.

We can conclude our rapid survey of Piaget's basic concepts with a brief reference to *equilibrium*. Bruner (1959), otherwise most sympa-

thetic, regards the notion of equilibrium as excess baggage, contributing to Piaget a comforting sense of continuity with biology, but offering little else. Perhaps the idea of disequilibrium is more easily described. A schema is in disequilibrium if adaptation (i.e., assimilation and accommodation) to the stimulus is incomplete.

It seems to me that the ideas of equilibrium and disequilibrium constitute most of Piaget's theory of motivation, which is a rather underelaborated part of his psychological system. The organism has a basic need to continue contact with an object as long as adaptation to it is incomplete — or, as Piaget would say, as long as the corresponding schema is in disequilibrium. The need for commerce with an object persists until the child's behavior has been wholly adapted to whatever novelty it presents, that is to say, it persists until the child has acquired mastery. Once accommodation is complete and assimilation is total, the schema is said to be "in equilibrium," and there is no further adaptation. There is, in short, no learning without a problem.

Further, two *schemata* are in disequilibrium until they have mutually accommodated and assimilated, and thereby been integrated into a new superordinate mental structure. This tendency to integrate schemata into more and more complex wholes is assumed by Piaget to be a native propensity of the mind, and as fundamental as the tendency toward equilibrium in physical systems. To put the matter in less cosmic terms, the person strives continually for more and more comprehensive mastery of his world. At each *stage*, however, he is concerned with those things which lie just beyond his intellectual grasp — far enough away to present a novelty to be assimilated, but not so far but what accommodation is possible. Phenomena too simple — i.e., already in equilibrium — and phenomena too complex for present adaptation are ignored in favor of those in the critical range. Anyone who has ever watched the persistence, and resistance to satiation, of a baby intent on mastering a developmental task — for example, learning to walk — will agree with Piaget as to the strength of the motivation, whether or not he accepts Piaget's thermodynamic metaphor.

What then are the general *stages* of intellectual development, and how may they be characterized? Piaget's stages are one of the best known aspects of his work, but he has not been altogether consistent either in the number of them or in the names assigned. Moreover, the stages are linked to particular chronological ages only rather loosely, and Piaget has himself offered data to show that the age at which a particular stage is reached differs for different content domains. For example, conservation (i.e., invariance under transformation) of a plastic object, such as a lump of clay, is acquired first with respect to mass, a year or so later with respect to weight, and a couple of years after that with respect to volume. Moreover, the Geneva group are concerned to demonstrate the invariance of the *sequence* of stages, not the age at which a given stage is achieved. In Martinique the children are 4 years retarded compared to those in Montreal (Laurendeau and Pinard, 1963), and certain Brazilian Indians appear never to achieve the last stage — but the sequence is everywhere the same.

When Piaget visited Berkeley, he deplored the preoccupation of American psychologists with accelerating a child's progress through the successive stages, and commented on recent work of Gruber, who found that kittens achieve awareness of the permanence of objects in 3 months, the human baby only in 9 months; but the important fact is that the cat never acquires the power to think in terms of formal logic, and the human being may!

The more recent books from Geneva usually divide development into four stages: the sensorimotor, from birth to 2 or 3 years; the preoperational stage, from around 2 to around 7 years; the stage of concrete operations, from roughly 7 years to 11 or 12; and finally the stage of formal operations. Each stage in turn has substages — no less than six for the sensorimotor period alone — which we shall not have time to describe today.

The sensorimotor period as a whole (i.e., from birth up to age 2) carries the child from inborn reflexes to acquired behavior patterns. It leads the child from a body-centered (i.e., self-centered) world to an object-centered one. During this period the various sensory spaces, of vision, touch, and the rest, are coordinated into a single space and objects evolve from their separate sensory properties into *things* with multiple properties, permanence, and spatial relationships to other objects. Altogether this stage comprises a most important set of intellectual achievements.

The preoperational stage (2 years to around 7 years) covers the important period when language is acquired. This permits the child to deal symbolically with the world instead of directly through motor activity, though his problem solving tends to be "action ridden." The child is himself still the focus of his own world, and space and time are centered on him. Time is only "before now," "now," and "not yet'; and space moves as the child moves. When he is taken for an evening walk, the moon follows *him*. Traces of this attitude are present even in adults, who often locate places and things in terms of distance and direction from themselves, rather than in terms of objective spatial relationships. By a process of "decentering," the child during this stage learns gradually to conceive of a time scale and of a spatial world which exist independent of himself. In dealing with physical objects and quantities, the child pays attention to one aspect to the neglect of other aspects. He concludes, for example, that there is more water in a glass graduate than in a beaker — though he has just seen it poured from the one vessel into the other — because in the graduate the column of water is taller, and the child neglects the reduction in diameter.

The stage of concrete operations has its beginnings as early as age 6 or 7. Now the child grows less dependent upon his own perceptions and motor actions and shows a capacity for reasoning, though still at a very concrete level. Among his "logical" acquisitions are classifying, ordering in series, and numbering. Asked to put a handful of sticks in order by length, he need no longer make all the pair comparisons but can pick out the longest, then the longest one left, and so forth, until the series is complete. When shown that Stick A is longer than Stick B, and Stick B is longer than Stick C, he can infer without actual demonstration that A is longer than C.

Here at Berkeley, my students and I have been developing test materials based on Piaget experiments, and intended to measure the abilities of children in the primary grades, i.e., at the transition point from the perceptual attitude of the pre-operational stage to the reasoning attitude of the stage of concrete operations. Thus far, fifteen tests have been developed and administered to more than 300 school children. Although we abandoned the *méthode clinique* for a strictly standardized psychometric approach, we have observed precisely the same types of behavior which Piaget had previously reported.

The last of Piaget's major stages of intellectual development begins usually somewhere around 11 or 12 years and matures a couple of years later. He calls it the stage of formal operations. Now the child can deal with abstract relationships instead of with things, with the form of an argument while ignoring its content. For the first time he can intellectually manipulate the merely hypothetical, and systematically evaluate a lengthy set of alternatives. He learns to handle the logical relationships of Identity (I), Negation (N), Reciprocity (R), and Correlation (C), which permit him to deal with problems of proportionality, probability, permutations, and combinations.

I have just referred to the INRC logical group whose acquisition marks the last stage of intellectual growth. In Piaget's writings over the years, the characteristics of each stage and the differences between them have increasingly been formulated in the notation of symbolic logic — a circumstance which does not increase the comprehensibility of his latest books for nonmathematicians.

Nevertheless, this transition to the language of formal logic is of profound importance for

Piaget's theory because it provides a set of explicit, mathematical models for cognitive structure, and serves as a vehicle to describe in a unified way the findings of experiments very different in content. The unity and economy of the logical theory as contrasted with his earlier multiplicity of explanatory terms — egocentrism, syncretism, animism, realism, etc. — is obvious. However, Piaget's critics have sometimes found the mathematical formulation strained, and have accused Piaget of distorting intellectual development to force it into the categories of formal logic.

Piaget's point of view may have been misunderstood. As he phrases it (1957),

> The aim is . . . to study the application of logical techniques to the psychological facts themselves. . . . The question whether the structures and operations of logic correspond to anything in our actual thought, and whether the latter conforms to logical laws is still an open one. . . . On the other hand, the algebra of logic can help us to specify psychological structures, and put into calculus form those operations and structures central to our thought processes. . . . The psychologist welcomes the qualitative character of logic since it facilitates the analyses of the actual structures underlying intellectual operations, as contrasted with the quantitative treatment of their behavioral outcome. Most "tests" of intelligence measure the latter, but our real problem is to discover the actual operational mechanisms which govern such behavior, and not simply to measure it [pp. xvii–xviii].

Many psychologists who acknowledge the brilliant originality of many of Piaget's experiments, and the enormous importance of his empirical contribution taken as a whole, continue nevertheless to reject the formal, mathematical theory which lies closest to Piaget's heart. Yet one of the most impressive parts of Piaget's discussions here in Berkeley concerned the isomorphism between his stages and the most basic structure of mathematics itself.

Piaget points out that if one considers not the content, but the architecture, as it were, of the various branches of mathematics, one discovers first a level where the prototype structure is the group and the type of reversibility is inversion or negation. Next comes a level where structures of order, such as the lattice, are typical, and reversibility is not inversion but reciprocity. Last comes the level of topology with key concepts of neighborhood, boundary, etc. Now the first of these three levels is the oldest, one part of it, Euclidean geometry, going back to the Greeks. The second level, typified by projective geometry, dates from the late seventeenth century; and the last, or topological, level is a product only of the nineteenth century. Taken in sequence, each level is more general, i.e., involves *fewer* axioms than the preceding, and the entire sequence might theoretically be expected to have developed in the opposite order. Now the curious part, is that the sequence of acquisition of mental operations by children follows not the historical sequence, but the theoretical sequence. Small children of 3 years of age, who for example are quite unable even to copy a simple geometrical figure such as a square, have no difficulty differentiating between a closed figure like a circle and an open one like a cross, and they can easily follow instructions in putting a second circle, however imperfectly drawn, inside, or outside, or even half in and half out of the experimenter's circle. Further evidence of young children's grasp of topological principles is seen in their sure knowledge of the forms into which a sphere, such as a balloon, can be deformed — i.e., sausagelike, flat sided, or dimpled figures, etc. — and those forms such as the torus or doughnut, which cannot be obtained by deformation of a sphere. Later, with the shift from the preoperational stage to the stage of concrete operations at age 6 or 7, the child learns to handle relations of order — seriation, transitivity, reciprocal relationships, and the rest to which I have already referred. Only with the approach of adolescence does he spontaneously utilize the propositional algebraic structures which are the oldest development in the history of mathematics.

What finally are the implications of Piaget's work for fields other than psychology and mathematics? Certainly they have a major bearing upon education.

If Piaget is correct — and much work now substantiates his empirical findings at least in broad outline — methods of education will be most effective when they are attuned to the patterns of thought which are natural to a child of the age concerned. It may not be true that you can teach a child *anything* if your approach is correct, but it does look as if you can teach him a great deal more than anyone might have guessed. Of course, teachers long before Piaget recognized intuitively that a child learned better when problems were approached at a concrete rather than at an abstract level. But there is more to it than that. Bruner, at Harvard, and others in this country are attempting to find ways to introduce children to some of the abstract ideas of mathematics — for example, the algebraic concept of squaring a number — by concrete, geometric models. They hope thus possibly to accelerate a child's progress — a goal which Piaget has his reservations about. Perhaps the most dramatic evidence of a revolution which owes a great deal of its impetus to Piaget is the new elementary school mathematics, in which children even in the lower grades are being taught, and learning, and actually enjoying learning basic arithmetical and geometrical ideas introduced via set theory, which most of their parents have never heard of.

I could not better conclude this appreciation of Piaget than by quoting from William James (1890) who wrote 75 years ago in his famous *Principles of Psychology* as follows: "To the infant, sounds, sights, touches and pains form probably one unanalyzed bloom of confusion [p. 496]." We can now go beyond the philosopher's speculations and describe in some detail how the unanalyzed "bloom of confusion" of the infant becomes the world of the child — in which not only objects, but time, space, causality and the rest acquire a coherent organization. And we owe this achievement in large measure to the analyses of Jean Piaget.

References

Bruner, J. S. Inhelder and Piaget's *The growth of logical thinking*. I. A psychologist's viewpoint.

British Journal of Psychology, 1959, 50, 363–370.

Flavell, J. H. Historical and bibliographic note. In W. Kessen and Clementina Kuhlman (eds.), Thought in the young child. *Monographs of the Society for Research in Child Development*, 1962, 27 (2, Whole No. 83).

Flavell, J. H. *The developmental psychology of Jean Piaget*. Princeton, N.J.: Van Nostrand, 1963.

Hunt, J. McV. *Intelligence and experience*. New York: Ronald Press, 1961.

Inhelder, Barbel. Some aspects of Piaget's genetic approach to cognition. In W. Kessen and Clementina Kuhlman (eds.), Thought in the young child. *Monographs of the Society for Research in Child Development*, 1962, 27 (2, Whole No. 83).

James, W. *The principles of psychology*. New York: Holt, 1890.

Koch, S. (ed.), *Psychology: A study of a science*. Vol. 3. *Formulations of the person and the social context*. New York: McGraw-Hill, 1959.

Laurendeau, Monique, and Pinard, A. *Causal thinking in the child, a genetic and experimental approach*. New York: International Universities Press, 1963.

Piaget, J. *The child's conception of the world*. New York: Harcourt, Brace, 1929.

Piaget, J. Autobiography. In E. G. Boring (ed.), A history of psychology in autobiography. Vol. 4. Worcester, Mass.: Clark University Press, 1952. (a)

Piaget, J. *The origins of intelligence in children* (2nd ed.). New York: International Universities Press, 1952. (b)

Piaget, J. *Logic and psychology*. New York: Basic Books, 1957.

Riesen, A. H. The development of visual perception in man and chimpanzee. *Science*, 1947, 106, 107–108.

Wohlwill, J. F. Developmental studies of perception. *Psychological Bulletin*, 1960, 57, 249–288.

Wolff, P. H. The developmental psychologies of Jean Piaget and psychoanalysis. *Psychological Issues*, 1960, 2 (1, Whole No. 5).

George A. Miller, Eugene Galanter, and Karl H. Pribram

Excerpt from Plans and the Structure of Behavior

Most psychologists take it for granted that a scientific account of the behavior of organisms must begin with the definition of fixed, recognizable, elementary units of behavior — something a psychologist can use as a biologist uses cells, or an astronomer uses stars, or a physicist uses atoms, and so on. Given a simple unit, complicated phenomena are then describable as lawful compounds. That is the essence of the highly successful strategy called "scientific analysis."

The elementary unit that modern, experimental psychologists generally select for their analysis of behavior is the *reflex*. "The isolation of a reflex," B. F. Skinner tells us, "is the demonstration of a predictable uniformity in behavior. In some form or other it is an inevitable part of any science of behavior. . . . A reflex is not, of course, a theory. It is a fact. It is an analytical unit, which makes the investigation of behavior possible."[1] Skinner is quite careful to define a reflex as a unit of behavior that will yield orderly data: "The appearance of smooth curves in dynamic processes marks a unique point in the progressive restriction of a preparation, and it is to this uniquely determined entity that the term reflex may be assigned."[2] This somewhat odd approach to the reflex — in terms of the smoothness of curves — results

[1] B. F. Skinner, *The Behavior of Organisms* (New York: Appleton-Century-Crofts, 1938), p. 9.
[2] *Ibid.*, p. 40.

from Skinner's consistent attempt to define a unit of behavior in terms of behavior itself instead of by reference to concepts drawn from some other branch of science.

Although Skinner's approach absolves the psychologist of certain burdensome responsibilities toward his biological colleagues, the fact remains that the reflex is a concept borrowed originally from physiology and made to seem psychologically substantial largely by the myth of the *reflex arc*: stimulus → receptor → afferent nerve → connective fibers → efferent nerve → effector → response. For many years all those elementary textbooks of psychology that mentioned the nervous system featured the traditional, simplified diagram of the reflex arc in a very prominent position. You may ignore a behaviorist when he tells you that the reflex is a fact, but you can scarcely ignore a physiologist when he draws you a picture of it. You might as well deny the small intestines or sneer at the medulla oblongata as to doubt the reflex arc. Even the most obstinate opponent of physiological explanations in psychology can scarcely forget the bloody tissue from which the reflex — even the reflex-sans-arc — originally grew.

But let us suppose, by a wild and irresponsible flight of fancy, that the physiologists and neurologists suddenly announced that they had been mistaken, that there was no such fact as a reflex arc and that the data on which the theory had been based were actually quite different from what had originally been supposed. What then would psychologists say? Would they persist in talking about reflexes? Has the reflex concept been so tremendously helpful that behaviorists could not afford to give it up, even if its biological basis were demolished?

There is some reason to think that the reflex unit has been vastly overrated and that a good many psychologists would like to get out from under it if they could. The reflex arc may have been helpful in getting psychology started along scientific paths, but the suspicion has been growing in recent years that the reflex idea is too simple, the element too elementary. For the most part, serious students of behavior have had to ignore the problem of units entirely. Or they have had to modify their units so drastically for each new set of data that to speak of them as elementary would be the most unblushing sophistry. After watching psychologists struggle under their burden of conditioning reflexes, Chomsky, the linguist and logician, recently summarized their plight in the following terms:

The notions of "stimulus," "response," "reinforcement" are relatively well defined with respect to the bar-pressing experiments and others, similarly restricted. Before we can extend them to real-life behavior, however, certain difficulties must be faced. We must decide, first of all, whether any physical event to which the organism is capable of reacting is to be called a stimulus on a given occasion, or only one to which the organism in fact reacts; and correspondingly, we must decide whether any part of behavior is to be called a response, or only one connected with stimuli in lawful ways. Questions of this sort pose something of a dilemma for the experimental psychologist. If he accepts the broad definitions, characterizing any physical event impinging on the organism as a stimulus and any part of the organism's behavior as a response, he must conclude that behavior has not been demonstrated to be lawful. In the present state of our knowledge, we must attribute an overwhelming influence on actual behavior to ill-defined factors of attention, set, volition, and caprice. If we accept the narrower definitions, then behavior is lawful by definition (if it consists of responses); but this fact is of limited significance, since most of what the animal does will simply not be considered behavior.[3]

Faced with the choice of being either vague or irrelevant, many psychologists have been restive and ill at ease with their borrowed terms. What went wrong? How was the reflex arc conceived

originally, and for what purpose? Can we supplant the reflex arc with some theory of the reflex that is more suited to our current knowledge and interests?

Sir Charles Sherrington and Ivan Petrovitch Pavlov are the two men who are probably most responsible for confirming the psychologist's Image of man as a bundle of S-R reflexes. Yet one may be permitted to speculate that neither of them would approve of the way their concepts have been extended by psychologists. In his *Integrative Action of the Nervous System* (1906) Sherrington is particularly explicit in his qualifications and warnings about the reflex. Again and again he states that "the simple reflex is a useful fiction" — useful for the study of the spinal preparation. He expressed considerable doubt that a stretch reflex, of which the knee jerk is the most frequently quoted example, represented his notion of a simple reflex and questioned whether it should be considered a reflex at all. The synapse was invented by Sherrington in order to explain the differences between the observed properties of nerve trunks and the properties that had to be inferred to describe the neural tissue that intervenes between receptor stimulation and effector response. Nerve trunks will transmit signals in either direction. Characteristically, the signals are of an all-or-none type. Reflex action, on the other hand, is unidirectional and the response is characteristically graded according to the intensity of the stimulus. How can these be reconciled? Sherrington resolved the differences by supporting the neuron doctrine: the nervous system is made up of discrete neural units that have the properties of nerve trunks; intercalated between these units are discontinuities which he christened "synapses," and these have the properties unique to reflexes.

In recent years, graded responses have been shown to be a prepotent characteristic not only of synapses but also of all excitable tissue, for example, of the finer arborizations of the nerve cells. The cerebral cortex, man's claim to phylogenetic eminence, "still operates largely by means of connections characteristic of primitive neuropil [which is] the most appropriate mechanism for the maintenance of a continuous or

[3] The passage quoted is from page 30 of Chomsky's review of B. F. Skinner, *Verbal Behavior*, in *Language*, 1959, 35, 26–58.

steady state, as contrasted to the transmission of information about such states."[4]

Moreover, additional data have come to light. Today we know that neural and receptor tissues are spontaneously active irrespective of environmental excitation. This spontaneous activity is, of course, altered by environmental events — but the change in spontaneous activity may outlast the direct excitation by hours and even days. Furthermore, we know now that the activity of receptors is controlled by efferents leading to them from the central nervous system. As an example, consider the events that control muscular contraction. (Similar, though not identical, mechanisms have also been described for the various sensory systems.) One third of the "motor" nerve fibers that go to muscle actually end in spindles that are the stretch-sensitive receptors. Electrical stimulation of these nerve fibers does not result in contraction of muscle; but the number of signals per unit time that are recorded from the "sensory" nerves coming from the spindles is altered drastically. It is assumed, therefore, that the central nervous mechanism must compare the incoming pattern of signals with the centrally originating "spindle control" signal pattern in order to determine what contribution the muscular contraction has made to the "spindle sensing" pattern. The outcome of this comparison, or *test*, constitutes the stimulus (the psychophysicist's *proximal* stimulus) to which the organism is sensitive. The test represents the conditions which have to be met before the response will occur. The test may occur in the receptor itself (e.g., in the retina) or in a more centrally located neuronal aggregate (as is probably the case for muscle stretch).

It is clear from examples such as this that the neural mechanism involved in reflex action cannot be diagrammed as a simple reflex arc or even as a chain of stimulus-response connections. A much more complex kind of monitoring, or testing, is involved in reflex action than the classical reflex arc makes any provision for. The only conditions imposed upon the stimulus

by the classical chain of elements are the criteria implicit in the thresholds of each element; if the distal stimulus is strong enough to surmount the thresholds all along the arc, then the response must occur. In a sense, the threshold is a kind of test, too, a condition that must be met, but it is a test of strength only. And it must have encouraged psychologists to believe that the only meaningful measurement of a reflex was its strength (probability, magnitude, or latency).

The threshold, however, is only one of many different ways that the input can be tested. Moreover, the response of the effector depends upon the outcome of the test and is most conveniently conceived as an effort to modify the outcome of the test. The action is initiated by an "incongruity" between the state of the organism and the state that is being tested for, and the action persists until the incongruity (i.e., the proximal stimulus) is removed. The general pattern of reflex action, therefore, is to test the input energies against some criteria established in the organism, to respond if the result of the test is to show an incongruity, and to continue to respond until the incongruity vanishes, at which time the reflex is terminated. Thus, there is "feedback" from the result of the action to the testing phase, and we are confronted by a recursive loop. The simplest kind of diagram to represent this conception of reflex action — an alternative to the classical reflex arc — would have a look something like Figure 1.

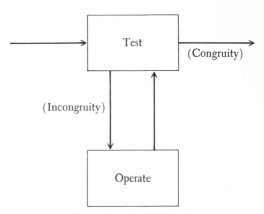

Figure 1. The TOTE unit

[4] George Bishop, The natural history of the nerve impulse, *Physiological Reviews*, 1956, 36, 376–399.

139

The interpretation toward which the argument moves is one that has been called the "cybernetic hypothesis," namely, that the fundamental building block of the nervous system is the feedback loop.[5] The development of a mathematical theory for servomechanisms, wedded to the physiological accounts of homeostatic mechanisms, has stimulated widespread discussion and speculation about devices closely akin to Figure 1. The argument, therefore, moves toward popular ground.

But what good is this alternative interpretation of the reflex? The psychologist was interested in reflexes because he thought they might provide the units he needed to describe behavior. But simple reflexes have been inadequate. And if reflexes based on afferent-efferent arcs would not turn the trick, why should we hope for better things from reflexes based on feedback loops? It is the reflex itself — not merely the reflex arc — that has failed, and repairing the neurological theory underlying it is not likely to save the day. What do we hope to gain from such a reinterpretation?

Obviously, the reflex is not the unit we should use as the element of behavior: the unit should be the feedback loop itself. If we think of the Test-Operate-Test-Exit unit — for convenience, we shall call it a TOTE unit — as we do of the reflex arc, in purely anatomical terms, it may describe reflexes, but little else. That is to say, the reflex should be recognized as only one of many possible actualizations of a TOTE pattern. The next task is to generalize the TOTE unit so that it will be useful in a majority — hopefully, in all — of the behavioral descriptions we shall need to make.

Consider what the arrows in Figure 1 might represent. What could flow along them from one box to another? We shall discuss three alternatives: energy, information, and control. If we think of *energy* — neural impulses, for example — flowing from one place to another over the arrows, then the arrows must correspond to recognizable physical structures — neurons, in the example chosen. As a diagram of energy flow over discrete pathways, therefore, the TOTE unit described in Figure 1 might represent a simple reflex. Or it might represent a servomechanism.

There is, however, a second level of abstraction that psychologists usually prefer. We can think of *information* as flowing from one place to another over the arrows. According to the method of measuring information that has been developed by Norbert Wiener and by Claude Shannon, information is transmitted over a channel to the extent that the output of the channel is correlated with the input.[6] We could therefore think of this second level of abstraction as the transmission of correlation over the arrows. In that case, we are concerned not with the particular structures or kinds of energy that are involved in producing the correlation but only with the fact that events at the two ends of the arrow are correlated. The situation is quite familiar to psychologists, for it is exactly what they mean when they draw an arrow leading from Stimulus to Response in their *S-R* diagrams or when they define a reflex as a correlation between S and R but refuse to talk about the neurological basis for that correlation.

A third level of abstraction, however, is extremely important for the ideas we shall discuss in the pages that follow. It is the notion that what flows over the arrows in Figure 1 is an intangible something called *control*. Or perhaps we should say that the arrow indicates only succession. This concept appears most frequently

[5] Norbert Wiener, *Cybernetics* (New York: Wiley, 1948). For a short review of the early development of this idea, see J. O. Wisdom, The hypothesis of cybernetics, *British Journal for the Philosophy of Science*, 1951, 2, 1–24. For more comprehensive discussion, see W. Sluckin, *Minds and Machines* (London: Penguin, 1954).

[6] A short introduction to these ideas written for psychologists can be found in G. A. Miller, What is information measurement? *American Psychologist*, 1953, 8, 3–11. A fuller account has been given by Fred Attneave, *Applications of Information Theory to Psychology* (New York: Holt, 1959). See also the highly readable account by Colin Cherry, *On Human Communication* (Cambridge: Technology Press, 1957).

in the discussion of computing machines, where the control of the machine's operations passes from one instruction to another, successively, as the machine proceeds to execute the list of instructions that comprise the program it has been given. But the idea is certainly not limited to computers. As a simple example drawn from more familiar activities, imagine that you wanted to look up a particular topic in a certain book in order to see what the author had to say about it. You would open the book to the index and find the topic. Following the entry is a string of numbers. As you look up each page reference in turn, your behavior can be described as under the control of that list of numbers, and control is transferred from one number to the next as you proceed through the list. The transfer of control could be symbolized by drawing arrows from one page number to the next, but the arrows would have a meaning quite different from the two meanings mentioned previously. Here we are not concerned with a flow of energy or transmission of information from one page number to the next but merely with the order in which the "instructions" are executed.

At this abstract level of description we are no longer required to think of the test as a simple threshold that some stimulus energy must exceed. The test phase can be regarded as any process for determining that the operational phase is appropriate. For example, to be clear though crude, we do not try to take the square root of "ratiocinate." We may know full well how to extract square roots, but before we can execute that operation we must have digits to work on. The operation of extracting square roots is simply irrelevant when we are dealing with words. In order to ensure that an operation is relevant, a test must be built into it. Unless the test gives the appropriate outcome, control cannot be transferred to the operational phase.

When Figure 1 is used in the discussion of a simple reflex it represents all three levels of description simultaneously. When it is used to describe more complex activities, however, we may want to consider only the transfer of information and control or in many instances only

the transfer of control. In all cases, however, the existence of a TOTE should indicate that an organizing, coordinating unit has been established, that a Plan is available.

In the following pages we shall use the TOTE as a general description of the control processes involved. The TOTE will serve as a description at only the third, least concrete, level. In its weakest form, the TOTE asserts simply that the operations an organism performs are constantly guided by the outcomes of various tests.

The present authors feel that the TOTE unit, which incorporates the important notion of feedback, is an explanation of behavior in general, and of reflex action in particular, fundamentally different from the explanation provided by the reflex arc. Consequently, the traditional concepts of stimulus and response must be redefined and reinterpreted to suit their new context. Stimulus and response must be seen as phases of the organized, coordinated act. We might summarize it this way:

> The stimulus is that phase of the forming coordination which represents the conditions which have to be met in bringing it to a successful issue; the response is that phase of one and the same forming coordination which gives the key to meeting these conditions, which serves as instrument in effecting the successful coordination. They are therefore strictly correlative and contemporaneous. [7]

Because stimulus and response are correlative and contemporaneous, the stimulus processes must be thought of not as preceding the response but rather as guiding it to a successful elimination of the incongruity. That is to say, stimulus and response must be considered as aspects of a feedback loop.

The need for some kind of feedback channel in the description of behavior is well recognized by most reflex theorists, but they have introduced it in a peculiar way. For example, it is customary for them to speak of certain conse-

---

[7] This passage is from an article by John Dewey entitled, "The Reflex Arc Concept in Psychology," an article as valuable today for its wisdom and insight as it was in 1896.

quences of a reflex action as strengthening, or reinforcing, the reflex — such reinforcing consequences of action are a clear example of feedback. Reinforcements are, however, a special kind of feedback that should not be identified with the feedback involved in a TOTE unit. That is to say: (1) a reinforcing feedback must strengthen something, whereas feedback in a TOTE is for the purpose of comparison and testing; (2) a reinforcing feedback is considered to be a stimulus (e.g., pellet of food), whereas feedback in a TOTE may be a stimulus, or information (e.g., knowledge of results), or control (e.g., instructions); and (3) a reinforcing feedback is frequently considered to be valuable, or "drive reducing," to the organism, whereas feedback in a TOTE has no such value.

When a TOTE has been executed — the operations performed, the test satisfied, and the exit made — the creature may indeed appear to have attained a more desirable state. It may even be true, on the average, that the TOTE units that are completed successfully in a given situation tend to recur with increased probability, although such a relation would not be necessary. Thus it is possible to discuss a TOTE in the language of reinforcements. Nevertheless, the TOTE involves a much more general conception of feedback. The concept of reinforcement represents an important step forward from reflex arcs toward feedback loops, but bolder strides are needed if behavior theory is to advance beyond the description of simple conditioning experiments.

Perhaps variations in the basic TOTE pattern will prove necessary, so for the purposes of the present discussion we shall continue to regard the diagram in Figure 1 as a hypothesis rather than a fact. The importance of this hypothesis to the general thesis of the book, however, should not be overlooked. It is, in capsule, the account we wish to give of the relation between Image and action. The TOTE represents the basic pattern in which our Plans are cast, the test phase of the TOTE involves the specification of whatever knowledge is necessary for the comparison that is to be made, and the operational phase represents what the organism does about it — and what the organism does

may often involve overt, observable actions. Figure 1, therefore, rephrases the problem ... How does a Plan relate the organism's Image of itself and its universe to the actions, the responses, the behavior that the organism is seen to generate?

Let us see what we must do in order to expand this proposal into something useful. One of the first difficulties — a small one — is to say more exactly what we mean by the "incongruity" that the test phase is looking for. Why not talk simply about the difference, rather than the incongruity, as providing the proximal stimulus? The answer is not profound: We do not want to bother to distinguish between TOTEs in which the operations are performed only when a difference is detected (and where the operations serve to diminish the difference) and TOTEs in which the operations are released only when no difference is detected. When the diagram is used to describe servomechanisms, for example, it is quite important to distinguish "positive" from "negative" feedback, but, because we are going to be interested primarily in the feedback of control, such questions are not critical. Rather than treat all these varieties as different units of analysis, it seems simpler to treat them all as examples of a more general type of "incongruity-sensitive" mechanism.[8]

A second difficulty — this one rather more important — is the question of how we can integrate this TOTE unit into the sort of hierarchical structure of behavior. How can the two concepts — feedback and hierarchy — be reconciled? One method of combining feedback components in a hierarchy has been described by D. M. MacKay,[9] who proposed to make the

[8] The notion of an "incongruity-sensitive" mechanism appears to the authors to be related to Festinger's conceptions of "cognitive dissonance," but we have not attempted to explore or develop that possibility. See Leon Festinger, A Theory of Cognitive Dissonance (Evanston: Row, Peterson, 1957).

[9] D. M. MacKay, The epistemological problem for automata, in C. E. Shannon and J. McCarthy, eds., Automata Studies (Princeton: Princeton University Press, 1956), pp. 235–251.

consequences of the operational phase in one component provide the input to the comparator of a second component; MacKay's suggestion leads to a string of such feedback components, each representing a progressively higher degree of abstraction from the external reality. Although MacKay's scheme is quite ingenious, we are persuaded that a somewhat different method of constructing the hierarchy will better serve a psychologist's descriptive purposes. A central notion of the method followed in these pages is that the operational components of TOTE units may themselves be TOTE units. That is to say, the TOTE pattern describes both strategic and tactical units of behavior. Thus the operational phase of a higher-order TOTE might itself consist of a string of other TOTE units, and each of these, in turn, may contain still other strings of TOTEs, and so on. Since this method of retaining the same pattern of description for the higher, more strategic units as for the lower, more tactical units may be confusing on first acquaintance, we shall consider an example.

R. S. Woodworth has pointed out how frequently behavioral activities are organized in two stages.[10] Woodworth refers to them as "two-phase motor units." The first phase is preparatory or mobilizing; the second, effective or consummatory. To jump, you first flex the hips and knees, then extend them forcefully; the crouch prepares for the jump. To grasp an object, the first phase is to open your hand, the second is to close it around the object. You must open your mouth before you can bite. You must draw back your arm before you can strike, etc. The two phases are quite different movements, yet they are obviously executed as a single unit of action. If stimulation is correct for releasing the action, first the preparatory TOTE unit is executed, and when it has been completed the stimulation is adequate for the consummatory TOTE unit and the action is executed. Many of these two-phase plans are repetitive: the completion of the second phase in turn provides stimuli indicating that the execu-

10 Robert S. Woodworth, *Dynamics of Behavior* (New York: Holt, 1958), pp. 36 ff.

tion of the first phase is again possible, so an alternation between the two phases is set up, as in walking, running, chewing, drinking, sweeping, knitting, etc.

We should note well the construction of a "two-phase" TOTE unit out of two simpler TOTE units. Consider hammering a nail as an

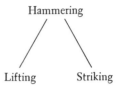

Figure 2. Hammering as a Hierarchy

example. As a Plan, of course, hammering has two phases, lifting the hammer and then striking the nail. We could represent it by a tree, or hierarchy, as in Figure 2. If we ask about details, however, the representation of hammering in Figure 2 as a simple list containing two items is certainly too sketchy. It does not tell us, for one thing, how long to go on hammering. What is the "stop rule"? For this, we must indicate the test phase, as in Figure 3. The diagram in Figure 3 should indicate that when control is transferred to the TOTE unit that we are calling "hammering," the hammering con-

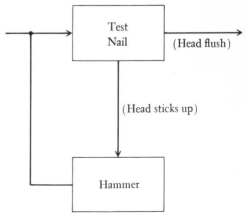

Figure 3. Hammering as a TOTE unit

143

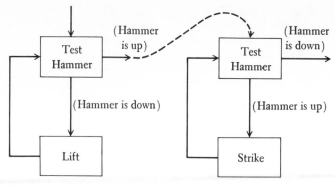

Figure 4. Dashed line indicates how two simple TOTE units are connected to form the operational phase of the more complicated TOTE unit in Figure 3.

tinues until the head of the nail is flush with the surface of the work. When the test indicates that the nail is driven in, control is transferred elsewhere. Now, however, we seem to have lost the hierarchical structure. The hierarchy is recovered when we look at the box labeled "hammer," for there we find two TOTE units, each with its own test, as indicated in Figure 4. When the pair of TOTE units combined in Figure 4 are put inside the operational phase in Figure 3, the result is the hierarchical Plan for hammering nails that is shown in Figure 5.

If this description of hammering is correct, we should expect the sequence of events to run off in this order: Test nail. (Head sticks up.) Test hammer. (Hammer is down.)Lift hammer. Test hammer. (Hammer is up.) Test hammer. (Hammer is up.) Strike nail. Test hammer. (Hammer is down). Test nail. (Head sticks up.) Test hammer. And so on, until the test of the nail reveals that its head is flush with the surface of the work, at which point control can be transferred elsewhere. Thus the compound of TOTE units unravels itself simply enough into a coordinated sequence of tests and actions, although the underlying structure that organizes and coordinates the behavior is itself hierarchical, not sequential.

It may seem slightly absurd to analyze the

motions involved in hammering a nail in this explicit way, but it is better to amuse a reader than to confuse him. It is merely an illustration of how several simple TOTE units, each with its own test-operate-test loop, can be embedded in the operational phase of a larger unit with its particular test-operate-test loop. Without such an explicit illustration it might not have been immediately obvious how these circles within circles could yield hierarchical trees.

More complicated Plans — Woodworth refers to them as "polyphase motor units" — can be similarly described as TOTE units built up of subplans that are themselves TOTE units. A bird will take off, make a few wing strokes, glide, brake with its wings, thrust its feet forward, and land on the limb. The whole action is initiated as a unit, is controlled by a single Plan, yet is composed of several phases, each involving its own Plan, which may in turn be comprised of subplans, etc.

Note that it is the *operational* phase of the TOTE that is expanded into a list of other TOTE units. If we wish to preserve the TOTE pattern as it is diagrammed in Figure 1, we cannot use it to build up more complicated tests.[11]

---

[11] The reason that the TOTE of Figure 1 can be expanded only in its operational phase is purely formal and can be appreciated by simple counting: There

The tests that are available, therefore, are conceived to be relatively fixed; it is the operational phase that may be quite various and complex. The operational phase may, of course, consist of a list of TOTEs, or it may terminate in efferent activity.[12] If we consider complex Plans — TOTE hierarchies in which the operation of one TOTE is itself a list of TOTE units — then some general properties of such systems become apparent:

The hierarchical structure underlying behavior is taken into account in a way that can be simply described with the computer language developed by Newell, Shaw, and Simon for processing lists.

Planning can be thought of as constructing a list of tests to perform. When we have a clear Image of a desired outcome, we can use it to provide the conditions for which we must test, and those tests, when arranged in sequence, provide a crude strategy for a possible Plan. (Perhaps it would be more helpful to say that the conditions for which we must test *are* an Image of the desired outcome.)

The operational phase can contain both tests and operations. Therefore the execution of a

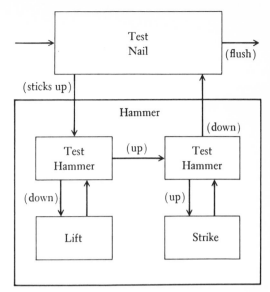

Figure 5. The hierarchical Plan for hammering nails

Plan of any complexity must involve many more tests than actions. This design feature would account for the general degradation of information that occurs whenever a human being is used as a communication channel.

In lower animals it appears that the pattern of their behavior is normally constructed more or less fortuitously by the environment — only man cherishes the illusion of being master of his fate. That is to say, the environment provides stimuli that "release" the next stage of the animal's activity. It is something of a philosophical question as to whether we wish to believe in plans that exist somewhere outside of nervous systems, so perhaps we should say merely that lower animals appear to have more tactics than strategy.

As we ascend the evolutionary scale we find in mammals an increasing complexity in the kind of tests the animals can perform. In man we have a unique capacity for creating and manipulating symbols, and when that versatility is used to assign names to TOTE units, it becomes possible for him to use language in order

---

are four arrows associated with Test; there are two arrows associated with Operate; and there are two arrows associated with TOTE as a unit. Therefore, if the two-arrowed TOTE is used to construct some component of another TOTE, the component it constructs must be the two-arrowed Operate, not the four-arrowed Test. However, rigid restrictions such as these are probably unrealistic and justifiable only in terms of pedagogic simplification. Anyone who has studied the hierarchically organized programs written by Newell, Shaw, and Simon to simulate human problem-solving will recognize how primitive and unelaborated these TOTE hierarchies really are.

[12] If we take seriously the suggested form of the TOTE, the system may be easily trapped into loops. For example, if the subtests in the expansion of an operational phase all pass, but the basic test fails, a loop will exist. In order to avoid loops we might insist that the basic test imply the disjunction of the subtests. A more realistic solution would accept the occurrence of loops as a signal that the Plan was not successful in producing the result for which the basic test was designed; it would then be necessary to provide further machinery for discovering and stopping such loops.

145

to rearrange the symbols and to form new Plans. We have every reason to believe that man's verbal abilities are very intimately related to his planning abilities. And, because human Plans are so often verbal, they can be communicated, a fact of crucial importance in the evolution of our social adjustments to one another. . . .

J. Richard Suchman

The Child and the Inquiry Process

Man's ability to understand and control his environment depends on how well he has conceptualized it — how closely his conceptual systems correspond to reality. When one person tries to shape the concepts of another by talking to him or showing him something or giving him something to read, we call it teaching. When a person tries to promote these conceptual changes for himself by gathering and processing information, the activity becomes inquiry.

If man could not inquire, he could not gather and process data, raise and test hypotheses, build theories and test them empirically; all of his learning would have to be programed for him by others. Data would have to be fed to him, inferences would have to be drawn for him, and he would have to be told at every turn what conclusions could be drawn. In short, he would be totally dependent as a learner and a thinker. It is obvious therefore that being able to inquire is a necessary condition for the independence and autonomy of learning.

Inquiry is a fundamental form of learning. Long before the child begins formal education he is gathering data from his environment. The infant grasps a pot, picks it up, feels it, turns it over, puts blocks in it, dumps them out, and so forth. These interactions with the environment help to form intuitive schemata by which the

J. Richard Suchman, "The Child and the Inquiry Process," *Intellectual Development: Another Look*, ASCD 1964 Yearbook. Washington, D.C.: Association for Supervision and Curriculum Development, 1964. Reprinted with permission of the Association for Supervision and Curriculum Development and J. Richard Suchman. Copyright © 1969 by the Association for Supervision and Curriculum Development.

child begins to internalize the properties of his environment.

Assimilation and Accommodation

As he grows older, the child learns to become more systematic in his searching and in his collection and processing of data. As his conceptual systems become broader and more complex, the methods by which he acquires and organizes data become more sophisticated. As a result he is able to build more elaborate and accurate conceptual structures which reflect more closely the complexities of the real world.

In analyzing the act of inquiry it is helpful to think in terms of two basic processes. The first of these consists of taking in and incorporating what we perceive in terms of what we know and understand. We process data in terms of our conceptual systems. A child sees an object that has a wooden handle and a long metal blade attached to it. It looks to him very much like a knife. We can say that the child has assimilated his perception of the object in terms of a well established conceptual system related to knives. The process of assimilation goes on continuously as we encounter familiar objects, events and situations. As long as we have the appropriate conceptual categories and models, there is no conflict, and assimilation occurs without difficulty.

Supposing that when the object is held over a flame, the blade bends downward. If the child has had experience with objects that melt and slump downward as the result of melting, he can apply this model to the perceived event and still can *assimilate* this experience. Next we plunge the blade into a tank of water whereupon it straightens out to its original shape. Then we place the blade back over the flame in an inverted position, and this time it bends upward instead of downward. If the perceiver is a sixth grade child, it is very likely that this experience will come as something of a shock. He is now confronted by a *discrepant event*, one which he could not have predicted and is not able to explain within the framework of his existing conceptual models. He faces a dilemma in the form of an experience which he cannot *assimilate*. Moreover, before he is able to assimilate this experience he will have to learn more about the properties of the blade and the circumstances under which the bending took place. He may have to create a new conceptual model by combining parts of old models. If he has no teacher to engineer this conceptual reorganization for him through explanation and demonstration, he will have to do this for himself by experimenting and gathering data, by trying out various combinations of conceptual models, and testing each of these experimentally until he finally arrives at a point where he has a model that seems to match the event.

This process of reshaping and reorganizing conceptual structures until they fit and account for perceived events is known as *accommodation*. Inquiry involves both assimilation and accommodation in complementary roles. The inquirer, faced with a discrepant event, may first attempt to break it down into component parts, to analyze it in terms of variables which he has already conceptualized. In the case of the knife that is not a knife (it is actually a bimetallic strip), he may try to find out what the blade is made of or how it is put together. He may try to determine the changing temperature of the blade or the temperature of the water in the tank. He may wonder about the size and shape of the blade and try to find out more about changes in these conditions throughout the observed event. Through the process of analysis he may have obtained enough information about the event to assimilate it entirely. If he is aware of the fact that metals expand with increases in temperature, and the fact that two different metals may expand at different rates, and if, in

addition, he discovers that the blade is made of two different metals welded together, he may arrive at the hypothesis that the bending was caused by stresses produced by the differential expansion within the blade. Analysis of this kind paves the way for conceptual reorganization. Yet before the child is able to assimilate the event, he must pull together the results of his analysis. To these analyzed data he tries to apply various combinations of explanatory conceptual models until he has constructed one that seems to account for what he has perceived. Accommodation provides for the necessary restructuring of concepts that enables the child to assimilate formerly discrepant events.

Through the dual processes of assimilation and accommodation a person is able to build theories, test them, incorporate them within a broader conceptual system and use them in finding greater meaning and unity in experience.

Inquiry in Contrast to Engineered Learning

It is possible for a teacher to engineer conceptual reorganization in a child and to bring about the child's accommodation to discrepant events by programing a series of experiences, by drawing on past experiences, and by focusing attention through verbal instruction and exposition on selected aspects of his environment. In order to be effective in doing this, however, it is important for a teacher to be reasonably well acquainted with the existing conceptual structures of the learner and to keep a constant check on the conceptual modifications that are taking place at every step along the way. This is very difficult even when the teacher-pupil ratio is one-to-one. It of course becomes more difficult as the number of pupils increases.

When the mode of learning is inquiry, however, the process of data gathering, analysis and experimentation is under the control of the learner himself. He is free to reach out in whatever direction he chooses for data and to gather this information in whatever sequence is most meaningful to him. Through inquiry, the learner influences and actually programs his own learning in terms of his own cognitive needs as dictated by his style of learning and his informational needs of the moment.

To summarize thus far, inquiry can be regarded as a fundamental learning process, which is under the autonomous control of the learner and promotes conceptual growth through the dual and complementary functions of assimilation and accommodation.

Developmental Changes in Inquiry

The course of development of thinking, as described by Inhelder and Piaget (1958), moves from the highly egocentric, intuitive and concrete toward the more decentralized, analytical and abstract. There is no mode of mental activity in which these developmental trends are more evident than the process of inquiry. At a very early age this process is seen as taking the form of sensorimotor learning. This is the seemingly disorganized interaction with the environment through which the child builds a repertoire of intuitive schemata representing the properties of his environment. These schemata are by-products of his attempts to manipulate and control his environment. Later, during the preschool years, data gathering takes on a somewhat more organized form. This stage is called "preoperational" because the child is still concerned with producing an effect rather than seeing a relationship. As yet he is unable to see his manipulations as tentative and reversible. He does not regard them as operations that can be done and undone or as experiments that can be replicated.

Once the child crosses over into operational thinking, his inquiry takes on more of the character of research. He can subdivide his activity into separate operations and can examine the effects of each operation independently from that which precedes or follows it. He is therefore able to experiment in a somewhat controlled fashion. At first he performs only concrete operations, that is, he manipulates the environment directly and groups his findings in ways that are likely to yield new ideas and conceptual organizations. In looking for an explanation of the bimetal strip, he might try varying the temperature first in one direction and then in another and observing the consequences of these changes. From this information, he might hypothesize a systematic relationship between temperature and the bending of the blade.

As the child approaches adolescence he becomes capable of going beyond concrete operations to the point where he can manipulate ideas and propositions and test hypotheses through formal logical operations. Thus, while the child at the stage of concrete operations might discover through the manipulation of materials that a bimetal strip will bend only when two different metals are used, the adolescent who has arrived at the level of formal logical operations might be able to deduce this same conclusion logically:

The metals must bend because they are fixed to each other along a common surface. The area of one becomes greater than the area of the other because they expand at different rates. Some internal stress must be produced. The only configuration that would permit the common surface to remain unchanged while one metal becomes larger than the other would be that of concentric circles.

The formal logical process by which the adult arrives at the conclusion that the blade had to bend seems far removed from the almost random exploratory manipulations of the infant, but they are both forms of inquiry because the learner increases his understanding of his environment through *self-directed* actions. There are many important changes in the way the autonomy of the learner is translated into plans and actions, into strategies and schemata. The infant centers on objects and comes to sense their properties intuitively by playing with them. The older child seeks to control the objects of his environment and learns how his manipulations as causes correlate with outcomes as effects. In time he abstracts from observed relationships concepts of causality. Perhaps it is more accurate to say that he constructs or invents these conceptual models of causality. Yet they are shaped by the events that he creates through his operations. He produces the data he needs in shaping, trying out, testing and revising his conceptual models of the real world.

The mature mind can go one step further and test the validity of a construct or test a hypothesis logically, and completely bypass certain empirical or concrete operations.

Motivation of Inquiry

Throughout these changes in the *form* of inquiry, its motivational basis is subject to very little change. The motivation to inquire is rooted partly in the need to assimilate perceived objects and events. At all levels of inquiry we pursue meaning, that is, we seek to relate new experience to old conceptual structures. Regardless of the level of sophistication that the pursuit takes, the activity of gathering and processing information is exciting and pleasurable. The ability to assimilate discrepant events is intrinsically rewarding, and the construction of new conceptual models that enable one to find new meaning in old events creates in the learner a sense of power. These are satisfactions that result from the act of inquiring or its immediate consequences and serve to motivate learning when it occurs in the inquiry mode.

One of the by-products of recent investigations dealing with new methods of instruction in science, mathematics, and social studies has been the almost universal recognition by the researchers of a kind of motivation that was not found in the traditional learning situation. Bruner (1961) has been one of the most articulate in describing this phenomenon. These new teaching methods have all involved the more or less inductive approach in which new understandings come to light through a form of discovery by the individual learner. It was sensed by Bruner and others that the act of discovery had a number of highly desirable consequences not the least of which was a high level of motivation. He noted that discovery tended to produce much activity and interest, a sense of intellectual potency in the learner, an increasing faith in the regularity of the universe. This faith seemed to promote a feeling of confidence in the child that prompted him to pursue his learning activities in search of more and more of these regularities.

150

Just what is discovery? Is it a highly creative act that involves the sudden recognition of something very new and unique? Or is it simply the recognition of order in what formerly appeared to be chaos? The term is used in a great many ways so that now it seems to be unwise to use it to describe any particular cognitive act. Yet the sense of discovery, the "aha" feeling does seem to turn up only under certain circumstances. It seems to happen only when assimilation is finally achieved after it is first blocked. When the discrepant event is suddenly rendered assimilable through cognitive reorganization there is a release of tension and a feeling of satisfaction.

Here then is reward that is directly associated with the process of inquiry. So long as a child can believe that a new discovery can result from inquiry, he will inquire without any outside pressure to do so.

Yet is there a motivation entirely *intrinsic in the act* of inquiry itself? Is the expectation of closure a necessary condition for the motivation of search? Hunt (1962) suggests yet another motivating force. He calls it the "motivation inherent in information processing and action." What he is saying in effect is that we have a need for cognitive activity, a need that can be met only by the intake of data, the processing of it, the drawing of inferences from it and the making of decisions. Another way of saying this might be that we have the need to inquire, not because inquiry leads to the joyous experience of discovery but simply because inquiry itself is a highly satisfying and stimulating activity.

One may then raise the question that if Hunt is right, why do we not find our schools filled with inquirers gathering data and satisfying this need? One answer may be that inquiry would be the dominant mode of learning in the school except that we have done a highly effective job of preventing this from taking place by utilizing ego and social needs to motivate children to conform rather than to inquire, to store facts and generalizations rather than to search and discover for themselves. Perhaps it has been that by providing a climate hostile to inquiry we have succeeded in preventing this motivational force from promoting inquiry activity and permitting children to develop the skills of inquiry and the attitudes that lead to its use.

Alpert (1960) has addressed himself to the problem of motivating curiosity in the schools. He suggests that we do this by utilizing the child's dependency on the teacher for social support. According to his plan the teacher acts toward the child *as though* the child is a curious person. The purpose is to shape the child's self-concept so that he comes to see himself as curious and then begins to take on curious behavior to correspond with this new self-image.

The theoretical implications of such an approach are most interesting. Can one expect a person to become curious because he has come to see himself as a curious person? Can we get a child to alter his self-image simply by giving social reinforcement to a new image? Will any resulting behavior change persist when the teacher is no longer around to reinforce the new self-image? We do not have answers to these questions, but it does seem that a more direct approach to promoting curiosity in anybody is to confront him with an event or object that is *discrepant enough to make him curious* — to build up irresistible pressures in the child to find a way of assimilating the event. As Bruner and others point out, the child who attains new understandings for himself gains a sense of intellectual power (Bruner, 1961), mastery (White, 1959), or accomplishment (Erikson, 1950). The new self-image that results grows out of what the child knows he has actually done. He sees himself as a curious person and an autonomous inquirer because he *has been* curious and autonomous. Once this image is established it is likely to promote more of the same kind of behavior.

Inquiry and Cognitive Style

The element of autonomy that characterizes inquiry has special psychological significance for conceptual growth because it allows the learner to adapt the learning process to his immediate cognitive needs. These needs are in part a function of the way the learner thinks. Each learner has a style of conceptualization which strongly influences the mode by which he gathers, processes and uses data. In other words, because inquiry is a self-directed mode of learning, it permits the learner to adapt the process of learning to match his own particular style of thinking.

Jerome Kagan at the Fels Research Institute and Irving Sigel at the Merrill-Palmer Institute have sampled these styles through a variety of instruments designed to reflect the basis upon which a subject prefers to associate elements of his perceived environment. They have been able to distinguish two and possibly three fundamental styles. These styles can best be illustrated by a sample test item. A child is presented with a card on which appear three pictures — a garden, a rake and a fork. The child is asked to pick the two pictures that seem to go together and to give the reason for associating these two. If the child picks the rake and the garden because a rake is used in a garden, he is relying on past associations. He is linking together entities which have been contiguous in his experience. This style is called "relational" because linkages are made on the basis of directly observed relationships and do not require the use of conceptual systems or abstractions. The relational thinker does not stray too far from his perceptions and the associations that have grown out of them.

If the child says that the fork and the rake go together because they both have tines, he is making his association on the basis of a breakdown of perceived wholes into meaningful components. This style is called "descriptive-analytical" because the associations are formed through the analysis of experience. He has linked the fork and the rake on the basis of a component characteristic of each of them which he was able to respond to only because he had first dissociated the parts of both objects and then compared them in terms of one or more of these parts. The rational thinker is more likely to rely heavily on impressions while the analytical thinker tends to reflect on his precepts within a systematic framework of conceptual categories.

Kagan, Sigel and Moss (1961) found these styles to have consistency within individuals over time and over a wide range of cognitive tasks. Boys tend to be more analytical than girls, and both become less relational and more analytical with age.

These styles affect the inquiry process. Children show inquiry strategies that correspond to these cognitive styles. A study by Suchman and Kagan, not yet published, found that children with highly analytical styles of thinking tended to inquire more analytically, gathering data primarily for the purpose of analysis. The relational (low analytical) children were more inclined to form hypotheses based on impressions, bypassing the analytical process. The children selected inquiry strategies that best suited their styles of thinking. Further investigations of the relationship between cognitive styles and inquiry are now in progress.

Inquiry and Conceptual Growth

It is well-known that you can get a child to become aware of a relationship or principle by exposing him to enough situations where the principle is operant. In time he will abstract the concept or generalize over the experiences. If the instances are carefully selected, one can guide or engineer the discovery of new relationships. Beberman's (1958) and Hendrix's (1961) approach to teaching algebra is based on this. They take the position that there is little point in talking about, let us say, the commutative principle unless the pupils have almost an intuitive understanding of just what the principle is. Too often when this is taught through a verbal didactic method, the pupils acquire merely a superficial, mechanistic understanding. They know what they have to do to get the answer but they do not know *why*. Beberman's method literally engineers the students into discovering the principle themselves. His pupils are given a series of mathematical operations to perform which can be done with simple arithmetic. The problems are arranged in order of increasing difficulty in that the numbers get larger and more difficult to handle arithmetically. However, it is possible to discover a short-cut that simplifies the calculation. By discovering this short-cut, the pupil has discovered the algebraic principle.

Without the benefit of a carefully programed set of experiences, one must go through a less-directed series of operations to arrive at a given concept. Before arriving at such a concept one might have to construct a number of intermediate and inadequate solutions in a succession of conceptual reorganizations. Is there any advantage in such trial and error thinking?

Smedslund (1961) wondered about this and tried to determine whether the emerging concept is different in the one case in which it results from a simple generalization drawn from a set of positive instances and in the other case in which it is the end product of a series of conceptual reorganizations. He worked with preschool children and used the concept of the conservation of weight. He got one group of children to discover empirically that the weight of a plasticene ball does not change as its shape is modified. He contrasted this with another group whose members had come to internalize the concept of the conservation of weight through the natural processes by which such concepts become internalized (Piaget, 1941). He found that concepts that are easily formed by simple generalizations are more readily discarded when data are discrepant to the concept. But when the concepts result from the resolution of conflicts in successive accommodations as in the normal course of conceptual growth, a conceptual structure is not easily given up even in the face of a heavy weight of discrepant data. Smedslund sneaked a little piece of clay away from the plasticene ball so that the children would not know he had done this. He then changed the shape of the ball and weighed it for the children so that they could see that its weight had changed as the shape was changed. Those children who had formed the concept of the conservation of weight simply through the generalization over several positive instances were quite ready to give up this concept in the face of *one discrepant event*. The other group,

152

however, refused to accept the data as valid and raised rather strong doubts as to the honesty of the experimenter presenting the demonstration.

This suggests certain weaknesses in any learning situation in which the conceptual increments toward each new structure are pre-programed for speed and ease of learning. It almost seems that when conceptual structures are formed by outside agents that obviate the learner's own accommodative struggles, the new concept is not hard-won or self-structured. It is less a part of the learner, less useful to him (Festinger, 1957). He is therefore more willing to relinquish the concept if new data challenge its validity.

The step-by-step path toward conceptual growth is typical of most teacher-directed learning. The primary objective is the attainment of a new concept. This attainment is engineered by starting with the familiar and moving with or without discovery toward the unfamiliar with the purpose of assimilating this in the framework of existing structures. The assumption is that all learners begin with conceptual structures and cognitive styles that are enough alike to permit a standard sequence of operations (or lesson plan) to bring them to the same level of conceptualization.

Yet children's conceptual models differ enormously in structure. Take the relatively simple phenomenon of floating bodies. What makes an air bubble rise to the surface of a liquid? Some children have very diffuse notions that involve the "lightness of air" or the "tendency for gases to rise." Some believe that water pressure has something to do with it and that water pressure acts only in a downward direction. Some children understand the depth-pressure relationships in liquids, but fail to see this at all as related to gravity.

If a child is going to reorganize his concepts of floating or sinking, he will have to be able to proceed from where he is and not from some hypothetical point of ignorance. He must have the opportunity to try out his conceptual models by using them to design experiments and make predictions. He must be free to gather the data he needs to resolve his cognitive conflicts

until he has evolved a conceptual system that lets him assimilate what he sees. In short, a realistic approach to conceptual growth must allow the learner to gather and process data in accordance with his cognitive needs of the moment, and this suggests he should be utilizing some form of inquiry.

Means of Promoting Inquiry

There is a wide range of cognitive skills involved in the inquiry process. This includes the gathering, organizing and processing of data, the trying out of conceptual models, the restructuring of these models to accommodate to new data, and the testing of models for validity. At times it is necessary to use exacting methods of sampling, control and analysis. At other times a wild intuitive leap might be the operation most needed. There are broad strategies and special tactics that help to make inquiry more productive. The one most dependable characteristic of inquiry is that there is no one fixed method of operation. To build and strengthen inquiry skills, one would be hard-put in trying to identify a set of specific component skills that would have to be independently exercised and strengthened. Even if it were possible to make children more perceptive or flexible by giving them special exercises in this kind of activity, it is very doubtful whether such a piecemeal approach would make a significant difference in the inquiry of children.

The element of creativity seems to play an important role in the inquiry process. Both in searching for new data and in restructuring conceptual systems to accommodate to new data the inquirer must act creatively. Torrance (1962), Getzels and Jackson (1962), and Guilford (1952) have made notable advances in identifying the conditions that appear to affect the creative process. Torrance lists the following conditions as necessary "for the healthy functioning of the preconscious mental processes which produce creativity":

1. The absence of serious threat to the self, the willingness to risk
2. Self-awareness — in touch with one's feelings

153

3. Self-differentiation — sees self as being different from others
4. Both openness to the ideas of others and confidence in one's own perceptions of reality or in one's own ideas
5. Mutuality in interpersonal relations — balance between excessive quest for social relations and pathological rejection of them.

These conditions seem to center about the ego and suggest that creativity increases as the ego is freed from inhibition and external domination, yet stays open to the intake of ideas from the outside.

Getzels and Jackson lend further support to the notion that creativity is promoted more through environmental conditions than through specific training. I quote from their book:

> Without passing premature judgment on the possibility of some positive effects from special instruction, we hold that boldness in thinking, free reign to the imagination, and creativity in performance will not be easily coming through piecemeal lessons and artificial stimulants. What is needed is a change in the entire intellectual climate in which we — the parents and the teachers — as well as the children function.

The findings of these researches point to the significance of attitudes and climates. They speak of the positive effects of "intellectual playfulness on creativity." Quoting again:

> The relevant educational issue might well be: Are there certain areas of instruction in which opportunities are provided for "discovering" as well as for "remembering"? Is there provision in the curriculum for playing with facts and ideas as well as for repeating them? Can we teach students to be more sensitive to the nature of problems? Can we teach them that a problem may have several different interpretations and solutions? Even if there is only one right answer as in a mathematics problem, can a student solve the problem in a number of different ways?

The build-up of a given set of response patterns is a lot simpler to achieve than the promotion of creative thinking. In the case of the former, high pressure through strong and repeated reinforcements will generally have the desired effect. But high pressure has a way of interfering with creativity in forcing children to rely on stereotyped behavior. Creativity seems to occur

most readily under conditions of low pressure.

One aspect of climate received extensive treatment in the research of Bruner *et al.* (1958) as reported in A *Study of Thinking*. One of the more significant outcomes of these studies was the identification of several search and concept attainment strategies and the recognition of the fact that the kinds of strategies used by the subjects were determined in part by the "pay-off matrix." That is, the way the subjects went about gathering data was largely a function of the kinds of performances that were being rewarded. When speed was rewarded, the subjects took greater risks and adopted a gambling strategy to save time. They leaped in to test hypotheses that had a far less than 50–50 chance of being valid. They also started testing hypotheses after they had gathered only a small portion of the available data. But when the time pressure was off and accuracy and economy of operations were made the important criteria for success, the strategy shifted. Stress on the economy of operations encouraged some to try to retain a maximum amount of data in their heads, although cognitive strain of this kind was generally avoided. When freedom from error was an important success criterion, the subjects took a slower but safer route.

These findings suggest that inquiry strategies are flexible and can be adjusted to the demands of the problem situation. The so-called "scientific method" is not a fixed sequence of operations such as (a) "define the problem," (b) "formulate hypotheses," and (c) "gather data," etc. Scientists have reported that *their* methods vary widely according to *their* problems, just as the strategies of Bruner's subjects do.

MacKinnon (1961) also found no set patterns in the searching and thinking of highly creative architects and engineers. He concluded that:

> If the widest possible relationships among facts are to be established, if what I would call the structure of knowledge is to be grasped, it is necessary that the student have a large body of facts which he has learned, as well as a large array of reasoning skills which he has mastered. . . . A knowledgeable person in science is not merely one who has an

accumulation of facts, but rather one who has the capacity to have sport with what he knows, giving creative rein to his fancy in changing his world of phenomenal appearances into a world of scientific constructs.

Bearing in mind that the process of inquiry has a large creative component, yet cannot depart from the realm of logic and reason, we shall turn now to the problem of developing inquiry in the elementary school.

The Inquiry Training Project

The Inquiry Training Project (Suchman, 1960, 1961, 1962) came into being because it seemed that the process of inquiry is basic to all intellectual activity, and because our pilot studies showed that elementary school children at the level of the intermediate grades did not seem to be either willing or able to inquire productively even when they were faced with events that aroused their curiosity. When they did make attempts to obtain closure, these attempts were highly dependent in the sense that the children merely asked for explanations. Apparently they had been accustomed to having their conceptual growth engineered for them by teachers and did not know how to achieve this autonomously by asking questions to gather information.

Although it has been modified in many ways since the time of its inception in 1957, Inquiry Training still retains the same basic form with which it started. The children work as a group. A concrete problem is posed in the form of a motion picture film of a physics demonstration. This film is designed to puzzle the children. The event is not one which an elementary school child would easily explain simply by observing. Many of the critical variables, the nature of the materials used, the conditions of the materials and the changes in these conditions are not observable in the film and must be verified in other ways.

The children are asked to find out why the events in the filmed episode occurred. The problem posed to them is one of constructing an explanatory system. In order to gather the information that they need they must ask questions. We restrict them to questions that can be answered by "yes" or "no" to prevent them from falling back into the open-ended type of inquiry in which the responsibility for structuring is in the teacher's hands. The yes-or-no question forces the children to think through and structure their own questions.

Inquiry sessions last between 30 and 60 minutes and each one is based on a different problem film. In structuring the inquiry sessions we try to provide the following three conditions:

1. A *problem that is real and meaningful to the children,* a discrepant event that they are unable to assimilate because: (a) they have not fully analyzed the event in terms of all the relevant variables, and (b) because they do not have the necessary conceptual models to assimilate the event in the way that they initially perceive it. The problem therefore is one of having to analyze and accommodate before assimilation can take place.

2. The second condition is the *freedom* given the children to gather whatever data they want in whatever sequence they desire. No attempt is made to guide or program the data given to the children beyond what is presented within the film itself. This condition allows the individual child to search in whatever direction he wants in gathering data to satisfy his own cognitive needs.

3. The third condition is *a responsive environment.* We attempt to provide the information asked for by the children as promptly and as accurately as possible so that the inquiry process is not blocked by delays or frustrations.

No external reinforcements or pressures are built into the program. Inquiry is motivated primarily by the satisfactions intrinsic in the process itself. Part of this, we believe, is gained through the progress the children make toward greater understanding of the problem episode. The other part of the motivation comes from the excitement inherent in gathering and processing data. Of course, one cannot keep out ego and social motivation. Children ask questions to impress other children with what they know, and many are driven by the need to have the satisfaction of finding the "right answer." However, the teacher tries to protect the children from these and other extrinsic pressures to allow the satisfaction to grow out of the activities themselves and not to have it artificially generated by outside agents.

The inquiry sessions enable the children to learn some of the effects of various strategies of data gathering and processing. However, this awareness of the dimensions of the inquiry process and the logical structures that are used in the construction of explanatory systems can be developed more rapidly and effectively if the children's attention is brought back to the process of inquiry itself after they are no longer engaged in the science problem. A "critique" is given as a follow-up of the inquiry session. A tape recording of the inquiry session is played back to the children so that the group can observe the effects of various types and groupings of questions. In examining and evaluating their own question asking, the children are able to see many of the dimensions of strategy.

The inquiry sessions and the follow-up critique sessions fulfill the major requirements of Inquiry Training. The children have a series of experiences in attempting to construct explanatory models for observed events and have a way of reviewing, examining and analyzing their previous inquiries so that they can be more effective and planful in future inquiry sessions.

In the academic year of 1960–61, we conducted an experiment to determine the effects of Inquiry Training over a 24-week period (Suchman, 1962). Twelve teachers were especially trained over the summer and each week during the experiment they spent an hour providing Inquiry Training for a full classroom of children. Each school that had an Inquiry Training group also had a control group. The control groups were given the same science content through the same films used to pose the Inquiry Training problems, but no practice or critiques relating to inquiry itself were given.

Evaluation of Inquiry Training posed a problem. None of the standardized aptitude or achievement tests could measure the kinds of

changes Inquiry Training effects in the children. Of special concern were the changes in the inquiry process itself, in the willingness and ability of the children to gather data autonomously and to attempt to build explanatory models on their own. There was interest too in conceptual growth, not in how many facts and generalizations the children had stored and could report verbally, but in the actual change in the children's internalized structure of physical relationships.

We had to devise our own instruments and it was this problem that gave the study some of its biggest headaches. To measure these two kinds of outcomes, we constructed two very different kinds of tests.

The analysis of the inquiry process could only be based on a sample of the child's inquiry. The "Questest" was designed to obtain just such a sample. Special problem films were used. Each child was given the test individually. He was shown the test film and then given 25 minutes to ask questions to gather the data he needed and to construct his explanatory system. We tape-recorded these individual inquiry sessions and used the tape as the basis of our analysis of each child's inquiry behavior.

While we actually identified some 12 question types that could be clearly differentiated, it is more meaningful to point out the three major categories of questions. One of these was *verification*. This category included all questions that are attempts to identify and analyze the parameters of the problem episode; questions about the names of objects, the materials they were made out of, the conditions of objects such as temperature, pressure, shape, size; the events of the episode, and the properties of objects in the episode.

The second major question type was what we call the *implication* question. These questions are probes used to test out ideas of causal relationships. They go beyond the verification of what happened into the realm of why things happen. Implication questions have two important subdivisions. Some questions in this category are attempts to verify relationships between variables in a direct, abstract way. This

156

question type is called "abstract-conceptual." An example of this would be: "Does the bending of the blade have anything to do with the heat?" The question is, in effect, a direct request for the verification of an idea. Abstract-conceptual questions are requests for judgments about causation and therefore short-circuit the process of inquiry. Because the questioner obtains a direct evaluation of his hypothesis he avoids the necessity of testing the hypothesis experimentally, of gathering data and making his own inferences.

The second type of implication question is called "concrete-inferential." These questions are more like experiments. An example would be: "If we made the flame hotter, would the blade bend further?" In this case the child is manipulating a variable and simply asking if a particular outcome would be the result of his manipulation. But he makes his own inference as to causality from the data he obtains.

Our attempt in Inquiry Training was to increase the amount of verification and the amount of experimentation and to decrease the abstract-conceptual "brain-picking" kind of questioning.

In our analysis of the Questest protocols for the experimental and the control groups, we found first of all that in every case the inquiry-trained groups asked significantly more questions than the controls. It was necessary therefore to control for fluency in comparing the groups in terms of the frequencies of the major question types. We found that where fluency was high the inquiry-trained groups asked significantly more verification questions than the controls and significantly less abstract-conceptual implication questions than the controls. There was no noticeable difference between the two groups in the use of experimentation.

With respect to conceptual growth, our finding was that in most cases conceptual growth through the inquiry approach was about the same as the growth attained under the more traditional didactic methods. We did have two groups, however, in which the inquiry-trained children had significantly higher scores on the concept test than the control children.

Of course, the real test of Inquiry Training would be the degree to which a child is able to transfer his inquiry skills to problems in other content areas. If inquiry is a mode of behavior and can be developed and strengthened through practice and through the deliberate shaping of strategies and techniques, then this behavior should be applicable in a wide range of problem situations.

We are now engaged in an investigation to test the transfer effects of Inquiry Training. New problem films are now being developed in economics and biology. Sometime next year we will give a group of sixth grade children Inquiry Training using our physics films and then determine how effective they are in solving economics and biology problems through the inquiry approach.

Implications for Curriculum

We do not see the specific techniques and methodology of Inquiry Training as we have used it thus far as the significant outcome of our work. We have been far more concerned with the theoretical implications of our findings. What has impressed us most in our observation of the inquiry process is that the autonomy of the learner has enormous importance for both motivation and conceptual growth. Take away from the child the element of choice in the learning process and you destroy one of the most potent forces for keeping the child involved in learning and for giving him an opportunity to influence the course of his own learning. Self-direction in learning is not a case of the blind leading the blind because the learner is in a position to know the nature and the location of his conceptual gaps. He is sensitive to his own informational needs. If he is not given an opportunity to modify and at least to some extent to direct his own data intake, his learning experiences may well miss the mark by a wide margin.

We have just begun to explore the possibilities of introducing the inquiry approach and Inquiry Training into the curriculum. This approach should not be brought in as a thing apart from "regular subjects," as a "gimmick" or special shot in the arm. Possibly what is needed is an inquiry-centered curriculum in which the children would find themselves launched into areas of study by first being confronted by concrete problem-focused episodes for which they would attempt to build explanatory systems. Part of their data gathering might well be in the question-asking mode and certainly along the way time would have to be spent in building inquiry skills through critiques and other such procedures. Yet there would also be room for helping the children enlarge their conceptual systems through more teacher-directed means. At times the teacher might work with groups in developing new conceptual models or in identifying variables that might be useful for analysis of the problem episode. Of course, the children would still be using the library and other materials, but always in relation to a particular problem of inquiry. Learning would always be in connection with moving from concrete events toward the construction of an explanatory model. Yet neither the analysis of the concrete events nor the particular models constructed to explain them would be the most important outcome of these inquiries. There would be three and possibly more by-products that would have far greater significance.

First there would be the development and strengthening of the inquiry process itself. Since learning would always be couched within the inquiry framework, the children would become more autonomous learners and their motivation in the process of learning would be greater. The second by-product would be the self-image that would develop in the children as a result of a greater autonomy in learning. The children would emerge with a sense of intellectual potency and a faith in the regularity of the universe and a greater skepticism toward any explanatory system as a final and ultimate truth. They would learn to question and test and to see themselves as able to move from data to theory under their own power. This should boost their self-confidence for making further inquiries and for resisting efforts by others to program them into accepting a predetermined conclusion.

A third consequence of such a curriculum would be the development of a greater depth of understanding of principles and concepts within the disciplines of study relevant to the problems posed for inquiry. The child who inquires into the bimetallic strip can never emerge with a complete explanation of the events observed, but he can come to grips with such fundamental physical principles as conduction, the theory of molecular structure, the relationship between volume and temperature in matter, the principles governing stress and strain in metals. In Bruner's terms he will penetrate the structures of the disciplines concerned and become rather intimately involved with some segments of those structures.

Finally, the inquiry-centered curriculum would break away from the rhetoric of conclusions which now dominates so much of the curriculum and would put the process and products of scientific inquiry back into their proper relationship.

References

R. Alpert. *The Shaping of Motives in Education.* Speech prepared for the Fifth ASCD Curriculum Research Institute, 1960.

M. Beberman. *An Emerging Program of Secondary School Mathematics.* Cambridge: Harvard University Press, 1958.

J. S. Bruner *et al. A Study of Thinking.* New York: John Wiley & Sons, 1958.

J. S. Bruner. "The Act of Discovery." *Harvard Educational Review* 31: 21–32; 1961.

E. Erikson. *Childhood and Society.* New York: W. W. Norton & Company, Inc., 1950.

L. Festinger. *A Theory of Cognitive Dissonance.* Evanston. Illinois: Row, Peterson & Company, 1957.

J. W. Getzels and P. W. Jackson. *Creativity and Intelligence.* New York: John Wiley & Sons, 1962.

J. P. Guilford *et al.* "A Factor-analytic Study of Creative Thinking." *Reports from the Psychology Laboratory.* Los Angeles: University of Southern California Press, 1952.

Gertrude Hendrix. "Learning by Discovery." *Mathematics Teacher* 54: 290–99; 1961.

J. McV. Hunt. *Piaget's Observations as a Source of*

Hypotheses Concerning Motivation. Paper read at the Annual Meeting, American Psychological Association, 1962.

Bärbel Inhelder and J. Piaget. *The Growth of Logical Thinking from Childhood to Adolescence.* New York: Basic Books, 1958.

J. Kagan, H. Moss, and I. Sigel. *The Psychological Significance of Styles of Conceptualization.* A paper read at a Conference on Basic Cognitive Processes sponsored by the Social Science Research Council, 1961.

D. MacKinnon. "Fostering Creativity in Students of Engineering." *Journal of Engineering Education* 52: 129–42; 1961.

J. Piaget and Bärbel Inhelder. *Le Développement des Quantités chez L'Enfant.* Dalachaux et Niestle, 1941.

Jan Smedslund. "The Acquisition of Conservation of Substance and Weight in Children." *Scandinavian Journal of Psychology* 2: 11–20, 85–87; 1961.

J. R. Suchman. "Inquiry Training in the Elementary School." *Science Teacher* 27 (7): 42–47; 1960.

J. R. Suchman. "Inquiry Training: Building Skills for Autonomous Discovery." *Merrill-Palmer Quarterly* 7: 147–69; 1961.

J. R. Suchman. *The Elementary School Training Program in Scientific Inquiry.* Illinois Studies in Inquiry Training. Urbana: University of Illinois, 1962. (Mimeographed.)

E. P. Torrance. *Guiding Creative Talent.* Englewood Cliffs, New Jersey: Prentice-Hall, Inc., 1962.

R. W. White. "Motivation Reconsidered: The Concept of Competence." *Psychological Review* 66: 297–333; 1959.

Jerome S. Bruner

The Act of Discovery

Maimonides, in his *Guide for the Perplexed*,[1] speaks of four forms of perfection that men might seek. The first and lowest form is perfection in the acquisition of worldly goods. The great philosopher dismisses such perfection on the ground that the possessions one acquires bear no meaningful relation to the possessor: "A great king may one morning find that there is no difference between him and the lowest person." A second perfection is of the body, its conformation and skills. Its failing is that it does not reflect on what is uniquely human about man: "he could [in any case] not be as strong as a mule." Moral perfection is the third, "the highest degree of excellency in man's character." Of this perfection Maimonides says: "Imagine a person being alone, and having no connection whatever with any other person; all his good moral principles are at rest, they are not required and give man no perfection whatever. These principles are only necessary and useful when man comes in contact with others." "The fourth kind of perfection is the true perfection of man; the possession of the highest intellectual faculties. . . ." In justification of his assertion, this extraordinary Spanish-Judaic philosopher urges: "Examine the first three kinds of perfection; you will find that if you possess them, they are not your property, but the property of others. . . . But the last kind of perfec-

Jerome S. Bruner, "The Act of Discovery," *Harvard Educational Review*, XXXI, 1 (Winter 1961), pp. 21–32. Copyright © 1961 President and Fellows of Harvard College. Reprinted by permission.

[1] Maimonides, *Guide for the Perplexed* (New York: Dover Publications, 1956).

160

tion is exclusively yours; no one else owns any part of it."

It is a conjecture much like that of Maimonides that leads me to examine the act of discovery in man's intellectual life. For if man's intellectual excellence is the most his own among his perfections, it is also the case that the most uniquely personal of all that he knows is that which he has discovered for himself. What difference does it make, then, that we encourage discovery in the learning of the young? Does it, as Maimonides would say, create a special and unique relation between knowledge possessed and the possessor? And what may such a unique relation do for a man — or for a child, if you will, for our concern is with the education of the young?

The immediate occasion for my concern with discovery — and I do not restrict discovery to the act of finding out something that before was unknown to mankind, but rather include all forms of obtaining knowledge for oneself by the use of one's own mind — the immediate occasion is the work of the various new curriculum projects that have grown up in America during the last six or seven years. For whether one speaks to mathematicians or physicists or historians, one encounters repeatedly an expression of faith in the powerful effects that come from permitting the student to put things together for himself, to be his own discoverer.

First, let it be clear what the act of discovery entails. It is rarely, on the frontier of knowledge or elsewhere, that new facts are "discovered" in the sense of being encountered as Newton suggested in the form of islands of truth in an uncharted sea of ignorance. Or if they appear to be discovered in this way, it is almost always thanks to some happy hypotheses about where to navigate. Discovery, like surprise, favors the well prepared mind. In playing bridge, one is surprised by a hand with no honors in it at all and also by hands that are all in one suit. Yet all hands in bridge are equiprobable: one must know to be surprised. So too in discovery. The history of science is studded with examples of men "finding out" something and not knowing it. I shall operate on the assumption that discovery, whether by a schoolboy going it on his own or by a scientist cultivating the growing edge of his field, is in its essence a matter of rearranging or transforming evidence in such a way that one is enabled to go beyond the evidence so reassembled to additional new insights. It may well be that an additional fact or shred of evidence makes this larger transformation of evidence possible. But it is often not even dependent on new information.

It goes without saying that, left to himself, the child will go about discovering things for himself within limits. It also goes without saying that there are certain forms of child rearing, certain home atmospheres that lead some children to be their own discoverers more than other children. These are both topics of great interest, but I shall not be discussing them. Rather, I should like to confine myself to the consideration of discovery and "finding-out-for-oneself" within an educational setting — specifically the school. Our aim as teachers is to give our student as firm a grasp of a subject as we can, and to make him as autonomous and self-propelled a thinker as we can — one who will go along on his own after formal schooling has ended. I shall return in the end to the question of the kind of classroom and the style of teaching that encourages an attitude of wanting to discover. For purposes of orienting the discussion, however, I would like to make an overly simplified distinction between teaching that takes place in the *expository mode* and teaching that utilizes the *hypothetical mode*. In the former, the decisions concerning the mode and pace and style of exposition are principally de-termined by the teacher as expositor; the student is the listener. If I can put the matter in terms of structural linguistics, the speaker has a quite different set of decisions to make than the listener: the former has a wide choice of alternatives for structuring, he is anticipating paragraph content while the listener is still intent on the words, he is manipulating the content of the material by various transformations, while the listener is quite unaware of these internal manipulations. In the hypothetical mode, the teacher and the student are in a more coopera-tive position with respect to what in linguistics would be called "speaker's decisions." The stu-dent is not a bench-bound listener, but is tak-ing a part in the formulation and at times may play the principal role in it. He will be aware of alternatives and may even have an "as if" atti-tude toward these and, as he receives informa-tion he may evaluate it as it comes. One cannot describe the process in either mode with great precision as to detail, but I think the foregoing may serve to illustrate what is meant.

Consider now what benefit might be derived from the experience of learning through discov-eries that one makes for oneself. I should like to discuss these under four headings: (1) The in-crease in intellectual potency, (2) the shift from extrinsic to intrinsic rewards, (3) learning the heuristics of discovering, and (4) the aid to memory processing.

1. Intellectual Impotency

If you will permit me, I would like to consider the difference between subjects in a highly con-strained psychological experiment involving a two-choice apparatus. In order to win chips, they must depress a key either on the right or the left side of the machine. A pattern of payoff is designed such that, say, they will be paid off on the right side 70% of the time, on the left 30%, although this detail is not important. What is important is that the payoff sequence is arranged at random, and there is no pattern. I should like to contrast the behavior of subjects who think that there *is* some pattern to be found in the sequence — who think that regularities are discoverable — in contrast to subjects who think that things are happening quite by *chance*. The former group adopts what is called an "event-matching" strategy in which the number of responses given to each side is roughly equal to the proportion of times it pays off: in the present case R70: L30. The group that believes there is no pattern very soon reverts to a much more primitive strategy wherein *all* responses are allocated to the side that has the greater payoff. A little arithmetic will show you that the lazy all-and-none strategy pays off more if indeed the environment is random: namely, they win seventy per cent of the time. The event-matching subjects win about 70% on the 70% payoff side (or 49% of the time there) and 30% of the time on the side that pays off 30% of the time (another 9% for a total take-home wage of 58% in return for their labors of decision). But the world is not always or not even frequently random, and if one analyzes carefully what the event-matchers are doing, it turns out that they are trying out hypotheses one after the other, all of them containing a term such that they distribute bets on the two sides with a frequency to match the actual occurrence of events. If it should turn out that there is a pattern to be discovered, their payoff would become 100%. The other group would go on at the middling rate of 70%.

What has this to do with the subject at hand? For the person to search out and find regularities and relationships in his environment, he must be armed with an expectancy that there will be something to find and, once aroused by expectancy, he must devise ways of searching and finding. One of the chief enemies of such expectancy is the assumption that there is nothing one can find in the environment by way of regularity or relationship. In the experiment just cited, subjects often fall into a habitual attitude that there is either nothing to be found or that they can find a pattern by looking. There is an important sequel in behavior to the two attitudes, and to this I should like to turn now.

We have been conducting a series of experimental studies on a group of some seventy school children over the last four years. The studies have led us to distinguish an interesting dimension of cognitive activity that can be described as ranging from *episodic empiricism* at one end to *cumulative constructionism* at the other. The two attitudes in the choice experiments just cited are illustrative of the extremes of the dimension. I might mention some other illustrations. One of the experiments employs the game of Twenty Questions. A child — in this case he is between 10 and 12 — is told that a car has gone off the road and hit a tree. He is to ask questions that can be answered by "yes" or "no" to discover the cause of the accident. After completing the problem, the same task is given him again, though he is told that the accident had a different cause this time. In all, the procedure is repeated four times. Children enjoy playing the game. They also differ quite markedly in the approach or strategy they bring to the task. There are various elements in the strategies employed. In the first place, one may distinguish clearly between two types of questions asked: the one is designed for locating constraints in the problem, constraints that will eventually give shape to an hypothesis; the other is the hypothesis as question. It is the difference between, "Was there anything wrong with the driver?" and "Was the driver rushing to the doctor's office for an appointment and the car got out of control?" There are children who precede hypotheses with efforts to locate constraint and there are those who, to use our local slang, are "pot-shotters," who string out hypotheses non-cumulatively one after the other. A second element of strategy is its connectivity of information gathering: the extent to which questions asked utilize or ignore or violate information previously obtained. The questions asked by children tend to be organized in cycles, each cycle of questions usually being given over to the pursuit of some particular notion. Both within cycles and between cycles one can discern a marked difference in the connectivity of the child's performance. Needless to say, children who employ constraint location as a technique preliminary to the formulation of hypotheses tend to be far more connected in their harvesting of information. Persistence is another feature of strategy, a characteristic compounded of what appear to be two components: a sheer doggedness component, and a persistence that stems from the sequential organization that a child brings to the task. Doggedness is probably just animal spirit or the need for achievement — what has come to be called *n-ach*. Organized persistence is a maneuver for protecting our fragile cognitive apparatus from overload. The child who has flooded himself with disorganized information from unconnected hypotheses will become discouraged and confused sooner than the child who has shown a certain cunning in his strategy of getting information — a cunning whose principal component is the recognition that the value of information is not simply in getting it but in being able to carry it. The persistence of the organized child stems from his knowledge of how to organize questions in cycles, how to summarize things to himself, and the like.

Episodic empiricism is illustrated by information gathering that is unbound by prior constraints, that lacks connectivity, and that is deficient in organizational persistence. The opposite extreme is illustrated by an approach that is characterized by constraint sensitivity, by connective maneuvers, and by organized persistence. Brute persistence seems to be one of those gifts from the gods that make people more exaggeratedly what they are.[2]

Before returning to the issue of discovery and its role in the development of thinking, let me say a word more about the ways in which information may get transformed when the problem solver has actively processed it. There is first of all a pragmatic question: what does it take to get information processed into a form best designed to fit some future use? Take an experiment by Zajonc[3] as a case in point. He gives groups of subjects information of a controlled kind, some groups being told that their task is to transmit the information to others, others that it is merely to be kept in mind. In general, he finds more differentiation and organization of the information received with the intention of being transmitted than there is for information received passively. An active set leads to a transformation related to a task to be performed. The risk, to be sure, is in possible overspecialization of information processing that may lead to such a high degree of specific organization that information is lost for general use.

I would urge now in the spirit of an hypothesis that emphasis upon discovery in learning has precisely the effect upon the learner of leading him to be a constructionist, to organize what he is encountering in a manner not only designed to discover regularity and relatedness, but also to avoid the kind of information drift that fails to keep account of the uses to which information might have to be put. It is, if you will, a necessary condition for learning the variety of techniques of problem solving, of transforming information for better use, indeed for learning how to go about the very task of learning. Practice in discovering for oneself teaches one to acquire information in a way that makes that information more readily viable in problem solving. So goes the hypothesis. It is still in need of testing. But it is an hypothesis of such important human implications that we cannot afford not to test it — and testing will have to be in the schools.

2. Intrinsic and Extrinsic Motives

Much of the problem in leading a child to effective cognitive activity is to free him from the immediate control of environmental rewards and punishments. That is to say, learning that starts in response to the rewards of parental or

---

[2] I should also remark in passing that the two extremes also characterize concept attainment strategies as reported in *A Study of Thinking* by J. S. Bruner *et al.* (New York: J. Wiley, 1956). Successive scanning illustrates well what is meant here by eposodic empiricism; conservative focusing is an example of cumulative constructionism.

[3] R. B. Zajonc (Personal communication, 1957).

163

teacher approval or the avoidance of failure can too readily develop a pattern in which the child is seeking cues as to how to conform to what is expected of him. We know from studies of children who tend to be early over-achievers in school that they are likely to be seekers after the "right way to do it" and that their capacity for transforming their learning into viable thought structures tends to be lower than children merely achieving at levels predicted by intelligence tests. Our tests on such children show them to be lower in analytic ability than those who are not conspicuous in overachievement.[4] As we shall see later, they develop rote abilities and depend upon being able to "give back" what is expected rather than to make it into something that relates to the rest of their cognitive life. As Maimonides would say, their learning is not their own.

The hypothesis that I would propose here is that to the degree that one is able to approach learning as a task of discovering something rather than "learning about" it, to that degree will there be a tendency for the child to carry out his learning activities with the autonomy of self-reward or, more properly by reward that is discovery itself.

To those of you familiar with the battles of the last half-century in the field of motivation, the above hypothesis will be recognized as controversial. For the classic view of motivation in learning has been, until very recently, couched in terms of a theory of drives and reinforcement: that learning occurred by virtue of the fact that a response produced by a stimulus was followed by the reduction in a primary drive state. The doctrine is greatly extended by the idea of secondary reinforcement: any state associated even remotely with the reduction of a primary drive could also have the effect of producing learning. There has recently appeared a most searching and important criticism of this

position, written by Professor Robert White,[5] reviewing the evidence of recently published animal studies, of work in the field of psychoanalysis, and of research on the development of cognitive processes in children. Professor White comes to the conclusion, quite rightly I think, that the drive-reduction model of learning runs counter to too many important phenomena of learning and development to be either regarded as general in its applicability or even correct in its general approach. Let me summarize some of his principal conclusions and explore their applicability to the hypothesis stated above.

I now propose that we gather the various kinds of behavior just mentioned, all of which have to do with effective interaction with the environment, under the general heading of competence. According to Webster, competence means fitness or ability, and the suggested synonyms include capability, capacity, efficiency, proficiency, and skill. It is therefore a suitable word to describe such things as grasping and exploring, crawling and walking, attention and perception, language and thinking, manipulating and changing the surroundings, all of which promote an effective — a competent — interaction with the environment. It is true of course, that maturation plays a part in all these developments, but this part is heavily overshadowed by learning in all the more complex accomplishments like speech or skilled manipulation. I shall argue that it is necessary to make competence a motivational concept; there is *competence motivation* as well as competence in its more familiar sense of achieved capacity. The behavior that leads to the building up of effective grasping, handling, and letting go of objects, to take one example, is not random behavior that is produced by an overflow of energy. It is directed, selective, and persistent, and it continues not because it serves primary drives, which indeed it cannot serve until it is almost perfected, but because it satisfies an intrinsic need to deal with the environment. [6]

I am suggesting that there are forms of activity that serve to enlist and develop the compe-

[4] J. S. Bruner and A. J. Caron, "Cognition, Anxiety, and Achievement in the Pre-adolescent," *Journal of Educational Psychology* (in press).

[5] R. W. White, "Motivation Reconsidered: The Concept of Competence," *Psychological Review*, LXVI (1959), pp. 297–333.
[6] *Ibid.*, pp. 317–18.

tence motive, that serve to make it the driving force behind behavior. I should like to add to White's general premise that the *exercise* of competence motives has the effect of strengthening the degree to which they gain control over behavior and thereby reduce the effects of extrinsic rewards or drive gratification.

The brilliant Russian psychologist Vygotsky[7] characterizes the growth of thought processes as starting with a dialogue of speech and gesture between child and parent; autonomous thinking begins at the stage when the child is first able to internalize these conversations and "run them off" himself. This is a typical sequence in the development of competence. So too in instruction. The narrative of teaching is of the order of the conversation. The next move in the development of competence is the internalization of the narrative and its "rules of generation" so that the child is now capable of running off the narrative on his own. The hypothetical mode in teaching by encouraging the child to participate in "speaker's decisions" speeds this process along. Once internalization has occurred, the child is in a vastly improved position from several obvious points of view — notably that he is able to go beyond the information he has been given to generate additional ideas that can either be checked immediately from experience or can, at least, be used as a basis for formulating reasonable hypotheses. But over and beyond that, the child is now in a position to experience success and failure not as a reward and punishment, but as information. For when the task is his own rather than a matter of matching environmental demands, he becomes his own paymaster in a certain measure. Seeking to gain control over his environment, he can now treat success as indicating that he is on the right track, failure as indicating he is on the wrong one.

In the end, this development has the effect of freeing learning from immediate stimulus control. When learning in the short run leads only to pellets of this or that rather than to mastery in the long run, then behavior can be readily "shaped" by extrinsic rewards. When behavior becomes more long-range and competence-oriented, it comes under the control of more complex cognitive structures, plans and the like, and operates more from the inside out. It is interesting that even Pavlov, whose early account of the learning process was based entirely on a notion of stimulus control of behavior through the conditioning mechanism in which, through contiguity a new conditioned stimulus was substituted for an old unconditioned stimulus by the mechanism of stimulus substitution, that even Pavlov recognized his account as insufficient to deal with higher forms of learning. To supplement the account, he introduced the idea of the "second signalling system," with central importance placed on symbolic systems such as language in mediating and giving shape to mental life. Or as Luria[8] has put it, "the first signal system [is] concerned with directly perceived stimuli, the second with systems of verbal elaboration." Luria, commenting on the importance of the transition from first to second signal system, says: "It would be mistaken to suppose that verbal intercourse with adults merely changes the contents of the child's conscious activity without changing its form. . . . The word has a basic function not only because it indicates a corresponding object in the external world, but also because it abstracts, isolates the necessary signal, generalizes perceived signals and relates them to certain categories; it is this systematization of direct experience that makes the role of the word in the formation of mental processes so exceptionally important."[9, 10]

[7] L. S. Vygotsky, *Thinking and Speech* (Moscow, 1934).

[8] A. L. Luria, "The Directive Function of Speech in Development and Dissolution," *Word*, XV (1959), pp. 341–464.

[9] *Ibid.*, p. 12.

[10] For an elaboration of the view expressed by Luria, the reader is referred to the forthcoming translation of L. S. Vygotsky's 1934 book being published by John Wiley and Sons and the Technology Press.

It is interesting that the final rejection of the universality of the doctrine of reinforcement in direct conditioning came from some of Pavlov's own students. Ivanov-Smolensky[11] and Krasnogorsky[12] published papers showing the manner in which symbolized linguistic messages could take over the place of the unconditioned stimulus and of the unconditioned response (gratification of hunger) in children. In all instances, they speak of these as *replacements* of lower, first-system mental or neural processes by higher order or second-system controls. A strange irony, then, that Russian psychology that gave us the notion of the conditioned responses and the assumption that higher order activities are built up out of colligations or structurings of such primitive units, rejected this notion while much of American learning psychology has stayed until quite recently within the early Pavlovian fold (see, for example, a recent article by Spence[13] in the *Harvard Educational Review* or Skinner's treatment of language[14] and the attacks that have been made upon it by linguists such as Chomsky[15] who have become concerned with the relation of language and cognitive activity). What is more interesting is that Russian pedagogical theory has become deeply influenced by this new trend and is now placing much stress upon the importance of building up a more active symbolical approach to problem solving among children.

To sum up the matter of the control of learning, then, I am proposing that the degree to which competence or mastery motives come to control behavior, to that degree the role of reinforcement or "extrinsic pleasure" wanes in shaping behavior. The child comes to manipulate his environment more actively and achieves his gratification from coping with problems. Symbolic modes of representing and transforming the environment arise and the importance of stimulus-response-reward sequences declines. To use the metaphor that David Riesman developed in a quite different context, mental life moves from a state of outer-directedness in which the fortuity of stimuli and reinforcement are crucial to a state of inner-directedness in which the growth and maintenance of mastery become central and dominant.

3. Learning the Heuristics of Discovery

Lincoln Steffens,[16] reflecting in his *Autobiography* on his undergraduate education at Berkeley, comments that his schooling was overly specialized on learning about the known and that too little attention was given to the task of finding out about what was not known. But how does one train a student in the techniques of discovery? Again I would like to offer some hypotheses. There are many ways of coming to the arts of inquiry. One of them is by careful study of its formalization in logic, statistics, mathematics, and the like. If a person is going to pursue inquiry as a way of life, particularly in the sciences, certainly such study is essential. Yet, whoever has taught kindergarten and the early primary grades or has had graduate students working with him on their theses — I choose the two extremes for they are both periods of intense inquiry — knows that an understanding of the formal aspect of inquiry is not sufficient. There appear to be, rather, a series of activities and attitudes, some directly related to a particular subject and some of them fairly generalized, that go with inquiry and research. These have to do with the *process* of trying to find out something and while they provide no guarantee that the *product* will be any *great* discovery, their absence is likely to lead to awk-

[11] A. G. Ivanov-Smolensky, "Concerning the Study of the Joint Activity of the First and Second Signal Systems," *Journal of Higher Nervous Activity*, I (1951), 1.

[12] N. D. Krasnogorsky, *Studies of Higher Nervous Activity in Animals and in Man*, Vol. I (Moscow, 1954).

[13] K. W. Spence, "The Relation of Learning Theory to the Technique of Education," *Harvard Educational Review*, XXIX (1959), pp. 84–95.

[14] B. F. Skinner, *Verbal Behavior* (New York: Appleton-Century-Crofts, 1957).

[15] N. Chomsky, *Syntactic Structure* (The Hague, The Netherlands: Mouton & Co., 1957).

[16] L. Steffens, *Autobiography of Lincoln Steffens* (New York: Harcourt, Brace, 1931).

wardness or aridity or confusion. How difficult it is to describe these matters — the heuristics of inquiry. There is one set of attitudes or ways of doing that has to do with sensing the relevance of variables — how to avoid getting stuck with edge effects and getting instead to the big sources of variance. Partly this gift comes from intuitive familiarity with a range of phenomena, sheer "knowing the stuff." But it also comes out of a sense of what things among an ensemble of things "smell right" in the sense of being of the right order of magnitude or scope or severity.

The English philosopher Weldon describes problem solving in an interesting and picturesque way. He distinguishes between difficulties, puzzles, and problems. We solve a problem or make a discovery when we impose a puzzle form onto a difficulty that converts it into a problem that can be solved in such a way that it gets us where we want to be. That is to say, we recast the difficulty into a form that we know how to work with, then work it. Much of what we speak of as discovery consists of knowing how to impose what kind of form on various kinds of difficulties. A small part but a crucial part of discovery of the highest order is to invent and develop models or "puzzle forms" that can be imposed on difficulties with good effect. It is in this area that the truly powerful mind shines. But it is interesting to what degree perfectly ordinary people can, given the benefit of instruction, construct quite interesting and what, a century ago, would have been considered greatly original models.

Now to the hypothesis. It is my hunch that it is only through the exercise of problem solving and the effort of discovery that one learns the working heuristic of discovery, and the more one has practice, the more likely is one to generalize what one has learned into a style of problem solving or inquiry that serves for any kind of task one may encounter — or almost any kind of task. I think the matter is self-evident, but what is unclear is what kinds of training and teaching produce the best effects. How do we teach a child to say, cut his losses but at the same time be persistent in trying out an idea; to

risk forming an early hunch without at the same time formulating one *so* early and with so little evidence as to be stuck with it waiting for appropriate evidence to materialize; to pose good testable guesses that are neither too brittle nor too sinuously incorrigible; etc., etc. Practice in inquiry, in trying to figure out things for oneself is indeed what is needed, but in what form? Of only one thing I am convinced. I have never seen anybody improve in the art and technique of inquiry by any means other than engaging in inquiry.

4. Conservation of Memory

I should like to take what some psychologists might consider a rather drastic view of the memory process. It is a view that in large measure derives from the work of my colleague, Professor George Miller.[17] Its first premise is that the principal problem of human memory is not storage, but retrieval. In spite of the biological unlikeliness of it, we seem to be able to store a huge quantity of information — perhaps not a full tape recording, though at times it seems we even do that, but a great sufficiency of impressions. We may infer this from the fact that recognition (i.e., recall with the aid of maximum prompts) is so extraordinarily good in human beings — particularly in comparison with spontaneous recall where, so to speak, we must get out stored information without external aids or prompts. The key to retrieval is organization or, in even simpler terms, knowing where to find information and how to get there.

Let me illustrate the point with a simple experiment. We present pairs of words to twelve-year-old children. One group is simply told to remember the pairs, that they will be asked to repeat them later. Another is told to remember them by producing a word or idea that will tie the pair together in a way that will make sense to them. A third group is given the mediators used by the second group when presented with the pairs to aid them in trying the pairs into

---

[17] G. A. Miller, "The Magical Number Seven, Plus or Minus Two," *Psychological Review*, LXIII (1956), pp. 81–97.

working units. The word pairs include such juxtapositions as "chair-forest," "sidewalk-square," and the like. One can distinguish three styles of mediators and children can be scaled in terms of their relative preference for each: *generic mediation* in which a pair is tied together by a superordinate idea: "chair and forest are both made of wood"; *thematic mediation* in which the two terms are imbedded in a theme or little story: "the lost child sat on a chair in the middle of the forest"; and *part-whole mediation* where "chairs are made from trees in the forest" is typical. Now, the chief result, as you would all predict, is that children who provide their own mediators do best — indeed, one time through a set of thirty pairs, they recover up to 95% of the second words when presented with the first ones of the pairs, whereas the uninstructed children reach a maximum of less than 50% recovered. Interestingly enough, children do best in recovering materials tied together by the form of mediator they most often use.

One can cite a myriad of findings to indicate that any organization of information that reduces the aggregate complexity of material by imbedding it into a cognitive structure a person has constructed will make that material more accessible for retrieval. In short, we may say that the process of memory, looked at from the retrieval side, is also a process of problem solving: how can material be "placed" in memory so that it can be got on demand?

We can take as a point of departure the example of the children who developed their own technique for relating the members of each word pair. You will recall that they did better than the children who were given by exposition the mediators they had developed. Let me suggest that in general, material that is organized in terms of a person's own interests and cognitive structures is material that has the best chance of being accessible in memory. That is to say, it is more likely to be placed along routes that are connected to one's own ways of intellectual travel.

In sum, the very attitudes and activities that characterize "figuring out" or "discovering" things for oneself also seems to have the effect of making material more readily accessible in memory.

Lee S. Shulman

Psychological Controversies in Teaching

The popular press has discovered the discovery method of teaching. It is by now, for example, an annual ritual for the Education section of *Time* magazine to sound a peal of praise for learning by discovery (e.g., *Time*, December 8, 1967 [7]). *Time*'s hosannas for discovery are by no means unique, reflecting as they do the educational establishment's general tendency to make good things seem better than they are. Since even the soundest of methods can be brought to premature mortality through an overdose of unremitting praise, it becomes periodically necessary even for advocates of discovery, such as I, to temper enthusiasm with considered judgment.

The learning by discovery controversy is a complex issue which can easily be oversimplified. A recent volume has dealt with many aspects of the issue in great detail [8]. The controversy seems to center essentially about the question of how much and what kind of guidance ought to be provided to students in the learning situation. Those favoring learning by discovery advocate the teaching of broad principles and problem-solving through minimal teacher guidance and maximal opportunity for exploration and trial-and-error on the part of the student. Those preferring guided learning emphasize the importance of carefully sequencing instructional experiences through maximum guidance and stress the importance of basic associations or facts in the service of the eventual mastering of principles and problem-solving.

Adapted from the article "Psychological Controversies in the Teaching of Science and Mathematics," by Lee S. Shulman, *Science Teacher*, 35, 1968 pp. 34–38, 89–90. Reprinted by permission of the publisher and author

Needless to say, there is considerable ambiguity over the use of the term *discovery*. One man's discovery approach can easily be confused with another's guided learning curriculum if the unwary observer is not alerted to the preferred labels ahead of time. For this reason I have decided to contrast the two positions by carefully examining the work of two men, each of whom is considered a leader of one of these general schools of thought.

Professor Jerome S. Bruner of Harvard University is undoubtedly the single person most closely identified with the learning-by-discovery position. His book, *The Process of Education* [1], captured the spirit of discovery in the new mathematics and science curricula and communicated it effectively to professionals and laymen. His thinking will be examined as representative of the advocates of discovery learning.

Professor Robert M. Gagné of the University of California is a major force in the guided learning approach. His analysis of *The Conditions of Learning* [3] is one of the finest contemporary statements of the principles of guided learning and instruction.

I recognize the potential danger inherent in any explicit attempt to polarize the positions of two eminent scholars. My purpose is to clarify the dimensions of a complex problem, not to consign Bruner and Gagné to irrevocable extremes. Their published writings are employed merely to characterize two possible positions on the role of discovery in learning, which each has expressed eloquently at some time in the recent past.

In this paper I will first discuss the manner in which Bruner and Gagné, respectively, describe the teaching of some particular topic. Using

169

these two examples as starting points, we will then compare their positions with respect to instructional objectives, instructional styles, readiness for learning, and transfer of training. We will then examine the implications of this controversy for the process of instruction in science and mathematics and the conduct of research relevant to that process.

Instructional Example: Discovery Learning

In a number of his papers, Jerome Bruner uses an instructional example from mathematics that derives from his collaboration with the mathematics educator, Z. P. Dienes [2].

A class is composed of eight-year-old children who are there to learn some mathematics. In one of the instructional units, children are first introduced to three kinds of flat pieces of wood or "flats." The first one, they are told, is to be called either the 'unknown square" or "X square." The second flat, which is rectangular, is called "1 X" or just X, since it is X long on

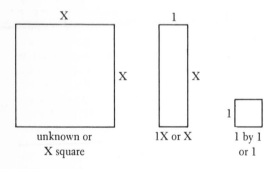

unknown or
X square
           1X or X
           1 by 1
           or 1

one side and 1 long on the other. The third flat is a small square which is 1 by 1, and is called 1.

After allowing the children many opportunities simply to play with these materials and to get a feel for them, Bruner gives the children a problem. He asks them, "Can you make larger squares than this X square by using as many of these flats as you want?" This is not a difficult task for most children and they readily make another square such as the one illustrated below.

Bruner then asks them if they can describe

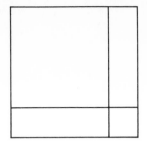

what they have done. They might reply, "We have one square X, with two X's and a 1." He then asks them to keep a record of what they have done. He may even suggest a notational system to use. The symbol $X^\square$ could represent the square X, and a + for "and." Thus, the pieces used could be described as $X^\square + 2X + 1$.

Another way to describe their new square, he points out, is simply to describe each side. With an X and a 1 on each side, the side can be described as $X + 1$ and the square as $(X + 1)(X + 1)$ after some work with parentheses. Since these are two basic ways of describing the same square, they can be written in this way: $X^\square + 2X + 1 = (X + 1)(X + 1)$. This description, of course, far oversimplifies the procedures used.

The children continue making squares and generating the notation for them. (See next diagram.)

At some point Bruner hypothesizes that they will begin to discern a pattern. While the X's are progressing at the rate of 2, 4, 6, 8, the ones are going 1, 4, 9, 16, and on the right side of the equation the pattern is 1, 2, 3, 4. Provocative or leading questions are often used Socratically to elicit this discovery. Bruner maintains that, even if the children are initially unable to break the code, they will sense that there is a pattern and try to discover it. Bruner then illustrates how the pupils transfer what they have learned to working with a balance beam. The youngsters are ostensibly learning not only something about quadratic equations, but more important, something about the discovery of mathematical regularities.

The general learning process described by

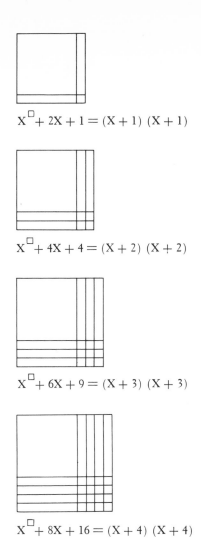

$$X^{\square} + 2X + 1 = (X + 1)\ (X + 1)$$

$$X^{\square} + 4X + 4 = (X + 2)\ (X + 2)$$

$$X^{\square} + 6X + 9 = (X + 3)\ (X + 3)$$

$$X^{\square} + 8X + 16 = (X + 4)\ (X + 4)$$

Bruner occurs in the following manner: First, the child finds regularities in his manipulation of the materials that correspond with intuitive regularities he has already come to understand. Notice that what the child does for Bruner is to find some sort of match between what he is doing in the outside world and some models or templates that he already has in his mind. For Bruner, it is rarely something *outside* the learner that is discovered. Instead the discovery involves an internal reorganization of previously known ideas in order to establish a better fit be-

tween those ideas and the regularities of an encounter to which the learner has had to accommodate.

This is precisely the philosophy of education we associate with Socrates. Remember the lovely dialogue of the *Meno* by Plato, in which the young slave boy is brought to an understanding of what is involved in doubling the area of a square. Socrates maintains throughout this dialogue that he is not teaching the boy anything new; he is simply helping the boy reorganize and bring to the fore what he has always known.

Bruner almost always begins with a focus on the production and manipulation of materials. He describes the child as moving through three levels of representation. The first level is the *enactive level*, where the child manipulates materials directly. He then progresses to the *ikonic level*, where he deals with mental images of objects but does not manipulate them directly. Finally he moves to the *symbolic level*, where he is strictly manipulating symbols and no longer mental images of objects. This sequence is an outgrowth of the developmental work of Jean Piaget. The synthesis of these concepts of manipulation of actual materials as part of a developmental model and the Socratic notion of learning as internal reorganization into a learning-by-discovery approach is the unique contribution of Jerome Bruner.

The Process of Education was written in 1959, after most mathematics innovations that use discovery as a core had already begun. It is an error to say that Bruner initiated the learning-by-discovery approach. It is far more accurate to say that, more than any one man, he managed to capture its spirit, provide it with a theoretical foundation, and disseminate it. Bruner is not the discoverer of discovery; he is its prophet.

Instructional Example: Guided Learning

Robert Gagné takes a very different approach to instruction. He begins with a task analysis of the instructional objectives. He always asks the question, "What is it you want the learner to be able to do?" This *capability* he insists, must be stated *specifically* and *behaviorally*.

171

By capability, he means the ability to perform certain specific functions under specified conditions. A capability could be the ability to solve a number series. It might be the ability to solve some problems in non-metric geometry.

This capability can be conceived of as a terminal behavior and placed at the top of what will eventually be a complex pyramid. After analyzing the task, Gagné asks, "What would you need to know in order to do that?" Let us say that one could not complete the task unless he could first perform prerequisite tasks *a* and *b*. So a pyramid begins.

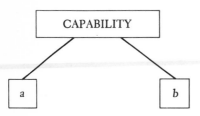

But in order to perform task *a*, one must be able to perform tasks c and *d* and for task *b*, one must know *e*, *f*, and *g*.

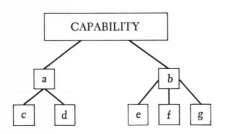

So one builds a very complex pyramid of prerequisites to prerequisites to the objective which is the desired capability.

Gagné has developed a model for discussing the different levels of such a hierarchy. If the final capability desired is a *problem-solving* capability, the learner first must know certain *principles*. But to understand those principles, he must know specific *concepts*, and prerequisite to these are particular *simple associations* or

facts discriminated from each other in a distinctive manner. He continues the analysis until he ends up with the fundamental building blocks of learning — classically or operantly conditioned responses.

Gagné, upon completing the whole map of prerequisites, would administer pretests to determine which have already been mastered. Upon completing the diagnostic testing, the resulting pattern identifies precisely what must be taught. This model is particularly conducive to subsequent programing of materials and programed instruction. When prerequisites are established, a very tight teaching program or package develops.

Earlier, we discussed the influences on Bruner. What influenced Gagné? This approach to teaching comes essentially from a combination of the neo-behaviorist psychological tradition and the task analysis model that dominates the fields of military and industrial training. It was precisely this kind of task analysis that contributed to successful programs of pilot training in World War II. Gagné was trained in the neo-behaviorist tradition and spent the major portion of his early career as an Air Force psychologist.

Nature of Objectives

The positions of Bruner and Gagné take very different points of view with respect to the objectives of education. This is one of the major reasons why most attempts at evaluating the relative effectiveness of these two approaches have come to naught. They really cannot agree on the same set of objectives. Any attempt to ask which is better — Michigan State's football team or the Chicago White Sox — will never succeed. The criteria for success are different, and it would be absurd to have them both on the same field competing against each other.

For Gagné, or the programed-instruction position which can be derived from him, the objectives of instruction are capabilities. They are behavioral products that can be specified in operational terms. Subsequently they can be task-analyzed; then they can be taught. Gagné would subscribe to the position that psychology has been successful in suggesting ways of teaching only when objectives have been made operationally clear. When objectives are not clearly stated, the psychologist can be of little assistance. He insists on objectives clearly stated in behavioral terms. They are the cornerstones of his position.

For Bruner, the emphasis is quite different. The emphasis is not on the *products* of learning but on the *processes*. One paragraph from *Toward a Theory of Instruction* captures the spirit of educational objectives for Bruner. After discussing the mathematics example previously mentioned, he concludes,

Finally, a theory of instruction seeks to take account of the fact that a curriculum reflects not only the nature of knowledge itself — the specific capabilities — but also the nature of the knower and of the knowledge-getting process. It is the enterprise par excellence where the line between the subject matter and the method grows necessarily indistinct. A body of knowledge, enshrined in a university faculty, and embodied in a series of authoritative volumes is the result of much prior intellectual activity. To instruct someone in these disciplines is not a matter of getting him to commit the results to mind; rather, it is to teach him to participate in the process that makes possible the establishment of knowledge. We teach a subject, not to produce little living libraries from that subject, but rather to get a student to think mathematically for himself, to consider matters as a historian does, *to take part in the process of knowledge-getting. Knowing is a process, not a product.* [2, p. 72] (Italics mine)

Speaking to the same issue, Gagné's position is clearly different.

Obviously, strategies are important for problem solving, regardless of the content of the problem. The suggestion from some writings is that they are of overriding importance as a goal of education. After all, should not formal instruction in the schools have the aim of teaching the student "how to think"? If strategies were deliberately taught, would not this produce people who could then bring to bear superior problem-solving capabilities to any new situation? Although no one would disagree with the aims expressed, it is exceedingly doubtful that they can be brought about by teaching students "strategies" or "styles" of thinking. Even if these could be taught (and it is possible

that they could), they would not provide the individual with the basic firmament of thought, which is subject-matter knowledge. Knowing a set of strategies is not all that is required for thinking; it is not even a substantial part of what is needed. *To be an effective problem solver, the individual must somehow have acquired masses of structurally organized knowledge. Such knowledge is made up of content principles, not heuristic ones.* [3, p. 170] (Italics mine)

While for Bruner "knowing is a process, not a product," for Gagné, "knowledge is made up of content principles, not heuristic ones." Thus, though both espouse the acquisition of knowledge as the major objective of education, their definitions of *knowledge* and *knowing* are so disparate that the educational objectives sought by each scarcely overlap. The philosophical and psychological sources of these differences will be discussed later in this paper. For the moment, let it be noted that when two conflicting approaches seek such contrasting objectives, the conduct of comparative educational studies becomes extremely difficult.[1]

Instructional Styles

Implicit in this contrast is a difference in what is meant by the very words *learning by discovery*. For Gagné, *learning* is the goal. How a behavior or capability is learned is a function of the task. It may be by discovery, by guided teaching, by practice, by drill, or by review. The focus is on *learning* and discovery is but one way to learn something. For Bruner, it is learning *by discovery*. The method of learning is the significant aspect.

For Gagné, in an instructional program the child is carefully guided. He may work with

---

[1] Gagné has modified his own position somewhat since 1965. He would now tend to agree, more or less, with Bruner on the importance of processes or strategies as objectives of education. He has not, however, changed his position regarding the role of sequence in instruction, the nature of readiness, or any of the remaining topics in this paper. [5] The point of view concerning specific behavioral products as objectives is still espoused by many educational theorists and Gagné's earlier arguments are thus still relevant as reflections of that position.

programed materials or a programed teacher (one who follows quite explicitly a step-by-step guide). The child may be quite active. He is not necessarily passive; he is doing things, he is working exercises, he is solving problems. But the sequence is determined entirely by the program. (Here the term "program" is used in a broad sense, not necessarily simply a series of frames.)

For Bruner much less system or order is necessary for the package, although such order is not precluded. In general Bruner insists on the child manipulating materials and dealing with incongruities or contrasts. He will always try to build potential or emergent incongruities into the materials. Robert Davis calls this operation "torpedoing" when it is initiated by the teacher. He teaches a child something until he is certain the child knows it. Then he provides him with a whopper of a counterexample. This is what Bruner does constantly — providing contrasts and incongruities in order to get the child, because of his discomfort, to try to resolve this disequilibrium by making some discovery (cognitive restructuring). This discovery can take the form of a new synthesis or a new distinction. Piaget, too, maintains that cognitive development is a process of successive disequilibria and equilibria. The child, confronted by a new situation, gets out of balance and must accommodate to achieve a new balance by modifying the previous cognitive structure.

Thus, for Gagné, instruction is a smoothly guided tour up a carefully constructed hierarchy of objectives; for Bruner, instruction is a rollercoaster ride of successive disequilibria and equilibria until the desired cognitive state is reached or discovered.

Readiness

The guided learning point of view, represented by Gagné, maintains that readiness is essentially a function of the presence or absence of prerequisite learning.

When the child is capable of d and e below, he is by definition ready to learn b. Until then he is not ready. Gagné is not concerned with genetically developmental considerations. If the

174

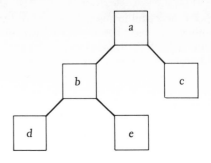

child at age five does not have the concept of the conservation of liquid volume, it is not because of an unfolding in his mind; he just has not had the necessary prior experiences. Ensure that he has acquired the prerequisite behaviors, and he will be able to conserve [4].

For Piaget (and Bruner) the child is a developing organism, passing through cognitive stages that are biologically determined. These stages are more or less age-related, although in different cultures certain stages may come earlier than others. To identify whether the child is ready to learn a particular concept or principle, one analyzes the structure of that to be taught and compares it with what is already known about the cognitive structure of the child at that age. If they are consonant, it can be taught; if they are dissonant, it cannot.

Given this characterization of the two positions on readiness, to which one would you attribute the following statement? ". . . any subject can be taught effectively in some intellectually honest form to any child at any stage of development." While it sounds like Gagné, you recognize that it isn't — it's Bruner! [2, p. 33] And in this same chapter he includes an extensive discussion of Piaget's position. Essentially he is attempting to translate Piaget's theories into a psychology of instruction.

Many are puzzled by this stand, including Piaget. In a recent paper delivered in the United States, he admitted that he did not understand how Bruner could make such a statement in the light of Piaget's experiments. If Bruner meant the statement literally; i.e., *any* child can learn *anything*, then it just is not true! There are always things a child cannot learn, especially not in an intellectually honest way. If he means it homiletically, i.e., we can take almost anything and somehow resay it, reconstruct it, restructure it so it now has a parallel at the child's level of cognitive functioning, then it may be a truism.

I believe that what Bruner is saying, and it is neither trivial nor absurd, is that our older conceptions of readiness have tended to apply Piagetian theory in the same way as some have for generations applied Rousseau's. The old thesis was, "There is the child — he is a developing organism, with invariant order, invariant schedule. Here, too, is the subject matter, equally hallowed by time and unchanging. We take the subject matter as our starting point, watch the child develop, and feed it in at appropriate times as he reaches readiness." Let's face it; that has been our general conception of readiness. We gave reading readiness tests and hesitated to teach the pupil reading until he was "ready." The notion is quite new that the reading readiness tests tell not when to begin teaching the child, but rather what has to be done to get him more ready. We used to just wait until he got ready. What Bruner is suggesting is that we must modify our conception of readiness so that it includes not only the child but the subject matter. Subject matter, too, goes through stages of readiness. The same subject matter can be represented at a manipulative or enactive level, at an ikonic level, and finally at a symbolic or formal level. The resulting model is Bruner's concept of a spiral curriculum.

Piaget himself seems quite dubious over the attempts to accelerate cognitive development that are reflected in many modern math and science curricula. On a recent trip to the United States, Piaget commented,

> . . . we know that it takes nine to twelve months before babies develop the notion that an object is still there even whan a screen is placed in front of it. Now kittens go through the same stages as children, all the same sub-stages, but they do it in three months — so they're six months ahead of babies. Is this an advantage or isn't it? We can certainly see our answer in one sense. The kitten is not going to go much further. The child has taken longer, but he is capable of going further, so it seems to me that the nine months probably were not for nothing.
>
> It's probably possible to accelerate, but maximal acceleration is not desirable. There seems to be an optimal time. What this optimal time is will surely depend upon each individual and on the subject matter. We still need a great deal of research to know what the optimal time would be. [6, p. 82]

The question that has not been answered, and which Piaget whimsically calls the "American question," is the empirical experimental question: To what extent it is possible through a Gagnéan approach to accelerate what Piaget maintains is the invariant clockwork of the order? Studies being conducted in Scandinavia by Smedslund and in this country by Irving Sigel, Egon Mermelstein, and others are attempting to identify the degree to which such processes as the principle of conservation of volume can be accelerated. If I had to make a broad generalization, I would have to conclude that at this point, in general, the score for those who say you cannot accelerate is somewhat higher than the score for those who say that you can. But the question is far from resolved; we need many more inventive attempts to accelerate cognitive development than we have had thus far. There remains the question of whether such attempts at experimental acceleration are strictly of interest for psychological theory, or have important pedagogical implications as well — a question we do not have space to examine here.

Sequence of the Curriculum

The implications for the sequence of the curriculum growing from these two positions are quite different. For Gagné, the highest level of learning is problem solving; lower levels involve facts, concepts, principles, etc. Clearly, for Gagné, the appropriate sequence in learning is, in terms of the diagram below, from the bottom up. One begins with simple prerequisites and works up, pyramid fashion, to the complex capability sought.

For Bruner, the same diagram may be appropriate, but the direction of the arrow would be changed. He has a pupil begin with *problem*

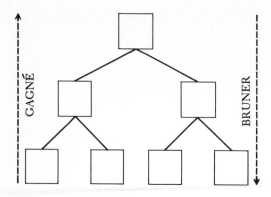

GAGNÉ BRUNER

solving. This process is analogous to teaching someone to swim by throwing him into deep water. The theory is that he will learn the fundamentals because he needs them. The analogy is not totally misbegotten. In some of the extreme discovery approaches we lose a lot of pupils by mathematical or scientific drowning. As one goes to the extreme of this position, he runs the risk of some drownings. For Gagné, the sequence is from the simple to the complex; for Bruner one starts with the complex and plans to learn the simple components in the context of working with the complex.

It is unclear whether Bruner subscribes to his position because of his concept of the nature of learning or for strictly motivational reasons. Children may be motivated more quickly when given a problem they cannot solve, than they are when given some little things to learn on the promise that if they learn these well, three weeks from now they will be able to solve an exciting problem. Yet, Bruner clearly maintains that learning things in this fashion also improves the transferability of what is learned. It is to a consideration of the issue of transfer of training that we now turn.

Transfer of Training

To examine the psychologies of learning of these two positions in any kind of comprehensive form would require greater attention than can be devoted here, but we shall consider one concept — that of transfer of training. This is probably the central concept, or should be, in

176

any educationally relevant psychology of learning.

Gagné considers himself a conservative on matters of transfer. He states that "transfer occurs because of the occurrence of specific identical (or highly similar) elements within developmental sequences" [4, p. 20]. To the extent that an element which has been learned, be it association, concept, or principle, can be directly employed in a new situation, transfer will occur. If the new context requires a behavior substantially different from the specific capability mastered earlier, there will be no transfer.

Bruner, on the other hand, subscribes to the broadest theories of transfer of training. Bruner believes that we can have massive transfer from one learning situation to another. Broad transfer of training occurs when one can identify in the structures of subject matters basic, fundamentally simple concepts or principles which, if learned well, can be transferred both to other subject matters within that discipline and to other disciplines as well. He gives examples such as the concept of conservation or balance. Is it not possible to teach balance of trade in economics in such a way that when ecological balance is considered, pupils see the parallel? This could then be extended to balance of power in political science, or to balancing equations.

Even more important, for Bruner, is the broad transferability of the knowledge-getting process — strategies, heuristics, and the like — transfer whose viability leaves Gagné with deep feelings of doubt. This is the question of whether learning by discovery leads to the ability *to* discover, that is, the development of broad inquiry competencies in students.

What does the evidence from empirical studies of this issue seem to demonstrate? The findings are not all that consistent. I would generalize them by saying that most often guided learning or expository sequences seem to be superior methods for achieving immediate learning. With regard to long-term retention, the results seem equivocal, with neither approach consistently better. Discovery learning approaches appear to be superior when the criterion of transfer of principles to new situations is employed [9]. Notably absent are studies which deal with the question of whether general techniques, strategies, and heuristics of discovery can be learned — by discovery or in any other manner — which will transfer across grossly different kinds of tasks.

Why is transfer of training superior in the discovery situation when the learning of principles is involved? There are two kinds of transfer — positive transfer and negative transfer. We call something positive transfer when mastery of task X facilitates mastery of task Y. Negative transfer occurs when mastery of task X inhibits mastery of task Y. Positive transfer is a familiar notion for us. Negative transfer can be exemplified by a piece of advice baseball coaches often give their players. They tell them not to play golf during the baseball season because the baseball swing and the golf swing involve totally different muscles and body movements. Becoming a better golf swinger interferes with the baseball swing. In psychological terms there is negative transfer between golf and baseball.

What is needed for positive transfer is to minimize all possible interference. In transfer of training, there are some ways in which the tasks transferred to are like the ones learned first, but in other ways they are different. So transfer always involves striking a balance between these conflicting potentials for both positive and negative transfer. In discovery methods, learners may transfer more easily because they learn *the immediate things less well*. They may thus learn the broad strokes of a principle, which is the aspect most critical for remote transfer, while not learning well the detailed application of that specific principle, which could interfere somewhat with successful remote transfer.

If this formulation is correct, we are never going to find a method that will both allow for tremendous specific learning of products and broad transfer, because we are dealing in a closed system in which one must make a choice. To the extent that initial learning is well done, transfer is restricted. The instructor may have to decide which is more important — an immediate specific product or broad transfer — and choose his subsequent teaching method on the basis of that decision. This is a pessimistic view, and I hope that future studies might find it flawed.

References

1. Bruner, Jerome S. *The Process of Education.* Harvard University Press, Cambridge, Massachusetts. 1960.
2. Bruner, Jerome S. *Toward a Theory of Instruction.* Belknap Press, Cambridge, Massachusetts. 1966.
3. Gagné, Robert M. *The Conditions of Learning.* Holt, Rinehart & Winston. New York. 1965.
4. Gagné, Robert M. Contributions of Learning to Human Development. Address of the Vice-President, Section I (Psychology), American Association for the Advancement of Science, Washington, D.C. December 1966.
5. Gagné, Robert M. Personal communication. May 1968.
6. Jennings, Frank G. "Jean Piaget: Notes on Learning." *Saturday Review;* May 20, 1967, p. 82.
7. "Pain & Progress in Discovery." *Time,* December 8, 1967, pp. 110 ff.
8. Shulman, Lee S., and Keislar, Evan R., editors. *Learning by Discovery: A Critical Appraisal.* Rand-McNally, Chicago. 1966.
9. Worthen, Blaine R. "Discovery and Expository Task Presentation in Elementary Mathematics." *Journal of Educational Psychology Monograph Supplement* 59: 1, Part 2; February 1968.

J. P. Guilford

Factors That Aid and Hinder Creativity

In the part of our current *Zeitgeist* pertaining to psychology and education, no word has had a more dramatic rise in popularity than "creativity." After generally ignoring the subject, psychologists have come to realize their backwardness in knowledge of this subject. Employers have been asking for more inventive scientists, engineers, and managers. Special courses on how to think creatively have been springing up by the score. Special institutes are being held on the subject. Teachers and educators are asking how they can make courses more stimulating and how they can arouse more productive thinking on the part of students.

The interest is international, as well it might be. The whole world faces two very critical problems — how to feed its exploding population and how to keep the peace. It has been estimated that in the next 20 years we shall need three times the number of scientists and engineers we now have, and they shall have to exercise all the ingenuity of which they are capable. We are reminded by the scriptures, however, that man does not live by bread alone. There is, I think, a very noticeable surgence of interest in the arts in all their forms. We wish to walk in beauty as well as in peace, freedom, and dignity. There is also good reason to desire increased creativity to achieve aesthetic goals.

Investigation of Creativity

My topic suggests that I give most consideration to the abilities and other traits of individu-

From *Teachers College Record*, 1962, 63, pp. 380–392. Reprinted by permission of the publisher and author.

als that make some of them creative and some not. Knowing these traits should help us to recognize which persons are likely to have the potentialities of becoming creatively productive. The same knowledge should help us in taking steps that should increase creative output in ourselves and in others, and other steps that may remove obstacles in the way of creative productivity. Our primary concern, then, will be the basic facts concerning the nature of creative thinking and of the more creative persons, with reference to the application of this information.

Serious investigation of creativity by psychologists began only in recent years. For centuries the common idea had been that only the exceedingly rare person is genuinely creative and that creativity is a divine gift. As such, it was not to be investigated, or at best, there was little hope of understanding it. Even after Darwin came upon the scene, when creativity came to be regarded as some kind of rare, hereditary blessing, there was still little incentive to attempt to understand it because there was thought to be little that one could do about it. In addition to being very rare, the highly creative person's behavior is sometimes eccentric. This has sometimes branded him as being abnormal and even pathological. Mental pathology was similarly avoided as a subject of study by scientific investigators for a long time.

Creativity became an object of scientific study primarily because of the general interest in individual differences. This approach recognizes that individuals differ psychologically in traits or attributes that can be conceived as continua or dimensions — that there can be varying degrees of a quality possessed by different individuals. This concept was eventually applied to creativity, but in serious ways only about a dozen years ago. This new way of looking at the matter permitted us to think that not only a few peculiarly gifted persons but individuals in general possess some degree of the same creative trait or traits.

This conception has opened the door to many kinds of research. We need no longer study creativity by catching the rare persons who are recognized as having creativity to high degree; a multitude of subjects is now available to investigators. We can discover the various aspects of the phenomenon called "creativity." We can find out the conditions under which creative performance occurs or does not occur.

As in the case of all psychological characteristics that make up personality, we may be forced to recognize that heredity establishes limits of development for an individual. But there is considerable faith among educators that rarely does an individual realize full development in any respect and that there is generally considerable room for improvement. This faith should also be applied to the creative aspects of personality.

Basic Traits and Creativity

There are a number of approaches to the investigation of the traits or characteristics in which creative individuals are most likely to excel. Some investigators appear to regard the phenomenon of creativity as a single dimension of personality. It is my view that the creative disposition is made up of many components and that its composition depends upon where you find it. Practically all investigators recognize that there are many potentially contributing conditions.

When the problem is approached from the standpoint of individual differences, the most natural scientific technique to apply is that of factor analysis. This is the approach that my associates and I have taken almost exclusively in the Aptitudes Project at the University of Southern California.

According to our original hypotheses (7), we expected to find the more creative individuals to think with greater fluency, with more flexibility, and with greater originality. The tests designed to measure fluency present very simple tasks, and the quantity of output determines the scores. When told to produce a list of items of information of a certain kind, how many responses can the examinee give in a limited time? Quality does not count, but, of course, the responses must be appropriate.

Flexibility in thinking means a *change* of some kind — a change in the meaning, interpretation, or use of something, a change in understanding of the task, a change of strategy in doing the task, or a change in direction of thinking, which may mean a new interpretation of the goal.

There has been some debate concerning the meaning of "originality." In our research and in that of others, originality means the production of unusual, far-fetched, remote, or clever responses. But there are some who say that an idea is not original or novel unless no human being has ever thought of it earlier. This conception is worthless to the scientist because there is no way of knowing that any idea has never existed before. It is somewhat better to say that a novel idea is a new one so far as the particular individual who has it is concerned. But unless we know the individual's past history of thinking, we cannnot be sure of meeting this criterion either.

Fortunately, we can resort to empirical signs of novelty in terms of the statistical infrequency of a response among members of a certain population that is culturally relatively homogeneous. This gives us some workable operations for applying the criterion of unusualness. The index of unusualness can therefore be purely objective. As for the far-fetched or remote associations and the clever responses, we have as yet no way to avoid some degree of subjectivity of judgment in assessing test performance to obtain an index of originality.

Another somewhat popular criterion of an original idea is that it is socially useful. Those who deal with practical affairs may be appropri-

179

ately concerned about this aspect of produced ideas. But such a criterion involves us in values in a way that science cannot deal with directly; hence, the criterion of social usefulness can be quickly dismissed by the psychologist. This does not mean that as a person he is unconcerned about social usefulness. It does mean that as a scientist he cannot afford to be so concerned and so restricted.

Fluency Factors

We shall now give closer attention to the various factors of fluency, flexibility, and originality. It turns out that in verbal tests alone there are three differentiated fluency factors (9). Ideational fluency has to do with the rate of generation of a quantity of ideas. The idea produced may be as simple as a single word, as complex as the title for a picture or a story, or as phrases and short sentences that convey unitary thoughts. In a test, we may ask the examinee to list all the things he can think of that are solid, flexible, and colored. He may respond with *cloth, leaf, rose petal, hair, skin, leather,* and so on. Any response that fulfills the specifications accepted and counts toward the total score. In other tests, we may ask the examinee to list the consequences of a certain action or event, the various uses of an object, or some appropriate titles for a given story. In all such tests, there are strict time limits.

It is easy to see where an operation such as that in tests of ideational fluency fit into problem solving of many kinds. Perhaps a problem situation, when interpreted in a certain way, calls for an object with a certain set of specifications in order to solve it. Once these specifications are realized, the person who can list pertinent possibilities most rapidly could, other things being equal, solve the problem most quickly.

Many a problem calls for a running through of the likely possibilities during the earlier stage of interpreting or structuring it as well as during the stage of finding solutions. This process also probably depends in some degree upon ideational fluency. Of course it is not necessary to run through *all* the logical possibilities in solv-

ing a problem. One can ignore the less promising ones. This point will be touched upon later.

Another kind of fluency is called "associational fluency." It pertains to the completion of relationships, in distinction from the factor of ideational fluency, which involves giving ideas that fit a class. As a test of associational fluency, we may ask the examinee to list all the words he can think of that mean the opposite, or nearly the opposite, of the word "good." He may respond with *bad, poor, sinful, defective, awful, terrible,* and so on. This ability is most obviously of use to the creative writer, who wants to find quickly a variety of verbal expressions without having to resort to a thesaurus.

The factor of associational fluency may have more general utility — for example, whenever we apply thinking by analogy as our strategy in solving problems. Thinking of a correlate is the completion of an analogy. Many solutions to new problems are achieved by the practice of thinking by analogy. The success of certain kinds of engineers in their work has been predicted to a small extent by means of a test of associational fluency as found by Saunders (21, 1956).

A third kind of fluency is called "expressional fluency." It has to do with the facile construction sentences. We ask the examinee to write as many four-word sentences as he can, all different, with no word used more than once. We may give the initial letters of the four words, the same four being specified for each sentence — for example, "W—— c—— e—— n——." To this task, he may reply "We can eat nuts." "Willie comes every night," "Wholesome carrots elevate nations," "Weary cats evade nothing," and so on. You will probably not be surprised when I tell you that in a ninth-grade sample, the girls obtained a higher mean score than the boys.

We do not know yet how much generality to attach to this factor, whether it is limited to tasks such as the writing of sentences or whether it is so broad as to pertain to organizing ideas into systems. If it is as broad as the latter suggestion, it should be of considerable consequence, perhaps in something as important as the trial-and-error development of a scientific theory. The factor has been found significantly related to ratings by psychologists of the creative performances of military officers.[1]

Flexibility Factors

One type of flexibility we first recognized as "spontaneous flexibility" because the tests that measure it do not even suggest that the examinee be flexible (5). Without his knowing it, he can make a good score if he varies his *kinds* of responses. If we tell the examinee to list all the uses he can think of for a common brick, the total number of uses listed is a good score for his status on the factor of ideational fluency. But we also score his performance in terms of the number of times he changes *category* of uses. For example, the person who responds with *build a house, build a school, build a factory*, etc., does not change his class of uses. Another person who responds with *make a paper weight, drive a nail, make baseball bases, throw at a cat, grind up for red powder, make a tombstone for a bird*, etc., changes class with each new response. He shows much more flexibility.

The person who makes a low spontaneous-flexibility score is rigid in the sense that he perseverates within one or a very few classes. As there are several kinds of flexibility in thinking, so there are several kinds of rigidity. When someone tells you that a certain person is rigid, beware of overgeneralization of the term. We do not find in normal (nonpathological) people a very general trait of rigidity vs. flexibility. We find several. This does not say that there are no individuals who are rigid in just about every respect, but the general rule is that they may be rigid in some respects and not in others, at least so far as thinking is concerned.

A new hypothesis may be considered in connection with the factor of spontaneous flexibility. Some advisers on how to think creatively

[1] From an unpublished study conducted jointly by the Aptitudes Project at the University of Southern California and the Institute for Personality Assessment and Research, University of California, Berkeley.

suggest that in starting to solve a new problem, we keep our thinking at a rather high level of abstraction. We think of it first in very general terms. Thus, the person who goes from class to class in the Brick Uses test is operating within the frame of reference of a much broader class within which there are subclasses. A higher level of abstraction may mean thinking in terms of broader classes. This has the effect of broadening the scope of the scanning process in searching for information. Going from one class to another in the Brick Uses test also means considering all the properties of a brick — its weight, its color, its texture, and so on. These are abstractions all lying within the class of the total nature of a brick. This is reminiscent of a stock method of practicing creative thinking, a method known as "attribute listing" and advocated by Crawford (3).

A second kind of flexibility has been called "*adaptive* flexibility" for the reason that in tests in which it was first found, the examinee, to succeed, must make changes of some kind — changes in interpretation of the task, in approach or strategy, or in possible solutions. Our current interpretation of the factor of originality is that it is adaptive flexibility in dealing with verbal information.

We have a kind of test, called Plot Titles, in which the examinee is told a very short story and that he is to suggest as many appropriate titles for the story as he can. One of the stories is about a wife who is unable to speak until a specialist performs the appropriate surgery. Then her husband is driven to distraction by her incessant talking until another surgeon eliminates his hearing, when peace is restored in the family.

The number of commonplace titles given to the story may be used as a score for ideational fluency. Such titles include,

A man and his wife
Never satisfied
Medicine triumphs
A man's decisions
Talking and hearing

The number of responses rated as "clever"

181

serves as a score for originality. Such titles are exemplified by

> The deaf man and the dumb woman
> Happiness through deafness
> Operation — peace of mind
> Yack, yack, hack

Several other types of tests serve to indicate individual differences in the factor of originality.

Elaboration

In the course of our investigations of abilities involved in planning (1), we found another kind of ability we have called "elaboration." In one test, given the bare outlines of a plan, the examinee is asked to produce the detailed steps needed to make the plan work. The more details he adds, the better is his score. We believe that the unique feature of this ability is that in tests for it, one item of information leads to another as a kind of extension or completion. In more technical language, we say that the examinee is producing a *variety of implications*.

It was eventually recognized that the abilities of fluency, flexibility (including originality), and elaboration are similar in that the tests of them call for a variety of answers. There is no right or fully determined answer in connection with the information given in the item. There are now parallel tests in which each item *does* have one right answer because it is fully determined by the information given or because there is one conventionally accepted answer. A distinction has therefore been made between *divergent* thinking and *convergent* thinking to represent the two classes of abilities. The abilities of which I have been speaking thus far belong in the divergent-thinking category. Because the individual has to generate his answer or answers, starting from given information, in both categories of abilities, we speak of diver-gent-*production* factors vs. convergent-*production* factors, respectively.

Quantity vs. Quality

Several questions arise concerning the relationship of quantity and quality of production. One debated and investigated hypothesis is that

"quantity breeds quality." This hypothesis holds that if a person produces a greater total number of ideas, he also produces a greater number of high-quality ideas in a limited time. Another view is that a mental set for quantity is inefficient because if a person spends his time producing a lot of low-quality responses, he cannot produce so many good ones.

There is another aspect of this controversy. When a person is set to give "good" answers, he is applying judgment or evaluation as he goes along. On the one hand, it is believed that an evaluative or critical attitude is generally inhibiting to the flow of ideas, good and poor alike. On the other hand, it is believed that the application of evaluation as one proceeds has a selective effect, holding back the low-quality responses and letting the high-quality responses come through.

The well-known brainstorming technique, attributed to Alex Osborn (18) and employed by many others, conforms to the first of these two schools of thought. One of its chief claimed virtues is that the separation of production and evaluation — in other words, suspended judgment — is better procedure. As originally applied, of course, brainstorming has other features, which include thinking in small groups rather than thinking by individuals in seclusion.

The experimental results bearing upon the issue of suspended judgment are somewhat mixed. Meadow *et al.* (16) report that with suspended judgment, the production of "good" answers was a little more than doubled. The problems were to suggest unusual uses for a wire coat hanger and for a broom. The criteria for "good" responses were "unique" and "useful."

In our Aptitudes Project (2), we gave the Plot Titles test with and without the specific instruction to give clever titles. It was expected that the instruction for clever titles would entail more evaluation. The effects of this instruction were shown by a reduction in the number of low-quality responses, an increase in the number of high-quality responses, and a higher average rating of degree of cleverness.

Hyman (13) found that his subjects generated 68% more responses under quantity instructions, but that this increase in "good" responses, where "good" meant uncommon and of "high quality," failed to keep pace with the total output. Hyman is probably right when he concludes that quantity may breed quality for some types of problems but not for others. It is also probably true that the *kind* of evaluative attitude applied by the thinker has much to do with the quantity and quality of responses he produces.

Divergent thinking is a matter of scanning one's stored information to find answers to satisfy a special search model. Evaluation comes into the picture in determining whether or not the produced information fits the search model. Relaxed evaluation would permit a broadening of the base of the search, whereas an evaluative attitude with some degree of strictness should narrow the search. In doing so, however, it may lead more efficiently to good answers. This should depend upon the clarity and accuracy of the search model. If the thinker has a good search model, the application of evaluation while he thinks should be helpful.

But if evaluation is of a more vague kind, such as that involving a fear of being unconventional, a fear of thinking socially unacceptable thoughts, or a fear of being wrong, it should be definitely better to suspend judgments based on such criteria. Evaluation incident to an overly strong desire for a quick solution would also be handicapping. But evaluation for the sake of efficient scanning, where there is good strategy in the scanning process, should be beneficial.

Hyman (13) has found that a general critical attitude can have rather broad transfer effects in solving problems. A group of engineers, in Hyman's experiment, read some previously given solutions to a certain practical problem under the instruction to list all the good points that they could see in those solutions. A second group was instructed to list all the faults they could see in the same solutions. Later, in solving the same problem and in solving a new one, the uncritical readers suggested solutions of their own that were rated higher on the average than those of the critical group. Thus, very general critical attitudes must be taken into account.

Group vs. Individual Thinking

The question of group thinking vs. individual thinking has received a great deal of attention. The virtue claimed for group thinking in brainstorming is that one person stimulates another. In support of this hypothesis, Osborn (19) reports that about a third of the ideas produced in group brainstorming are of the "hitchhiking" type. In such a case, one person's idea is based upon another person's idea.

There are results which do not support his hypothesis, however. Taylor *et al.* (23) found a larger number of unrepeated ideas produced by individuals working alone than by those working in groups, where both kinds of thinkers were working under the condition of suspended judgment. Taylor points out that the group condition may have the effect of channeling thinking in similar directions, reducing the variety and therefore the quantity of unrepeated ideas.

Perhaps neither the group nor the isolation condition is best under all circumstances or for all individuals. It is quite possible that both can be applied to advantage. The preference of the thinker should have something to do with the choice of condition. A great deal is made of the point that the highly creative person is an independent thinker and that his creation may be a highly personal thing. Torrance (21, 1959) found that the more highly creative child (as indicated by his test scores) in a small group often works by himself or is somehow induced by the others to do so.

Whatever the outcome of brainstorming sessions in particular instances, experiments show that courses on creative thinking that are heavily weighted with brainstorming exercises seem to leave the students with beneficial results, and these results have some degree of permanence (15, 20). How much of the improvement to attribute to the brainstorming technique and to which aspects of it the improvement should be attributed are open questions.

Context of Creation

From the discussion thus far, one may conclude that creative performances are to be identified psychologically as a small number of divergent-production operations. Two different qualifications must be introduced. One exception is that two of the factors that we in the Aptitudes Project regarded from the first as being pertinent to creative thinking fall outside the divergent-production group. The other exception is that I have not yet told the whole story regarding the divergent-production factors. I shall make good on the latter omission first.

I have repeatedly stated that the tests on the factors thus far described are *verbal* tests. They pertain to verbally stated information. There are other kinds of information, and the question comes up whether the same person is usually equally creative in handling different kinds of information, material, or content. From our analytical results, we can say that it can happen, but we should rarely expect the same person to be equally capable of creativity in science, in the arts, mathematics, administration, and musical composition. Highly creative individuals in many of these different areas may have outstanding qualities in common, but psychological study indicates that they also have some marked differences.

In the area of divergent-production abilities alone, we find that individuals may be uneven in handling verbal vs. concrete vs. symbolic material. Symbolic material is the kind with which the mathematician deals — numbers and letters. Fluency, flexibility, and elaboration in dealing with concrete (perceived) material are probably of greater importance to the inventor of gadgets, the painter, and the composer, whereas the same kinds of abilities for dealing with verbal material or content are more important for the creative writer and the scientist. In other words, there are parallel abilities for dealing with concrete (or figural) material, symbolic material, and verbally meaningful (or semantic) material.

One of our earlier hypotheses (7) was that the unusually creative person has a high degree of sensitivity to problems. One person notices

something wrong or in need of improvement, whereas another fails to observe defects, deficiencies, or errors. The observation of imperfections starts the creative person on his way to creative production. The observation of inadequacy of solutions also keeps the creative thinker at work on his problem (17).

Factor analysis has consistently upheld this hypothesis by finding an ability common to a variety of tests calling for the noticing of defects and deficiencies in such things as common household appliances, social customs, or in solutions to problems. Such an ability, however, seems to fit better in the general category of evaluative factors than it does in that of divergent production.

Not being satisfied with things as they are is a matter of evaluation. We hear a great deal about the "divine discontent" of the creative person. It is said that Thomas A. Edison frequently admonished his workers with the comment, "There must be a better way. Go and find it." The uncreative, in contrast, are often willing to settle for half-way measures and tolerably successful solutions to problems.

Another of our initial hypotheses was that many an invention or new idea is the revision of something that is already known. But the revision is not an obvious one. It takes quite a change in the meaning, interpretation, or use of an object to achieve such an innovation. One of our tests, designed for such an ability, asks which of five objects or their parts could be most reasonably adapted to be used to start a fire when there are available the following items: a fountain pen, an onion, a pocket watch, a light bulb, and a bowling ball. The accepted answer is "pocket watch," since the cover of the watch face could be used as a condensing lens. Since this and other such tests call for one best answer, this factor falls logically in the convergent-production category. The feature that makes a contribution to creativity is that a *transformation* must occur; objects must be redefined. Individuals who are clever at improvising seem to show this kind of ability.

There are other abilities outside the divergent-production category that make some contribution to creative performances in their own

184

ways. We have seen that one of the evaluative abilities — sensitivity to problems — has a function in getting the creative thinker started. Other evaluative abilities should have their uses, whether judgment is suspended or not, in determining whether the products of thinking are good, useful, suitable, adequate, or desirable. If the creator is to finish his job, he will eventually appraise his product, and he will revise it if he feels that revision is called for.

Cognition and Memory

Thus far I have spoken of three major categories of intellectual factors — abilities of divergent production, convergent production, and evaluation. There are two other major categories — cognitive abilities and memory abilities — all distinguished from those in the first mentioned categories and from each other. Cognitive abilities have to do with discovery, recognition, or comprehension of information in various forms. Memory abilities have to do with storage or retention of information.

Many people, including some teachers, have for some reason disparaged memory and memory abilities. Some of them, who emphasize the importance of thinking, seem wrongly to believe that good thinking and good memory are incompatible qualities, perhaps even negatively correlated. Actually, good memory contributes to good thinking.

It is not a good, well-stocked memory, as such, that is bad, for even the most creative people have given due credit to stored information. It is the way in which storage is achieved and organized that makes the difference between the graduate who is sometimes described as "merely a walking encyclopedia" and the graduate who has a usable and fruitful fund of information. Memory abilities thus make their indirect but important contribution to creative performance.

The question often arises concerning the relation of creativity to intelligence. In connection with this question, the usual conception of "intelligence" is that which is measured by such tests as the Stanford Binet, the Wechsler scales, or the California Test of Mental Maturity.

In discussing abilities related to creativity, I have referred to them as intellectual factors. It is very doubtful whether these abilities, particularly those in the divergent-production category, are represented to any appreciable degree in standard IQ tests. IQ tests were designed to predict success in school learning, particularly in reading, arithmetic, and the subject-matter or informational courses. But we now know that there are many other kinds of intellectual abilities.

Studies of groups of research scientists and engineers (22) show that such groups have high average scores on IQ tests. They would need to have higher-than-average IQs to have passed all their academic hurdles, most of them including the PhD. But only a fraction of these are outstanding for creative performance. But within groups of scientists and engineers, the correlation found between IQ-test scores and creative performance is usually rather low. This is due in part to the restriction of range of IQ within such groups. The evidence seems to indicate that although the qualities in traditional IQ intelligence may be of some help to the creative scientist or engineer, they are by no means sufficient.

The low correlation between creativity and IQ is also found at younger age groups. In high school students, Getzels and Jackson (21, 1959) found that if the highest 20% of the subjects on IQ were selected as "gifted," 70% of those who stood in the highest 20% in terms of divergent-thinking tests would have been missed. Torrance (21, 1959) has reported a similar finding in the elementary grades. In both instances, it was reported that the teachers knew their high-IQ students better and liked them better. The high-creative without high IQs were often regarded as nuisances, and they were somewhat estranged from other students. Those with both high IQ *and* high creativity were recognized as having unusual but sound ideas, to be good in planning and improvising, and effective in getting attention (21, 1959).[2]

---

[2] For systematic treatments of a unified theory of intelligence see references (8, 11).

Non-Aptitude Traits

The assessment of traits of temperament, interest, and attitude in connection with creativity has been approached in various ways. One approach has been to find the most outstandingly creative individuals in different professional groups, such as architects, writers, and scientists, and to assess them quite thoroughly by methods that are available. If a creative group differs systematically from the general population or, better, some group outside the profession but matched with it for age, sex, and educational level, it is concluded that this creative group stands apart or is distinguished by the personality trait or traits in question.

There are obvious dangers in drawing conclusions from studies of this kind, unless an appropriate control group has been used. When it is found that creative architects, scientists, mathematicians, and writers alike tend to score highest on theoretical and esthetic interest on the Allport-Vernon-Lindzey *Study of Values*, this may occur just because any high-IQ group would do the same (14). When it is found that the creative males tend to score relatively in the direction of femininity on the masculinity-femininity scale of the *Minnesota Multiphasic Personality Inventory* scale, we remember that Terman and Miles (24) found that as members of the two sexes are more intelligent and better educated, they respond more alike to test items on masculinity vs. femininity. Nor should it be surprising that the creative groups just mentioned should tend to score high on the Strong *Vocational Interest Blank* scales for architect, psychologist, and author-journalist.

A somewhat better approach is to obtain two samples from the same profession, composed of highly creative and less creative individuals, respectively. The groups can then be compared with respect to various assessed qualities. Sometimes the groups are distinguished on the basis of judgments by their teachers (4, 12). In still other studies, subjects of mixed occupations but similar in IQ and educational level have been tested with measures of creative aptitude and of non-aptitude traits (10).

186

Non-Aptitude Differences

We have had to recognize that creative occupational groups share parallel but different exceptional abilities. We should expect the various groups to show some non-aptitude qualities in common and also to show some differences. One difference, for example, has been noted between creative students of art and of science. The more creative art student has been reported to be more of an observer than a participant in what is going on (12). The more creative science student is reported to be more of a participant than the less creative student (6). Such observations should prevent our generalizing conclusions obtained from one creative group to all other creative groups.

There are many ways in which creative people of many groups are alike, however. There is general agreement that the highly creative person, particularly the original person, is self-confident. Which comes first, originality or self-confidence? It is a little like the old hen-and-the-egg problem. Probably, it works both ways: Originality yields success and hence self-confidence, and self-confidence leads the individual to attempt to solve problems where others would give up. In some instances, self-confidence goes over into conceit, as we have all been aware. Sometimes this is fed by the adulations of admirers. Sometimes it may suggest an underlying hypersensitivity to criticism.

Along with self-confidence, there is usually self-assurance or social boldness. The creative person is especially confident about his own judgment and his own evaluations of his work. He is often described as an independent thinker, which includes having an independent set of values. If he thinks his product is good, he discounts the criticisms of others and may disparage their judgments.

Not only is he more or less independent of other people's judgments, he may be self-sufficient in that he can take people or he can let them alone. He is likely to find ideas more important than people, though he is not necessarily a social recluse. These qualities do not add to his popularity with others, so he is in danger of becoming estranged from his parents, his teachers, and his peers. Contributing to this state of affairs also is a lack of mutual understanding. The creative child and his associates may need special counseling to smooth over some roughness in interpersonal relationships. This can be done without curbing development along creative lines.

We have found that young men who stand high in one or more kinds of fluency are likely to be somewhat impulsive, cheerful, and relaxed. Those who score high in tests of originality tend to have strong esthetic interests, and they like to indulge in divergent thinking. They do not feel much need for meticulousness or for discipline. Somewhat surprisingly, they show no particular dislike for conventional or socially approved behavior, nor do they show signs of neuroticism.

One of the striking traits found by Getzels and Jackson (21, 1959) among high school students who stand high in divergent-thinking tests is a strong sense of humor. This is shown particularly in the kinds of stories they tell in response to pictures. For example, one picture showed a young man working at his desk at six-thirty in the morning. A bright but less creative student wrote the following kind of story: "This young man is very ambitious to get ahead. He comes early every morning to impress his boss so he will be promoted." A more creative student told the following kind of story: "This picture is the office of a firm that manufactures breakfast cereals. It has just found a formula to produce a new kind of cereal that will bend, sag, and sway. The man is a private eye employed by a rival firm to obtain the formula. He thinks he has found it and copies it. It turns out to be the wrong formula, and the competitor's factory blows up."

Such stories usually involve some novel twist or transformation, such as the expression regarding the cereal that will "bend, sag, and sway." Many stories derive their humor from such a source. The person who makes up such stories is exhibiting verbal or semantic transformations, which is a sign that he has a fair degree of the factor of originality. Since this is a

semantic ability, and since Getzels and Jackson's tests were verbal, we may well question whether the affiliation of humor and the ability to produce transformations extends to other kinds of content, figural or symbolic. It is probably true, however, that creative painters, composers, and mathematicians also experience a certain amount of enjoyment, if not amusement, in playfulness with their own kinds of materials.

Final Suggestions

Although the temperament and motivational qualities can help us somewhat in identifying potentially creative people, no one of them is a dependable sign, nor would all of them collectively be sufficient. Neither do these qualities help us very much in understanding the nature of the creative processes. On the whole, we have less chance of changing individuals with respect to these qualities in order to increase their creativity, except for changing certain attitudes.

Our chief hope, then, of either identifying the more creative persons or enhancing their creative performances lies with the aptitude factors. If we regard the intellectual factors as distinct but somewhat generalized thinking skills, this statement seems more reasonable. We develop skills by practicing them. The question, then, is one of what kinds of practice can best be applied and under what conditions.

An understanding of the nature of the skills is one of the most important steps either for the teacher or the student. When we know what kind of skill is to be developed, we have a more clearly defined goal toward which to work. Torrance (21, 1959) reports that even after 20 minutes of instruction on the nature of divergent-thinking processes, grade-school children showed a clearly observable improvement in performing tasks of this type.

Although special courses on creative thinking have proved beneficial, our whole educational system can be of greater help by giving more attention to this subject. There is abundant opportunity to teach almost any subject in ways that call for productive thinking rather than rote memory. Even the multiplication tables can be taught in ways that give the pupil insight into properties of the number system.

In some experimental courses at the University of Illinois in which mathematics is taught from the lower grades on by what is called a "discovery" method, instead of telling the child the axioms and other principles of mathematics, the teacher lets him discover them for himself by exposing him to appropriate examples. Also at the University of Illinois, science is being taught to children by a discovery method. Some natural phenomenon is demonstrated without explanations to the class, perhaps in motion-picture form. From then on, it is a matter of the students' asking questions, with minimum information being given by the teacher, until the student develops his own satisfactory hypothesis.

Education in this country has unfortunately been too much dominated by the learning theory based upon the stimulus-response model of Thorndike, Hull, and Skinner. People, after all, are not rats (with a few exceptions), and they are not pigeons (with similar exceptions). Let us make full use of the human brains that have been granted to us. Let us apply a psychology that recognizes the full range of human intellectual qualities. We must make more complete use of our most precious national resource — the intellectual abilities of our people, including their creative potentialities.

References

1. Berger, R. M., Guilford, J. P., and Christensen, P. R. A factor-analytic study of planning abilities. *Psychol. Monogr.*, 1957, 71, (Whole No. 435).
2. Christensen, P. R., Guilford, J. P., and Wilson, R. C. Relations of creative responses to working time and instructions. *J. exp. Psychol.*, 1957, 53, 82–88.
3. Crawford, R. P. *Techniques of creative thinking.* New York: Hawthorn Books, 1952.
4. Drevdahl, J. E. Factors of importance for creativity. *J. clin. Psychol.*, 1956, 12, 21–26.
5. Frick, J. W., Guilford, J. P., Christensen, P. R., and Merrifield, P. R. A factor-analytic study of flexibility in thinking. *Educ. psychol. Measmt.*, 1959, 19, 469–496.
6. Garwood, D. S. Some personality factors related to creativity in young scientists. Unpublished doctoral dissertation, Clarement Graduate School, 1961.
7. Guilford, J. P. Creativity. *Amer. Psychologist*, 1950, 5, 444–454.
8. Guilford, J. P. Three faces of intellect. *Amer. Psychologist*, 1959, 14, 469–479.
9. Guilford, J. P., and Christensen, P. R. A factor-analytic study of verbal fluency. *Rep. psychol. Lab.*, No. 17. Los Angeles: Univer. Southern California, 1957.
10. Guilford, J. P., Christensen, P. R., Frick, J. W., and Merrifield, P. R. The relations of creative-thinking aptitudes to non-aptitude personality traits. *Rep. psychol. Lab.*, No. 20. Los Angeles: Univer. Southern California, 1957.
11. Guilford, J. P., and Merrifield, P. R. The structure of intellect model: its uses and implications. *Rep. psychol. Lab.* No. 24. Los Angeles: Univer. Southern California, 1960.
12. Hammer, E. F. *Creativity.* New York: Random House, 1961.
13. Hyman, H. *Some experiments in creativity.* New York: General Electric, Relations Services, 1960.
14. MacKinnon, D. What do we mean by talent and how do we use it? In *The search for talent.* New York: College Entrance Board, 1960.
15. Meadow, A., and Parnes, S. J. Evaluation of training in creative problem solving. *J. appl. Psychol.*, 1959, 43, 189–194.
16. Meadow, A., Parnes, S. J., and Reese, H. Influence of brainstorming instructions and problem sequence on a creative problem solving test. *J. appl. Psychol.*, 1959, 43, 413–416.
17. Merrifield, P. R., Guilford, J. P., Christensen, P. R., and Frick, J. W. A factor-analytical study of problem-solving abilities. *Rep. psychol. Lab.*, No. 22. Los Angeles: Univer. Southern California, 1960.
18. Osborn, A. F. *Applied imagination.* New York: Scribner's, 1953.
19. Osborn, A. F. *Development of creative education.* Buffalo, N. Y.: Creative Education Foundation, 1961.
20. Parnes, S. J., and Meadow, A. Evaluation of persistence of effects produced by a creative problem solving course. *Psychol. Reports*, 1960, 7, 357–361.
21. Taylor, C. W. (ed.) *Research conference on the identification of creative scientific talent.* Salt Lake City, Utah: University of Utah Press, 1956, 1958, 1959.
22. Taylor, D. W. Thinking and creativity. *Ann. N. Y. Acad. Sci.*, 1960, 91, 108–127.
23. Taylor, D. W., Berry, P. C., and Block, C. H. Does group participation when using brainstorming facilitate or inhibit creative thinking? *Admin. Sci. Quart.*, 1958, 3, 23–47.
24. Terman, L. M., and Miles, Catherine C. *Sex and personality.* New York: McGraw-Hill, 1936.

Richard S. Crutchfield

Nurturing the Cognitive Skills of Productive Thinking

One of the cardinal aims of education is to develop cognitive skills, the skills of acquiring, understanding, creating, and using knowledge. In pursuit of this aim, traditional school-work has concentrated mostly upon the simplest of these skills, those concerned with the sheer acquisition of subject matter. Relatively neglected, and often ignored, have been the higher-level skills of productive thinking and problem solving.

Traditional curricula are so heavily weighted with the learning of specific subject matter content that there is little room in the program for anything else. Since the skills related to this kind of subject matter acquisition have been regarded as much more easily developed than the more advanced skills of thinking, there has been in elementary schoolwork a preoccupation with the former kinds of skills and a temporary putting aside of the latter. Yet this postponement has more often been permanent than temporary; for secondary schools make no more than minimal efforts to deal with the skills of productive thinking, and even institutions of higher learning do very little in this regard. (Notice that they are not called "institutions of higher thinking"!)

Underlying this comparative neglect of the training of thinking skills seem to be at least two implicit assumptions, both ill-founded and

Abridged Version — Richard S. Crutchfield, "Nurturing the Cognitive Skills of Productive Thinking." *Life Skills in School and Society*, ASCD 1969 Yearbook, Washington, D. C.: Association for Supervision and Curriculum Development, 1969. Reprinted with permission of the Association for Supervision and Curriculum Development and Richard S. Crutchfield. Copyright © 1969 by the Association for Supervision and Curriculum Development.

mutually incompatible. One view is that these skills *cannot* be trained. The other view is that they *do not need* to be trained. The first view — that productive thinking and problem solving are simply not trainable — is based on the assumption that the marked individual differences found at all ages in ability to think and solve problems are a function of basic intellectual abilities of a deep-seated kind not readily susceptible to modification. There is gradually accumulating evidence that this assumption is wrong. A number of quite different approaches are showing success in direct attempts to facilitate the productive thinking and problem-solving performance of students at all ability levels. Some relevant evidence of this kind will be presented later in this paper pertaining to the successful promotion of such thinking skills in the upper elementary grades.

The second view — that the highly advanced skills of productive thinking and problem solving do not require direct training — is based on the assumption that they will more or less automatically develop as the student learns more and more subject matter; in short, the higher-level cognitive skills are assumed to be merely an extension and elaboration and adding together of the simpler cognitive skills. It is very doubtful that this assumption is correct. There seems no good reason to suppose that the higher-level mental skills can be counted on to emerge automatically out of the simpler ones. Productive thinking and problem solving are complex processes which require direct attention in and of themselves. They are not just the additive end products of simpler cognitive processes.

Indeed, the view we present here is quite the opposite: In their fullest sense, *all* cognitive

189

skills, even the simplest of the skills of acquiring information, are properly to be conceived of as integral parts of the more general processes of productive thinking. Productive thinking should not be conceived of as something special, rarefied, and removed from the usual mental activity of the individual. It is what goes on, or should go on, whenever the individual is engaged in cognitive work. And that is true equally of the young child and the mature student. Viewed in this way it becomes artificial to separate cognitive skills into simpler ones which do not require thinking and more complex ones which do. At every age and at every level of complexity, the training of cognitive skills should be seen as the training of productive thinking.

As we have said, the simplest cognitive skills have to do with the acquisition of information. A major part of the student's schoolwork in the traditional educational setting is the exercise of this function: He memorizes facts, and he regurgitates the facts on command. Put thus baldly, it would appear that the individual's cognitive task in acquiring information is straightforward and uncomplicated and that the requisite skills are simple and few. Certainly there would seem to be nothing involved in the way of productive thinking. Indeed, the only "problem" to be solved in this kind of schoolwork seems to be that of passing the test or of otherwise satisfying the teacher that the facts have been learned. Viewed in this way there would seem to be little of significance to add to what has already been said repeatedly by educational psychologists about the best ways of training for the skills of efficient memorization of facts, e.g., repetition, distribution of practice, and use of incentives.

The Acquisition Process

What is at fault here is a misleading description of the acquisition process. This process has been too narrowly conceived in much of traditional educational practice, being viewed mainly as one of sheer intake and output of unmodified information. It should properly be thought of in quite a different way — as a process of *assimilation*, in which the incoming information must be operated upon by the individual, restructured and transformed and fitted meaningfully into his preexisting conceptual world. It is this problem of assimilating the new information into what is already there which requires productive thinking by the individual whenever he learns subject-matter content.

Reformulated in this way, it becomes clear that the requisite cognitive skills for assimilating information are by no means mundane; indeed they are essentially *creative*. For the problem posed by the intake of a given piece of information is unique to each individual. He must seek to assimilate the new information in a way which successfully fits it into and reshapes *his own* conceptual world. And since no two individuals possess an identical conceptual world, his solution must be to some degree distinctive and innovative.

Figuratively speaking, the person must make the fact his own. In becoming "part of himself," the fact has necessarily been changed in some degree. It is no longer the "same" fact that it was, nor is it now the "same" fact that exists in other people's minds. He must render the fact relevant and meaningful, and he must do this through a process of directed mental activity which has as its end the complete ingesting, metabolizing, and incorporating of the fact in such a way that is becomes widely "distributed" throughout the diverse reaches of his conceptual system.

When we consider the customary manner in which facts are taught and learned in school, the foregoing description of the essential cognitive process occurring in the assimilation of new information may seem overly elaborate, exaggerated, or even downright wrong. Yet that is because what we customarily have in the classroom is the routine acquiring of trivial facts, or of potentially significant facts that are taught and learned in a trivializing fashion. What the school should be dealing with, instead, are clearly non-trivial facts — those which have widespread implications, those which can (if the student will but think) connect with and modify many diverse parts of his ideational world. And what the school should be concerned with is the presentation of such potentially significant facts in a non-trivializing way. Each significant piece of information, properly presented, constitutes a problem for assimilation. The student should be brought to attack the problem — to engage in productive thinking about it, to analyze the information, to consider its many implications, and to see how and where it fits, or fails to fit, with his other knowledge. Though the necessary hard, elaborative, cognitive work can be aided by the teacher and facilitated by class discussion, it must in the last analysis be done by the individual student himself.

The effective training of any skill, such as this skill in assimilating new information, requires methods for assessing the progress and outcomes of the training. For evaluating the sheer acquisition of unmodified facts as customarily required in the school, the method is a simple testing of how accurately the student can regurgitate and reproduce the memorized facts. But for assessing the outcomes of the productive thinking process involved in assimilating new information in the way described above, the evaluative approach must be both deeper and more comprehensive in scope. Evidence must be sought that the new information has indeed made a discernible difference in the individual's mind, in diverse and widely ramified aspects. Evidence is needed that the given fact, in the process of being assimilated into the total belief-system of the student, has produced changes in other contexts and structures of his belief-system, especially when the new fact is in some degree inconsistent with his preexisting beliefs.

Evidence is also needed on the extent to which the newly assimilated information has come to assume a proper salience in the individual's mind. This might be obtained, for example, by determining the ease with which the information appears "spontaneously" in a variety of mental contexts in the absence of explicit direction, and by determining the threshold for retrieval of the information under conditions of direct inquiry. This foregoing account of the extensive requirements for an adequate testing of how well a piece of new information has been assimilated by the student brings into sharp relief the distinction between this kind of productive thinking process and the commonplace, low-level process of sheer routine acquisition of facts.

The purpose of this lengthy excursion into the nature of the skills of assimilating information has been to substantiate the earlier assertion that all cognitive skills, simple as they may appear to be, are properly to be conceived of as requiring the exercise of productive thinking and problem solving. It seems perfectly clear, therefore, that the school must concern itself directly with the training and nurturing of productive thinking and problem-solving skills in all students and at all levels. The remainder of this paper will consider the nature of the thinking skills which are involved in problem solving and what can be done to train and nurture these skills.

The Skills of Problem Solving

We should make clear at the outset that in this discussion of problem-solving skills the term "problem" is meant broadly, pertaining to all kinds of subject matter and all domains of human activity. Both simple and highly complex problems must be included; so must precisely stated and well-structured problems as well as those which are loosely defined and weakly structured. The spectrum of problems must include the briefest, lasting but a few seconds, and those which stretch out over prolonged periods of time with many sessions of work by the individual. And problems may not only be fixed and static in nature, but may also be such as to undergo constant changes in structure and conditions as they are worked on.

Problems include those for which there are unique solutions as well as those for which there are multiple solutions; those with partial solutions and those with complete solutions. Problems differ in the type of solution sought: some pertain to the achievement of understanding, as in the assimilation of new information described previously; others pertain to explanation, as in the accounting for a puzzling phenomenon in science; others pertain to the creation of an innovative way of accomplishing an end, such as in resolving a conflict in human relations.

Although problems are usually defined and evaluated within an objective framework common to all individuals, they sometimes must be viewed within a purely individual and subjective framework. Some problems can be defined meaningfully from the perspective of the person himself; the success of the artist who seeks to construct on canvas a painting that "fits" what he has in mind can be judged only from his own frame of reference. How successfully he communicates to the viewer what he has in mind is a quite different, more objective, problem. Whether or not the solution to a problem is judged "creative" will depend in part upon the particular circumstances of the individual, how much relevant information he possessed, and how much he knew of other people's prior solutions to the problem.

For all of these diverse types of problems — simple and complex, brief and protracted, partial and complete, objective and subjective — the problem-solving process involves a large variety of thinking skills. We shall first discuss each of the specific skills and then consider the manner in which they are organized and integrated through the operation of a master thinking skill. We conceive of these various skills as *generalized,* that is, as transcending any particular kind of problem or subject matter. The importance of the role played by any specific skill will vary, of course, depending upon the particular problem and subject matter. Some problems will require a relatively large amount of attention to clarification of the questions, others a great amount of analysis of data; some problems will require a relatively large amount of idea generation, others a large amount of testing and checking out of ideas. But to some degree all these, and the other skills, will enter into virtually every problem.

Problem Discovery

One main set of skills has to do with *problem discovery and formulation.* The individual must, in the first place, somehow become aware of a problem — either through recognizing a problem which already exists, or by creating a novel problem out of his own incessant mental activities.

This crucial stage in the productive thinking process tends to be short-circuited or completely omitted in the typical problem solving which the child does in school. For example, a mathematics problem or a science problem is usually given to him in an already neatly packaged and labeled form. The relevant terms and conditions of the problem are clearly and specifically stated, and the question to be answered is explicitly put. Obviously, under these special circumstances, the student is not called upon to exercise or train in the important skills having to do with detecting and defining problems. But these special, and somewhat artificial, circumstances are not representative of most of the "real life" problem solving in which the individual engages. In most cases he is not the passive recipient but rather the active seeker and discoverer of problems. And in most cases the problems he discovers are not clearly demarcated and explicitly defined but are imprecisely structured and difficult to formulate.

As the individual experiences and copes with complex situations and phenomena, he seeks to make some kind of sense of them. In so doing he may detect something puzzling, something which demands explanation or accounting for. He may notice an apparent inconsistency among several facts, an incongruity of some kind, something strange which violates what is to be expected, a causal gap. The accomplished problem solver has a sharpened sensitivity to such puzzling things and is adept in narrowing down and pinpointing the source and nature of the puzzlement.

Although such skills are especially in demand during the origin and initiation of problems, they are also germane at all stages of the problem-solving process. The total problem may need to be broken up into several subproblems, each of them requiring separate specification. Moreover, at any point during work on a problem the person needs to be open to the discovery of wholly *new* problems, arising unexpectedly out of the old problem, and leading into entirely different directions. It is, indeed, one of the hallmarks of the truly creative thinker that he has this continuous set toward problem discovery — a readiness to find problems everywhere, to be puzzled by the obvious, to see the extraordinary in the ordinary, to make the familiar into the strange.

For a problem to be discovered is, of course, the first essential. Yet to attack the problem effectively requires that it then be *formulated* in a meaningful way by the individual; he must state the problem to himself in a form which points up the crucial issue to be solved and which avoids a misleading set. For example, the problem should not be stated in a way that implies a certain answer or range of answers to the exclusion of other possible answers. This skill in problem formulation is a difficult one and requires a great deal of training. The individual must be able to counteract a strong disposition toward conventional or traditional ways of stating the issue. A problem that has been worked on by others may prove intractable just because the individual too readily falls in with formulating the problem in the identical terms previously used. New solutions to old problems often occur because the new formulation of the problem is a more appropriate or powerful one. The inexperienced problem solver may not realize how much scope there generally is for alternative formulations of an issue. Part of the training he needs is to be shown the various possibilities and to be given practice in discriminating and choosing among these alternatives.

Processing Information

A second broad set of problem-solving skills has to do with the *organizing and processing of problem information*. Having formulated the problem for himself, the individual must now get the essentials of the problem well in mind. He must identify the boundary conditions of the problem and the circumstances which govern it; he must get an overview of the facts, and must put the facts into some orderly form; he must distinguish the relevant facts from the irrelevant; he must recognize gaps in the available information and specify what other data are needed to fill these gaps.

The organizational and analytical mental skills involved in these various requirements are fairly obvious ones. We shall not dwell upon these skills, partly because they have been given disproportionately large emphasis in traditional work on thinking which concentrates most heavily upon logical reasoning, critical thinking, and analytical functioning, rather than upon the kind of productive or creative thinking which concerns us here. However, it should be mentioned that the manner and degree in which these skills are called upon in problem solving depend heavily upon the type of problem. In the highly structured problem exercises that the student is often given in school, e.g., in mathematics or science, the problem information is substantially "predigested" for the student; the problem conditions are rigorously specified, the relevant facts are clearly stated, and all irrelevant facts are omitted. Obviously in these cases the student requires little use of the skills we are here describing. It should also be noted that this manner of problem presentation is highly artificial and unrepresentative of the kinds of problems customarily encountered in the everyday thinking of the person. In more realistic circumstances, problems are "messy" and cluttered with confusion and irrelevancy. A crucial part of successful problem solving in these cases is the adept use of skills in organizing and processing the information.

Another point is that problems vary widely along a dimension of sheer complexity. Simple problems are likely to involve a small amount of information; complex problems tend to be embedded in the context of very large bodies of information. In the latter, the problem solver must be able to exercise skills of rapid mental and perceptual scanning, of flexible deployment of attention, of efficient categorizing, and the like.

Idea Generation

A third broad set of problem-solving skills has to do with *idea generation*. Having formulated the problem; having gotten the relevant information well in mind, the individual must now come up with possibilities for solutions, directions to be investigated, hypotheses to be tested. These skills of idea generation are the very core of the problem-solving process. It is what happens at this fateful point, perhaps more than anywhere else, that determines whether the problem solver will succeed or fail in his quest. And what does happen here depends heavily upon the level to which these idea generation skills are developed in the individual.

In light of this, it is especially significant that of all cognitive skills, the typical school does *least* with the nurturing of idea generation. Depressingly little attention is given to stimulation of ideas in most schoolwork at most levels. This is partly because of the deadening influence of the conventional curriculum and teaching methods with their heavy stress upon the "authority" of established knowledge. Also, it reflects an uneasiness in some teachers about being able to cope with classroom creativity. It also stems from an implicit assumption on the part of many educators that "ideational fluency," "creative thinking," and the like, are deeply-rooted individual traits not at all susceptible to training.

It is certainly true that we do observe enormous individual differences in these idea-generation skills at all ages from young children to adults. Yet we also find evidence from many sources that these skills *are* subject to training, that the individual can be made better able to think of productive ideas. Studies of so-called "brainstorming" are but one such example. The successful use of "inquiry" methods in some of the new curricula is another example. Later we shall offer additional direct evidence on the point.

Part of the strengthening of idea-generation skills depends upon sheer repeated practice in thinking of ideas, something of which we have said the schools provide too little. Such practice is made meaningful by the learning and use of certain *strategies* of idea generation. One such strategy, for example, is the sequential scanning systematic listing of attributes of each element

as a source of ideas. Another strategy is the orderly exploration of the ramifications of "idea-trees," by proceeding from the enumeration of general possibilities to the spelling out of specific ideas. Another strategy that the individual can learn to use is that of analogical and metaphorical thinking. Through searching for parallels and similarities with other perceived phenomena he can often come to discover whole new sets of ideas relevant to his problem.

Still another strategy is to plumb systematically the rich source of ideas which lies in what he has previously experienced and stored away in memory having to do with related phenomena, and with potentially applicable facts, concepts, and principles. How readily accessible these are to him as he works on a problem will — to revert to our earlier point — depend heavily upon the skill with which he has originally assimilated and stored them. Here we see a particularly compelling example of the way in which the various cognitive skills are inextricably interrelated.

The most creative ideas usually derive from some sort of *restructuring* of one's conception of the problem. The earlier way of looking at the problem must be abandoned and a wholly new perspective discovered. Tacit and misleading assumptions and rigid preconceptions must be overcome. A questioning and even skeptical stance must be assumed. These skills in insightful mental reformulation are perhaps the least studied and least understood. Yet there is every reason to believe that they, like the other skills of thinking, are susceptible to training. Some evidence on this will be mentioned later.

Evaluation of Ideas

The final set of problem-solving skills which we will mention has to do with the *evaluation of ideas*. This is, as some would call it, the stage of hypothesis testing. What is required of the individual here is a fairly high-level kind of critical and logical thinking. He must check to determine how consistent his idea is with respect to the detailed requirements of the problem. He must engage in a process of inferential thought in which the consequences or implications or likely outcomes of his idea are explicated. He must decide what specific evidence would be relevant to the confirmation or the rejection of the idea. Eventually, he must gather and marshal the evidence and come to a decision about the validity of the idea — whether it is to be accepted, modified, or abandoned as a solution to the problem.

In simple problems having clearly defined solutions, the skills of idea evaluation are relatively straightforward. The correct answer may be immediately evident once it has been thought of, or it may easily be checked in a rigorous and unambiguous way against the problem statement. Yet in complex problems involving a great amount of data, incomplete information, and the possibility of multiple alternative answers, the evaluation process may be considerably more difficult. The correctness of an answer or the validity of an idea may only be ascertained after a considerable amount of work. And in many cases, perhaps most cases, the evaluation cannot be made with complete certainty. Often the best that can be said is that a particular answer or idea is "likely" or "unlikely." In short, the individual must have the skill of weighing evidence and coming up with a probable decision. In the face of overwhelming complexity and unresolvable uncertainty, the superior problem solver may have to be able to exhibit an intuitive "feel" for the rightness or wrongness of a tentative idea.

For convenience in exposition we have chopped up the total process of problem solving into the skills of problem formulation, information processing, idea generation, and idea evaluation. But this gives a false picture of the actual process. Problem solving does not always, or even usually, proceed in these tidily ordered stages. Typically, the stages are overlapping and intertwined. The process does not necessarily begin at the beginning and end at the end. Often an idea occurs to the person *before* he has adequately stated the problem; a period of information processing may precede rather than follow the emergence and formulation of a problem; an answer may wander in search of an appropriate question. There may be direct insightful leaps from problem to solution with the intervening steps of logical thought not filled in until after the fact. Moreover, for complex problems which involve many facets and many steps, the individual will often be working on several different subproblems simultaneously, each at a different stage of development.

In short, the problem-solving process is not a cut-and-dried sequence of steps executed in the orderly manner of the pre-established program of a computer. This is not the appropriate model for either the student thinking productively in the classroom or the scientist experimenting in the laboratory. It should be noted that despite the venerable dogma of the "scientific method," much testimony agrees that productive thinking by scientists proceeds very differently from the "textbook" accounts of it. Creative thinking of scientists, like that of other creators, is often a wild and even chaotic process whose history is retrospectively tamed and rectified so as to fit better the stereotyped image of rational scientific thought.

It is clear that the process of solving problems is highly complicated, involving a great number of separate but interrelated cognitive skills. Whether or not the individual succeeds in solving the problem depends heavily upon his ability to marshal these skills in an effectively coordinated way. He must know which step to take at a given point, which plan of attack to adopt. He must know how to employ sensible "stop strategies," for instance, to be able to decide when it is time to stop collecting information and to start generating ideas, when it is time to stop generating ideas and to start evaluating them, and when it is time to abandon one direction of thought and to embark on another. He must be able to balance and harmonize the often contradictory demands which arise in the problem. For as we have seen, at times he needs to be rigorously analytical, at other times freely unconstrained and imaginative; at times he needs to be intensely involved in the problem, at other times capable of detachment from it to gain perspective; at times he may need to give free rein to an impulsive jumping to conclusions, at other times a patient reflectiveness is required.

A Master Thinking Skill

The ability of the individual to manage all these diverse and disparate requirements in the problem-solving process has been termed the *master thinking skill*.[1] This is a metaskill which enables the effective coordination, integration, and utilization of the many specific skills we have already enumerated. Without this overall master thinking skill, an individual may be able to accomplish some parts of the process, but not others. He may be capable of an outpouring of ideas but be unable at the same time to distinguish the good from the poor. He may be able to see the flaw in the evidence but utterly unable to come up with a new conception of the issue. On the other hand, in possessing a sufficiently developed master thinking skill, the individual will be enabled to make progress toward problem solution in all these interacting functions. The ultimate objective criterion for an adequate degree of development of this master thinking skill is, quite simply then, the person's success in achieving *solutions* to problems.

The educational implications of these comments about the master thinking skill are clear. If we seek to nurture the student's ability to think, then we must give him appropriate

[1] R. S. Crutchfield. "Creative Thinking in Children: Its Teaching and Testing." In: O. G. Brim, Jr., R. S. Crutchfield and W. H. Holtzman. *Intelligence: Perspectives, 1965. The Terman-Otis Memorial Lectures.* New York: Harcourt, Brace & World, Inc., 1966, pp. 33–64.

training on the many specific skills we have described. But in order to do this most effectively — so as to practice these skills in a mutually reinforcing way and to make for optimal transfer — we should train them simultaneously in the context of whole problems which have considerable scope, complexity, and meaningfulness. In this fashion the student will practice using his productive mental processes in the integrated way they must be used for genuine problem solving in his school studies and in other "real life" situations.

To practice one of the specific component skills without reference to its place in the integrated performance pattern would be analogous to a pianist exercising the pressing of the foot pedal without any reference to the synchronization of the hands on the keyboard, the visual input from the music sheet, or the auditory feedback from the sound of the keys. The pianist's purpose is to produce music, and his skill in using the pedal is but a single part of the organized whole; as such it must constantly be coordinated with all of the other specific skills of the whole performance. Similarly, the thinker's purpose is to solve a problem by using many specific cognitive skills. These skills must be effectively coordinated with one another if the problem-solving process is to go forward to a successful conclusion. The perfecting of one of these specific cognitive skills is thus as much a matter of learning how to integrate it with the other concurrently operating skills as it is a matter of practicing this skill by itself. In short, what is required is the development and strengthening of the master thinking skill.

John Holt

Excerpt from How Children Fail

June 20, 1960

How can we tell whether children understand something or not? When I was a student, I generally knew when I understood and when I didn't. This had nothing to do with marks; in the last math course I took in college I got a respectable grade, but by the end of the year I realized I didn't have the faintest idea of what the course was about. In Colorado, I assumed for a long time that my students knew when they did, or did not, understand something. I was always urging them to tell me when they did not understand, so that with one of my clever "explanations" I could clear up everything. But they never would tell me. I came to know by painful experience that not a child in a hundred knows whether or not he understands something, much less, if he does not, why he does not. The child who knows, we don't have to worry about; he will be an A student. How do we find out when, and what, the others don't understand?

What first comes to mind is some external test. But what kind? By now I have many times seen children crank out right answers to problems without the faintest idea of what they were doing. They are blind recipe-followers. Some can even parrot back my explanations, but again without knowing what they mean. On the other hand, there are many children who are so paralyzed by their fear of tests that they can't show what they do know, while others who understand clearly what they are doing

get confused and scared when they try to put it into words.

Part of the answer to the problem may be to give children the kind of tests I used this year, in which there was a mixture of problems. These tend to throw the automatic answer-finding machinery out of gear and to make them do some thinking about what they are doing. It may help, too, to give problems in a form new to them. But what do we do when the result of such tests is to show that hardly any of our pupils understand anything of what we have been trying to teach them during the year?

It may help to have in our minds a picture of what we mean by understanding. I feel I understand something if and when I can do some, at least, of the following: (1) state it in my own words; (2) give examples of it; (3) recognize it in various guises and circumstances; (4) see connections between it and other facts or ideas; (5) make use of it in various ways; (6) foresee some of its consequences; (7) state its opposite or converse. This list is only a beginning; but it may help us in the future to find out what our students really know as opposed to what they can give the appearance of knowing, their *real learning* as opposed to the *apparent learning*.

There are many, of course, who say that this distinction does not exist. It's their handy way of solving the knotty problem of understanding; just say there is no such thing. Apparently this view is currently in fashion among psychologists. According to many of them, if you can say that 7 x 8 = 56, you know all there is to know about that particular fact, and you know as

197

much about it as anyone else who can say it. The mathematician, the third grader, and, presumably, a well-trained parrot, would all have an equal and identical understanding of this fact. The only difference between the mathematician and the child is that the mathematician carries around in his head many more such facts. So as to make children into mathematicians all we have to do is train them, condition them, until they can say many such facts. Teach them to say everything that Einstein knew, and hey, presto! another Einstein!

It's amazing what nonsense people will believe.

Of course, this notion fits neatly into behaviorism, which is also still very much in fashion, despite all it cannot explain. It is also comforting to teachers, who have felt all along that their job is to drop, or push, one at a time, little bits of information into those largely empty minds that are moving slowly before them down the academic assembly line. And finally, it has set into motion the apparently endless gravy train of programed instruction and machine teaching, onto which everyone and his brother seem to be happily clambering.

But pieces of information like 7 x 8 = 56 are not isolated facts. They are parts of the landscape, the territory of numbers, and that person knows them best who sees most clearly how they fit into the landscape and all the other parts of it. The mathematician knows, among many other things, that $7 \times 8 = 56$ is an illustration of the fact that products of even integers are even; that 7×8 is the same as 14×4 or 28×2 or 56×1; that only these pairs of positive integers will give 56 as a product; that 7×8 is $(8 \times 8) - 8$, or $(7 \times 7) + 7$, or $(15 \times 4) - 4$; and so on. He also knows that $7 \times 8 = 56$ is a way of expressing in symbols a relationship that may take many forms in the world of real objects; thus he knows that a rectangle 8 units long and 7 units wide will have an area of 56 square units. But the child who has learned to say like a parrot, "Seven times eight is fifty-six" knows nothing of its relation either to the real world or to the world of numbers. He has nothing but blind memory to help him. When memory fails, he is perfectly capable of saying that $7 \times 8 = 23$, or that 7×8 is smaller than 7×5, or larger than 7×10. Even when he knows 7×8, he may not know 8×7, he may say it is something quite different. And when he remembers 7×8, he cannot use it. Given a rectangle of 7 cm. $\times$ 8 cm., and asked how many 1 sq. cm. pieces he would need to cover it, he will over and over again cover the rectangle with square pieces and laboriously count them up, never seeing any connection between his answer and the multiplication tables he has memorized.

Knowledge, learning, understanding, are not linear. They are not little bits of facts lined up in rows or piled up one on top of another. A field of knowledge, whether it be math, English, history, science, music, or whatever, is a territory, and knowing it is not just a matter of knowing all the items in the territory, but of knowing how they relate to, compare with, and fit in with each other. It is the difference between being able to say that a room in your house has so many tables, so many chairs, so many lamps, and being able to close your eyes and see that this chair goes here and that table there. It is the difference between knowing the names of all the streets in a city and being able to get from any place, by any desired route, to any other place.

Why do we talk and write about the world and our knowledge of it as if they were linear? Because that is the nature of talk. Words come out in single file, one at a time; there's no other way to talk or write. So, in order to talk about it, we cut the real, undivided world into little pieces, and make these into strings of talk, like beads on a necklace. But we must not be fooled; these strings of talk are not what the world is like. Our learning is not real, not complete, not accurate, above all not useful, unless we take these word strings and somehow convert them in our minds into a likeness of the world, a working mental model of the universe as we know it. Only when we have made such a model, and when there is at least a rough correspondence between that model and reality, can it be said of us that we have learned something.

What happens in school is that children take in these word strings and store them, undigested, in their minds, so that they can spit them back out on demand. But these words do not change anything, fit with anything, relate to anything. They are as empty of meaning as parrot-speech is to a parrot. How can we make school a place where real learning goes on, and not just word swallowing?

Caleb Gattegno

The Powers of Children

Most of the things that are without importance to educators today, are the source of what is going to make us do a much better job in education.

What is the task of education? Is it not to provide students with the means to meet the future?

There is one thing that we all agree about with respect to the future, and this is that it is unknown — unknown absolutely if we project far enough and relatively if we consider the relationship of tomorrow to yesterday, which seem not so different.

In devising a system of education, man may wish to stress what remains constant after the passage time, but he can equally well stress that our world is becoming more and more "man-made" as against "natural," and that in such a world we would be on very shaky ground if we identified what will be with what is. The only way to be properly prepared and secure in a changing world is if we accept the future as unknown. (But really the world is always changing.) Such a view is all the more persuasive when we see that it leads to suggestions for doing the job of education that are at least as good as those that follow if we separate the remote and near future and treat them differently. That we must prepare for the unknown is my approach to education — and in a sense is everyone's approach.

Teachers in traditional schools — the schools we have today — know that what they know and have to teach is unknown to the learners. And

they believe that they are making the unknown known by imparting their knowledge to their students. But has this belief proved right? How many readers of this book, for example, understand everything their teachers taught them? Or sixty or forty percent? And to what extent has the sixty or forty percent enabled them to meet what is new and strange? The answers are self-evident. Unfortunately, the traditional approach has not worked well. On the other hand, a method of educating for the future does exist — if we know how to acknowledge what is given us and already is in us, and with this, encounter what is but is not yet part of us.

It happened that every one of us as a child did precisely this. For a while we did not talk, we did not speak, and after a while we did both. That is to say, we met what was and we managed to make it our own. So every one of us as a child was really facing the unknown, meeting the unknown, and developing the techniques for doing it. But when we went to school, we found another technique in use: someone told us what was supposed to be known by us. Teachers told us, "You should know it," and the reason was, "Because I told you" — arrived at by putting together two ideas that are entirely unrelated: the pronouncement by the teacher and the retention or understanding by the student.

Two roughly drawn diagrams will assist us in comparing the way of working that is from the teacher to the student — the traditional method of schooling — and the way of working that is from the student to the world — the method of subordinating teaching to learning. The first diagram portrays the standard way of teaching.

In this approach, knowledge is conceived as

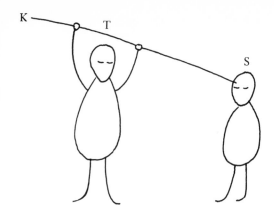

pre-existing and as coming down, through the teacher, from those gifted people who managed to produce it. (Let us note that in this country, the phrase "knowledge industry" expresses just such a view of knowledge.) It is stored in special places called libraries which have books and more modern forms of containers. People who want knowledge have to go there and pick it up, in much the same way that they would acquire any other manufactured product.

Teachers are those people who take knowledge down from the shelves where it is displayed and hand it out to students who presumably need only memory in order to receive it. This process is conceived as the way the student comes to own knowledge. The key to this view — and to the whole traditional way of teaching — is the tacit belief that memory is a power of the mind.

Obviously it is. But still, memory can be strong or weak. La Rochefoucauld said around 1660 in a very short statement: "Man gladly complains of his memory, but not of his intelligence." Was he correct in his implication that memory is in fact a weak power of the mind?

To see that it is we need go no farther than to look at what is done by teachers in order to insure that their students retain the knowledge handed down to them.

Teachers give a *lesson*, thinking that they are passing knowledge on to their students, but since they do not actually know whether they

have succeeded, they proceed to give the students *exercises*.

Why do they give exercises? So that what they themselves cannot do, the exercises will do: get the knowledge securely into their students.

But exercises usually are not sufficient, so teachers also give *homework*. What does homework do? What a teacher cannot do. If the teacher could finish the job in school during school hours, there would not be any need for any homework. That is why students get homework.

It does not end there either. There are also *reviews*. On Monday morning the class reviews what was done the week before. In January the class reviews what was done last term. And next year what was done the previous year. Teachers not only review and review, they also *test* whether students still hold the knowledge. And they do not stop with one cycle of reviewing and testing. Reviewing and testing goes on for years because teachers know that many of their students do not retain the knowledge they are presented with.

So there is this accumulation of props, all to sustain the poor weak memory.

But nobody says that exercises, homework, reviewing, testing, then more exercises, more homework, more reviewing, more testing, and on and on, are there because memory is weak. We do not say that the whole traditional education is based on something that is weak, and that therefore the basis of education should not be memory. Yet the education offered in traditional schools — at least when we are concerned with transmission of knowledge — is described with precision by the above remarks.

This we call the subordination of learning to teaching, illustrated in the first diagram. I hope no reader believes I am trying to ridicule the situation with this diagram. For me, it is an exact illustration. The teacher with one hand gets some knowledge and with the other hand gives it out: that is the operation.

An advantage of such a teaching procedure is that it can be explained at the college level. Professors can explain to teachers how to present a subject and how to refine a presentation. Indeed, in their explanations they use the same approach they are passing on. The diagram applies equally to the work done at institutions of higher learning.

To understand that there once was good reason for Man to choose memory as the channel of instruction in spite of its inadequacies we need only to look back and place ourselves at a time when ways of recording events had not yet been invented. In our individual experience, then and now, we find that much of what we know how to do — talk, walk, breath while eating, etc. — expresses itself in automatic unconscious functionings often difficult to objectify and thus inaccessible to other people. On the other hand, the content of tales, legends, stories, gossip, etc., if repeatedly told, gains an existence of its own which we can attempt to preserve per se as we do objects. When recording of events was not available, the quality of the mind socially most valued was faithfulness (fidelity in the modern electronic sense), and verbatim retention became the highest attribute of a good mind. Since as children we show retention best after we have learned to talk, verbal retention understandably became the object of the care of teachers whether at home, in the forum, or at school. Tests in such a social setting were tests of retention for those who carried the tribal traditions.

When recording appeared, the attribute of retention could be weaker per se since it was supported by the record, and in fact it soon became second best to the record. But this change did not make societies discard the use of memory as the basis for teaching. There still was a stress on traditional transmission; no more individually oriented method of transmission had yet become acceptable to the Establishment. A stable society uninterested in questioning tradition was served well by transmission of well-preserved statements about wisdom and truth.

But in a changing world one discovers that the ability to forget is needed as much as the capacity to retain and that there is no value in taking the time to fix in one's mind what no longer obtains. No one in such a world is prepared to pay a heavy price for what is no longer

functional. This is the situation today. The success, such as it is, of the present system of education through memory results in fact from our own spontaneous use of ourselves as we go beyond the epistemology that describes our growth as greater and greater retention and shift ourselves to other ways of knowing.

Now, what is the alternative to the use of memory?

The alternative is to build on strength. And strengths exist. These I call the *functionings of children,* and they are the basis of all individual education, and now can be made the basis of institutional education.

What are the functionings of children? They could all become known to us because we all have been children. We have used these functionings, we have them in us, and we did with each such a good job, mastering it so successfully, that we do not have to do it again (except in an extreme situation, as with an accident that takes, say, half of one's brain, after which one has to learn to use the other half for the functionings involved with the missing half). On the whole, for example, we learned so well to sit that we do not have to learn to do it ever again. Sitting is one of the functionings of children.

When I was in my crib I worked tremendously hard. I knew that if (while lying on my back) I lifted my legs — which were quite easy to lift — with muscles reachable by my will, I was helping myself to learn to sit. Nobody showed me how to sit. Was any reader of this book taught to sit? Each person looked toward himself and saw for himself the problem of being on one's back and of learning to sit. One cannot say that sitting is instinctual. It takes months to learn. A man is not a little goat who is born having already practiced lots of things and an hour after its birth is standing on its feet. At six months I had not sat before. My mother did. I did not. I had to learn how to sit, and this I did for myself, as every reader did it for himself, in the crib.

If a child's accomplishments in his crib are not impressive, then nothing is impressive. There is no end to the (extraordinary) functionings we all accomplished as children. One of the most impressive is learning to speak. In my crib I discovered that if I worked on the muscle tone of my lips, that would permit me to gain entry into the field of the sounds of speech. I knew that I had to act on the muscle tone first, and by the sixth or seventh or ninth week of my life, I had learned the ways of doing this. And as I produced these ways I used my lips straightaway to produce new sounds, which in turn made me aware of other ways and so on.

As a child, nobody reading this book ever heard a word. In fact nobody ever heard a word. Ears hear voices. And voices are all different. We hear voices, and they differ in pitch and in stresses. There are all sorts of variations: one can have a deep voice or a smooth voice, a very quick speech or slow speech, and so on. And out of all these voices that represent the reality of the environment, each of us has picked up that component that we learned to call word. Every one of us has recognized words as being something one can add to the functioning of the throat one owns so that a sound comes out in a particular guise and is recognized by others as having been produced by one's voice. Children do not learn by imitation, otherwise they would speak at different pitches to the various people they come in contact with. That they do not is one reason that makes us say that children learn to make words through the use of their own mental powers — and learn to do it so well that for their whole life thereafter (barring an unusual accident) they continue to make words without any conscious preparation. (There are other reasons: how can a child even *see* the tongue movements that, if he learned speech through imitation, he necessarily would have to duplicate in order to talk?)

What do we learn about the mental powers of children from the fact that the ability to make words becomes one of their functionings? We learn first of all that children are equipped — we are all equipped — with the power of *extraction*, which obviously is very competent since it can find what is common among so large a range of variations.

Second, we have to acknowledge that children have the power to make *transformations*, for to learn to speak is to use transformations

constantly. In every verbal situation in which someone is trying to tell us something, the words are to be used by us as they are by the others. The words cannot simply be repeated.

If someone says to me, "*This* is *my* pen," and I repeated it, I would be wrong; and if we were children, we might quarrel. Then perhaps I would see that I have to say something else to be at peace with the other person, and I might learn very quickly. In any case, I eventually will learn to say, "*That* is *your* pen."

Again, if I look at one person, a woman, and I talk to her, I will use the word "you." But if I look at her and talk of a third person, a man, I must say, "he." Such transformations go on all the time. Indeed, there would be no pronouns in a language if there were no such thing as transformation.

So this is a second power used by children in the process of speaking and developed by it.

Further, everyone who has learned to speak has demonstrated an enormous competence in handling *abstractions*, for no particular word has an exclusive meaning of its own.

Words are signs, arbitrary signs, since each object, for example, can have as many names as there are languages. Not only do children have to extract words from the full packages represented by the voices they hear, they must also attach meaning to the words. Meaning must precede the grasp of what is used by the environment to refer to it.

Nouns, for example, cover classes of objects (*car* applies to all cars, *glass* to all glasses, whatever the make, shape, color, etc.). Verbs cover multitudes of actions or states (*jump* applies to a continuum of distances from the ground, *cry* to any cause for this kind of behavior). Adjectives cover spectra of impressions (*red, rectangular*, etc.) and so on. Children must learn to make the proper abstractions so as to give to words their particular agreed upon meaning, and they do learn.

No one can retain a noun without making allowance for all the changes in lighting, distance, angle of vision, etc., which constantly accompany our constant displacements in the environment.

So to talk I have to learn that I have to demonstrate that I can pick up — extract — something that is as subtle as words. I must recognize the word within the voice that is used. I must also recognize what transformation is required in going from one situation to another. And I must learn, which I do through my powers of abstraction, the meanings attached to words. Therefore I have a functioning as a speaker at the age of two, that could give me a doctorate, for no doctoral student in a university has ever done as good a job equivalent to what we all did when we were one and two years of age finding by ourselves how to acquire the extremely complicated system called language (which in English is more complicated than in many other languages).

Indeed because we all did it, it does not impress us very much. And in my career, in my work with developing new solutions to the problems of education, I have often been considered a fool for having been impressed. But when we look at children as owning the powers they actually have and at how they function, we are overwhelmed with the possibility for education. We are not discouraged, as we are when we look at memory as the only basis for progress.

There is one universal functioning without which nothing is noticed. This is the *stressing* and *ignoring* process.

Without stressing and ignoring, we can not see anything. We could not operate at all. And what is stressing and ignoring if not abstraction? We come with this power and use it all the time. I know that the pitch of my brother and the pitch of my father differ but I ignore the difference so as to comprehend that the words of one are comparable to the words of the other. I ignore that it is only the eye of my mother that I can see when she comes close to my cheek and kisses me. If I did not, the eye, quite likely would frighten me. But I ignore this, and I stress the smell of the person. From this I know it is my mother. That is, I can shift my attention to another attribute that also belongs to her. If I did not do that I would not know that it was my mother that kissed me. To stress and ignore *is* the power of abstraction

that we as children use all the time, spontaneously and not on demand, though in its future uses we may learn to call it forth by demand. And teachers insist that we *teach* abstraction to children through mathematics at the age of twelve!

What does it mean to possess a functioning, to know as children know how to eat, how to sit, how to speak?

What reader of this book literally remembers his native language? Not one. None of us remembers it, we function in it, we have at our disposal the "know-how" to do it. This is what it means to have a functioning.

The know-how leads to skill, the know-how is what we have within us that does not require conscious recall. It is just there. If I had to remember my speech, I would never be able to talk. Anyone observing himself will see that to have an intention to speak is sufficient for all of one's verbal elements to be available and for finding them adequate for one's intention. An individual need not call in these elements one by one; they come, the intention brings the appropriate words in and excludes the others.

Further — and here we move to another point and another power of children — when the words come out, it is the will that acts upon the speech organ for the words to be spoken in the way that the language expects them to sound.

Hence, there must be within us a control system that guides the making of these sounds.

We have established this system in our crib, the feedback mechanism that exists between our utterances and our hearing. All day long the vigilant ear attends to our speech. And what we developed as a result is reliable most of the time. An individual knows when he has made a mistake. He says: "Oh, that is not what I wanted to say." It is the ear that tells him this, not the throat. This task of organization and coordination does not exist when we are first born, we discover it in our crib, and we use it, practice it, refine it, and make it more powerful until it becomes an instrument for knowledge — knowledge that is meaningful within the criteria we have.

Now, as soon as we shift from acquiring facts through memory to acquiring them through functionings, we unify our experience in the duration of one life — for we always build on and integrate with what already exists and do not simply pile one fragment of information upon another — and we recognize that inner meaning is more important than outside authority. Meaning for our psychosomatic organism exists if it either falls readily within the sense of truth already at work or can be integrated in an enlarged functioning of the sense of truth. But in either case it is the person doing to himself what is required in order to receive the new. Hence the person is judging whether there is a reality (within him or outside) that agrees with the existing functionings or requires the widening of oneself to integrate the new. This adaptation of the self to the world is proof both of the malleability of the self and, more directly to the point in this context, of the existence of inner conscious criteria capable of ordering either immediate integration or immediate change in order to achieve integration.

Such inner criteria, which all children have, are the epistemological consequence of the shift from an outside vision of man to one aware of individuals functioning for themselves in their world.

An approach to education that rests on the powers of children — the approach that I call the subordination of teaching to learning — can be illustrated in the following way.

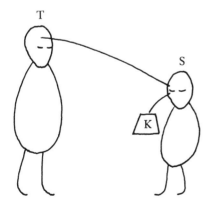

Its contrast to the diagram illustrating the traditional approach is obvious.

Despite all that children know, in school we do not allow them to trust their own perception, only their teachers. At school, to the question "2 plus 3?" some children answer — "Five?" They do not answer "Five!" because they have not been allowed to use the basis of surety that exists in their perception. They have not been allowed to believe in their sense of truth. So knowledge becomes something that is passed on to them. Not something they own. This is the consequence of teaching through memory and not by functionings, and it brings us to the one last power developed in the functionings of children that we need to examine for our present purposes.

The schools have a curriculum that is based upon the teachers providing children with showers of knowledge. Knowledge is so vast that, to make this approach manageable, we take a stretch of knowledge and divide it among thirteen or so years by separating it into little bits. And in its piecemeal quality, Chapter 1 of the first textbook resembles Chapter n of the last.

In the books for teaching a foreign language, for example, all the lessons have the same format. As if having learned something of the language does not change one. One always begins the same way and the lesson invariably follows the same pattern, ending in a test.

In this approach, there is no concern with one of the things that all of us know — that all of us go through — and that is, that practice gives one the capacity to undertake bigger tasks, to be involved in greater challenges. Is this not so? Is it not something that everybody knows, that practice provides us with the capacity to attack bigger tasks?

In my own case, I learned this as an adolescent when I lifted weights. Lifting weights teaches one a lot if one can learn more than lifting weights. I recognized that lifting weights made me have muscles that allowed me to lift bigger weights, and that when I lifted bigger weights, I got bigger muscles which allowed me to lift bigger weights.

205

But this is not the approach that we have imbedded in the curriculum. Instead we work in the same way throughout the entire curriculum and do not take into account that there is a law — *the law of the cumulative effect of learning* — which can be described by saying once you have learned something, once you have mastered something, then you can attack a bigger task. The curriculum should be like a fan, opening up to more and more things, to bigger and bigger things.

These comments point the way to what we can learn from studying the functionings of children.

Additional Resources

Books

Bruner, Jerome S. *On Knowing: Essays for the Left Hand.* New York: Atheneum, 1962.
In this book of essays, Bruner examines how we know what we know and how we can help others to know.

Furth, Hans G. *Piaget for Teachers.* Englewood Cliffs, N.J.: Prentice-Hall, 1970.
Of particular interest to this content area are letter 2, "Piaget's Perspective," letter 6, "The Role of Language in Thinking," and letter 10, "Creative Thinking."

Getzels, Jacob W. and Philip W. Jackson. *Creativity and Intelligence.* New York: Wiley, 1962.
This is a report of a study that questioned the relationship of creativity to intelligence in adolescents; of special value is chapter 3, "On Creative Thinking: The Findings in Theoretical and Educational Context."

Holt, John. *How Children Fail.* New York: Pitman, 1964.
Part 3 contains many interesting classroom episodes that illustrate and develop Holt's concept of real learning.

————. *How Children Learn.* New York: Pitman, 1967.
Holt describes ways in which young children learn effectively without extensive adult direction.

————. *What Do I Do Monday?* New York: Dutton, 1970.
Sections 2, 3, and 4, "The Mental Model," "The Worlds I Live In," and "Learning As Growth," discuss how the learner perceives and acts on reality.

Jones, Richard M., ed. *Contemporary Educational Psychology.* New York: Harper and Row, 1966.
This anthology contains essays that collectively integrate Bruner's concepts of cognition and Kubie's theories about affective learning.

Postman, Neil, and Charles Weingartner. *Teaching as a Subversive Activity.* New York: Delacorte Press, 1969.
Chapter 3, "The Inquiry Method," and chapter 6, "Mean Making," are recommended for expanding the major concepts of this content area.

Shulman, Lee S., and Evan R. Keislar, eds. *Learning by Discovery: A Critical Appraisal.* Chicago: Rand McNally, 1966.
This book offers a wide range of views presented at a conference on the topic of learning by discovery.

Articles

Eisner, Elliot N. "Critical Thinking: Some Cognitive Components." *Teachers College Record* 66 (1965): 624–634.
This article discusses the components of critical thinking and emphasizes their importance in developing the kind of behavior necessary for coping with an increasingly complex environment.

Gagné, Robert M. "Learning Research and Its Implications for Independent

Learning." In *The Theory and Nature of Independent Learning*. Scranton, Pa.: International Textbook Co., 1967.

Gagné discusses the concept of mediation and relates it to stimulus-response models of learning.

Getzels, Jacob W. "Creative Thinking, Problem Solving, and Instruction." In *Theories of Learning and Instruction, NSSE 63rd Yearbook*, edited by Ernest R. Hilgard. Chicago: University of Chicago Press, 1964.

Getzels offers ways that people deal with the "unknown," drawing upon thinkers such as Piaget, Guilford, and Freud.

Gordon, Ira J. "New Conceptions of Children's Learning and Development." In *Learning and Mental Health in the School*, edited by W. B. Waltjen and R. R. Leeper. Washington, D.C.: ASCD, 1966.

Emphasizing the theories of Piaget, Bruner, and Hebb, this overview of cognitive development presents the human organism as an active, information-seeking, and information-processing system.

Hunt, J. McVicker. "The Implications of Changing Ideas on How Children Develop Intellectually." *Children* 2 (May–June 1964) : 83–91.

Hunt discusses the development of intelligence and its implications for preschool programs for disadvantaged children.

Scheerer, Martin. "Problem Solving." *Scientific American* 208 (April 1963) : 118–128. Reprint available from W. H. Freeman and Company, 660 Market Street, San Francisco, Calif. 94104.

This fascinating article illustrates with several problems the shifts in thinking that are necessary for solving them.

Shulman, Lee S. "The Study of Individual Inquiry Behavior." Paper presented at meetings of the American Psychological Association, Washington, D.C., September 2, 1967.

Shulman describes a basic model of inquiry that can be used for classroom inquiry, research, and the teaching inquiry skills.

Films

The Mind of Man, produced by National Educational Television, British Broadcasting Corporation, and Swedish and Bavarian Television. Audio-Visual Center, Indiana University, Bloomington, Indiana.

Areas included in this film are mind development in children, brain structure, reasoning, and the power of the mind in controlling bodily functions.

Why Man Creates. Pyramid Film Producers, P.O. Box 1048, Santa Monica, California 90406.

This creative film allows the viewer to examine conditions that allow man to create.

Materials

Cuisenaire Rods. Cuisenaire Company of America, Inc., 9 Elm Avenue, Mt. Vernon, N.Y. 10550.

These materials, designed to help students discover mathematical relationships, can be used to examine "concrete operations" in children.

Soma (Cube Puzzle Game). Parker Brothers, Inc., P.O. Box 900, Salem, Mass. 01970.

These blocks, mentioned in Holt's article "The Mind at Work," challenge one to think in three dimensions by placing pieces to form a cube.

Suchman Inquiry Box. Science Research Associates, Inc., 259 East Erie Street, Chicago, Ill. 60611.

This device poses problems for inquiry using various combinations of strings, springs, spools, pulley and dowel rods.

Resolution Activity

At the beginning of this content area it was argued that examining how the mind works is a critical part of any inquiry into the teaching-learning process. Implicit in the argument was the notion that learning is largely an internal event; that is, it is more significantly a phenomenon of inner mental reorganization than a process of external forces influencing behavioral responses. Such a conception of learning and cognitive activity, it was suggested, had important consequences for educational practice.

The resources that have been presented have, by and large, supported and expanded this point of view as well as they have suggested educational implications. The statement that follows is to help you bring your search of these resource materials to some resolution, so that your own ideas might be sufficiently articulated and concretized to allow for developing practical applications.

There are many ways of treating this statement, but one particularly interesting possibility is to assume that a school principal has expressed considerable interest in it. He has requested more elaboration as well as critical evaluation of the ideas it contains, especially those concerning classroom implications. Imagine further that the author of the statement has asked you to help him on this task. From a review of the readings and activities you have experienced during this content area, what would be the major ways in which you could assist him?

One of my main questions concerns how people actually learn anything. A good deal of the research that has been done, and the theory that is related to it, support a compelling model. The key idea of this model is that learning can be equated with observable changes in behavior. Learning is defined as such a change, and it is referred to as a response. Stimulus conditions are regarded as capable of directly causing responses, and something is said to be learned well if the relationship between the stimulus and response is predictable. It has also been shown that reinforcement plays an important role in establishing this relationship. This model has many implications for the classroom teacher. Some of the more important ones include the need to carefully organize the material to be presented, the need to require observable changes in the students' behavior, and the need to make positive rewards available to shape desired responses.

In contrast to this model, I have observed in myself and others that learning usually seems to take place in a very different manner. First of all, learning appears to be going on all the time — irrespective of any specific stimulus-response units or reward conditions. Indeed, just as I cannot stop my mind from thinking, I often find that I cannot turn off my mind from learning something. As a model of learning, thinking activity is clearly more important than changes in behavior; learning is an internal change in the mind brought about by ongoing mental processing: testing, formulating, and acting on information. As evidence of its validity, it has been shown that children and adults engage naturally in such information processing when they are given adequate opportunity. I think that learning conceived in this way has implications in conflict with the other model. The organization of materials, observable changes, and rewards would have lower priorities than student direction, nonobservable thinking, and intrinsic interest in what is to be learned. This conflict is worthy of careful consideration.

Feedback

When you have completed your inquiry into cognitive functioning, you can evaluate the materials by using this form and sharing your views with others. Feedback can be used as a tool for examining how helpful the materials were to yourself as well as to groups or to the class as a whole.

Rate the relative usefulness of the resources you have used in your inquiry into cognitive functioning. Leave blank the selections you did not read. Use the following ratings:

1 = not very useful
2 = moderately useful
3 = very useful

_____ Yanoff, "The Functions of the Mind in the Learning Process"
_____ Holt, "Excerpt from *How Children Learn*"
_____ Tuddenham, "Jean Piaget and the World of the Child"
_____ Miller, Galanter, and Pribram, "Excerpt from *Plans and the Structure of Behavior*"
_____ Suchman, "The Child and the Inquiry Process"
_____ Bruner, "The Act of Discovery"
_____ Shulman, "Psychological Controversies in Teaching"
_____ Guilford, "Factors That Aid and Hinder Creativity"
_____ Crutchfield, "Nurturing the Cognitive Skills of Productive Thinking"
_____ Holt, "Excerpt from *How Children Fail*"
_____ Gattegno, "The Powers of Children"

Rate your general interest and involvement in your inquiry into the cognitive processes.

1	2	3	4	5	6	7	8	9
Low								High

How much do you feel you have learned during this content area?

1	2	3	4	5	6	7	8	9
Little								A lot

Describe any insight you have gained as a result of your inquiry into cognitive processes.

Evaluate in what ways this content area allowed you to fulfill your personal expectations.

What aspects of your inquiries do you think will help you to facilitate students' thinking?

Part 3
The Teaching Process

The Problem: What Should Teachers Offer Students?   Developing Ways of Thinking About Open Classrooms

In the first two content areas, problems concerning the emotional needs, intrinsic motives, and cognitive processes of the learner were presented. Some implications for the act of teaching have no doubt emerged from these inquiries. It is important, however, to give more focused attention to ways of approaching teaching. Classroom teaching is a complex affair; it involves not only a concern for specific instructional techniques but also the design of the classroom environment, the development of instructional materials, the programming of learning experiences, and the building of meaningful relationships with students. Many factors are missed if teaching is conceived at one extreme to be merely a monitoring of prescribed learning tasks or at the other extreme to be solely a matter of making materials and oneself available to students. Teaching should not be viewed so simplistically.

Critical problems especially exist for a teacher who believes that his students should actively share in the direction of the teaching-learning process. First of all, he needs to determine how he can guide his students without inhibiting their sense of self-direction and without interfering with their individual patterns of thinking. And secondly, there is a need to determine what kinds of learning experiences are likely to facilitate the interests of students and at the same time fulfill the teacher's educational values. It is highly improbable that a teacher could find teaching personally meaningful if his own goals, skills, and knowledge did not have a significant role in his relationship with students. Every teacher ought to be responsive both to the needs of his students and to his own expectations. With some degree of student direction in mind, it is even more important to face the problem of developing plans that are open-ended and flexible, and ways of achieving congruence between the goals of the teacher and those of the students.

The concept of the open classroom is an aid to considering the problems of student direction. It is a significant breakthrough for thinking about the teaching-learning process because it provides active roles for both teacher and students and because it allows for meaningful dialogue between them. The classroom environment envisioned is neither authoritarian and rigid nor permissive and unstructured. The concept supports learning by inquiry and creative expression, yet it is not indifferent to the development of basic skills. What is needed for its practical application are personal ways of thinking about the open classroom so that the idea does not become a monolithic, dogmatic conception of teaching. The materials and resources provided in this content area will help you inquire toward this end.

Initiating Activities

The initiating experiences that follow are designed to increase your awareness of the values and ideas that you have about teaching. Any one of them should also help you to examine aspects of the problem that has just been raised. After completing one or more of these activities, list the ideas that emerged during this experience and place them in these categories:

1. ideas that contradict each other
2. ideas that lack evidence or philosophical support
3. ideas that seem incomplete

Engaging in this process should enable you to select relevant and helpful topics and readings.

1/Facing Students

A problem teachers face is how to interact with students in ways that make the educational process meaningful to everyone involved. In this activity you are to think about practical alternatives for interacting with students.

Ask yourself how you might respond to a student in the following situations:

1. You sense a problem but a student does not.
2. A student is defensive about some work he has completed.
3. You want to criticize a student without closing his mind to your ideas.
4. A student raises a question that is obviously irrelevant.
5. A student is thinking very fast, and you feel he should consider more alternatives.

Group Activity
Discuss how a teacher can respond in each of these instances. List alternative ways of handling each situation arising in group discussion and examine the implications of each for both the student and the teacher.

Individual Activity
Imagine yourself in each of these situations. Without giving yourself too much time for reflection, decide how you would intuitively respond in each case. After doing this, consider more carefully approaches other than those you initially used.

2/Conceptions of Teaching

The following statements reflect two students' conceptions of teaching after they had completed a student-directed introductory course in educational psychology.[1] They were asked to describe the things they would most like to accomplish when teaching and to indicate how they thought they would achieve them.

Examine these two responses and evaluate the students' suggestions concerning the act of teaching.

Student A

The greatest thing that a teacher can accomplish is to lead his students in experiences which will "teach" them to think independently and critically about all aspects of life. If this is the teacher's aim, learning will never cease even though the student eventually leaves the learning environment that is school. My other major aim in teaching, and this is closely related to the first, is to make the learning experience of my students a positive one.

How am I going to accomplish my goals? Right now that is still a difficult question to answer, but I'm getting closer to some conclusions all the time.

I know that my role will have to be one of guidance counselor. Since I expect to be working in the traditional school setting where a prescribed amount of content is to be covered each year, my job as a guide is going to be a difficult one. I must learn how I can allow a student choices and when my authority as teacher must interfere with his choices. I have to learn how to impose this authority without being authoritarian in the traditional sense.

Allowing the student to work on a topic of his choice at the time of his choice is only the first step in achieving my goals. I feel convinced now that the mind naturally goes through a process of identifying and solving problems. It is only when the external world imposes restrictions that this process is interrupted and learning becomes more difficult. If your class is any grade besides first, this process of thinking has already been ruined and the damage is proportional to the grade level. At Summerhill, they told the children that they were free to do whatever they want whenever they want and sometimes it was quite a while before they even went to classes. If I did this, I would be fired. However, I think that if I lead children through the problem solving practice at first they will be able to do it themselves as the year progresses.

As for creating a positive experience with learning, I think that this will be a natural outcome of my whole teaching theory. The student will have a sense of achievement because he is handling something that he has chosen and is within his intellectual grasp. Both teacher and student are then free to react humanly to the experiences of the classroom.

[1] We wish to thank Sharon Dunbar and Dennis O'Neill for giving us permission to reprint these statements.

217

When I teach, I would like to involve my class both as a group and as individuals in such a way that the experience they encounter can be solved in a problematic way. That means that I would employ an inquiry approach in as many situations as possible. I would expect students to pose problems to themselves. I would encourage them to use outside resources and to find solutions to their problems. In order to develop decision making in my students, I would offer as many choices in as many situations as I could think of. I believe these are all important steps in teaching children how to think.

I hope not to instill my values or some other predetermined set of values in the children but rather provide an environment which helps them realize their own values.

I know there were times in my own education when I had to memorize something and forgot it very rapidly. I want to be able to have a classroom where real learning and understanding of actual life situations are encountered.

Hopefully by accomplishing all of the above the students will feel a sense of responsibility for their own education. They will also understand that this education will be beneficial for them when they face new experiences and provide them with tools for understanding the society in which they live.

Group Activity

In a small group or with the whole class, compare these two conceptions of teaching. Pick out issues on which you would like to focus. Also evaluate ideas that seem to be incomplete or those that need refinement.

Individual Activity

Read the two conceptions of teaching. Ask yourself what major issues are conveyed in each of them. For contrast, outline what your conception of teaching would be if you were given this task formally.

3/Behavioral Objectives

Behavioral objectives are specific statements by a teacher concerning the exact changes in behavior he expects to see in his students as a result of particular acts of teaching. Many of today's educators advocate their use as a way of understanding and planning for teaching and learning. The concept of the open classroom, however, challenges the use of behavioral objectives because they negate the students' responsibility to share in the planning of the teaching-learning process. This activity will allow you to examine the strengths and weaknesses of behavioral objectives.

Imagine that, as a teacher, you were sent the following note from your principal. Consider what issues ought to be examined in a faculty discussion of the note at a later date.

Many educators advocate that teachers should plan their class activities with clearly stated behavioral objectives. The theory is that teaching is more efficient and effective when teachers are aware of the changes in behavior they want to facilitate and when they specifically communicate them to their students. One of the good things about this approach, I see, is that it places a great deal of responsibility on the teacher if students fail to achieve the objectives. It makes sense to assume that if all doesn't go well, something is wrong with the teaching methods or the objectives themselves (rather than with the students). One of the problems, on the other hand, is that this approach demands close scrutiny of learning activities and only observable learning is counted. I think it may also tend to detract from a student's responsibility for his own learning. By thinking out these ideas carefully and using them intelligently, however, I think a teacher could avoid most of the disadvantages. I would like to see more of this approach in our school.

Group Activity

Each individual in a small group or the whole class should list the arguments for or against behavioral objectives that he would like to raise when the group comes together. In the discussion, one person can act as moderator to make sure that all the differing points of view are heard, considered, and debated.

Individual Activity

Imagine that the note asked for a written response. Consider your arguments as logically as you can and then outline a note back to the principal. It might also be helpful to share your reply with other students.

4/Understanding the Teacher's Role

A task that confronts all teachers is determining the role most likely to accomplish the goals they want to achieve. This activity is to help you examine your own ideas of what the teacher's role ought to be.

Consider all the statements on the next page and ask yourself whether you agree with them.

Group Activity

Begin by having each person respond to the statements privately. Afterward, there can be a discussion of the items receiving the greatest disagreement. It would be useful as well to examine the reasons for agreeing or disagreeing with the statements. Doing this may reveal conflicting ideas that deserve further exploration.

Individual Activity

List separately all the items with which you strongly agree and those with which you disagree. After examining these two lists, construct a brief personal statement that accounts for your views of the role of the teacher.

	Agree strongly	Agree somewhat	Disagree
1. It is best to enter a class without a plan of action in order to allow for spontaneity.	____	____	____
2. Feedback should be given mainly when students request it.	____	____	____
3. The first thing to do at the beginning of the school year is to find out what your students' interests are.	____	____	____
4. Students should view their teacher as a kind of learning expert.	____	____	____
5. Students' plans should be challenged if they are not meaningful to the teacher.	____	____	____
6. Ideally, a teacher should emulate psychotherapists.	____	____	____
7. A teacher has a greater responsibility to consider *how* a student learns than *what* he learns.	____	____	____
8. It is desirable to communicate one's basic expectations to students before the teacher-student relationship develops.	____	____	____
9. Socrates really understood the role of the teacher.	____	____	____
10. The teacher should stay out of his students' way as much as possible.	____	____	____

Topics of Study

These topics of study are different points of focus for examining the teaching process.

1. Structuring Learning Experiences. This topic provides for an exploration into how instruction can merge open-ended guidance and students' interests.
2. Instructional Materials and Programs. This topic examines different forms of recorded communication and innovative programs that a teacher could make available to students.
3. Teacher-Student Interaction. This topic is concerned with alternative ways that teachers can verbally interact with students in order to stimulate thinking.

"Structuring Learning Experiences" is the broadest and most general of the three. While concerned with the overall process of teaching, the other topics treat more specific problems of the planning and interactive aspects of teaching. Jerome S. Allender's article "New Conceptions of the Role of the Teacher" serves as introductory reading for the entire content area. Including it as part of future activities may be useful. You are urged to read it and explore each topic of study to determine how it relates to the personal interests and questions that have emerged from the initiating experiences in which you participated.

1/Structuring Learning Experiences

The teacher who wants to establish some degree of student direction in his class needs to think about structuring open-ended learning experiences. Since most of us were educated in traditional ways, they may not be easy to imagine. The possibilities of facilitating student involvement and inquiry, however, will be enhanced by developing personal approaches to the theories and ideas underlying the concept of the open classroom. At this point, you may be thinking about many issues that are difficult to put into words, but perhaps some reflection on the following questions will bring into focus your particular concerns:

1. What is the role of the teacher in an open classroom?
2. What kinds of learning experiences can a teacher plan to help students develop ways of inquiring?
3. How do open-ended activities personalize learning?
4. What expectations are needed for students in an open classroom? For teachers?

Barbara Biber and Patricia Minuchin, "The Changing School" (pp. 239–250)

Biber and Minuchin compare the philosophy and practice of two different styles of education — one centering on traditional forms and one drawing its outlook from dynamic theories of human growth and learning. The article is useful as a comprehensive review of the concepts in the previous content areas and their implications for education. The broadest of the recommended readings, it is a discussion of the entire scope of educational programs in the "changing school."

Bernice J. Wolfson, "Pupil and Teacher Roles in Individualized Instruction" (pp. 251–257)

This article is especially helpful for developing ways of thinking about the role of a teacher. Wolfson contrasts two analogies — the teacher as a doctor and the teacher as a travel consultant — which do not precisely conceptualize the teachers' role but do clarify how individualizing instruction can be based on radically different styles of teaching and how the degree of open-endedness differs from one approach to the other. The article also contains a review of some of the studies concerning student-directed learning and brief descriptions of innovative teaching.

Herbert Kohl, "Excerpt from *36 Children*" (pp. 258–260)

This excerpt from *36 Children* describes an episode in Kohl's sixth grade Harlem classroom that illustrates how teaching can be based on open-ended experiences. Kohl, taking his leads from a name-calling incident between two of his students, develops a discussion about the origin of a word into a class-wide inquiry concerning the nature of language. This is the most descriptive of the recommended readings because it provides a clear picture of the ongoing process in an actual classroom. It might be helpful to explore in what way other learning environments can be structured to allow for spontaneous experiences such as the one described here.

Herbert A. Thelen, "Some Classroom Quiddities for People-Oriented Teachers" (pp. 261–268)

In a critical analysis of our schools, Thelen argues that the natural tendencies of children should be used, rather than suppressed and ignored, to educate students. He discusses how potentially educative tendencies fit together within a coherent, sequential model of inquiry for use in the classroom. The section of the article that describes this model, "The Educative Process," deserves careful reading because it contains principles for generating inquiry-oriented learning experiences. Particularly helpful is Thelen's discussion on how confronting activities can be used to initiate an inquiry.

2/Instructional Materials and Programs

Recorded instructional materials and innovative training programs have extended the teacher's ability to provide relevant information and exciting activities and have increased the teacher's capacity to personalize learning and individualize instruction. As a consequence of these developments, part of the teacher's role in modern education is to evaluate the suitability of materials and programs as well as to adapt those selected to individual circumstances. It is, therefore, important to inquire into the problems created by this aspect of the teacher's role. These questions might focus such an inquiry:

1. How does programmed instruction individualize learning?
2. In what ways do teaching machines compete with or augment the role of the teacher?
3. How do the goals and effects of instructional materials and training programs differ?
4. How can recorded forms of communication be used without destroying the realness of learning?

Readings

Philip W. Jackson, "Excerpt from *The Teacher and the Machine*" (pp. 269–273)

In this excerpt from Jackson's *The Teacher and the Machine* there is an insightful discussion of different meanings of the term "individualizing instruction." Jackson points out that teaching machines can be helpful in only limited ways, and he identifies the qualities of human teachers that machines cannot replace. Near the end of the selection is a particularly cogent argument about how children are likely to feel toward technological devices. Jackson's ideas are also useful for thinking about other ways of individualizing instruction in the classroom.

John Holt, "The Wholeness of Learning" (pp. 274–275)

Holt describes in this excerpt from *What Do I Do Monday?* his experience working with programmed instructional materials in mathematics. He describes the efficiency with which he learned the material but complains that many of his personal questions were left unanswered. His experience illustrates some of Jackson's arguments. You will find it helpful to consider a brief statement in the beginning of this reading concerning the assumptions on which Holt is basing his remarks.

Carl R. Rogers, "The Facilitation of Significant Learning" (pp. 276–284)

In this article, Rogers describes alternative ways of implementing what he calls "significant experiential learning." They include inquiry training, programmed instruction, and sensitivity training. In addition, there is a discussion of two contrasting approaches to learning in terms of focus, aims, and assumptions about the educational process. The contrast is helpful for evaluating the utility of instructional materials and programs.

Donna S. Allender and Jerome S. Allender, "I Am the Mayor: Inquiry Materials for the Study of City Government" (pp. 285–291)

In this selection is described a set of programmed materials that departs radically from the typical format. The materials allow students to play the role of a mayor of a small town and to develop inquiry skills. They encourage participation in open-ended learning activities where the problems and their solutions are not predetermined. "I Am the Mayor" is also useful as a model from which a teacher can generate his own inquiry materials for other subjects.

Melvin L. Silberman, Jerome S. Allender, and Jay M. Yanoff, *The Psychology of Open Teaching and Learning*

This entire book can be viewed as a set of instructional materials aiming to facilitate an inquiry into the teaching-learning process. It may be worthwhile to examine the structure and contents of this book in terms of your personal experience using it. These questions might be helpful:

1. How does the book succeed or fail in involving you in its subject matter?
2. How effectively does the book allow for a personal inquiry?
3. In what ways could the organization of this book be used as a basis for a textbook in a different subject matter or at a different level of education?

3/Teacher-Student Interaction

Regardless of the amount of planning that a teacher does before he meets with his students, his influence on them is greatly determined by classroom verbal interaction. Among the things he needs to consider are how his patterns of interacting with students encourage reflective thinking and dialogue and how the language he uses respects students' autonomy and feelings of self-worth. These questions about teacher-student interaction are worth pursuing:

1. What are the effects of different styles of teacher-student interaction?
2. How can a teacher accept and build upon students' ideas and feelings?
3. What kinds of verbal behavior facilitate reflective thinking in students?
4. How can a teacher maximize meaningful peer interaction?

Readings

Ned A. Flanders, "Intent, Action and Feedback: A Preparation for Teaching" (pp. 292–302)

Flanders describes "interaction analysis," a technique that involves analyzing one's own classroom verbal behavior on the basis of an observer's record or a tape recording. He discusses in detail ways of interpreting the data collected by using this technique. There is also a discussion of two contrasting styles of teacher behavior — direct and indirect — and their typical effects on students. The article is extremely useful for developing alternative ways of responding to students.

Herbert Kohl, "Excerpt from *36 Children*" (pp. 258–260)

Beyond the general significance of this excerpt, discussed on page 222, this is an excellent illustration of how a teacher can interact with students to build upon their feelings and ideas rather than reject them. Kohl skillfully demonstrates how to question students without interrogating them and how to guide a discussion without creating debilitating periods of silence and confusion.

John Holt, "The Wholeness of Learning" (pp. 274–275)

In this excerpt from *What Do I Do Monday?* Holt describes an incident in which he helped a student to understand calculus. The discussion is particularly valuable because it shows how a teacher can assist a student by giving him a way of thinking about a problem he is facing. After reading this excerpt, it would be helpful for you to take a learning problem you have and ask someone to guide you following Holt's style.

Herbert A. Thelen, "Some Classroom Quiddities for People-Oriented Teachers" (pp. 261–268)

An important aspect of this article is Thelen's discussion of students' natural tendency to seek meaning from each other. This tendency, Thelen argues, prompts students to want to talk about their ideas and speculations with friends. He suggests ways of promoting this form of peer interaction to aid in the process of group inquiry.

Inquiry Activities

A successful search for relevant information about the teaching process mainly involves an ability to see the applicability of other people's ideas to one's own present or future situation. Because of its complexity, though, teaching should be examined from as many angles as possible in order to create from the different views your own image of what needs to be done. It is valuable, therefore, to plan activities that consider the major concepts and suggested ways of practicing teaching. Of importance are:

1. Thelen's model of inquiry learning
2. Wolfson's conception of the teacher as a travel consultant
3. Flanders' system of interaction analysis
4. Jackson's views of individualized instruction

After you have read any or all of the selections, it is appropriate to try to attach and build personal meaning into the ideas set forth in them. The following inquiry activities are to assist you in this task.

1/Planning Inquiry Experiences

Thelen discusses principles for generating ideas for inquiry-oriented learning experiences, particularly in secondary schools. In this activity you are to use Thelen's model to develop inquiry materials and activities.

It may be worthwhile to examine Thelen's model of inquiry before you begin this activity. Then, either alone or in a group, select one of the suggested topics and plan a week of teaching that would facilitate inquiry. Pay particular attention to how you would initiate the inquiry; keep Thelen's suggestions in mind.

1. Study history to find evidence of prejudiced views.
2. Examine the scientific method in terms of deductive and inductive thinking.
3. Compare and contrast English with French or Spanish.
4. Consider the social and psychological effects of pollution.
5. Study the relationship of bacteria and health.
6. Determine how a person could learn about a vocation.

After you have completed your plans, share them with other students. Discuss how the plans either satisfy or violate some of the natural tendencies of students and how you think they would be reacted to if you actually implemented them.

2/Two Views of the Teacher's Role

This activity is designed to explore Wolfson's images of the role of the teacher in an individualized classroom. You are asked to compare the goals you imagine the teacher would have as a "doctor" and as a "travel agent."

Assume that you are in a teacher-pupil conference, a one-to-one situation, in the following circumstances:

1. discussing something a student recently read
2. looking over a paper a student has written
3. discussing a picture a student has painted
4. examining why a group discussion went poorly

For each of the situations, ask yourself how the conference would differ given the two approaches. What do you imagine would be the content of such a conference in each case? When would you utilize the "doctor" or "travel agent" approach in a classroom? You may want to respond individually in writing to these questions and then discuss your thinking in a small group or with the class.

3/Evaluating Educational Programs

Rogers discusses the meaning of significant experiential learning and lists five criteria he feels must be met for such learning to occur. He also contrasts two sets of assumptions — one implicit in current education and one relevant to the educational experiences he advocates. In this activity you are to use these criteria and assumptions to evaluate an educational experience.

View any educational television program designed for children (*Sesame Street*, for example) and evaluate it using Rogers' criteria. Determine what educational assumptions listed by Rogers serve as the basis for the program. If you are working in a small group or with a whole class, it will be worthwhile for everyone to see the same program and then to discuss individual evaluations.

Ask yourself what effect the program has on the learner. To what extent do you think it encourages significant learning? If you were to recommend changes in the program, what experiences would you want children to have? How could the changes be implemented?

4/Designing Inquiry Materials

The Allenders describe a set of programmed materials designed to allow students to actively participate in an inquiry; the materials, "I Am the Mayor," suggest new ways for teachers to think about using programmed materials. In this activity you are to consider the possibility of applying the "I Am the Mayor" format to other subjects.

Given the topics that follow, try to figure how you could adapt the ideas of "I Am the Mayor." You may want to consider ways that a teacher could provide information without having to create a file system such as the one used in "Mayor." You can offer alternatives to directly providing questions from which to choose. You may want to suggest other approaches for arriving at resolutions. Choose one of these topics:

1. a high school social studies class investigating the legal system in the United States
2. a kindergarten class studying the role of policemen
3. a science class pursuing factors related to placement of atomic energy plants
4. a junior high class examining the impact of political cartoons on newspaper readers
5. an English class criticizing Shakespearean literature
6. a mathematics class trying to develop a new system of mathematics called Martian Math

Suggest how you could initiate the inquiry, develop question asking, provide for information seeking, and allow for well thought out resolutions.

5/Analyzing Classroom Interaction

Interaction analysis allows for an examination of the verbal interaction of students and teachers. It also helps to suggest to the teacher specific patterns of behavior that might prove to be useful for his personal goals. This activity is to help you learn how to use this technique. You are asked to examine the interaction patterns of a teacher and to discuss your interpretations of them. It is necessary to read Flanders' article carefully as preparation for this activity.

	1	2	3	4	5	6	7	8	9	10
1				1						
2				3	3	1	1		2	
3					4					
4								10		7
5				10	12	4			9	6
6								8		4
7								4		6
8		6	4	2	9	3	1	2	1	
9	1	4		1	6	1	4		5	2
10					7	3	4	4	7	
Total	1	10	4	17	41	12	10	28	24	25

A high school English teacher has been displeased with the lack of involvement and development of ideas in class discussions. On the basis of the interaction analysis matrix above (derived from observation in the teacher's classroom), what helpful feedback could you give this teacher to improve his leading of discussions? Derive your information from an examination of the frequencies of (1) each major category (for example, how often the teacher praises students is equal to the number of tallies in the 2 row or column); (2) particular cells (for example, how often the teacher's questions are followed by silence is reflected in the 4–10 cell), and (3) specific areas of the matrix (for example, how a teacher responds to students is revealed in the 8 and 9 rows through column 7).

6/Conducting Discussions

The episodes in the selections by Holt and Kohl illustrate two teachers' efforts to make the study of a difficult subject meaningful to students. In this activity you are to consider their styles and apply them to different situations. At the same time, the activity enables you to examine different approaches to group interaction.

Assume that your goal is to introduce the learning of a new math skill to elementary school students or the study of a new period in American history to high school students. Your task is to discuss approaches to doing this based on Holt's and Kohl's styles. For approximately thirty minutes, conduct a discussion in a rather deliberate, organized fashion. For example, you might begin by reviewing the episodes in the readings. Select the aspects of them that are relevant to introducing new topics in a way meaningful to students. Next, there might be an exploration of how the relevant sections of the readings apply to the goal you have assumed. A final step could entail a summary of the helpful ideas that have emerged, with a test of the validity of each, and a consideration of the problems that remain. However the discussion is structured, it is important that participants keep a common focus and work orientation. When the allotted discussion time has elapsed, the group should begin again, with a looser, more spontaneous consideration of the task. Avoid structuring the discussion and allow for tangents and "brainstorming." The only thing to be kept in mind is to accept and build upon each other's thoughts and feelings. Conduct this discussion for approximately thirty minutes, also.

Conclude the activity by evaluating the two approaches to discussion. Since it is unlikely that one discussion was clearly better in every respect than the other, using several evaluative criteria would be helpful. For example, how did group interaction differ? In which discussion was there wider participation? Which discussion was more involving? Which was more productive?

Readings

Jerome S. Allender

New Conceptions of the Role of the Teacher

The active development of new roles for the teacher begins with the re-creation of the context within which teaching takes place. Great satisfaction with the traditional roles of the teacher is not evidenced by general support coming from any corner; this fact, alone, is a sufficient argument for the direct application of innovative ideas to education. By carefully exploring different ways in which new contexts can be created, a teacher puts himself in a position of being able to make a rational decision concerning the degree of change he wants to attempt. Depending on the extent, this can range from an involvement in the normal evolutionary process that affects teaching to a radical approach to change.

Currently, several developments provide helpful bases for thinking about changing the context of teaching. Because it has been recognized for some time that individual differences have a significant effect in all learning, it is feasible to consider individualizing most of the instruction that goes on in one's class. Although less widely supported, the need to emphasize increased independent study and freedom of movement under less teacher direction, in what is called an *open classroom*, has also been strongly argued. Possibilities for implementing these ideas should be explored because both are conducive to the reconceptualization of the role of the teacher. A more progressive approach is to create a positive role for the teacher in an open classroom; this would involve reconstruct-

Adapted from chapter 5 of Jerome S. Allender, *A Radical Psychology of Learning*. Manuscript in preparation. Copyright © 1972 by Jerome S. Allender.

ing the context of teaching from the standpoint of a theory of student-directed learning. Rather than trying to follow the best avenues of traditional teaching or simply reducing the degree of directiveness, the development of new roles for the teacher can be attacked by focusing on the establishment of common meaning with students, the cooperative planning of teaching and learning, and the provision of choice at all times. In many schools, even for the experienced teacher, this approach may never be practical. However, it is worth reflecting on the kind of direction it can possibly give to teaching; and seeing how quickly the everyday world around us is changing, it may be impractical, particularly for the teacher-in-training, not to take this more radical approach.

I

The most general basis for individualizing instruction comes from the broad study of individual differences including the varying points of view of biology, society, the school, the curriculum, and the teacher (Henry, 1962). Whether they are the result of genetic predispositions, varying abilities, previously acquired skills, or personal style, it is clear that individual patterns play an important role in learning. The problem posed for the teacher is that every child's program should somehow be geared to his unique learning needs. This supports the idea of making as much individual help available to students as possible, and it shows an advantage for grouping children who have similar needs. The main practical outcome has been the increased availability of materials that allow children to work at their own level of readiness and at their own pace. In many schools, it is expected that ordinary classroom materials should be made available on an individual basis whenever possible, and a variety of individualized materials will be ordered if requested.

As a part of the emphasis on instructional materials, programed instruction was conceived and introduced (Pressey, 1964; Lumsdaine, 1964). Following Skinner (1968) for the most part, it is based on a theory that reinforcement is necessary for learning, or at least its best facilitator. Thus, programed texts characteristically have carefully sequenced short items or questions requiring easy-to-guess answers, and the correct answers are nearby for a student to check his own responses. It is assumed that a student's learning is reinforced whenever he finds that the response he gave to a particular question is correct. A body of research was undertaken to demonstrate the effectiveness of programed instruction, and not surprisingly, the evidence suggests that its utility depends on the materials, the students, and the teacher's goals (Allender, 1967). At times, though, it can be used quite effectively to help a group of students learn a given body of knowledge, and as a consequence of these encouraging results, another source of individualized materials in many subject-matter areas has become available. A broader concept of programed instruction has involved the use of computer-like approaches and actual computers (with multiple student stations) for the presentation of programed materials (Allender, 1967; Atkinson, 1968; Hansen, 1968). Easily capable of immediately indicating to students whether their answers are correct, they have also been used to implement programs of study involving complicated forms of feedback — like those that might be given by a tutor — to assist in the learning process.

The teacher's major role in a school where the majority of emphasis is on individualized instruction is obviously not to transmit information. Students are expected to be dependent mainly on instructional materials for acquiring knowledge, and the significant function of the teacher is to make sure that each student always has materials that are particularly appropriate for him at any given time. In an analysis of developing teacher roles, Wolfson (1968, p. 358) likens this role of the teacher to that of a doctor: "The most popular interpretation of individualized instruction is that the teacher makes specific recommendations and assignments for each pupil. This interpretation rests on the teacher-as-doctor analogy.... That is, she diagnoses needs, deficiencies, or problems and prescribes appropriate treatment." As critical as the design of materials, it is argued that a teacher should specify behavioral objectives (Mager, 1962; Plowman, 1971): these are observable and measureable changes in behavior that he expects in his students as a result of working through a program of study. One such program, called Individually Prescribed Instruction (IPI), is based on the importance of sequencing materials so that students can be required to demonstrate their competence with one set of ideas or skills before they are given new work that is more difficult (Lindvall and Cox, 1969). These ideas, in general, have even been used to think about making major changes in the organization of the school and the curriculum (Goodlad, 1966), and developments in technology are largely responsible for many new practical possibilities (Gleason, 1967A).

Opportunities for dramatic individualization of instruction are best in schools which have added learning centers to their traditional structures (Brown, 1968; Hellerich, 1969). The advantage of having learning centers is that a wide range of instructional resources, including materials and equipment, can be offered to students over a large span of grade levels. Whether they are used in addition to or instead of regular classroom work is an issue that needs consideration, but either way, the availability of a learning center in a school greatly facilitates the development of new roles for the teacher.

II

Impetus for the creation of open classrooms comes from a number of sources. For sometime, there has been an active interest in forming independent study programs (Beggs and Buffie, 1965; Gleason, 1967B). Most schools make

231

some provision for independent learning, and the potential that increased freedom has for enhancing a student's involvement in learning is usually recognized. The drawback of these programs is that they are only available under special conditions, while it is the history of their success that has provided a background of experience on the basis of which to build more general programs. With a more direct focus on the open classroom, theoretical support stems from two lines of argument. From one side, both Neill (1960) and Rogers (1969), in spite of the fact that they have very different views of psychology, argue that it is essential for students to have control over their own learning. Neill argues for the importance of self-regulation and Rogers emphasizes the role of individual meaning, but both would agree that the control is critical for personal growth and the development of the thinking skills that are needed in our culture today. A second argument stems from the application of Piaget's work to education (Furth, 1970; Piaget, 1970). The fact that intellectual growth follows natural stages of development is a logical basis for arguing that a teacher should beware of interfering with critical aspects of the learning process. Practical proposals have been made by teachers who have experimented with these ideas (Kohl, 1969; Holt, 1970), and Featherstone's work (1971) is particularly informative because it is based on observations of English primary schools where the concept of the open classroom has been applied extensively. The strength of these proposals is in their demonstrated practicality; because they are based on experience, their viability has been at least partially tested.

The concept of the open classroom combines an awareness of the significance of individual differences with an interest in changing the focus of present-day educational goals. The chief aims include providing the opportunity for learning how to learn and allowing for the full development of a student's potential. For this reason, paradoxically, the move to create open classrooms is as much contrary to the principles of individualized instruction as it is opposed to the traditional organization of the classroom. The locus of the conflict is in the different goals. Individualized instruction can be dependent for the most part on the use of programed materials because the outcomes of learning are specifically identified. The goals of the open classroom, however, are usually much more general, and the degree of teacher direction that is implicitly given by such materials is inconsistent with these goals.

The two approaches are least incongruent in relation to the use of learning centers. More precisely, the open classroom can be accurately described as a kind of learning center. The availability of materials and equipment is as important as it is for individualized instruction. Characteristically different, though, from a situation with behavioral objectives, is the nature of the materials that need to be available. In addition to those that would normally be found in a classroom, there need to be many open-ended materials designed to elicit curiosity and raise questions rather than focusing on teaching of specific knowledge and skills. Less teacher direction in the use of facilities is also critical. Instead of specifying objectives, a teacher is expected to help children when they ask for assistance and otherwise allow them to direct their own learning as much as possible. Using another analogy, Wolfson (1968, p. 362) clarifies the role of the teacher in the open classroom by likening him to a travel consultant: "The teacher's role would be primarily that of consultant and resource person to the learner. She would be a manager of the classroom environment, supplying a variety of materials and at times initiating new experiences. She would help pupils learn to plan, to evaluate, and to consider alternatives. She could bring her own interests and inquiry into the classroom. The main focus of her activity would be to promote self-direction." Although the line between the role of the teacher and the student needs to be better understood, Wolfson does show how one can begin to think about teaching in an open classroom in innovative ways.

III

For designing an educational environment, almost completely anew, on the basis of a theory of student-directed learning, the initial problem is to determine how conflicts between teacher's and students' meaning can be resolved. In the traditional classroom, such conflicts are minimized because the teacher is expected to make all decisions concerning goals, materials, rules, etc. The context is basically the same in a classroom where the major emphasis is placed on individualized instruction. But when a teacher begins to consider the possibility of teacher student planning, as one would within the context of an open classroom, a set of problems different from those traditionally experienced is created. The inclination has been in the operation of open classrooms to solve such problems intuitively. It is feasible, though, to anticipate the kinds of conflicts that are likely to occur and to create a classroom environment which is conducive to their resolution.

A general view of the problem reveals that uncertainty is caused by open-ended environments; this is in contrast to the traditional classroom where the roles of the teacher and the student are relatively well defined. For the teacher, the goals that he has, his ideas about relevant subject matter, and the minimum rules that he thinks students must follow to function within a group have to be open to discussion, challenge, and change. And the student in such a situation has to be willing to articulate what is meaningful for him: his goals, his interests, and his ideas about rules. The resolution of conflict between these two viewpoints depends on the existence of common goals, mutual interests, and agreement about the social conventions that are to be followed. It is reasonable to believe that an educational environment which is designed to help teachers and students reach these kinds of common meaning has to have specific structures within which they can be developed.

What is significantly missing in any uncertain social context is an automatic basis for trust. In terms of template theory,[1] the underlying basis of trust is to withhold the use of the testing mechanisms in the brain that judge the value of one's relationships with others. When a person discovers that he has some important meaning in common with another person, this is the way in which he can enhance the quality of subsequent interaction. Equally important, however, is the need for people to suspend judgment of each other, if only temporarily, in an effort to *develop* common meaning. The process appears to be cyclical, and out of it, it should be possible to arrive at teacher-student goals, commitments concerning time and work, and an assurance that the methods of evaluation will not be unfair to students (or the teacher) if the commitments are fulfilled. This does not mean that extensive trust can be created instantly, but it is a context within which it can be deliberately built up.

It might be argued that conflicts could easily be minimized if a teacher were willing to help students plan without imposing his own expectations; this is no more tenable, though, than asking students to place complete trust in their teachers and not to bring their personal expectations to the learning process. A more realistic approach to the resolution of conflicts in meaning requires a willingness to modify one's expectations and an interest in finding areas of commonality. It begins with an awareness of the determinants that seem to be given and a sharing of expectations with the purpose of uncovering underlying conflicts. This can be partially accomplished through discussion, but it would seem to be facilitated by activities which are based on temporary commitments. The teacher's role would be to initiate the learning experience within the context of some minimally agreed-upon goals. The student would need to not judge the experience while participating in it and he would have to allow himself to become involved. A successful *initiating ex-*

[1] For an explanation of the term "template" see Yanoff's article "The Functions of the Mind in the Learning Process."

perience might broadly define an area of subject matter, cause positive feelings of tension, and/or provide the opportunity for sensing relevant problems. On the basis of this experience, a teacher and his students could also engage in a dialogue searching for new areas of commonality. The process can be appropriately viewed as initiating teacher-student planning, and it should be generally helpful toward building trusting relationships.

The practical application of initiating experiences to teaching will be hindered mostly by disagreements over the pressure of time. Without agreement on overriding broad goals as to what needs to be accomplished in a given period of time, either the teacher or the student can easily create a failure situation by prolonging unduly any aspects of the initiating process. There is a limit to how much can be communicated in an orientation to students just as an excessively long presentation of a teacher's expectations can make a discussion meaningless. Similarly, students' unwillingness to follow basically the instructions that have been prepared for an initiating experience can delay its completion and deflate the tensions and interest in an inquiry that it was meant to produce. These kinds of problems are not foreign to the teacher in a traditional classroom, but they are much more critical in the context of an open classroom. For one, if there is a commitment to cooperative planning, the authority to keep the process moving is no longer completely in the power of the teacher. Secondly, initiating experiences facilitate only the beginning of an inquiry; if adequate time is not allowed for other phases of inquiry, the total process is undermined.

The success of an initiating experience seems to depend on a teacher's ability to design an activity which is within the range of the students' interests and to obtain a loose agreement concerning what has to be done to complete the activity. How often a teacher might provide such initiating experiences is an open question just as is the determination of its particular nature for any given learning situation. Initiating experiences will probably be quite different for times

when one is first meeting a group of students compared to times when one is simply introducing a new subject-matter area. With these questions in mind, though, a practical hypothesis is tenable: that adequate common meaning to serve as a basis for meaningful teacher-student planning can be established through the combination of a short orientation, a sharing of expectations, participation in an initiating experience and a discussion of that experience.

A decision to encourage cooperative planning also creates a number of difficult problems for the teacher. In one way, they are not intrinsically different from those associated with the establishment of common meaning. Planning is basically the creation of a relationship of long-range trust and this means that the two processes are very interdependent. The kinds of activities, however, involved in planning are different and their potential for tangible and immediate consequences is greater. In addition, where the initiation of learning can depend on the usual willingness of people to engage themselves in temporary commitments for a while, the prospect of longer-range commitments tends to make people wary. The most basic problem has to do with closed-mindedness on the part of both the teacher and the students. Such closedness is not unusual for the teacher in the traditional classroom, and it is not automatically dissolved for someone who is trying to create a new educational context. Mainly, it interferes with a teacher's ability to value and build upon a student's past experience and current thinking, and it supports any tendency that students have within the freer context of an open classroom to disregard a teacher's knowledge and experience. The latter is an important part of what the teacher has to offer his students, and the planning process is greatly handicapped without it. This problem, from either side, causes an imbalance in the dialogue that leads to cooperative planning, and it would seem to necessarily impede the process.

Should a productive dialogue actually be established, other problems can come into focus. A teacher and his students may agree on their overall goals and still be in conflict over the specific direction that plans take. Even when their views of relevant subject matter are not in conflict, the evaluation of plans in terms of their probability of success can differ significantly. Of equal importance, a willingness to become involved in a learning activity can be frustrated by a plan which is only capable of generating high initial interest and unable to sustain it for the extended time that the plan might require. The solution of these problems usually falls solely to the judgment of the teacher; structures are needed to create a context within which teacher and students can make them together.

Theoretically, planning learning activities particularly when they are related to the teaching of inquiry skills, is a kind of problem formulation. The unique characteristic of cooperative planning is that common templates are formed in the minds of the teacher and the students. The functional difference between individual and group formulation of plans has to do with the subprocesses that are involved. For the teacher who plans by himself, there is no need to allow systematically for every aspect of information processing that is important to problem formulation. With a little awareness, it is possible to coordinate aspects of planning that are related to the subject matter, the learning process, and the likelihood of student interest. In cooperative planning, though, because the processing of information is going on in many minds at once, it is easier to avoid subprocesses and/or to not allow for the increased need for time that is involved in the formation of common templates. One individual should not have responsibility for judging the utility of the process in which the group is engaged.

It is necessary, therefore, that time be allocated for each subprocess that is considered to be critical, and they need to be kept somewhat distinct. First of all, there must be an adequate opportunity for the input of information into the planning process. For the teacher, this means that he has a responsibility to create an awareness of the different ways in which relevant problems can be formulated and the kinds of information, including the range of materials and activities, that can be made available. For the students, this means that there is an opportunity to formulate and reformulate problems sensed in initiating experiences, to raise questions that will facilitate an inquiry into these problems and to propose actvities that will be helpful for resolving them. Secondly, there must be points at which a teacher and his students can negotiate between their two positions. There are an unlimited number of planning problems that might develop, but it is assumed that working agreements can be reached on the basis of a reasonable amount of time spent negotiating. For example, when the formulation of a plan by students requires materials that a teacher is unable to make available, he would ask them to reconsider it. Or, if a teacher judges that a proposed activity is too difficult to undertake, his students might insist that he help them plan a comparable activity that is easier. Thirdly, time needs to be allowed for formalizing plans. Depending on whether students were working individually, in small groups, or as a class, their structure might differ widely, but they would be helpful, in any case, for students and teachers alike. A completed plan for students serves as a detailed guide for a sequence of learning activities, and, for the teacher, such plans direct his preparation and allow for meaningful evaluation.

The application of the theory is easiest if it is actually conceptualized in terms of planning activities. Their order and number might be varied according to differences in subject matter, students, and teachers, but invariably there seems to be a need for the three kinds of activities that have been distinguished. From the input of information, students would gain an overview of the subject matter in a short period of time. From the negotiation, there would result a new level of common meaning — one that is conducive to immediate action. The completed plans of the students and the teachers can almost be considered as an end in themselves. The activities, which logically can be thought of as *pre-formulation*, *negotiation*, and *post-formulation*, constitute structures that are hypothesized to facilitate the planning process. These structures are not likely to be found in a present-day school, and their practical development will surely be enhanced by experience and research. Their strangeness, though, might begin to be undone by looking to models outside of education. Cooperative planning is basic to democratic institutions and there could not be a more appropriate model in our society for the design of this aspect of an educational environment.

The design of an educational environment to provide for choice is the least difficult to imagine and implement. Part of the ease is related to the experience of traditional education. Although the overriding goal for most teachers may be the direct transmission of information, it is not always assumed that only a single channel of communication should be used. It is doubtful, indeed, that any challenging classroom environment is devoid of choice. Many teachers are able to make available several channels of communication at the same time, and over the period of a day, a week, or a semester, a child has a fair opportunity to match what he is learning with his interests. This demonstrates how, when a variety of different kinds of relevant information are provided, students' learning of specific knowledge and skills can actually be facilitated. Advances in the development of individualized materials and technology also make problems connected with the provision of choice less of an obstacle than they might appear at first.

For goals of teaching that include the development of inquiry skills, other new developments and changes in emphasis make the offering of appropriate kinds of choice feasible. A context like that of an open classroom is expected to promote learning how to learn and, hopefully, directly help children learn thinking skills. Ordinarily, the kinds of choice that have been offered in schools would not accomplish these goals, but some of the new self-instructional materials are helpfully focused on problem solving and creativity tasks. Another problem, in connection with direct inquiry experience, has to do with the quantity of information that is needed. Much more must be on hand when children are encouraged to engage in high-level information processing than would ever be offered in a traditional classroom. The problem is beginning to disappear, however, because of the introduction of a wide range of inexpensive techniques for reproducing information and new means for reducing the amount of space required for storing it. A related problem has to do with the need for open-ended materials. This is more a matter of mental set than one of technology. If one looks to the total body of information that is readily and practically available in our society instead of to that which is usually used in schools, there is no shortage of materials that can be used to raise questions and serve as pools of data necessary for open-ended inquiries.

Toward a radical reconceptualization of the classroom, a general approach to design along these lines is missing only a theory for the organization of choice. All the problems that have been identified are related to students' finding information. This is equally true for learning specific knowledge and skills, for learning general thinking skills, and for engaging in a personal inquiry. The solution is not to create a special oranizational structure for each of the different kinds of goals that are involved. The essential element is the opportunity for search activity. What is necessary is an overall structure that facilitates searching for information at as many levels as possible. Thus we return to the idea that the classroom should be designed like a learning center. Two overlapping concepts serve as a basis for accomplishing this kind of reorganization in its most radical form. The first involves recognizing that there are different basic sources of information and it is appropriate for a teacher to use all of them in an effort to make the maximum amount of choice available. The second shows how different kinds of information can be offered at the same time. The clarification of these two concepts, involving sources and kinds of information, illustrates how they might be applied.

It is reasonable to regard *experience, observation,* and *knowledge* as the primary bases for obtaining information in place of conceptualizing the teacher as the major source of in-

236

formation for his students. There is nothing unusual about a teacher who is willing to share his own experiences — particularly as they relate to the learning activities of his students. It would be equally helpful, though, for students to have an opportunity to gain their own relevant experience as it relates to their studies, either in the school or in the community. The significance attached to laboratory work and the history of apprenticeships and work-study programs make this idea less foreign than it might initially seem. Similarly, the extensive expansion of the idea of field trips might make systematic observation of any aspect of society or nature an important source of learning. Its general relevance to science is an argument for its value to education. Obviously, the most important source of information in school usually will be knowledge; it is an error, though, to assume that the teacher is its largest storehouse. No person can vie with the amount of knowledge that can be stored and transmitted via recorded communication. Highly innovative educational technology aside, books, programed texts, all other printed instructional materials, and audio-visual aids are so integral to teaching that their unique role can be missed. In addition, a student's previously acquired knowledge and his ability to generate new knowledge through his own thinking can be too easily dismissed. Recorded communication, the student, and the teacher are all valid sources of knowledge upon which to draw.

A look at how different kinds of information can be useful to students reveals a second dimension. Where the student has identifiable questions or skills that he wants, for which established knowledge exists, it would be foolish to look elsewhere for such information. To do otherwise is what makes "discovery learning" a phony process. Similarly, during the planning of an inquiry, it is relevant to directly learn strategies that are equivalent to broad thinking skills and information that are necessary for initiating experiences. They may need to be restructured in terms of a student's personal information processing style, but they clearly are the simplest means for facilitating an inquiry. Yet a

third kind of information is needed to create pools of data toward which the search phase of an inquiry can be directed. This would be an unusual kind of material to find in a classroom because it can include relatively disconnected information which only acquires meaning to the extent that it becomes a part of a student's search activity. These categories are not mutually exclusive; there is a need to plan for each of them separately, though, if they are all to be included in an educational environment.

In general, if care is taken to muster as many opportunities for experience, observation, and gaining knowledge as possible, and a broad view is taken concerning the kinds of information that are relevant, a teacher will have an excellent basis for providing a wide variety of choice. The teacher's minimal role would be to make available a sufficient range of sources and kinds of information to allow for plans that have been negotiated. With the accumulation of materials and experience, though, it is easy to imagine a classroom environment which would actually begin to stimulate searching for information. Sometimes a teacher would be called upon, as a resource within that environment, to transmit knowledge directly; the teacher's main role, though, in relation to search activity, would be to continue developing the design of the environment and to keep it organized.

Summary

An attempt has been made to show how there is a range of possible ways to design an innovative educational environment. Relatively close to the context of traditional education, it is possible to create a classroom setting in which most instruction is individualized. Secondly, it is possible to organize an open classroom by simply reducing the directive role of the teacher. Not only is instruction highly individualized, but there is also a great deal of freedom for students with regard to goals, subject matter, movement within the classroom, etc. The third alternative is to develop a structured open classroom by designing an environment on the basis of a theory of student-directed learning. From this vantage, new kinds of structures would be introduced with the specific aim to facilitate the establishment of common meaning between a teacher and his students, to encourage the cooperative planning of learning activities, and to make as much choice of materials and activities available to students as possible. A teacher's task is to determine the learning environment that would be personally supportive of the kind of role that is most consistent with his conception of teaching.

References

Allender, Jerome S. "The Importance of Recorded Communication." AV Communication Review 15 (1967): 412–422.

Atkinson, Richard C. "Computerized Instruction and the Learning Process." American Psychologist 23 (1968): 225–239.

Beggs, David W., III, and Edward G. Buffie, eds. Independent Study. Bloomington, Ind: Indiana University Press, 1965.

Brown, Robert M. "The Learning Center." AV Communication Review 16 (1968): 294–300.

Featherstone, Joseph. Schools Where Children Learn. New York: Liveright, 1971.

Furth, Hans G. Piaget for Teachers. Englewood Cliffs, N.J.: Prentice-Hall, 1970.

Gleason, Gerald T. "Technological Developments Related to Independent Learning." In The Theory and Nature of Independent Learning, edited by Gerald T. Gleason. Scranton, Pa.: International Textbook Co., 1967. Pp. 65–78. A

————, ed. The Theory and Nature of Independent Learning. Scranton, Pa.: International Textbook Co., 1967. B

Goodlad, John I. School, Curriculum, and the Individual. Waltham, Mass.: Blaisdell, 1966.

Hansen, Duncan. "Computer-assisted Instruction and the Individualization Process." Journal of School Psychology 6 (1968): 177–185.

Hellerich, Robert L. "The Creative Learning Center." Elementary School Journal 69 (1969): 259–264.

Henry, Nelson B. Individualizing Instruction. 61st NSSE Yearbook, Part I. Chicago: University of Chicago Press, 1962.

Holt, John. What Do I Do Monday? New York: Dutton, 1970.

Kohl, Herbert R. The Open Classroom: A Practical Guide to a New Way of Teaching. New York: Vintage Books, 1969.

Lindvall, C. M., and Richard C. Cox. "The Role of Evaluation in Programs for Individualized Instruction." In Educational Evaluation: New Roles, New Means. 68th NSSE Yearbook, Part 2, edited by Ralph W. Tyler. Chicago: University of Chicago Press, 1969. Pp. 156–188.

Lumsdaine, A. A. "Educational Technology, Programed Learning, and Instructional Science." In Theories of Learning and Instruction, 63rd NSSE Yearbook, Part 1, edited by Ernest R. Hilgard. Chicago: University of Chicago Press, 1964. Pp. 371–401.

Mager, Robert F. Preparing Instructional Objectives. Palo Alto, Calif: Fearon, 1962.

Neill, A. S. Summerhill: A Radical Approach to Child Rearing. New York: Hart, 1960.

Piaget, Jean. Science of Education and the Psychology of the Child, translated by Derek Coltman. New York: Orion Press, 1970.

Plowman, Paul D. Behavioral Objectives: Teacher Success Through Student Performance. Chicago: Science Research Associates, 1971.

Pressey, Sidney L. "Autoinstruction: Perspectives, Problems, Potentials." Theories of Learning and Instructions, 63rd NSSE Yearbook, Part 1, edited by Ernest R. Hilgard. Chicago: University of Chicago Press, 1964. Pp. 354–370.

Rogers, Carl R. Freedom to Learn. Columbus, Ohio: Merrill, 1969.

Skinner, B. F. The Technology of Teaching. New York: Appleton-Century-Crofts, 1968.

Wolfson, Bernice J. "Pupil and Teacher Roles in Individualized Instruction." Elementary School Journal 68 (1968): 357–366.

Barbara Biber and Patricia Minuchin

The Changing School

In this paper we will be considering the school's role in the socialization of competence from a vantage point relevant to the recent explorations in education but rooted in trends which have been evolving over a period of several decades. The changing conceptions with which we will deal were based originally on growing knowledge, as it accumulated in the 20th century, concerning the processes of learning and motivation, the structure and complexity of human personality, and the dynamics of child development. The implications of this knowledge dictated pervasive changes in the atmosphere and teaching practices of at least a small proportion of the nation's schools; many more followed suit with partial changes, while others continued in relatively traditional pathways, with little change in their assumptions, goals or methods.

The Province of Education:
Extension in Scope and Responsibility

In redefining its role as an educating and socializing force, the changing school has first of all broadened its scope. It has taken explicit responsibility for fostering growth in areas of child functioning that were not traditionally part of the school's self-defined province. One

Excerpt from Barbara Biber and Patricia Minuchin, "The Role of the Schools in the Competence of Socialization," a paper presented at the Conference on Socialization for Competence, Social Science Research Council, Puerto Rico, April, 1965. Reprinted by permission of the authors.

The ideas in this paper are presented more fully in *The Psychological Impact of School Experience* by P. Minuchin, B. Biber, E. Shapiro, and H. Zimiles. New York: Basic Books, 1969.

would include among these areas: (1) the school's concern with the child's intellectual functioning in a group context, where he must pool his work and ideas toward achievements that are cooperative in process and mutual in product; (2) the school's concern with vitality, depth, and effectiveness in interpersonal relationships, defining this as interpersonal competence or as effective interaction with the human environment; (3) the school's concern with the child's capacity to express what is personal, fantasy-rooted, and unique, to handle without constriction relatively open situations as well as those requiring finite problem solution, mastery of structured material, and impersonal skills; (4) the school's concern for the child's self-knowledge and for the extent to which this knowledge gains in differentiation, reality, and usefulness as the child grows.

Are these indeed all aspects of competence? Do they flood the concept, in the effort not to narrow it unduly? Are some of these necessary conditions for competent functioning but not evidence of "competence" per se? Can they be systematically investigated? These are difficult questions to answer. It might be noted, at the least, that the changing schools have taken on responsibility for educating in these varied areas, though they are saved our particular conceptual — or semantic — problem of deciding whether these are all a matter of educating for competence. They see these areas as a crucial part of the equipment and experience the child must build to function well in his current and future world. In this sense they are conceptualized as part of his growing competence, though they are also relevant to a broader theory of optimal personal growth.

239

Perhaps examples in one area would illustrate how such goals are actually mediated in the classroom. The following pertain to the area of group intellectual effort, in which the child's competence is surely involved, though the context and purpose is extended beyond individual processes and products:

The six-year-olds are re-creating the city with building blocks — the waterfront, bridges, highway arteries for the flow of the people and material in and out of the city, as they have been reading about it, discussing it, visiting and observing its workings in their weekly trips. They work in groups: several on the new bridge, some on the heliport, some on the piers and roads. Their product is interconnecting, like the city itself.

The second-grade children are writing a group story. They have been to a small, homestyle bakery and to a large, modern, automated bakery, and they are recording their impressions of the contrasts and similarities, the size and movement of the machines, the "gummy, sticky, yellowish" dough, the steps of the process, and the smell of the baking. The teacher is the scribe. She regulates the flow of contributions where they tumble and interfere, and she discusses obscurities. The ideas of the children build on each other, and the story is a rich recall of pooled impressions and learnings.

The fourth grade spends a day in the country. They have been studying colonial America, the way it lived and supplied its needs. They have probed the principles of water power and water wheels as these operated to work the old mills. They spend the day building a dam and setting up a water wheel till it functions. Their research and planning has been careful and cooperative. They divide their labor, pour their ideas into the handling of emergencies, produce a working product that represents the intense efforts of the entire group.

The seventh grade is charting the major social, economic, and political events in America, Britain, and Europe between 1620 and 1850. They work in subgroups, mediate the assignment of individual responsibilities — not without conflict — and reassemble in smaller and larger

groups to pool their information and argue the problems of categorization and implication. (Can one call the American Revolution primarily an American or British affair, or does it need to appear twice? Is the Reign of Terror really a political matter — was it not certainly social or perhaps even economic?) The process is not peaceful but it is lively and productive, and the final chart is more than the sum of its parts.

In these situations, the school sets the child into a context where his individual contributions are vital but the product is not his alone. The school here is offering experience and guidance in working with others, aiming toward effective and committed interaction, the meshing of ideas and efforts toward a mutual goal. It sees this as calling for skills somewhat different from those involved in independent work and regards the education of these skills as part of the school's extended teaching responsibility, both in the service of social goals and in the service of the individual intellectual growth assumed to be inherent in such experience.

Intellectual Mastery: A Revision in Concepts and Goals

Within the clearly acknowledged province of the school — the sphere of intellectual growth — the school has also been changing its viewpoint and practices. Intellectual mastery is conceived less in terms of fact acquisition, more in terms of the organization of knowledge and a complex, active stance toward learning.

In such schools high priority is placed upon stimulating as great a degree of organization of experience as is suitable to the stage of cognitive maturity. According to the developmental theorists Werner (1957) and Piaget (1958), cognitive maturing is seen as a progression from diffuse, global awareness to an increasingly differentiated condition, until a new level of integration is attained. This progression is related to chronological stages but occurs as well on exposure to new, complex experience or ideas at any age.

The teacher has a definite and important role in advancing this process. He extends and sharpens sensitivity by using every opportunity for differentiated observation, accepting the noting of detail and nuance whether the material is perceptual or ideational. This technique and its purpose is not unlike what Suchman (1961) calls Stage 1 of his Inquiry Training Technique.

It is the teacher's further task to help the child systematize factual data by activating processes of comparison. He guides the search for origins, the recognition of change over time, the ordering and classification of experience to achieve generalization, the process of abstracting for the sake of arriving at principles. Consider the exploration of the environment outside the school as an example of the teaching technique. In this framework, a walk around the block is not an outing or a desultory ramble. Depending on the educational level, it is expected to yield awareness that different stores sell different things, or that modern streets follow old country lanes and that is why Fourth Street strangely crosses Tenth Street, or that the new zoning laws explain why all the new tall buildings are on the corners, or that there is a question to be pursued as to why this neighborhood did not qualify for a slum clearance project.

The technique of discussion is another important tool — one example of the techniques employed toward the basic goal of enriching the experience between the question and the answer (Biber, 1959). As currently used in the changing schools, it is a period where questions have the status of problems to be explored and issues to be considered, where the teacher's role is to bring children to awareness of the multiple facets involved in weighing issues and evidence, to indicate fact-finding sources and guide their probing for significant relationships among the relevant facts. Conceived in this way, the technique of discussion is not a replica of the traditional recitation period — not a time for short quick answers to short, quick questions or for guessing the single correct answer the teacher has in mind for the question he has posed.

Perhaps the best of the Dewey influence on the philosophy and practice of the modern school is represented in the general climate as well as in techniques developed for active learning. The school looks like a workshop; the climate of interchange encourages open questioning, allows for difference of opinion and the frank admission of not knowing. The techniques place high value on the child's participation and on a sequence of exploration and consolidation so guided that gratification in achievement is deepened by the pleasure of discovery. The technique developed by Mitchell (1944) for study of the environment is perhaps the best single illustration of the enactment of these principles. Basically, this involves direct encounter with an environmental phenomenon, observation, and questioning *in situ* (a talk with the ferry boat captain about tides and navigation or with the U.N. delegate from Thailand about his country's shift in attitude toward the United States). Back in school, pursuit of the exposure takes multiple forms, depending again on developmental level. The impressions may be relived in mural painting or free dramatizing; the questions raised may be followed through in individual library research; the consolidation may take the form of reports to the class or for the school newspaper. No matter what the content, the elements are exposure, observation, questioning, pursuit, fact gathering and analysis, and, finally, integration through re-expression in verbal and non verbal media.

In the last few years there has been a felicitous convergence of what we have described as the modern school's approach to learning and the work of psychologists — Bruner (1961), Hilgard (1964), Suchman (1961), Ojemann (1961), and others — in emphasis on learning through active discovery, organization of knowledge by governing principles, inductive reasoning, and the basic stance of vital questioning and probing search. There is, however, an important difference in the enactment of this common orientation. The modern school has developed a mode of teaching that attempts to create a pervasive intellectual climate, reflecting in all its parts this goal for learning; the psychologists have developed specific techniques, sometimes exercises, for the furtherance of these same goals. These techniques are an important development, but we can look forward to appreciable advance educationally only to the extent that they can be integrated into a generalized learning climate consistent with their goals.

We need to recognize, of course, that such learning climates are not easily established. They require well informed teachers with flexibly organized knowledge, with a process orientation toward achievement, and well schooled in appropriate teaching techniques. Teaching machines and programmed learning have a place, though a distinctly limited one, in this kind of learning climate. As Hilgard (1964) and Wohlwill (1962) have pointed out, an extended use of such techniques endangers the development of an active stance toward learning, a flexibility of thinking, and a high skill in communicating with other people — goals central to the conception of education outlined here. The method of programmed learning, with its emphasis on efficiency, and the discovery method, with its emphasis on active and autonomous search, represent divergent influences from psychology to the field of education, at this point in time.

The changing schools and those psychologists whose work is syntonic with their methods have a common orientation concerning the stance the child will need to take toward a changing world. They look upon the kind of learning in which the child must be an active and consolidating thinker as a way of equipping him with tools for analysis and decision making and with propensities for the adaptation and flexibility essential for competence in the unforeseeable, much-changed world of his adult years. Having been helped to perceive all knowledge as moving and changing, never coming to finality, the child may be readier to conceive of and utilize knowledge as an instrument for change. Ideally, the facts he acquires will come under disciplined cognitive control, and his intellectual mastery will serve toward making an impact on his changing world.

The World of Knowledge and Individual Meaning: Fusion of the Objective and the Subjective

The growing recognition of the need to educate for greater competence in terms of hard core intellectual mastery and independent thinking has been paralleled by concern that we develop individuals in whom propensities for divergent thinking are also highly developed (Getzels and Jackson, 1962; Guilford, 1959; Torrance, 1962). If one uses the stock phrases — creativity, originality — all schools will consider these to be worthwhile goals, except perhaps those that have been bludgeoned into eliminating all "frills." For the traditional school, however, the meaning of these terms is circumscribed. Creative activities are a subject matter domain and the style of teaching for this subject matter shares the dominant approach to mastery in the traditional school — curtailed exploration, premature imposition of standards of technical proficiency and precision, focus of interest and evaluation on the final product rather than on the multiple processes out of which it emerges, and application of formalized standards that encourage uniformity rather than diversity.

For the changing school, originality and creativity, as they appear in the end products of learning experience, are seen as evidence that an integrative process has taken place — that some part of the child's perception of objective reality has filtered through his own existing pattern of meanings and feelings and reappears, in his expressive output, as a new blend of the personal and the impersonal. It is because this integrative process is so highly valued as the culmination of learning that this kind of school offers an extended variety of materials and modes for the re-expression of experience. The paints, the clay, the dance class, the woodworking shop are the appurtenances in support of this integrative process. The variety in which they are offered is in recognition of the fact that language, which can serve the same end, is only one means toward this goal, and that there are differences among children as to which modality serves them best as a medium for the re-expression of what has been assimilated.

In this kind of school, broad general views on the nature of human experience on the one hand, and highly specific techniques on the other, influence the content and course of the integrative process through which the children are guided. These can be condensed into four points:

1. Though adeptness in the processes of logic is clearly vital, the span of experience would be seriously restricted if intuitive processes, full use of feeling and impulsivity and the reorganization unique to fantasy were denigrated or neglected. These classrooms not only tolerate but value feelings and emotion: The six-year-old who tempestuously spills out the story of his Sunday trip to see the new baby seal at the zoo is not stopped midstream with a reminder that he is not standing in the proper position at his desk for telling things to the class. The twelve-year-olds who want to portray a sit-down in the South for their assembly performance are not discouraged in favor of choosing some more "suitable" topic. The goal is to develop people whose deep feelings remain generative in connection with their intellectual functioning and channel and qualify the nature of their performance.

2. The major teaching techniques specific to this goal of merging subjective meanings with objective reality deal with the life of pretending and portraying. For the young child's fusion of thinking and projection of affect the play mode appears to be the idiomatic form. In illustration: Several five-year-olds have built a square barn with windows, into which they have put the sheep, cows, and horses. All the animals are facing the wall; they are "chained" there. When it is time for them to eat they are put out to pasture (a large enclosure surrounding the barn) with the sheep dogs to watch them. On top of the barn is a box with a "sick cow" in it. Mike explains "that's what they do when a cow is sick — they put him in a separate place," as he brings cylinders from the shelf, "these are the silos." George adds a small enclosure to the side of the barn, "that's a cell — to put the bad farmers in." Shortly after, they put all the farmers into the cell and cover them up. The animals are covered up, too, and the boys leave the play, announcing it is night time.

Free dramatic play is supported with ample time, classroom space, physical materials for macrocosmic and microcosmic forms of reproducing experience and a great variety of objects, in raw and representative form — colored cubes, trains, planes, people. The teaching in connection with play is subtle. Symbolic distortions of reality are not interfered with or corrected, but the cue for the direction in which the children are ready to extend their factual knowledge is picked up by the teacher and followed through systematically.

For the older children, who no longer allow themselves such free shifts from reality to fantasy, the writing, producing, and performing of original plays are an analagous vehicle. They are usually the culmination of some part of a social studies program, worked out through a complex group process in which the artifacts, ideas, points of view of people of a given time and place have been studied and reflected upon and in which the characters are treated as people, not archetypes. In a play created by a group of nine-year-olds who had been studying ancient Egypt, the importance of water supply in that culture is communicated through an incident that has many layers of meaning. A boy, spilling a cup of water, is scolded by his mother and warned of the god who punishes evil. In the boy's guilt-laden dream, the gods appear and preside over the weighing of his good and evil deeds. To the relief that comes to the boy on awakening, the children add a profound touch and an element of mystery as the boy, finding a prop that belonged to the dream sequence, asks if it was really a dream. In the dramatic productions of the traditional school, where a play is selected and assigned to the children for memorization, the integration of subjective and objective is, by definition, not comparable.

3. It is inevitable that, where the processes of absorption and re-expression of experience follow these lines, diversity rather than uniformity is the outcome. The children are not only working through their own integrative processes, developing their own idiomatic styles, but the educative process is enriched through interaction with the multiple forms in which the re-expression of other children appears.

4. Finally, it is presumed that knowledge acquired in this matrix of meaning vital to the self takes on a charge that strengthens commitment and propels the individual to act in his world.

The Sequence of Education: Development Characteristics and Their Relation to Curriculum

In the modern school there is basic investment in individuality — its uniqueness, complexity, and malleability. But there are important commonalities in the sequence of growth of all children; every design for schooling — modern or traditional — is conditioned by its conceptual framework for projecting individuality against the patterns of advancing maturity. For the modern school, neither normative chronological descriptions nor the deviation of achievement from IQ scores is suitable. Instead, the concept of stages of development, delineated by important qualitative shifts in interests, motivation, and productive capacity — according to the models of Erikson (1959), Piaget (1958), and Werner (1957) — has proved a more useful theoretical tool.

The sources in psychology for characterizing a stage of growth are multiple — psychodynamic theory, cognitive process research, studies of creativity — and there is also, from the field of education, a substantial reservoir of understanding of childhood in the minds of teachers who have been in the forefront of changing education. Drawing on all these sources, the modern school builds curriculum on a broad, inclusive purview of each stage of development,

asking: What are the known capacities? Are they being fully exercised? What are the key confusions and conflicts? What are the major sources of gratification? Where are the areas of greatest vulnerability? What are the crucial learning idioms and the specific directions of the urge to master?

An illustration of how the teacher's focus differs according to the stage of development can be taken from the area of language skills. The teacher of the very young children is aware of several key facts about the relation between language and communication while the child is still a somewhat primitive talker: His verbal skills, as tools, are weak; his perspective is too fixed to put his meanings into other words when he is not understood — the words and meanings are fused. At the same time the teacher recognizes his forward thinking processes in the kind of experimental sorties that end with words like "interestering" and the thinking by analogy that makes "goodest" the superlative of "good." The teacher is aware that, at this stage, verbal discourse is just developing as a means for communicating feelings and ideas to other people and strengthening the connection of self with other selves. The teacher acts primarily, therefore, as the sensitive, helping recipient of meaning, responsive to the child's spontaneous innovations, more the protector of the good underlying thinking than the monitor of the incorrect word form.

For the older child, in the primary or elementary years, the focus shifts as the teacher reacts to the changed direction which the urge to master has taken. The child is now eager to become skilled in the ruled, structured aspects of experience. He gains ego-strength in proportion to the degree that reality — the reality of the adult world — can begin to come under independent control. Mastery of the rules of language, accuracy, and proficiency in the built-in rules of this "game" is a specific goal; it matches the child's general motivational organization at this period. The teacher accordingly takes the responsibility for active teaching toward such mastery. The teaching task is more complex: For communication to be most effective the child needs to find channels for his individualized meanings within the restrictions of form and accepted usage. The sequence and balance in the teacher's evaluation of a written composition is illustrative. In an essay about flight the teacher deals first with the child's efforts to contrast imagery of birds and planes and then with the paragraphing mechanisms for better clarity. In the traditional schools, the formal elements are given more central attention; these schools are less apt to conceptualize communication systems as changing synchronously with other changes in the child's position in the adult world.

The question of how best to facilitate progression from stage to stage — to educate — can become an issue between acceleration and fulfillment. The changing school has not accepted the meaning of acceleration which is vested in earliest possible mastery of specific skills. It is aligned with the psychodynamic concept of fulfillment for each stage of development. It is equally concerned, however, with preparatory experiences geared toward future competence. The problem of what shall be regarded as salient preparatory experience for future mastery is a dividing line among educators as it is among psychologists. The changing school does not follow the theorists whose conceptions of learning stress cumulative practice of specific skills as the major road to mastery. Curriculum decisions are more consistent with theories of epigenetic progress in learning, with the concept as stated by Hunt (1964) that "the experiential roots of a given schema will lie in antecedent activities quite different in structure from the schema to be (later) observed and measured."

An illustration of how this works out in practice becomes clear in Mitchell's (1934) exposition of sequential progress toward broad geographic thinking. The "experiential roots" of the ten-year-old's ability to deal with geographic abstractions such as projection, sphere, and equator are seen, for instance, as far back as the six-year-old's groping with space concepts in painting a scene where the boats lie along the riverbank and the bridge must be shown to cross the river. The block play of five-year-olds

has "embryonic map form" in the relationships reified by the placement of trains inside a roundhouse structure or by the re-creation of connecting tunnel and highway systems. The intrinsic experience with space relations is evident even in younger children; their nonrepresentational block building is regarded by Mitchell as relevant to, and preparatory for, the symbolic thinking and knowledge of space relations necessary for mature geographic conceptualization.

The Generality of Competence: Attitudes Toward General Effectiveness

Perhaps it is useful to conceptualize the idea of general competence in two ways. The first is a matter of performance adequacy over a wide range of tasks; it might be described as a *high plurality of skills*. The second is a matter of resourcefulness in many situations — an active, flexible, generally effective stance; it might be described as a *high generality of competence*. These are alternative ways of being effective, sometimes co-existent and sometimes not, and the school has some role in relation to each of them.

In relation to the first aspect — the high plurality of skills — the changing school shares with the more traditional school a self-assignment to educate for basic skills and information over a wide variety of subject matter. This induction of the child into the symbol systems, skills, basic facts, and ideas of his culture and era represents a basic charge to the school in its role as a socializing force for competence, and all schools strive to fulfill this charge.

In the teaching of skills, however, the modern school may be said to differ from its more traditional counterpart in several ways:

1. It strikes a different balance between rehearsing specific content and skills and offering learning at more integrated and cross-sectional levels. The traditional curriculum is apt to be relatively fragmented; the school teaches and expects learning to occur predominantly through specific rehearsal and in pockets of content. The

245

modern school ties its teaching of skills and basic content into more complex units, though it uses practice and rehearsal as well. The modern school continues to search for the optimal proportion of these methods for different children, but it asks its second-grade children, for instance, to spend less time copying words and practicing penmanship as they learn to write, and more time writing stories of their own or recording the daily changes in the Monarch butterflies they have been watching through their cycle of change and growth.

2. The modern school is apt to highlight a somewhat different roster of skills. It places greater stress, for instance, on the skills of communication. It devotes time and teaching to the organization and presentation of ideas in ways that facilitate communication and interchange with other people. It also gives more "prime time" to the teaching of art skills, wishing to provide its students with the hard tools (the techniques, modes, skills) for competent expression in those areas that give them pleasure and expressive satisfaction.

3. It has a less standardized conception of adequate progress; the expectation and acceptance of individual patterns is greater. Uneven performance across areas is taken, at least in part, as an expression of legitimate variation rather than as evidence that effort has not been applied. The teacher needs to decide when to regard potential as present but ineffective, requiring teaching efforts to move the child toward its better use, and when to accept unevenness as intrinsic. Within this framework, the evaluative system is not as apt to judge the child with the highest plurality of skills as automatically the "best and smartest."

It is in relation to the second concept of generality, however, that the changing schools have departed most from the traditional. They place great value on the kind of competence that is expressed in a general resourcefulness, a resilience, a predisposition to assess a situation and find one's way in it. These schools have geared much of their theory and practice to developing such attitudes and effectiveness. The mediating processes here include the following:

1. The first is rather nonspecific. It involves a general learning climate which communicates the sense that the world is knowable and that the child has power to be effective in it. This is conveyed in ways that have been discussed earlier: When questions are raised, they tend to be pursued, conveying the sense that this pursuit is both right and possible; the child himself is made the active agent of discovery and learning; curriculum is developed in child-relevant terms, so that the child's sense of contact with what he learns will be strong; there is a differentiated reaction to individual functioning, with reinforcement for evidences of adequacy and minimization of gross failure experiences.

2. The second technique is specific. It involves the development of skills for finding out about the environment. These skills, discussed in the earlier section on Intellectual Mastery, encourage a differentiated and objective perception of circumstances and provide tools for moving counter to need distortion and stereotype. They have generality beyond the specific content to which they are applied and are meant to provide the child with experiences and methods for understanding his environment as a prerequisite for effective functioning in it. As such, this approach represents an education for general competence in a variety of circumstances.

3. Lastly, the structure of the modern classroom is less fixed and rule dominated than the traditional classroom; it therefore offers the child more experience in finding his niche and his role in any given situation. The search for "where I fit into this" is more open in such schools and proceeds with teacher support and guidance. The

child finds his function in the class play by working on scenery; in the Book Fair by preparing posters; in using his math skill by helping another child; in study of the westward movement by special research on wagon construction; in class conviviality at lunch time by take-offs on TV personalities. The many settings with leeway for varied functioning and the many combinations of interacting groups, as structured in these schools, offer him guided practice in developing his own way of functioning effectively in a variety of circumstances. If all schools provide this to some extent, these changing schools have tended to provide it more, both through their more flexible structure and through the teacher's interest in guiding the process. In this sense these schools are trying to foster effectiveness that becomes a general part of the personality style and is applicable over a wide range of circumstances and situations.

Competence Motivation:
Its Roots and Maintenance

Traditional education has been geared primarily to the effectiveness of performance. It has tended to ask few questions about how strong the child's learning drive is — unless to wonder why he is "not trying" — but it has built its learning climate on certain assumptions.

It has been traditionally assumed, for instance, that the child's motivation for effective performance is rooted primarily in his strong dependence on adults. He works and learns in order to win approval and avoid trouble or pain, and that pleasure or pain follow directly from the reactions of adults to his efforts. It has been further assumed that the competitive drive is strong vis-à-vis other children and that effort can be mobilized in the interest of surpassing competitors and garnering the lion's share of praise and approval. This effort has been so mobilized, without particular concern either for its side effects or for its possible alternatives. Lastly, it has been assumed that self-discipline and other superego virtues enable the child to

apply himself persistently to his work and that it is not the work itself that has major compelling power; this is, in some instances, a self-fulfilling prophecy. By this concept of competence motivation, the setting of clear and extrinsic standards is essential; grades, teacher approval and disapproval, comparison with the group, etc., are the mobilizers of motivation.

The changing school system has worked and taught on the basis of other assumptions. Psychologists have come only lately to dealing with the urge to explore and to master, arguing its place in dynamic theory and the origins of its energy (White, 1959). Educators have been little concerned with these theoretical problems, but they have a somewhat longer history of central contact with this energy and curiosity. At least from the time of Dewey, a whole wing of American education has systematically built its teaching methods on the assumption that the child has a strong and intrinsic drive to explore, to extend his world, to gain in understanding, and to make an impact. They have assumed that this exploration and learning is inherently pleasurable and that it is the business of education to offer such experiences as will keep this force alive. The changes in education have built on competence motivation conceived in terms of the pleasure and power that are inherent in mastery.

Beyond the intrinsic motivation to master, the changing schools have built on two other sources of motivation, as they conceive them: the identification with learning goals developed through the teacher-child relationship, and the identification with group work goals developed through peer group interaction.

It would be an error to imply that for learning motivation the adult in the changing schools is not comparable in importance to the adult in the traditional schools. The contrast is in the particular conception of role and function. The aim of the teacher in the modern school is partly to provide a model for intensive and zestful attitudes toward learning and for a vigorous approach to gathering and organizing knowledge. More specifically, however, he attempts to establish a personalized and differentiated relationship to each child as an individual, hoping to make it possible thereby for the child to internalize the teacher's particular goals for his learning — to understand and adopt the relevance to himself. The quality of the teacher-child relationship changes in the form and extent of closeness as the child grows older, but it always aims for communication that will enhance internalization of meaningful learning goals rather than for reinforcement of specific behavior through approval and disapproval.[1]

It is assumed in these schools, further, that peer group ties are deeply important to the school age child and that there is considerable motivational impetus to perform well when effective functioning has implications for peer relationships. These schools provide for learning in varying group combinations as well as in individual work and study. The block building of the city, the group bakery story, the water wheel construction, and the historical chart serve as illustrations. The child's competence in such a context has social implications. If his contribution is important for something the group values, then it is assumed that his peer loyalty and his need to be accepted and valued by other children will be interwoven with motivation from other sources. He will wish to work well and responsibly as an intrinsic member of his group.

It is perhaps repetitious to note the educational processes that mediate motivation, conceived in these terms, but a brief summary may be in order: There is an attempt to design curriculum that is relevant and meaningful to children, so that learning enthusiasm is not extinguished; an attempt is made to set learning goals at a point that is manageable but challenging enough to keep interest high; the teacher builds a relationship that is personal in quality and that communicates her particularized goals

[1] See the detailed description of two teachers, fifth- and sixth-grade levels, in Sears and Sherman (1964). They represent a "modern" and a relatively "traditional" teacher, in our terms, and exemplify in part the distinction described here.

248

for the individual child; the peer group is utilized as an important and serious work group, capable of mobilizing the child's competence motivation on an additional plane.

Feelings of Competence: A Pivotal Construct

The difference between traditional and changing schools in their attitudes toward self-feeling is not, perhaps, a sheer matter of difference in conceptions or assumptions; it is a basic difference in the extent to which such a construct enters into the teaching philosophy or system. The traditional school is concerned with the confidence with which the child performs and presents himself, and the child who is competent within this system often feels pride and satisfaction with himself as a by-product of his performance, but deep feelings about capacity and self-image as a learner are not, in themselves, within the province of the traditional school.

For the changing school, self-concept and feeling is a pivotal factor. The school is concerned that the child know himself well, to the extent possible at his age level, and that he feel adequate and capable at any age. Self-contact, realistic evaluation of oneself, and feelings of confidence and competence are assumed to mediate effective functioning — the child's capacity to learn, to meet the environment, and to act on it.

The modern school actually assumes an interconnected triumvirate of feeling, motivation, and performance, all of which affect each other, and the school maintains a teaching alertness toward all levels. The teaching support for positive self-feeling starts at the preschool stages, with the provision and bolstering of experiences that permit the child to experience himself and his power (on the jungle gym; with a hammer, a puzzle, a paint brush; with equipment to play fireman or doctor; with help in a situation where power resides in the capacity to channel anger). The school helps him to differentiate himself from his environment, establish who he is and the fact that he can make an impact. It goes on through the grades building on the assumption that this feeling, and the self-knowledge that enables one to use oneself well, helps to mediate competent behavior.

The school attempts to reinforce this feeling in several ways — and if they seem to overlap with the methods for sustaining motivation the overlap is not accidental; motivation and feeling are assumed to reinforce each other.

The teacher-child relationship is one element, and it has perhaps two qualities, when well enacted, that are especially relevant. The first is a supportive quality, warm and objective, in which the teacher conveys a sense of partnership with the child in his learning; he is there to teach and facilitate, not to criticize or "show him up." The second is a quality of specificity and differentiation in the way he relates to the child as an individual. He attempts to foster through this kind of relationship a growth in the child's knowledge about himself.

The kind of learning challenge set for the child is another element. The attempt is made, as noted before, to set him to work at a level that extends his boundaries and makes achievement worthwhile, but which is nonetheless within his reach. It is assumed that tasks well beyond the child's ability have inherent in them a gross failure experience and that both motivation and the sense of adequacy suffer from repeated exposure of this kind. To find the optimal range is a difficult teaching decision — it is seldom equivalent for all children in a class — but the teacher who works from this theoretical framework assumes he must select for the child's efforts what he can manage, albeit with help, if he does not wish to lose him as a confident and effective learner.

Lastly, the nature of assessment and reaction to the child's performance is directed toward maintaining a sense of adequacy as well as objective evaluation. The teacher accepts the child's product at its own level, rather than in terms of the adult standard he will eventually get to. The five-year-old's painting of a girl and her dog is crude and inaccurate by objective standards, but the teacher is neither condescending nor amused. He accepts its vitality and color, the struggle to master and techniques of rendering an image in paint, and the competence of the product in five-year-old terms. The teacher is apt also, especially though not exclusively at older age levels, to present the child with a delineated reaction to the product, in which analytical comment and acceptance are combined. The impassioned essay of the 12-year-old on the population explosion may be corrected at the level of grammar and organization, opened to discussion at the level of social complexities, but accepted at the same time for the intense, well thought out seventh-grade product that it is; the recognition of what is competent about his work drives the thinker on. There is the further important assumption, however, that assessment must be, in the end, a matter of self-evaluation based on individual meaning. The child is asked and helped to internalize a standard that is relevant to his own capacities, and here it is assumed that the struggle to meet a "standard of excellence" that is personal and internalized is most apt to be sustained, to generate pleasure, and to build a sense of meaningful accomplishment and adequacy.

If one were to summarize the theory and assumptions of traditional and changing education, then, in the terms by which we have described them, one might say that traditional education has concerned itself with competent performance, rooted in subject matter mastery, drawing on motivation that is competitive and approval-oriented in nature, and concerning itself only in part with the child's feeling of competence or adequacy. Changing education has also concerned itself with competent performance but has defined this differently, through a broader range of life areas, a more personalized quality of impact, and through a definition of meaningful cognition that stresses the tools and principles for intellectual exploration, the organization of knowledge, and the breadth and flexibility of its application. It has assumed and drawn on a different motivational system — intrinsic curiosity and the internalization of learning goals — and has given to feelings of competence and adequacy the status of a key mediating factor in the socialization of competence.

References

Biber, Barbara. "Premature Structuring as a Deterrent to Creativity." *American Journal of Orthopsychiatry* 24 (2) (1959): 280–290.

Bruner, Jerome. "The Act of Discovery." *Harvard Educational Review* 31 (1961): 21–32.

Erikson, Erik H. "Identity and the Life Cycle." *Psychological Issues* 1 (1959): 18–171.

Getzels, J. W., and P. Jackson. *Creativity and Intelligence.* New York: Wiley, 1962.

Guilford, J. P. "Three Faces of Intellect." *American Psychologist* 8 (1959): 469–480.

Hilgard, Ernest R. "Issues Within Learning Theory and Programmed Learning." *Psychology in Schools* 1 (April 1964): 129–139.

Hunt, J. McV. "The Psychological Basis for Using Pre-school Enrichment as an Antidote for Cultural Deprivation." *Merrill-Palmer Quarterly* 10 (3) (1964): 209–248.

Mitchell, Lucy S. "Research on the Child's Level: Possibilities, Limitations, and Techniques." University of Pennsylvania Bulletin (1944).

————. *Young Geographers.* New York: John Day, 1934. (Reprinted New York: Basic Books, 1963.)

Ojemann, R. H. "Investigations on the Effects of Teaching an Understanding and Appreciation of Behavior Dynamics." In *Prevention of Mental Disorders in Children,* edited by G. Caplan. New York: Basic Books, 1961.

Piaget, Jean. *The Growth of Logical Thinking in the Child.* New York: Basic Books, 1958.

Sears, Pauline S., and Vivian S. Sherman. *In Pursuit of Self Esteem.* Belmont, Calif.: Wadsworth, 1964.

Suchman, J. Richard. "Inquiry Training: Building Skills for Autonomous Discovery." *Merrill-Palmer Quarterly* 7 (July 1961): 147–169.

Torrance, E. P. *Guiding Creative Talent.* Englewood Cliffs, N.J.: Prentice-Hall, 1962.

Werner, H. *Comparative Psychology of Mental Development.* New York: International Universities Press, 1957.

White, R. W. "Motivation Reconsidered: the Concept of Competence." *Psychology Review* 66 (September 1959): 297–333.

Wohlwill J. F. "The Teaching Machine: Psychology's New Hobbyhorse." *Teachers College Record* 64 (November 1962): 139–146.

Bernice J. Wolfson

Pupil and Teacher Roles in Individualized Instruction

We have been hearing a persistent call for better education. Yet, the people who join in making this appeal are far from agreement in their criticisms of present school conditions and in their views of what is required to effect improvement (1).

"Better education" may mean more up-to-date knowledge, faster achievement, better teachers, introducing new disciplines in the early grades, preparing every child for college, or, less often, changing education to make it more relevant to the lives of today's children. On the one hand, the emphasis may be on "more-and-better" of the school's traditional pattern and role. On the other hand, the focus may be on finding some new pattern for the institution and for the processes to occur within it.

Why Individualize?

With the second focus in mind, many of us in education are committed to the idea of individualizing instruction. Again, we find a variety of reasons for this commitment. Some of us hope to teach more efficiently than we have taught under some form of group instruction. We want children to achieve the same learnings we have been striving for but at different rates and possibly with greater amounts of enrichment. Others want to encourage greater individuality among pupils and a wider variety of learning outcomes. Still others perhaps want to go beyond our current view of the classroom to transform our present goals and ways of working into

a new image made possible by individualized instruction. No doubt, there are additional purposes. But it seems to me that each of us must know why he wants to individualize instruction. What makes it a desirable thing to do?

Personally, I believe that individualizing instruction can enable us to change our educational direction. I would like to see less emphasis on conformity and more on initiative and individuality. I would like to see us break out of the box of "covering content" as defined in grade level steps or predetermined sequences. Particularly, I would like to see more opportunities for children to ask questions of real concern to them, to make choices and plans, to evaluate and think independently, and to develop individual interests and commitments. I am well aware that many thoughtful and gifted teachers have sought to provide such opportunities with varying degrees of success. I believe that organizing to individualize instruction — or, more accurately, to encourage personalized learning — will strengthen efforts to move in these directions.

What Is Individualization?

Even though we might develop some agreement about reasons for individualizing instruction, our definition of the process is not quite clear. In fact, observations in classrooms where teachers say that they are individualizing instruction reveal a wide variety of practices. Teachers may be using traditional textbooks and workbooks and allowing each child to work at his own pace. Teachers may have conferences with individual children. They may instruct small groups in particular skills. In some classrooms pupils may use programmed materials or textbooks as-

251

signed by the teacher on an individual basis, as she decides they are appropriate. In other classrooms small groups of children who share some common interest may work together, and individual children may select their own materials from the available resources.

It is not at all certain that these practices provide individualization. Take a pupil-teacher conference. This procedure obviously provides a one-to-one relationship. But the teacher may be doing the same thing that she would do in a directed reading lesson with a group. In fact, she may be doing what she does with many of the other pupils, one at a time. I would not consider these conferences examples of individualized instruction. The use of programmed learning materials and textbooks with individual pacing is not truly an example of individualized instruction. These materials provide for differences in rate of learning, but are not responsive to other kinds of variation among pupils, such as motivation, style of learning, energy level, attitudes, previous learning, and complex personality factors.

At present, the most popular interpretation of individualized instruction is that the teacher makes specific recommendations and assignments for each pupil. This interpretation rests on the teacher-as-doctor analogy, an analogy seriously in need of examination. According to this view, the teacher functions as a doctor; that is, she diagnoses needs, deficiencies, or problems and prescribes appropriate treatment.

Admittedly there is something appealing about this analogy. Part of its appeal is probably due to the high status doctors have in our society. To say that teachers behave like doctors is therefore seen as a compliment. However, I think that the attractiveness of this analogy is due mostly to the apparent simplicity, precision, and neatness of the model: One assesses the present condition, diagnoses the nature of the problem, prescribes the appropriate treatment, and a cure is effected.

However attractive this model may be, teaching really does not fit such a design. (And I doubt that doctoring does either.) Surely teaching is more complicated than doctoring, has

more dimensions, and, in spite of intensive efforts, has not developed clear-cut criteria for treatment success.

Let us examine this model further as it might be applied in a hypothetical classroom. Consider the plight of the teacher who must diagnose and prescribe for thirty pupils in many subject areas over an extensive period of time. Does she really know what each pupil is ready for or what specific learning experiences he needs next? She may have some general hunches, and perhaps she could get some helpful suggestions from the pupil. But how would she make her diagnosis and prescription? She might decide that a pupil is ready for third-grade work or for subtraction or for addition with bridging. She might decide that he needs practice in recognizing beginning sounds. Or she might merely decide that he has successfully completed one section of his workbook and is ready to start the next section. In many so-called nongraded schools she would decide that he is ready to read at Level 11.

Most of these decisions, it seems to me, are arbitrary and often not relevant to the pupil's understanding of his world. Somehow I do not believe that these are meaningful ways of planning for individual, continuous learning. Furthermore, since the teacher is the chief source of evaluation, her relationship with the pupil is necessarily judgmental and the pupil continues to be dependent on her evaluation of his efforts. Finally, the inappropriateness of this model becomes clearer when we recognize that the teacher as a diagnostician is led to focus on needs, disabilities, and problems instead of attending to the pupil as a person who is constantly growing and learning. If the doctor analogy is inappropriate, what analogy might be more fitting?

Recently, I have been exploring the notion that the teacher is more like a travel consultant. Suppose you want to take a trip to the Orient. You tell the travel consultant what you think you would like to see. He will have some questions: How much time do you have? What are you most interested in seeing? How much money do you want to spend on this venture?

How do you prefer to travel? He may suggest other possibilities you did not know existed. A good travel consultant will help you to plan loosely, so that you will not find yourself dashing from one place to another. He will also help you to plan flexibly, so that if you find a place that you particularly enjoy you can make arrangements to stay longer.

Among the interesting features of this analogy, at least as far as I have taken it, are the implications for outcomes. It seems to me that this analogy implies that the primary outcome is not simply to get to the Orient. The outcomes are the kinds of experiences you have along the way and while you are there. Some of these outcomes are completely unpredictable — the people you happen to meet, the experiences you could not anticipate. These unpredictable outcomes might be, in the long run, the most vital aspects of your trip — the ones you remember forever, in contrast to the general clear-cut objective of getting to the Orient or of seeing certain sights that you decided on in advance. Furthermore, other travelers can choose other destinations.

This analogy, in contrast to the medical analogy, is in large part open-ended, responsive to persons (rather than to deficiencies), and clearly allows for self-direction. Still, after all has been said, analogies are merely vivid pictures that may help us see new relationships but that necessarily fall short of describing the realities we are discussing. Instead of exploring analogies, then, let us consider how teachers and pupils might function to promote the kind of individualized and personalized learning that is truly responsive to, and supportive of, individuality.

Beliefs We Can Question

For a discussion of this kind we must first eliminate some of the constraints that inhibit our thinking about new roles. These constraints are both conceptual and institutional. The first conceptual constraint I would discard is the idea that there is a necessary sequence for learning certain skills, or a particular set of sequences that is best for all children. Also I would discard

the idea that certain predetermined sequences are necessary to develop understanding in a content area. These two assumptions underlie programmed learning and the "structure-of-discipline" approach to curriculum. In addition, I do not believe that we know what knowledge and skills all children should have. Knowledge is neither certain nor permanent. As for skills, I think there are certain agreements in our culture. For example, in order to learn you have to be able to read, and reading involves a variety of interrelated skills. However, there is great difference of opinion as to what constitutes reading skill and how children learn to read. Commonly held assumptions inhibit our view of curriculum.

I would also discard the premise that the learner is primarily a receptive, reactive organism responding to stimuli presented by the teacher and by teaching materials, as well as to reward and punishment, or approval and disapproval, as meted out by the teacher. I would reject the view, still common among teachers, that intelligence tests measure the child's ability, or potential for learning, and that this potential is fixed and almost entirely genetically determined. Assumptions of this kind limit our perceptions of children.

I disagree with those who believe that grade level is a meaningful and useful way of organizing schools and curriculums. I do not believe that the teacher directly controls what is learned by the class. Nor do I believe that certain specific content or concepts must be covered during a school year. Finally, I cannot accept the current conviction that specific behavioral objectives provide the best guidelines for the planning of teaching and learning.

All these commonly accepted assumptions can, I believe, be challenged and rejected. Here I will discuss only the first assumption: that there is a best or desirable sequence for learning.

A study by Mager (2) raises some interesting questions about learning sequence. Six adults were studying electronics in a learner-directed program. Each subject in this study was treated individually and took part in one to seven sessions that lasted sixty-five minutes on the average.

In the experimental group, the instructor's role was merely to respond to the questions and requests of the learner. These requests could be for information, for demonstration, for reviews, for whatever the learner felt he needed at the moment.

Some interesting findings emerged. The author reported: "Subject-matter commonality in the learner-generated sequences was greatest at the outset of instruction. As instruction progressed the learners moved into their areas of special interest in electronics. . . . The instructor-generated sequences began with an entirely different topic than did the learner-generated sequences. This suggests that the sequence most meaningful to the learner is different from the sequence guessed by the instructor to be most meaningful to the learner" (2: 3). In fact each learner pursued a different path of instruction. The instructor found it difficult to follow the questions of the learner. Mager commented: "If the instructor finds it difficult to keep up when the sequencing of content is controlled by the student, what kinds of obstacles must the student be facing when the instructor controls the sequence?" (2: 3).

Also, although the subjects were convinced that they knew absolutely nothing about electronics before this experiment, it turned out that they actually had a large body of relevant background information from which the instructor could draw. In addition, from the learners' behavior, the way they raised questions and used the information they got, it appeared that they "were continuously attempting to tie new information to information they already knew, whether correct or incorrect" (2: 3).

Finally, the author concluded, "The data suggest that the learner's motivation increases as a function of his control, or apparent control, of the learning situation. Subjects' comments indicated that they terminated their sessions because they felt unable to absorb more material rather than because they were bored" (2: 3).

Mager started out to compare the effectiveness of instruction using the traditional meth-

ods with the effectiveness of instruction using programmed materials. He found that he saved time when he used the program. However, he saved even more time when he used learner-directed instruction. This investigation, it seems to me, encourages us at least to question the conviction that we can determine the best sequence for teaching and learning.

Roles Redefined

A willingness to question many commonly held assumptions will make it possible to visualize a new model of the classroom. We must, of course, be aware that the same actions at different times and in different contexts will have different meanings. We cannot say that behaving in a certain fashion is necessarily consistent with our goal of developing individuality. Furthermore, each classroom is a unique environment for learning. It could not be otherwise. Each teacher is unique, and each combination of individuals who make up a class is unique. The resultant mix of personalities, attitudes, interests, resources, and materials can never be duplicated.

How then might pupils and teachers, having discarded the old assumptions, function in these environments? I will describe some possible roles that I believe would encourage the individual development of the pupil.

Principally, the pupil could play a more significant role in determining his learning activities. He could be involved in significant decisions — not just in the unimportant ones we usually allocate to him. Within broad limits, he could choose what he will learn and in whose company. He could plan and evaluate for himself. He could be free to raise questions important to him and to explore his world outside the classroom as part of his planned learning. He could be encouraged to clarify his personal meanings and values. In short, he could be a self-directing, active learner, a role not often emphasized in today's schools.

The teacher's role would be primarily that of consultant and resource person to the learner. She would be a manager of the classroom environment, supplying a variety of materials and at times initiating new experiences. She would help pupils learn to plan, to evaluate, and to consider alternatives. She could bring her own interest and inquiry into the classroom. The main focus of her activity would be to promote self-direction (4). Of course, each teacher's approach is unique. But if a teacher does not intend to promote self-direction, she will not truly allow children to make choices. Her intent, therefore, will influence how she and her pupils organize their class.

In these classrooms there would be a flexible mix of individual activities, small-group activities, and large group activities. There would be frequent pupil-teacher conferences. Small groups might ask the teacher to confer with them. Temporary interest-centered groups would develop and disband as they completed their plans. At times the entire class would meet at the request of the teacher or a pupil. A wide variety of materials in many media would be available. Resources outside the classroom would also be used. The significant element in organizing and using resources would be the co-operative planning of pupils and teacher.

A word of caution is appropriate here. Many of the features I have been describing may be found in classrooms that are not focused on the educational purposes I have been emphasizing. Furthermore, we cannot conclude that the presence of these features will in themselves further individualized instruction and the development of self-direction. The intent and the functioning of the teacher will have an important influence on the pupils. Are they actually learning to be self-directing, or are they merely learning how to give the teacher what she expects? The teacher's attitudes, values, perceptions, and communications contribute to the formation of classroom climate and to the pupil's perception of his role in school.

New Roles in Action

Let us turn now to some examples of efforts to achieve the type of educational experience I have been discussing. Three projects seem to me to incorporate the spirit of this conception. There are undoubtedly other examples.

The first project was reported in an article called "Mississippi's Freedom Schools: The Politics of Education." In that article Florence Howe described her experience as a teacher and director of a Freedom School one August. Most of her work was with a group of eleven-to-fourteen-year-olds. Her description seems to communicate the realities of the situation. Take the following remarks about the teacher role:

> The teacher's main problem was to learn to keep quiet, to learn how to listen and to question creatively rather than to talk at the students. He had to discard whatever formal classroom procedures he had ever learned and respond with feeling and imagination as well as with intelligence and good humor to the moods and needs of the group. Above all, the students challenged his honesty: he could not sidestep unpleasantness; he could not afford to miss any opportunity for discussing differences (5: 155).

These comments, it seems to me, convey an awareness of the need for "real" people as teachers. They also remind us that teaching consists of confronting problems. One cannot support a particular approach to teaching in the hope that it will eliminate all problems. Teachers and pupils must choose to confront the problems that they feel are meaningful. These are not necessarily the problems that other people consider meaningful.

A second example of an effort to achieve the type of educational experience I have been describing is an experimental high school in California. A report of the first year of the school describes the problems and the development of a school designed for "maximum student involvement and maximum freedom for individual growth" (6: 1). In discussing curriculum and the related teacher-student roles the authors state:

> In the classroom the student is shown that he should feel free to be himself. Our teachers try not to hide behind their teacher role; they, in turn, urge students not to hide behind theirs. They all begin their courses as students, the teachers only perhaps farther along in their questioning. Teachers encourage their students to formulate and share their own questions. By sharing in the inquiry, students will hopefully be drawn by their own natural curiosities into a search for the heart of each subject, and to the basic questions which draw disciplines together. They are made free to explore . . . the

student learns to take more and more charge over his own education. By making choices available, by encouraging individual and small-group projects, by fostering an open, non-threatening atmosphere, by encouraging divergence of approach and opinion, by allowing ample room for unscheduled exploration, by aiding in the formation of individual goals, and by giving each student some personal attention and understanding, the teacher in the classroom makes constructive use of the individual learning pattern and goals of each student (6: 4).

In this description, too, we can see an awareness of the need for teachers to be "real" people to their students. Admittedly, it is easy to describe an experimental school in glowing terms without providing corroborative evidence of its practices. I have spoken with the writers of this report, but I have not yet observed the school in action. Still, the direction of the effort clearly speaks to the kind of possibilities I am exploring.

For a third example, I would like to describe some observations made by teachers with whom I have been working, who teach in multiage, heterogeneous classrooms. As you can imagine, working with randomly assigned six-, seven-, and eight-year-olds (or nine-, ten-, and eleven-year-olds) in one classroom requires one to individualize instruction and to provide a wide variety of materials and learning opportunities.

In some of these classrooms I have seen evidence of extensive changes in teacher and pupil roles. Some teachers report that they experience a new kind of relationship with their pupils. At times, as pupils become increasingly self-directing, the teachers wonder how much they are needed. They note that pupils feel free to come to the teacher for help on various problems, but often the pupils also seek help from other pupils. Teachers express amazement at the capabilities of some of their pupils, capabilities that were completely unexpected. Some teachers also report that they do relatively little direct instruction, and are surprised to see growth in skills on achievement tests without specific instruction.

In these classes pupils appear to learn to accept differences in other children and to work

willingly with individuals who would ordinarily be in other grades. Many pupils pursue individual or small-group projects for an extensive period. One boy at the primary level spent much time studying continents and then proceeded to study air currents. Two boys (who would have been in third and fourth grade in a traditional organization) worked together for a long time studying about various animals.

I could give many examples (4) but to describe what one may see in a class of this kind, or to describe the activities a teacher and her pupils engage in, does not get to the heart of the matter. To provide the type of environment for learning I have been trying to describe, the teacher must have a view of man, and of children in particular, that allows her to see them as growing creatively, rather than as moving in predetermined paths. She must be able to interact honestly and realistically with her pupils. Living in schools can be real, not just playing the game of beating the system. To me individual and personalized learning means really living in school.

There is little research on the conception I have tried to develop. Most current research about teaching seems to me to be based on a mechanistic rather than an organismic model of man. The classroom observation and analysis research done in recent years by Anderson, Withall, Flanders, Smith, Hughes, Medley and Mitzels, and others (7) have produced observation and category systems that purport to describe and analyze the teacher's behavior, mostly verbal behavior. The result of these efforts is a relatively superficial labeling or categorizing of the teacher's verbal acts. These categories describe a limited dimension of teaching behavior, but they are not really pertinent to what the teacher thinks she is doing. Nor are they particularly crucial dimensions of the teacher's actions. It seems to me that this type of analysis is equivalent to using the linear dimensions of an automobile and the names of some of its parts in an effort to describe and explain its functioning. Research of this kind assumes that the teacher's verbal behavior is meaningfully described by discrete units of activities in categories such as "asks questions" or "accepts feelings." This research also assumes that these bits, when added together in each category and examined for proportional distribution, will characterize some significant differences among teachers.

I have no objection to researchers who observe teaching and try to describe and even measure what they see. I would hope they might uncover some meaningful relationships. However, for the teacher of teachers and for the teacher herself, study of this kind has not yet yielded much useful information. I have already suggested that these studies fail because of the mechanistic nature of their analysis. I would also like to suggest that it is a mistake for the teacher to look to research for specific answers to her concerns as a practitioner. Like the aesthetician, who may possibly add to the artist's generalized thinking about art, but not directly affect how he goes about creating a painting, the student and researcher of teaching may possibly add to our generalized understanding about teaching, but not directly affect how we go about teaching.

How Teachers Know

It seems to me that our most vital questions as teachers cannot, at least at present, be answered by the researcher, the curriculum specialist, or the principal. Each of us must draw our working answers from our personal interpretation and integration of our current knowledge and experience. Indeed, our "tacit knowledge" (8) guides our actions whether in wisdom or in error.

I would like to close with the reminder that science is but one way of knowing, no doubt an extremely useful way but still, as Bronowski said, uncertain. Bronowski went on to say:

Not all experience is got by observing nature. There is a second mode of knowledge which differs from the procedures of science. In our relations with people, and even with animals, we understand their actions and motives because we have at some time shared them, so that we know them from the inside. We know what anger is, we learn an accent or the value of friendship, by directly entering into the experience. And by identifying ourselves with the experience of others, we enlarge our knowledge of ourselves as human beings: we gain self-knowledge (9: 83).

In my view of individualized and personalized learning, the teacher is working with her knowledge from the inside as well as with her observations from the outside. It is, I believe, through some combination of both kinds of knowledge that we must continue to search for the heart of the matter in struggling with the concepts of teaching and learning I have been discussing. The teacher cannot relinquish either focus, or indeed separate them, if she is concerned with her own and her pupils' personal learning.

Notes

1. This article is based on a paper originally presented at a Workshop on Individualized Instruction, University of California, Los Angeles, July, 1967.
2. Robert R. Mager. "On the Sequencing of Instructional Content," reported by Millicent Alter in *Programmed Instruction*, 4 (November, 1964), 3–4.
3. See: Robert F. Mager and John McCann. "Learner-controlled Instruction." Palo Alto, California: Varian Associates, 1961.
   Robert F. Mager and C. Clark. "Explorations in Student-controlled Instruction," *Psychological Reports*, 13 (August, 1963), 71–76.
   Vincent N. Campbell and Madalynne A. Chapman. "Learner Control vs. Program Control of Instruction," *Psychology in the Schools*, 4 (April, 1967), 121–30.
4. Bernice J. Wolfson. "The Promise of Multiage Grouping for Individualizing Instruction," *Elementary School Journal*, 67 (April, 1967), 354–62.
5. Florence Howe. "Mississippi's Freedom Schools: The Politics of Education," *Harvard Educational Review*, 35 (Spring, 1965), 144–60.
6. Raymond J. Roberts and Carolyn Schuetz. "Monte Vista High School — The First Year." San Ramon Valley Unified School District, Danville, California, 1966 (Mimeographed).
7. Nathan L. Gage. *Handbook of Research on Teaching*. Chicago: Rand McNally and Company, 1963.
8. Michael Polanyi. *The Tacit Dimension*. Garden City, New York: Doubleday and Company, 1966.
9. J. Bronowski. *The Identity of Man*. Garden City, New York: The Natural History Press, 1966.

Herbert Kohl

Excerpt from 36 Children

One day Ralph cursed at Michael and unexpectedly things came together for me. Michael was reading and stumbled several times. Ralph scornfully called out, "What's the matter, psyches, going to pieces again?" The class broke up and I jumped on that word "psyches."

"Ralph, what does *psyches* mean?"

An embarrassed silence.

"Do you know how to spell it?"

Alvin volunteered. "S-i-k-e-s."

"Where do you think the word came from? Why did everybody laugh when you said it, Ralph?"

"You know, Mr. Kohl, it means, like crazy or something."

"Why? How do words get to mean what they do?"

Samuel looked up at me and said: "Mr. Kohl, now you're asking questions like Alvin. There aren't any answers, you know that."

"But there are. Sometimes by asking Alvin's kind of questions you discover the most unexpected things. Look."

I wrote *Psyche*, then *Cupid*, on the blackboard.

"That's how *psyche* is spelled. It looks strange in English, but the word doesn't come from English. It's Greek. There's a letter in the Greek alphabet that comes out *psi* in English. This is the way *psyche* looks in Greek."

Some of the children spontaneously took out their notebooks and copied the Greek.

"The word *psyche* has a long history. *Psyche* means mind or soul for the Greeks, but it was also the name of a lovely woman who had the misfortune to fall in love with Cupid, the son of Venus, the jealous Greek goddess of love. . . ."

The children listened, enchanted by the myth, fascinated by the weaving of the meaning of *psyche* into the fabric of the story, and the character, Mind, playing tricks on itself, almost destroying its most valuable possessions through its perverse curiosity. Grace said in amazement:

"Mr. Kohl, they told the story and said things about the mind at the same time. What do you call that?"

"*Myth* is what the Greeks called it."

Sam was roused.

"Then what happened? What about the history of the word?"

"I don't know too much, but look at the words in English that come from *Cupid* and *Psyche*."

I cited *psychological, psychic, psychotic, psychodrama, psychosomatic, cupidity* — the children copied them unasked, demanded the meanings. They were obviously excited.

Leaping ahead, Alvin shouted: "You mean words change? People didn't always speak this way? Then how come the reader says there's a right way to talk and a wrong way?"

"There's a right way now, and that only means that's how most people would like to talk now, and how people write now."

Charles jumped out of his desk and spoke for the first time during the year.

"You mean one day the way we talk — you know, with words like *cool* and *dig* and *sound* — may be all right?"

"Uh huh. Language is alive, it's always changing, only sometimes it changes so slowly that we can't tell."

Neomia caught on.

"Mr. Kohl, is that why our reader sounds so old-fashioned?"

And Ralph.

"Mr. Kohl, can't we study the language we're talking about instead of spelling and grammar? They won't be any good when language changes anyway."

We could and did. That day we began what had to be called for my conservative plan book "vocabulary," and "an enrichment activity." Actually it was the study of language and myth, of the origins and history of words, of their changing uses and functions in human life. We began simply with the words *language* and *alphabet*, the former from the Latin for tongue and the latter from the first two letters of the Greek alphabet. Seeing the origin of *alphabet* and the relationship of *cupidity* to Cupid and *psychological* to Psyche had a particularly magical effect upon the children. They found it easy to master and acquire words that would have seemed senseless and tedious to memorize. Words like *psychic* and *psychosomatic* didn't seem arbitrary and impenetrable, capable of being learned only painfully by rote. Rather they existed in a context, through a striking tale that easily accrued associations and depth. After a week the children learned the new words, asked to be tested on them, and demanded more.

"Vocabulary" became a fixed point in each week's work as we went from Cupid and Psyche to Tantalus, the Sirens, and the Odyssey and the linguistic riches that it contains. We talked of Venus and Adonis and spent a week on first *Pan* and *panic*, *pan-American*, then *pandemonium*, and finally on *demonic* and *demons* and *devils*. We studied *logos*, *philos*, *anthropos*, *pathos*, and their derivatives. I spun the web of *mythos* about language and its origins. I went to German (*kindergarten*), Polynesian (*taboo*), or Arabic (*assassin*), showing what a motley open-ended fabric English (and for that matter any living language) is. The range

of times and peoples that contributed to the growth of today's American English impressed me no less than it did the class. It drove me to research language and its origins; to reexplore myth and the dim origins of man's culture; and to invent ways of sharing my discoveries with the children.

The children took my words seriously and went a step further. Not content to be fed solely words that grew from sources that I, the teacher, presented, they asked for words that fitted unnamed and partially articulated concepts they had, or situations they couldn't adequately describe.

"Mr. Kohl, what do you call it when a person repeats the same thing over and over again and can't stop?"

"What is it called when something is funny and serious at the same time?"

"What do you call a person who brags and thinks he's big but is really weak inside?"

"Mr. Kohl, is there a word that says that something has more than one meaning?"

The class became word-hungry and concept-hungry, concerned with discovering the "right" word to use at a given time to express a specific thought. I was struck by the difference of this notion of rightness and "the right way" to speak and write from the way children are supposed to be taught in school. They are supposed to acquire correct usage, right grammar and spelling, the right meaning of a word, and the right way to write a sentence. Achievement and I.Q. tests give incomplete sentences and the child is instructed to fill in the "right" word. Many teachers correct children's writing on the basis of a canon of formal rightness without bothering to ask what the children's words mean. I did the same thing myself.

I noticed that the children frequently said that they were bad at their friends, or their parents, or some teacher who angered them. They insisted upon describing a certain type of anger as "being bad at," and I kept telling them that it was wrong because "to be bad at" someone doesn't exist in English. And in a way I was "right"; it didn't exist, nor did the concept it was trying to express exist in English as I spoke and wrote it. But the children did mean "to be bad at," and meant something very specific by it. "To be bad" is a way of defying authority and expressing anger at the same time, as indicating one's own strength and independence. The use of "bad" here is ironical and often admiring. One child explained to me that down South a "bad nigger" was one who was strong enough and brave enough to be defiant of the white man's demands no matter how much everyone else gave in. . . .

I think that before we talked about language and myth the children, if they thought about it at all, felt that most words were either arbitrary labels pinned on things and concepts the way names seem to be pinned onto babies, or indicators of connections amongst these labels. These "labels" probably represented the way the adult world capriciously decided to name things. I doubt whether the children ever thought of adults as having received language from yet other adults even more remote in time. My pupils must have found the language of their teachers strange and arbitrary indeed. The "right" language of school texts and middle-class teachers must have seemed threatening and totalitarian, especially since the only living words the children knew and used were the words they used on the streets, words teachers continually told them were "wrong" and "incorrect."

The idea that words were complex phenomena with long and compelling histories was never presented to the children. I doubt many teachers entertained it. The canons of the schools pretend that a small preselected segment of the language of the moment is an eternally correct and all-inclusive form. This form is embodied in basic word lists and controlled vocabulary readers, as if the mastering of language consists of learning a list of fifty or a hundred words by rote. The use of language in human life is continually avoided or ignored, as if it poses too great a threat to "correctness" and "rightness." No wonder then that the children showed so persistently and ingeniously how much they feared and avoided the language of the schools.

Herbert A. Thelen

Some Classroom Quiddities for People-Oriented Teachers

To an objective and impartial behavioral scientist (like me), practically all classroom discussions (except yours) are self-flagellating activities in celebration of a monstrous and unnatural educational (?) tradition. The major effect of this tradition is the flouting of most of what we now know about the circumstances under which experiences in groups are meaningful and/or productive.

Reluctantly eschewing the promise of further polemical goodies anticipated by this statement, I shall present the grounds for my judgment, consider the sacred beliefs that maintain the tradition, and then paint a picture of an educative classroom. For those of you who remember the old story, I shall play the ant to your grasshopper.

Engagement Without Learning

Let me begin with a proposition that seems unassailable: that "society" puts a lot of time and energy into sending children to school because children cannot be counted on, by themselves, to learn the things we say they "need" to learn. Schooling is expected to alter their behavior and attitudes through (a) causing them to *engage in* certain activities (e.g., reading, experimenting) they are not likely otherwise to engage in, and (b) supervising this participation

Reproduced by special permission from *The Journal of Applied Behavioral Science*, "Some Classroom Quiddities for People-Oriented Teachers," by Herbert Thelen, pp. 270–285, Copyright © 1965, NTL Institute for Applied Behavioral Science.

Previous publication: Earlier draft under same title in *Bulletin of the Bureau of Social Service* (Lexington, Ky., College of Education), June 1964, 36, (4), 39–52.

in such a way that the child will *learn from* it the lessons we think are important. Engagement and learning are two different things, namely, a and b, and they are worth distinguishing. It is possible for a child to go through a programmed text, making all the required responses correctly, and then not remember any of the ideas he has been dealing with. It is possible for a child to work through a chemical experiment in the laboratory manual and still not be able to say what he has seen and what principle it illustrates. It is possible for a child to study spelling for seven years and still not be able to spell. It is possible for a man to engage in churchly activities all his life and still be spiritually unwashed; for a business man to engage in one business activity after another and end up broke. (And for a professor to study education for 20 years and still not have any different or new ideas.) It is one thing to engage in activities, producing socially demanded and acceptable behavior; it is another thing to learn anything from the experience — except, possibly, how to play roles.

"Socialization" Without Education

One thing that happens to most children in the classroom is that they learn to play the roles required by the teacher. There are many who do not learn even that; we call them "culturally deprived," or we label them "problem children." The existence of the whole body of lore known as "classroom management" testifies to the fact that with respect to most children some of the time and some children all of the time, we have difficulty in getting them to engage in the activities and produce the role performance we want from them. These difficulties are problems of socialization of the child. Most college teachers get the roles they want to the extent they want them because they deal only with children who have already been more or less successfully classroom-socialized.

Difficult as it is to achieve socialization in some situations, education — the process of learning useful things from participation in activities — is even harder to come by. Socialization is transactional and has a visible component of overt behavior. You can condition a child to do math homework because you can identify behaviors to reward and punish. But education proceeds through covert and sneaky processes of internal reorganization of thoughts and feelings. You cannot even find the behavior to reward or punish in order to make math homework *educative*. You can train the child to make the right reply to a question, but you cannot force him ever to use the idea for any other purpose. We occasionally have Ph.D. candidates who have been socialized or trained over the years to make acceptable responses on tests and yet cannot think up a research proposal (let alone commit themselves to it) to save their lives. Those learnings which are justified primarily as attributes of an "educated" social class may be considered the fruit of socialization, not education. What the "culturally deprived" child is deprived of is, to some extent, "culture"; but what irks the teacher is his lack of socialization in the pleasantries of toilet training for the middle class.

It seems to me, then, that classrooms as now constituted are primarily instruments of socialization rather than of education. The successful student participates properly in activities and learns to produce the consistently demanded responses (becomes test-wise). And, after so many years of it, he is accorded entry into the social class known as "college graduates." At this point, certain jobs are open to him and others are closed; and a host of social expectations define his probable position in society. The socialization we produce is aimed at creating "good" members in organizations, and we react to and deal with the child's talents primarily with this end in view. The commendable desire

262

to produce effective citizens has been denigrated to the development of sterile organization men. And as a result, "society" is rapidly losing its capacity to adapt itself to changing conditions. We have turned out in increasing numbers an "educated" citizenry that so far has not signally saved the world; and our communities just sit there, bleating helplessly in the face of such "issues" (not opportunities) as civil rights, increasing job deficits, and continually decreasing degrees of freedom for the individual. Very few "educated" persons allow themselves to be jockeyed into the kinds of participant roles which would give them the sorts of challenges and problems an education (if they had one) could apply itself to.

They do not get into these roles because through the years of schooling we have not merely not encouraged them to do so — we have actively suppressed any sign of such an interest on their part. The most general factors we found in a study of 750 pupils from 11 high schools, distributed in grades VIII through XI, were submissiveness, dependency on the teacher, and undiscriminating liking for *all* classroom activities. High school students today have only two alternatives: to become the organization men our noneducation is pointing them toward, or to reject the whole thing and become "delinquents." If they had any real alternative to school — such as productive youth communities — most present schools would be half empty.

Sacrosanct Practices

There have, of course, been some good educational conceptions developed from time to time during the last 2,000 years. These notions have succeeded in enriching the pedagogical vocabulary, but not in changing pedagogical practices. For what the schools do is school, not educate, the child; and the practices of schooling are sacrosanct. Procedures change with each new fad, but the attitudes — the spirit — that animate schooling keep change from reaching any vital organ. Under these conditions, the new vocabulary merely promotes hypocrisy — the hypocrisy of schoolmen masquerading as educators. Thus we want children to inquire into matters meaningful to them — so long as they can pass tests made up with no knowledge of what is meaningful to them. We recognize individual differences so that we can select the ones we want to deal with, or so that we can immediately "sweep them under the rug" through some type (mostly futile, as judged by research findings) of "homogeneous grouping." We would like to have free discussion in which pupils say what they think and feel — not as the basis for autonomous investigation, but merely so we can "correct" them more effectively. We even justify having some teachers be S.O.B.'s on the invalid grounds that students have to learn to deal with other S.O.B.'s they will meet later. If, occasionally, we get them excited and involved in something, we suppress their efforts to talk about it among themselves. We decide to have them be "self-directing," and we do it in such ways that they have to spend all their time trying to find out what we want them to do. We put them through the most extraordinary lockstep ever conceived, namely, Skinner-Crowder programs, and represent these as ways to "increase educational motivation." We talk about the need for people who can make mature judgments and then assign grades on the basis of tests of everything else but.

There is much criticism of our schools today. Most of the critics — at least the noisier ones — seem to be arguing that our schools are ineffective as judged by the sacred educational tradition, whereas I am arguing that it is the educational tradition itself that is at fault. Moreover, as experience in large cities is showing more clearly every year, the tradition is becoming faultier all the time. In Chicago, the 25 or 30 per cent of students for whom schooling made no sense ten years ago is now close to 60 per cent. There are some troubles, as in an ineffective psychoanalysis, which can sometimes be cured by stepping up the demand and effort along the same lines; but there are other troubles, as when a bureaucratic organization breaks down, for which the answer is not more of the same but rather drastic alteration along different lines. The ideal, of course, is not to have a perfect situation but merely to have one that can be self-corrective. This we do not have in schools today; what we do have is a succession of "innovations" that make things different at the procedural level but leave the spirit malingering in the same dark cave. Self-correction requires that there exist a strong commitment to principles which are regarded as fundamental and enduring.

The Educative Process

To be able to direct our own thinking about a body of phenomena, we need to assert a proposition about how we intend to seek understanding. I submit that the most significant and inclusive proposition for illuminating the study of teaching is that *in any situation there are some tendencies "going our way" and some going in other ways.* The teacher's job is to maximize the first and minimize the second. He must set such conditions as are under his control in such a way that whatever educable tendencies the child has become actualized to a greater extent than tendencies in other directions. But — and here is something many teachers would like to forget — the teacher has to deal with *both* sorts of tendencies, for conflict between the two types is the normal condition of the learner at the beginning of a new unit or activity; and the teacher's behavior decides which kind of tendency will dominate. To a high degree, the art of the sophisticated teacher manifests itself in the ability to capitalize on the wide range of natural tendencies that exist in the class: to work with them rather than suppress them and to teach the child socially constructive, higher-reward behaviors through which his tendencies can be expressed. Thus, for example, behaviors which express resistance and opposition to the work and to the teacher are capitalized on by one teacher and their energy is channeled into useful learning; whereas another teacher attempts to punish or suppress them. One teacher accepts any and all responses as challenges and weaves the contradictory and inconsistent behaviors of the students into a reality-seeking dialogue; whereas the other teacher acts like a censor, calling the responses he wants "relevant"

263

and the others "irrelevant." For his students, the experience is one of continually trying to guess what the teacher has in mind — up to the time when they find out that the reward they can get is incommensurate with the effort. (From then on, they simply seduce the teacher into giving his lecture, which is what he really has been wanting all along. But who listens?)

What, then, are these "natural tendencies" and under what conditions do they occur? Let us "walk through" a lesson being taught in the classroom.

Consider first the natural tendencies through which persons get "involved." At the beginning of a lesson, the teacher hopes to get the students "involved," interested, intrigued, "ready" to learn more. The tendencies he needs to facilitate are those through which the student "takes on" some part of the environment and has thoughts and feelings about it. There are (at least) three tendencies that can be capitalized on: (a) if stimuli are too sparse, the tendency is to "fill out" the picture by speculation (projection); (b) if stimuli are overwhelming, the tendency is to select certain ones and ignore others; (c) if stimuli violate expectations, the tendency is to try to rationalize away the inconsistency.

The teacher capitalizes on these tendencies, respectively, when he (a) presents a chemical demonstration silently and then asks the students to decide what were the hypotheses, the data, and the conclusions; or when he hands the student a document and asks him to reconstruct the way of life and community out of which the document came. To "overwhelm" (b) calls for a "rich" experience: a field trip, a dramatic movie, an exciting role-played scene. The invitation that unleashes the tendency is simply the question: What is the thing that strikes you as most important (significant, interesting, troublesome, and so on) about the field trip, movie, or other? That is, given all these things we might talk about, what things do you have the most need to talk about? The third tendency (c) is set in motion when expectations are violated: the demonstration that doesn't work, the prediction that fails, the be-

havior that is unexpected. Professor Bruner thinks that children have intuitive feelings about such things as levers and weights; and when the yardstick balance tilts up instead of down, the pupils become highly "involved." Any unaccustomed behavior of the teacher will involve the students and preoccupy them; and if the unaccustomedness is related to the subject discipline, it may develop readiness to learn; but if it is related to interpersonal manners, it is more likely to develop readiness to react defensively to the teacher — which is not the same thing.

In short, speculation, selection, and resolution of inconsistency are behaviors most persons "normally" engage in when given the opportunity. To get the students to do these things, the teacher must give them the chance; and he does this by carefully arranging the input from the environment.

The two most usual ways to prevent these normal tendencies from taking over are: (a) to make oneself (i.e., the teacher's person) the object of concern, and this is easily accomplished by threatening behavior which arouses interpersonal anxiety; and (b) to do all the work oneself, so that the students really have no role at all except that of bystanders.

Consider second the tendency of "involved" persons to seek "meaning." When most persons are "involved" in something, they tend to want to talk about it with certain other persons. These other persons do not normally include the teacher; the other persons are peers, and, more especially, friends. The need, following initial involvement and arousal, is to "get hold" of the experience both emotionally and conceptually, and this requires one to formulate thoughts and name the feelings one has. This is a risky enterprise, and it calls for interpersonal support from someone who has neither the power nor the inclination to engage in reprisals for what may turn out to be deviate or antisocial thoughts and feelings. In a classroom, after getting the children involved, the teacher actualizes this second tendency most effectively when he asks them to select themselves into small groups to compare notes and decide what they think and feel about the confronting involvement situation.

The tendency to associate with others in order to cope with one's own feelings, doubts, and anxieties is the fundamental cause of "friendship" or "psyche" groups, such as bull sessions. When members of a large group, such as a class, are forced to associate with one another day after day, smaller psyche groups form; students, we say, begin to "relate" to one another interpersonally; and, especially when the lesson is dull, they fill in the void and the anxiety it produces by talking with one another. (This annoys many teachers, and they seek advice on "classroom management"; they hope to suppress this busy-buzz, this "inattentiveness," these cliques. A tug of war develops between teacher and class, and the teacher is likely to resort to threats and punishment: he makes and enforces "rules," preaches, punishes by making the lesson even duller. In short, he tries to suppress a very basic and very natural tendency instead of either arranging to capitalize on it or by setting conditions under which the tendency is minimized.)

Consider third the tendency to seek closure amidst semi-conflicting and untested opinions. After finding out that one has many different ideas, and that his friends have additional ideas, one seeks to know what is "right" or "true." That is, to seek authority (authorization, legitimization) for an answer rather than to leave the perceptual-cognitive field wide open. But this is not a strong tendency because the psyche group, through its "acceptance" of ideas and its nonreprisal basis of operation, actually encourages toleration of all personal or subjective opinions — which is why it works so well in encouraging people to formulate and express their ideas. In effect, for the truth-seeking (or rationalizing) tendency to be strong, we have to reverse the field of the small subgroups. This reversed field can be found in the *class-as-a-whole*, a miniature society with an authoritative leader, with interpersonal competition for recognition and scarce rewards (grades) and (most important for learning) with a sense of common purpose in planning and carrying out activities.

To distinguish it from the psyche group, Jennings named it a sociogroup; or it could also be called a "work" group.

When the teacher brings the class back together, he has the problem of capitalizing on the wide range of ideas the students have just formulated and rehearsed with one another. There are three ways in which he might proceed. He could ask the class what they think is the *right* answer to some question that was presumably introduced along with the confronting stimuli: What do you think this document is? What was the purpose of the silent demonstration I showed you? In the ensuing discussion, he would respond (in effect) with "right" or "wrong" to whatever the students said. He would, presumably, be noting which students were right or wrong, and they would understand that this would influence their grades. He would also, probably, compliment the right ones and ignore, correct, or punish the wrong ones. A second possibility would be to ask for the *best* answer, thus inviting students to try to "top" one another. Focus on the right answer appeals to desire for certainty, whereas focus on the best answer invites competition.

Seeking authoritative answers and competing with others are indeed natural human activities. But encouragement of these by the teacher is less educative than a third possibility which depends on the sociogroup's sense of common purpose. Under common purpose, cooperation rather than competition is dominant; for the members join forces to cope with some situation, achieve some objective, meet some demand made on the group as a whole. The chief requirement for the cooperative situation is that each individual believes that he needs the others in order to do something he needs or wants to do: in other words, he is a member of the group in order to put his contributions together with those of others in order to get something done that he cannot do by himself. If the others are to help him in this undertaking, then it follows that they, too, must value the undertaking (for some reason); and to proceed effectively, there must be some agreement on what the undertaking is and what its purposes are. It

265

is by no means required that the individuals must want or value the undertaking for all the same reasons (which is lucky, because such a condition never occurs); but it is required that there be public agreement and understanding of at least the conditions external to the group that their activity is to change.

Thus, for example, the class can agree to design and carry out an experiment. This requires that they decide what objects to manipulate through what actions, but it does not require that all the students achieve or even seek the same personal gratifications. To one individual, the experiment is a situation in which to imagine himself a scientist; to another, it means checking some hunches against nature; to a third, it might mean mostly taking on a challenging task and completing it successfully. Cooperation, then, is the coordination of roles taken by the students as members of the group, not the development of identical personal views and feelings.

We conclude, then, that following the free exchange in subgroups, the teacher should draw out the opinions of the students and then invite the group to plan some further activity. In the planning discussion, opinions are neither *right* nor *best*; they are useful. And the reward comes not from the teacher as authoritative expert nor as encouraging father but rather from the satisfaction of influencing the class through its adoption of or "building" on one's ideas. The teacher's role under these conditions is that of methodologist-consultant, helping the class put its ideas together, confronting them with further facts in order to get them to sharpen, qualify, or assess the usefulness of their ideas.

So far, we have considered three tendencies: (a) the tendency of persons to get "involved" under certain conditions; (b) the tendency of psyche groups to form from "involved" persons so they can come to terms with their own involvements; and (c) the tendency, in sociogroups, to assess ideas and give them some backing more authoritative than personal hunches. These tendencies, properly encouraged, produce some of the most important activities of educational learning.

The class, like most other groups, either alternates or blends the two characters, psyche and socio. The artistic teacher knows when to "push" on the task and when to "break the tension" by encouraging more intimate and expressive behaviors. The student has a place in both the psyche and socio structures: sociometrically, he is part of a friendship network; in relation to tasks, he has a reputation and a range of roles that people come to expect of him. To be secure, he needs to know (or at least not be anxious about not knowing) his place in *both* structures.

Let us look at the teacher's use of the sociogroup to help students follow up the ideas they expressed in their small psyche groups. I think that seeking authoritative "truth" (right answers) and competing with others for scarce rewards (best answers) may well express tendencies in *individuals*, but I do not believe that carrying out these activities is a legitimate or natural purpose of groups. Groups do not get together to see who is right, and they do not get together merely to engage in intermember competition. These things can go on in groups, but then only for reasons that should not exist in the classroom. Granted that individuals want authority and want to compete — or at least some of them do, an effective voluntary group seduces the authority only when it needs to agree on some assumption that cannot be tested within their experience and yet has to be settled in order to be able to take further steps in planning; and it engages in intermember competitive struggles only when it has not yet developed satisfactory leadership. On the other hand, planning and carrying out activities together and on behalf of the individuals is, of course, the whole rationale for society.

On Not Educating

You can now see the basis for my opening blast in which I characterized present classroom groups as monstrous, artificial, maladaptive, and so on. Neither of the two proper reasons for getting together in a confined space and talking exists in the usual classroom. When the students try to operate like a psyche group, the teacher suppresses them. And the opportunity to act like a sociogroup is denied them because the teacher has presented them with no particular challenge they have to meet interdependently, as a group — rather than collectively and in parallel, as it were. The usual classroom group is a botched-up mess because the teacher wants to have some group characteristics and some non-group characteristics at the same time, and he wants to be free to take whatever he wants and ignore or suppress the rest. Thus when it comes to most discussion, which goes back and forth between the teacher and a succession of pupils, the teacher wants a collective conversation, a series of one-to-one interactions which he hopes, somehow, will deal with each participant individually. From this stand-point, group discussion is intended to approximate a series of semi-private individual conversations. But on the other hand, the teacher is also talking to the bystanders, and some of what he does to the current participant is really intended for them. Such behaviors tend to include presenting further information, but mainly, I think, they have more to do with setting standards for the group. If the teacher wants students to "think critically," by the time he has responded to the first eight discussants he rather expects the ninth to show some evidences of "critical thinking." My own impression is that the teacher is making a series of case demonstrations to the class, and that what he is demonstrating and defining is the role he wants the students to take in the remainder of the discussion period. At the same time, the teacher has in mind a line of argument to be developed, but more often than not he is the only one who can go away from the discussion with any sense of having built anything or produced anything. The only common purpose — and a real one it is — is to placate the teacher. This is, the group meets primarily to satisfy the teacher, just as the Siamese court dancers met to entertain the king. Except that the king respected their art and left it up to them as to how they would organize themselves, what specific message they would work up, and the like. In a word, the teacher wants each individual to play with him the games he

has in mind, but he wants the group to set standards that will put further pressure on the members to play these games.

What about teacher lecturing? Is this also a monstrous and unnatural situation? Is there a natural tendency for persons to come together, not primarily to reduce anxiety among friends or to do a job, but simply to hear some speaker? If so, how does that fit into the psyche-socio distinction? I would answer as follows: We know there is a tendency for a crowd to collect at fires, lynchings, baseball games, plays, and other such dramatic events. These are nonreality-tested, nonfeedback, private, projective experiences in which the persons give one another support. They are on the psyche-group side — that is, having to do with private emotion. Perhaps the essence of these experiences is caught in the observation that many people, surrounded by an audience, will cry at movies when they would not cry at the same things in "real life." This sort of audience situation seems to me to be basically an extended psyche group at a very low level in the sense that there is no demand for awareness of one's thoughts and feelings.

In some small way, each of us, as lecturer, has something of Billy Graham, President Johnson, and a three-alarm fire. In our own institutions, we have curiosity and stimulus values for some of the students. If they knew about us and came to our lectures on their own initiative, there would be nothing monstrous involved. There would also be very little of a planned educational quality about it, but some of the students would be better off for the experience. But I feel that this is too haphazard a basis for serious educational effort, and I do not think making the lectures compulsory does much to help.

But surely I must be off the beam? Who among us would be willing to say right out loud that he is an entertainer, an inspirer, a dramatic tragedy? Our task is to communicate useful information — it is to teach. Very well, then, my reply is that I think people come together voluntarily to be taught when there is something that it is important for them to learn, when there is a real use for the information, when some valuable activity over and beyond the "activity" of listening is contemplated. In other words, under socio-group conditions. If you have ever run a human relations training group or a cooperative research seminar, you will recognize what I am getting at: there are times when groups with shared purposes need organized information, know that they need it, and will listen avidly to it. And at these times, a 20-minute lecturette will "cover" more ground and produce more results in changed behavior than will eight hours of lecturing under the more usual circumstances.

Position Reviewed

Perhaps we had better take a minute to get a "fix" on this argument. I said that learning begins in a confrontation, and I listed three sorts of activities — speculation, selection, and conflict reduction — as producing "involvement" by capitalizing on normal spontaneous tendencies in the three appropriate stimulus situations. Then I suggested that the "involved" person tends to seek safe people — friends — to try out his ideas on and, in the process, become aware of them. This, I alleged, would develop "readiness" for several possible kinds of further activities; and these are the activities through which one moves from the private and semi-private subjective world to the public world. In this public world, one seeks to have a place, to participate in the culture, to define his role, to know what to count on by way of tested, accepted, or true ideas. But I argued that the public world, society, exists because there are jobs to be done, functions to be carried out vis-à-vis the environment, and that the natural, spontaneous, and potent reason we know instinctively that we have for moving into this world is that most of our needs must be met interdependently.

My position has been that to the extent that teaching can build on these natural tendencies and rationales, the better and more educative it will be.

The conclusion as applied to the classroom group is that its purpose should be to plan and carry out activities in pursuit of shared goals. Under such "natural" conditions, morale would be high, students would be "involved," and management problems would be practically nil because the demand of the job would impose a legitimate and understandable "discipline."

You may feel that what I am pleading for is a voluntary association of learners, and you are right. You may agree with this as being nice, but also tell me that carrying out projects is not particularly educative and that, anyway, in your subject (foreign language, math) there are not any good projects to carry out. To which I will reply that I know what you mean, but am a lot less ready to reach that conclusion. Let me add a couple of comments.

I think that much of the feasibility of my behavioral science approach for education will have to rise or fall by our understanding of the discipline of our subjects and, more especially, how we locate inquiry within the discipline. The two major alternatives are: (a) the discipline of the subject is confined to knowing the ideas as organized by someone else and as sampled by achievement tests (in which case everything I have said is a waste of your time and mine); and (b) the discipline of the subject is an orientation metatheory and methods of investigation of phenomena comprehended in the corresponding field of knowledge (in which case the activity of the sociogroup is *cooperative investigation of phenomena*). If you see education as society's provision for helping people cope with the world, then, in a world of rapid change like ours, education must develop the primitive but natural capability of inquiry; if you see education as society's provision for locating each person in some segment in which he can "belong," then education must be concerned only with developing common discourse and vocabulary among groups of students sorted out in terms of the social groups to which they shall belong. Except that I would call that socialization rather than education.

268

Philip W. Jackson

Excerpt from The Teacher and the Machine

The individualization of instruction, as embodied in a tutorial system, has been an educational ideal for centuries. Indeed, the tutorial arrangement of a one-to-one ratio between teachers and students is described in our earliest accounts of teaching and continues to exist in many parts of the world today. During this century, in particular, there have been countless efforts to modify group instruction in such a way as to make it resemble more closely the ideal pairing of one teacher to one student.

Providing each student with his own tutor, or with an exclusive portion of his teacher's time, however, will not necessarily achieve the goal of individualization. The essential requirement is not that the teacher be alone with his student, but that he respond to the student's uniqueness with pedagogical wisdom. The condition of not having other students present merely increases the likelihood that the teacher will treat the student as an individual; it certainly does not guarantee it. A teacher who is blind to the subtleties of his student's behavior, and who has a narrow repertoire of pedagogical alternatives on which to draw, cannot possibly individualize instruction in anything more than a superficial sense, no matter how many hours he spends alone with his charge.

Several of the educational benefits assumed to accompany the individualization of instruction concern what might be called the economics of learning. They deal principally with the speed and efficiency with which the student

Reprinted from *The Teacher and the Machine* by Philip W. Jackson by permission of the University of Pittsburgh Press. Copyright © 1968 by the University of Pittsburgh Press

masters the material to be learned. These benefits are among those most frequently mentioned when the case for individualization is under discussion. Though interrelated, they can be grouped roughly into three broad classes:

The first has to do with the rate of learning. In an individualized setting, the learner supposedly can move along at a pace that is comfortable to him. He need not wait for his slower peers to catch up, nor must he struggle to keep abreast of his intellectual superiors. The speed with which other learners progress is simply an irrelevant consideration when there are none to serve for comparison.

A second class of alleged benefits focuses on the goodness of fit between the learner and the curriculum. In an individualized setting, the student apparently is presented with learning tasks that are uniquely appropriate to his level of proficiency and that take into account his special strengths and weaknesses. Moreover, the introduction of new tasks is solely dependent on the student's mastery of the old. On the one hand, he will be prevented from wasting time by continuing with a topic or a skill after he has mastered it, and on the other hand, he will not be forced to leave an activity before mastery has been achieved.

A third set of benefits has to do with the continuous monitoring of the student's progress. With a teacher in almost constant attendance, the student will not be allowed to persist in errors, and thus he will avoid learning things that only have to be unlearned at some later date. At the same time, he will be afforded a prompt and continuing appraisal of his educational growth.

Although these seem to be among the most frequently mentioned reasons for seeking the individualization of instruction, they are by no means the only arguments that could be made in its favor. In addition to the benefits that focus on the economics of learning there are those that concern what might be called the dynamics of instruction. These have less to do with questions of speed and efficiency than with the quality of the learning experience and the attitudes engendered by it. Again, it is difficult to discuss these advantages singly, for they are all interrelated, but they too can be classified into three major types.

First are those conditions affecting the psychological distance between the learner, his materials, and his instructor. In the individualized setting, there is commonly a greater intimacy between teacher and student than is true under other circumstances. This intimacy is achieved in part by greater physical proximity (in tutorial sessions the teacher tends to speak in softer tones and often sits beside the learner rather than standing in front of him), but it is enhanced by other conditions as well. Not only is the teacher closer to the learner in a physical sense, he also is likely to reveal more of his personal life to the learner, and vice versa. (It is worth noting that tutoring is often done in the home of the teacher or the student, rather than in an "outside" institution.) The result is a greater psychological proximity than that which obtains when the teacher is working with a large group of students. Even the learning materials, to the extent that they are tailored to fit the student, are "his" in a more profound sense than when he is working in a collective setting.

Closely related to the reduction of psychological distance in the learning situation is the degree of importance that comes to be attached to the experience itself. The enhancement of this importance comprises a second class of benefits associated with the dynamics of individualized instruction. An activity requiring the full attention of a knowledgeable person is likely to be perceived as more important than one requiring only his divided attention. If a teacher spends a large amount of time with one student, his actions not only contain an implicit evaluation of the activity itself, they also reflect on the worth of the individual with whom he is working. Thus, when instruction is individualized, conditions are established in which it is possible for the student to learn not only that the process of instruction is very important but also that he, the learner, is worthy of personalized attention. Whether or not this message actually gets across is another matter entirely.

A third type of benefit associated with the dynamics of instruction and likely enhanced by individualization has to do with the communication of feeling between the teacher and his student. When the teacher is in constant attendance he is available not only to call attention to errors and to affirm correct responses, but also to beam with pleasure and to frown with disappointment. In short, he is on hand to communicate his concern as well as to instruct. The teacher's involvement and his emotional entanglement with his students can also flourish in a crowded classroom, but he is probably freer to "let himself go" in an affective sense when the student in question is the sole object of his concern.

Here, then, is an overview of the chief advantages of individualized instruction. Although the benefits most frequently mentioned are those having to do with the speed and efficiency of learning, they are clearly not the only reasons that make this situation a desirable one. When instruction is individualized it is also, in an important sense, personalized. As this happens, the student comes to know and to be known by a mature adult who demonstrates, by action and by thought, his personal concern for the student's progress. The communication of this concern may be more important, in the long run, than the more obvious benefits on which educators have focused their attention.

When the complexities of individualized instruction are revealed even to this limited extent, the potential of technical advances for achieving this end is brought into serious question. This is not to say that machines can be of no help in the process. But they are clearly not the only answer to the problem, as is suggested by some critics. In fact, the aspects of individualization that might make the fullest use of the machine's power — such as the goals of varying learning rates and providing constant feedback — are precisely the ones about which there seems to be the greatest need for further discussion and debate.

It has been reported that with the aid of a computerized tutorial system the brightest child in a class may move along at a rate five or ten times faster than that of the slowest child in the room. This statement may be startling to persons unacquainted with classroom affairs, but as most experienced teachers know, differences as large as that are a commonplace in today's schools. Even without the aid of a computer it is not at all unusual to have some students finish in ten minutes an assignment that it takes others an hour to complete; every teacher knows that some students will read ten pages in the time it takes others to read one.

Unfortunately, the educational problem created by these differences in ability is not solved simply by creating conditions under which each student may move along at his own rate. A recognition of variability in learning speed does not tell us what to do about it. If Billy can complete in five minutes an arithmetic assignment that takes Sammy fifty minutes to complete, should Billy spend an additional forty-five minutes on arithmetic, thus moving far ahead of Sammy? Perhaps he should, but then again, maybe not. It may well be that Billy would be better off spending his "extra" time on his language arts workbook, or finishing his science project, or casually browsing through the books on the library shelf. Perhaps by breezing through his arithmetic lesson in five minutes Billy is also learning that arithmetic is "a snap," whereas another forty-five minutes would convince him otherwise. As the problem is posed no one knows for sure what to do with Billy, except perhaps the teacher who works with him daily, and even he must have his doubts. The point is that individualization of instruction involves much more than clearing the educational path of obstacles so that students may hobble or dash along as fast as their intellectual legs can carry them.

In point of fact, the greatest barrier to coping with differences in individual learning rates is the graded school system, not the human teacher. Miss Jones, with little effort, could move some of her third graders along to fifth grade mathematics but the tradition of not overstepping her legally defined boundaries, coupled with the practices of textbook packaging, prevent her from easily doing so. Machines alone will not solve this problem, although their mass adoption could well bring the issue to a head.

The goal of fitting learning materials to the unique characteristics of the student entails another set of practices requiring serious scrutiny before we conclude that the machine can do the job better than humans. As it is commonly discussed, the concept of an ideal match between the learner and his materials or between the learner and an instructional methodology is probably as romantic and as unrealistic a notion as the concept of an ideal marriage. Just as all marriages, outside of storybooks, involve compromise and adjustment, so too, in a more trivial sense perhaps, do all learning encounters. The teacher, or the machine, may hope to locate just the right exercise or the perfect example for Billy at a given moment of instruction, but chances are they will miss the mark by at least a little bit. Happily, the miss will probably not matter very much insofar as Billy's learning is concerned. Even with an approximate fit, Billy seems to make do and appears to benefit from the experience. The marriage between the learner and his materials can surely benefit from some behind-the-scenes maneuvering, but as an educational matchmaker it is doubtful that the machine's capacities are significantly greater than those of the teacher.

The advantages of having the machine in constant attendance to monitor the student's successes and failures is another topic about which there is room for further discussion. At first glance, it would seem beneficial to have errors and misunderstandings corrected immediately. If a pupil adds five and three and gets nine, or reads "was" for "saw," surely he will be better off if the teacher informs him of his mistake as soon as it happens. But the validity of this assumption is not as great as it might appear. Consider, as an instance, the pre-school child who is pretending to read or who is just learning how to count. Is it better, pedagogically, to correct his many errors as they occur, or should we applaud his efforts while smiling inwardly at his naïveté? The experimental evidence may be unclear on this point, but the intuitive wisdom of generations of parents is almost unanimous and cannot be lightly brushed aside.

There is certainly much that we do not know about how to inform a student of his progress, but most teachers would probably agree that there are times when it is unwise to tell a student he is wrong, even if he is. At times it may be better to allow a student to think he can do something even when we know he cannot. Perhaps a belief in one's powers precedes their realization.

Even if it were possible, therefore, to monitor each and every student's response and to provide instant feedback on the current status of educational growth, there is at least some question about whether we should hasten to provide such a service. Even if it were shown that students would learn more rapidly under conditions of constant surveillance, the issue would not be settled, for it would still be necessary to show that no attitudinal damage had been done.

The line between simply informing a person of his weaknesses and nagging him about them is sometimes easily crossed. Among the conditions that increase the likelihood of crossing this boundary are the frequency and consistency with which errors are pointed out. A nagging housewife may succeed in having her husband walk the straight and narrow if she keeps after him enough, but her success is often accomplished at some risk to the stability of her marriage. Even after a few hours of human surveillance most students are glad to get out for an afternoon. If machines greatly increased the frequency of watchfulness and prodding in the classroom, the desire to escape might be even

greater. We must certainly be cautious about doing anything that could inflate the educational divorce rate.

When it comes to the personalization of learning — as contrasted with the individualization of such things as learning rate, materials, and feedback — machines, even those that only exist in the dreams of inventors, do not begin to compete with the human teacher. The reason for this lack of competition is simply that a machine is not a person. It is embarrassing to have to state the obvious, but unfortunately, this basic fact often seems to get lost in the shuffle in discussions of the potential of the machine in the classroom. Although a computer can store almost countless pieces of information about a student, it cannot *know* him as one person knows another. Moreover, it cannot *know* the subject a student is studying, even though its memory cells are packed to capacity. A machine may be able to dispense praise and reproof according to the most complicated set of instructions — it may even, when so doing, exude the mellifluous tones of an Everett Dirksen — but this marvelous performance should not allow us to overlook the fact that the machine cannot begin to *care* whether the student learns anything or not. Only humans care about humans, machines never do. Thus, what is here being called the personalization of instruction lies completely outside of the machine's capacity. The most elaborate computer ever developed will never know a student in the same sense as does the bus driver who takes him home in the afternoon, nor will it ever care more about his progress than does the janitor who shuffles past him in the hall.

This fundamental incapacity of the machine deserves further comment. As our technology develops, so too does our ability to produce machines with a greater number of humanoid features. Computer experts talk optimistically about the time, in the not-too-distant future, when machines will converse with students, reason with them, and presumably even emit a kindly chuckle or two when their electronic scanners brush over a harmless mistake. These added touches of realism are indeed impressive as feats of engineering, but they do not significantly reduce the gap between the human and the non-human. From the standpoint of personalizing the learning encounter, the advantages of lifelike mechanical instructors are dubious indeed. Some understanding of why this is so can be gained by considering the difference between playthings and real things.

In recent years, toy manufacturers have gone out of their way to produce objects that stimulate reality. Dolls that *really* cry, trucks that *really* roar, irons that *really* get hot, and other just-like-the-real-thing contraptions crowd the shelves of our toy departments. Many children seem to like these simulated wonders, or at least their parents do, for thousands of them are purchased each year. Yet children, as they mature, begin to grow tired of the artificial and increasingly insist on dealing with genuine objects rather than toys. This gradual rejection of the artificial has little to do with the toy's superficial realism or lack of it. Toy manufacturers cannot keep teenage girls in the dolls' corner by adding salt to the doll's tears or by producing a Raggedy Ann who speaks in complex sentences. Even a locomotive belching real smoke will not keep a gang of adolescent boys on their hands and knees for very long. This is so because the child's separation from his toys is brought on not by any disappointment with the facsimile as such, but by his increasing need to distinguish sharply between fantasy and reality. Gradually he comes to realize that toys remain toys no matter how realistic they might become. No manner of magic, except the pre-logical rationality of the young child, can bridge the gap between the plastic truck on the living room floor

and the real McCoy rumbling by on the street outside.

The same tendency that leads to the ultimate rejection of make-believe will likely have some effect on the student's willingness to "converse" and "reason" with a computer console. Engineers can add sound, color, canned applause, and even low-heeled oxfords, but their product will forever remain a toy teacher, not a real one. This does not mean that the machine is unable to perform instructional tasks; we have long known that even the crudest toy can have educational value. But young people have a way of casting toys aside long before they have learned all they might from them. All things considered, this is a sign of health and we must be quite as willing to applaud it in the classroom as we do on the playground.

Although we typically associate individualized instruction with the achievement of a one-to-one teacher/pupil ratio, there is no reason why a considerable amount of individualization cannot go on while the teacher is working with a group of students. As he responds to a student's query during class discussion, as he pauses to clear up another student's misunderstanding, even as he snaps his fingers to bring the inattentive day-dreamer back into the center of things, the teacher is achieving a degree of individualization even though thirty pairs of eyes happen to be on him. When the richness of the teacher's knowledge of individual students and the complexity of his pedagogical moves, even in a crowded classroom, are compared with those of any of the machines now available, it is easy to see why many teachers are inclined to be suspicious of the programmer's use of the term "individualized instruction."

John Holt

The Wholeness of Learning

Let me sum up what I have been saying about learning. I believe that we learn best when we, not others, are deciding what we are going to try to learn, and when, and how, and for what reasons or purposes; when we, not others, are in the end choosing the people, materials, and experiences from which and with which we will be learning; when we, not others, are judging how easily or quickly or well we are learning, and when we have learned enough; and above all when we feel the wholeness and openness of the world around us, and our own freedom and power and competence in it. What then do we do about it? How can we create or help create these conditions for learning?

Perhaps I can make more clear what I mean by the wholeness of learning or experience by talking about my own discovery of mathematics. At school, I was always a fairly good math student. It bored me, but it didn't scare me. With any work at all, I could get my B. But after many years I knew that although I could do most of the problems and proofs and remember the theorems and formulas, I really didn't have the slightest idea what it was all about. That is, I didn't see how it related to anything — where it had come from, what it was for, what one might ever do with it.

Some years after I left the Navy I came across a series of books, written to help people with little or no math training understand some of the new and large ideas in mathematics. They

274

were written by a Mr. and Mrs. Lieber. The first of them was *The Education of T. C. Mits*. There was a character called SAM, whose initials stood for Science, Art, and Mathematics. The point of the books was that people should not be afraid of new ideas in these fields, and that if they took the plunge, exposed themselves to them, they would find them not so terrifying or difficult.

The books themselves were very well done. Mr. and Mrs. Lieber, in one sense at least, were excellent teachers. They would have been very good at writing out programs. They understood how easily and quickly a learner, moving into new territory, is frightened by uncertainty, contradiction, or logical steps that cover too much ground. So they were very careful to define their terms in words the learner would understand, to move ahead slowly and patiently, taking time to illustrate their points and to reassure the reader. Anyone who didn't panic could follow them through their argument.

But at the end of each of their books, though I had enjoyed being able to follow them on their journey, and liked the feeling of knowing something I hadn't known before, I was still uneasy, dissatisfied. I was not sure why. It seemed that there must be more to this new idea than I had been told. I was not able to bring my unease into focus, to get hold of it, find words for it, until I had finished their book on *Galois and the Theory of Groups*. I had been able to follow them, step by step, to the end of the book. But at the end I felt as if I had been blindfolded and then led along a carefully prepared path. "Now put your foot here, easy now, that foot there . . ." I didn't stumble, but

I wanted to take the blindfold off and say, "Where are we, anyway? How did we get here? Where are we going?" What had led Galois to invent this theory? What had made it seem worth inventing? Had he been working on a problem that he and others had not been able to solve? What was the problem, what had he and the others been doing to try to solve it, what had started him in this direction? As it was presented to me, the Theory of Groups seemed disconnected from everything, or at least anything I could imagine. And once Galois had started to work on it, had he made any false starts, gone down any dead ends? Or did he go straight along, like the Liebers? And then, when he got the theory worked out, came to where I was at the end of the book, what did he do with it, how did he use it, where did he go next? Did it help him with the problem he had been trying to solve, and how?

In short, I felt like saying to my patient and hard-working guides, the Liebers, "Thanks for your help, but you haven't told me anything important, you've left out the best part."

Some years later, a former pupil and good friend of mine, then at college, was meeting calculus for the first time. Like many people, he was having trouble. He had the feeling I had had years before of being able to go through the motions, writing formulas and doing problems, but without any idea of what they were all about, seeing them only as a kind of mumbo-jumbo, meaningless recipes for getting meaningless answers to meaningless questions. He asked me one day if I would try to make some sense of it for him. I said I would. I began by trying to give him a very rough idea of the problem, philosophical as much as mathematical, that had started man on his search for the calculus. (What little I knew about all this I had picked up after I left school.) So I talked about the Greeks trying to think about instanta-neous motion, described some of the Paradoxes of Zeno — the arrow, Achilles and the tortoise, etc. At any instant the arrow is not moving, since motion is distance covered in time; but then, since time is made up of a sum of instants, how can motion be possible? It is easy to say, if a car traveled five miles in ten minutes, its average speed in that time was thirty miles per hour. But what does it mean to ask how fast it is going at any instant, and how can we find out?

My friend saw the sharpness of the dilemma. I then showed how Cartesian or coordinate geometry made it easier to think about the problem, and thus prepared the way for men to solve it, by giving us a way to make a picture or map of something moving at various rates in space and time. We simply plot a graph of distance traveled against time. It could then be seen that the average speed between two points could be seen as the slope of the line joining them on the graph. From there we could see that the question: How fast is this object going at a particular instant?, could be asked as: What is the slope of the curve, or the tangent to the curve, at that particular point? We had then to find out what happened to that slope as the interval of time became smaller and smaller, and indeed what it meant to have something approach zero as a limit. My friend and I did some arithmetic, some algebra, derived the general formula for the differential at a point — all stuff he had had in the course. But now he said, "So that's it. Why didn't anybody tell me that? It's so simple when you see what it's about."

Exactly. What I had done, clumsily enough, was not to try to hand him a lump of knowledge, which people had already handed him and which he could not take hold of, but to take him on a kind of human journey with the people who had first thought about and discovered these things.

Carl R. Rogers

The Facilitation of Significant Learning

In this chapter, I would like to describe two types of learning, two possible aims for education, and two sets of assumptions upon which the educational process can be based. It will be clear that for me the second member of each of these pairs seems more suitable for today's world. I shall then try to indicate some of the ways in which this second view might be implemented.

Two Types of Learning

Cognitive Learning

Some learning appears to be primarily cognitive, primarily the fixing of certain assocations. A child can learn his letters and numbers in this fashion; at a later date he may learn to "rattle off" the multiplication table; at a still later date he may learn the rules for solving a binomial equation or the irregular verbs in French. Only very imperceptibly do any of these learnings change *him*. They are like the nonsense syllables which the psychologist asks him to learn as a participant in an experiment. They are learned as part of a task set before him, part of a "body of knowledge" which he is to acquire. Such learning is often painfully difficult and also often quickly forgotten.

Experiential Learning

The other type of learning is primarily experiential, or significant or meaningful. The student

Abridged version of "The Facilitation of Significant Learning," in *Instruction: Some Contemporary Viewpoints* (Ed.) Lawrence Siegel, 1967, pp. 37–54. Reprinted by permission of Intext Educational Publishers and author.

I am indebted to Miss Ann Dryfuss for her assistance in various aspects of this chapter.

says, "I am discovering — drawing in from the outside and making that which is drawn in a real part of *me*." The adolescent who devours everything he can read or hear about gasoline engines in order to make his hot rod faster and more efficient exemplifies this type of learning. The child who is trying to draw a realistic house reads or hears a few simple rules of perspective. He reaches out to grasp this material, make it his, use it. This is another instance of meaningful learning. Still another is the child who goes to books and the library to satisfy his curiosity about earthworms or the hydrogen bomb or sex. The feeling in regard to any experiential learning is, "Now I'm grasping what I *need* and *want*."

I shall define a bit more precisely the elements which are involved in such significant or experiential learning.

1. *It has a quality of personal involvement.* The whole person in both his feeling and cognitive aspects is involved in the learning event.
2. *It is self-initiated.* Even when the impetus or stimulus comes from outside, the sense of the discovery, of reaching out, of grasping and comprehending, comes from within.
3. *It is pervasive.* It makes a difference in the behavior, the attitudes, perhaps even the personality of the learner.
4. *It is evaluated by the learner.* "This is not quite what I want — doesn't go far enough — ah, this is better, this *is* what I want to know." The locus of evaluation may be said to reside definitely in the learner.

5. *Its essence is meaning.* When such learning takes place, the element of meaning to the learner is built into the whole experience.

Two Possible Aims for Education

To Transmit Stored Knowledge

For the most part, the current educational system is geared to the aim of inculcating in the young the stored knowledge already accumulated, together with the values which have guided men in the past. Its natural product is the informed, essentially passive conformist.

Historically, there has been much to be said for this point of view. Because of a recent visit in Australia, I have been reading and hearing about the Australian aborigine. For twenty thousand years he and his kind have survived in a most inhospitable environment in which modern man would die. He has survived by passing on every bit of knowledge and skill he has acquired about a relatively unchanging world and frowning upon or tabooing any new ways of meeting the relatively unchanging problems. This has been the description of American educational goals as well.

To Nurture the Process of Discovery

But modern man is face to face with a situation which has never before existed in history. The world — of science, of communication, of social relationships — is changing at such a pace that knowledge stored up in the past is not enough. The physicist cannot live by the stored knowledge of his science. His confidence, his basic trust, is in the *process* by which new knowledge is acquired. In like fashion, if society is to be able to meet the challenges of a more and more rapidly changing world — if civilization is to survive — people must be able increasingly to live in a process manner. The public, like the physicist, will have to put their trust in the *process* by which new problems are met, not in the *answers* to problems of the past.

This need implies a new goal for education. Learning how to learn, involvement in a process of change — these become the primary aims of an education fit for the present world. There must evolve individuals who are capable of intelligent, informed, discriminating, adaptive, effective involvement in a process of change. Such involvement develops only in the individual who has discovered that significant learning is, though threatening, even more deeply rewarding; who has recognized that it is satisfying to take the risk of being open to his experience, both of his feelings and reactions within and of the evidence his senses bring him about the world without. Such an individual is in process of change, is continually learning, is constructively meeting the perplexities of a world in which problems are always spawning much faster than their answers. He has learned that the process of change is something in which he can live more comfortably than in rigidity, that the ability to face the new appropriately is more important than being able to repeat the old. This is a new type of aim for education.

Two Sets of Assumptions in Education

Assumptions Implicit in Current Education

From an observation of educational institutions at all levels (first grade through graduate study), I have attempted to abstract from the behavior of the educators those assumptions or principles upon which they act. It should be clear that these six assumptions are implicit, rather than explicit — that they are drawn from what teachers *do*, rather than from what they *say*.

1. *The student cannot be trusted to pursue his own learning.* The attitude of most teachers and faculty members tends to be one of mistrustful guidance. They look suspiciously on the student's aims and desires and devote their energies to guiding him along the pathway he "should" follow. I believe it is extremely rare that students have the feeling that they are being set free to learn, on their own.
2. *Presentation equals learning.* This assumption is evident in every curriculum, every lesson plan. It is especially clear if one ob-

277

serves a faculty committee trying to decide what topics a course shall "cover." It is clear that what is presented or covered is what is learned. Anyone who has used any method which taps the actual experience of students in a class knows that this assumption could not be further from the truth; yet it persists.

3. *The aim of education is to accumulate brick upon brick of factual knowledge.* There must be a "foundation of knowledge." These clearly defined building blocks must be assimilated before the student can proceed to learn on his own. Though this assumption flies in the face of everything known about the curve of forgetting, it remains an unquestioned assumption.

4. *The truth is known.* In almost every textbook, knowledge is presented as a closed book. "These are the facts" — about chemistry or history or literature. The student has almost no opportunity to realize that in every field it is the *search* for knowledge which is important and that the "knowledge" already gained is only the best working hypothesis that can be formulated at the moment. Only in recent years, in such developments as the teaching of the "new mathematics" has there been the slightest dent in this assumption.

5. *Constructive and creative citizens develop from passive learners.* There seems to be great unanimity in the verbalized aim of producing good citizens, able to act constructively, with an independence and originality adequate to the complex problems of today. Yet it is equally evident that the main virtue encouraged in classrooms at all levels is that of passively learning material which is presented by the instructor, which in turn has been selected by some educational group as being important for the student to learn. This is clearly the way in which it is assumed that an independent citizenry is developed.

6. *Evaluation is education, and education is evaluation.* Taking examinations and preparing for the next set of exams is a way of life for students. There is little or no thought of intrinsic goals, since the extrinsic have become all-important. Rarely does the student ask himself, "What aspect of this subject or this book interests me?" or "How could I find out about this particular aspect of life?" The sole question is, "What will be asked on the examination?" It has gradually come to be assumed by teachers, students, and parents that report cards and grades *constitute* education. When a faculty member asked a student what he got out of a certain course, the student's response was what one would expect in this system: "I got a B."

Assumptions Relevant to Significant Experiential Learning

It is my belief that in the next few decades there is likely to be a revolution in education which will deeply challenge the foregoing assumptions. My reason for believing that such a revolution will occur is that I question whether our culture can afford to permit its citizens to develop under such an educational system. It cannot afford to develop citizens who are passive, whose knowledge is settled and closed, whose ways of thinking are rigid, who have no feeling for the *process* of discovering new knowledge and new answers.

The question for this newer approach to education will be, "How can the incorporation of the *process* of learning and changing be made the deepest purpose of the educational experience?" In endeavoring to answer this, I list below a new set of assumptions which, I believe, will replace the present principles.

1. *Human beings have a natural potentiality for learning.* They are curious about their world, they are eager to develop and learn, and they have the capacity for making constructive discriminations between learning opportunities. This potentiality for learning, for discovery, can be released under suitable conditions (which I discuss

below). In short, the student's desire to learn can be trusted.

2. *Significant learning takes place when the subject matter is perceived by the student as having relevance for his own purposes.* When an individual has a goal he wishes to achieve and when he sees the material available to him as relevant to achieving that goal, learning takes place with great rapidity. How long does it take an adolescent to learn to drive a car? A very reasonable hypothesis is that the time for learning various subjects would be cut to a small fraction of the time currently allotted if the material were perceived by the learner as related to his own purposes. The evidence from various sources indicates that in many instances one-third to one-fifth of the present time allotment would be sufficient.

3. *Much significant learning is acquired through doing.* When a student is attempting to cope with a problem which is directly confronting him, effective learning is likely to occur. The brief, intensive courses for teachers, doctors, farmers — individuals facing immediate problems — provide ample evidence of learning through doing. The class group which becomes involved in a dramatic production — selecting the play and the cast, costumes, coaching the actors, selling tickets — provides similar evidence.

4. *Learning is facilitated when the student participates responsibly in the learning process.* This assumption is closely related to the preceding. When he chooses his own directions, helps to discover his own learning resources, formulates his own problems, decides his own course of action, and lives with the consequences of each of these choices, then significant learning is maximized. There is evidence from industry as well as from the field of education that participative learning is much more effective than is passive learning.

5. *Self-initiated learning, involving the whole person of the learner — feelings as well as intellect — is the most pervasive and lasting.* This hypothesis has been discovered in psychotherapy, where it is the totally involved learning of oneself by oneself which is most effective. This is not learning which takes place "only from the neck up." It is a "gut-level" type of learning — profound and pervasive. It can also occur in the tentative discovery of a new self-generated idea, in the learning of a difficult skill, or in the act of artistic creation — painting, poetry, sculpture. One of the most important aspects is that in these situations the learner knows it is his own learning, and thus can hold to it or relinquish it in the face of a more profound learning, without having to turn to some authority for corroboration of his judgment.

6. *Creativity in learning is best facilitated when self-criticism and self-evaluation are primary, and evaluation by others is of secondary importance.* Creativity blossoms in an atmosphere of freedom. The best research organizations, in industry as well as in the academic world, have learned that external evaluation is largely fruitless if the goal is creative work. The individual must be permitted to make his own evaluation of his own efforts.

7. *The most socially useful learning in the modern world is the learning of the process of learning, a continuing openness to experience, an incorporation into oneself of the process of change.* I have already discussed this assumption in speaking of the second aim in education.

Some Practical Ways of Encouraging Experiential Learning

Keeping in mind the conditions which have been described, I turn now to some of the newer developments in education, practical approaches which may be used to facilitate a more experiential type of learning and which may be used to implement the hypotheses basic to the second educational goal. I have selected three

279

examples which apply specifically to classroom instruction, and one which applies both to the classroom and to the training and supervision of the instructor himself.

The Conduct of Inquiry

A specialized type of participative and experiential learning which has been receiving increasing emphasis in the last few years has been developing in science. Various individuals and national groups have been working toward a goal of helping students to become inquirers, working in a fluid way toward discovery in the scientific realm.

The impetus for this movement has grown out of an urgent need to have science experienced as a changing field, as it is in the modern world, rather than as a closed book of already discovered facts. The possession of a body of knowledge about science is not an adequate qualification for the teacher today. Hence the aim is to get the teacher away from the misleading image of science as absolute, complete, and permanent (Schwab, 1960). Suchman (1961, 1962) is one of those who have given rather specific details regarding the implementation of this aim. In trying to strengthen the autonomous processes within the learner, Suchman advocates a new approach in which special training is necessary for teachers of science. The teacher sets the stage of inquiry by posing the problems, creating an environment responsive to the learner, and giving assistance to the student in his investigative operations. This climate makes it possible for pupils to achieve autonomous discoveries and to engage in self-directed learning. They become scientists *themselves*, on a simple level, seeking answers to real questions, discovering for themselves the pitfalls and the joys of the scientist's search. They may not learn as many scientific "facts," but they develop a real appreciation of science as a never-ending search, a recognition that there is no closure in science.

It is obvious that if prospective teachers are to stimulate the spirit of inquiry among their pupils, they must have experienced it themselves. Therefore, courses in the teacher-training

institution must be taught in the same fashion as Suchman describes if teachers themselves are to experience the satisfaction of self-initiated discovery in the scientific realm. This new development in the area of science constitutes a deep challenge to present concepts of teaching. According to the evidence, current educational practice tends to make children less autonomous and less empirical in their search for knowledge and understanding as they move through the elementary grades. This tendency is strictly at variance with the aim of those who focus on inquiry. When children are permitted to think their way through to new understandings, the concepts they derive in the process have greater depth, meaning, and durability. The children have become more autonomous and more solidly based in an empirical approach.

Simulation

The trend toward a more experiential type of learning shows up in the increasing use of simulation in the classroom. The essence of this procedure is that a complex situation is simulated — the relationships among several nations (Solomon, 1963; Guetzkow, 1963), a historical situation, a social conflict, a problem in interpersonal relationships — and the students take the parts of those participating in the event. Though there is no conclusive research as yet indicating the outcome of this type of learning as compared with more conventional procedures, it is already being successfully used in half a dozen universities and a number of high schools. Since it is a relatively new type of approach, I shall outline a hypothetical example.

A social studies or civics course might well simulate a problem in community policy regarding education. Different pupils might be assigned respectively to be the mayor, the head of the board of education, the members of the board of education, the superintendent of schools, the president of the PTA, the head of the taxpayers' league. Now the problem is posed to them — from their own community or from any other community where the facts are available to them — that members of the board of education want a new bond issue to expand the building plant and hire new teachers. They prepare to take their parts in the simulated situation.

What are the types of learning that would follow upon this simulation? First, each student would turn to the factual resources in order to develop his own stance on the issue and to justify his point of view. There would be a degree of self-discipline involved in searching for this factual material. The student would find it necessary to make a personal decision based on his own informed stand. He would be involved in the handling of interpersonal relationships with those who hold different points of view. He would find himself bearing the responsibility for the consequences of his own decisions and actions. Throughout the experience, there would be necessary a disciplined commitment to learning, decision, action. Such an experience would appear to develop a positive type of learning rather than a negative, critical type of thinking. Current education often develops individuals who can readily criticize any proposal or idea but cannot make a positive plan or decision regarding constructive action.

Another interesting example of the use of a type of simulation is described by Ronald Lippitt (1962). A fifth-grade class was concerned about youngsters who were know-it-alls. The whole class participated either as actors or observers in dealing with the problem. As they did so, the pupils developed a real understanding of why know-it-alls behave as they do; the class came to recognize the insecurity which so often underlies such behavior. Gradually, an attitude evolved of working *with* the problem rather than *at* it. In the process, individual students showed significant personal development, and the class as a group showed increased freedom of communication, which encouraged and supported greater individuality of participation. It was a living experience in behavioral science.

Programed Instruction

As educators well know, there has been a vast and explosive development in programed instruction (Skinner, 1961; Fry, 1963; Gage,

1963; Pressey, 1963). This is not the place to review these developments or the theory of operant conditioning upon which this work is based. It is appropriate, however, to point out that programed instruction may be used in a variety of ways. Programing can be seen as potentially providing for all learning, or it may be seen as one new and very useful tool in the facilitation of learning. As Skinner has pointed out, "To acquire behavior the student must engage in behavior" (1961, p. 389).

It is of particular interest to note that in the development of programed instruction there is a tendency toward shorter, "plug-in" programs, rather than toward the development of whole courses covering a total field of knowledge. To me, the development of these shorter programs suggests the more fruitful way in which the student may be involved in the use of so-called teaching machines. When learning is facilitated in line with the second set of assumptions presented, the student frequently comes upon gaps in his knowledge, tools which he lacks, information which he needs to solve the problem he is confronting. Here the flexibility of programed instruction is invaluable. A pupil who needs to know how to use a microscope can find a program covering this knowledge. The student who is planning to spend three months in France can utilize programed instruction in conversational French. The pupil who needs algebra, whether for the solution of problems of interest to him or simply to get into college, can work on a program of instruction in algebra.

Used in these ways, a competently developed program undoubtedly gives the student immediate experiences of satisfaction, enables him to learn a body of knowledge when he needs it, gives him the feeling that any content is learnable, and fosters a recognition that the process of education is an intelligible and comprehensible one. He can work at his own rate and finds that the carefully designed program presents him with coherent, interrelated steps. Its stress on immediate reinforcement and reward rather than on punitive or evaluative measures is another factor in its favor. If programed learning is used flexibly, it can constitute a large forward step in meeting the massive needs for functional learning of subject matter as the number of pupils grows sharply.

Programed learning is developing in new and unexpected fields. Berlin and Wyckoff (1963) are developing programs for the improvement of interpersonal relationships in which two people work together at mutual tasks assigned by the programed text, not only learning some of the cognitive concepts in regard to interpersonal relationships but also gradually experiencing deeper and deeper communication with each other. Both industry and educational institutions have begun to make use of this developing series of programs, impressed by the fact that the learnings involve both feelings and intellect and that they have significant personal meaning for the learner.

It should be obvious that programed learning has great potential risks if it is unwisely used. It it becomes a substitute for thinking in larger patterns and gestalts, if it becomes a way of stressing factual knowledge more than creativity, than real damage may be done. But if it is perceived as an instrument which can be used by educators to achieve flexibility in education, then it is one of the most powerful tools which psychology has as yet contributed to the field.

"Sensitivity Training"

The final example of a new development which fosters a climate for experiential or significant learning is so-called sensitivity training. This is an approach which is of help in educating administrators and teachers for the newer goals in education. It also has relevance to the classroom situation.

Though not widely used as yet in educational institutions, there has been a burgeoning use of the intensive group experience in the development of business executives and government administrators. Under a variety of labels — the T-Group, the Laboratory Group, the Sensitivity Training Course, the intensive Workshop in Human Relations, the Basic Encounter Group — this approach has become an important part of the training function.

It is difficult to describe briefly the nature of such a group experience, especially since it var-

ies greatly from group to group and from leader to leader. (See Wechsler and Reisel, 1959, for one description.) Essentially, the group begins with little imposed structure, so that the situation and the purposes are ambiguous and up to the group members to decide. The leader's function is to facilitate expression and to clarify or point up the dynamic pattern of the group's struggle to work toward a meaningful experience. In such a group, after an initial "milling around," personal expressiveness tends to increase and involves an increasingly free, direct, and spontaneous communication among members of the group. Façades become less necessary, defenses are lowered, basic encounters occur as individuals reveal hitherto hidden feelings and aspects of themselves and receive spontaneous feedback — both negative and positive — from group members. Some or many individuals become much more facilitative in relationships to others, making possible greater freedom of expression.

In general, when the experience is a fruitful one, it is deeply personal, resulting in more direct person-to-person communication, sharply increased self-understanding, more realness and independence in the individual, and an increased understanding and acceptance of others. While much still remains to be learned about the intensive group experience in all its forms, it is already clear that it helps to create in most members of the group attitudes which, among other things, are highly conducive to experiential learning.

Perhaps a few examples will convey a more meaningful picture of what is already being done. The National Training Laboratory has begun to conduct "college labs" at Bethel, Maine (Bradford, Gibb, and Benne, 1964, p. 109). Each of the T-Groups in these laboratories contains several students and several faculty members from the same college. As they share in the exploration of their interpersonal attitudes and relationships and of their work goals, their learnings have often been highly significant. There are reports that at least one department of English has been revolutionized by its experience in this college lab.

Various leaders in the group-dynamics field

(Gibb, Herold, Zander, and Coffey) have transformed courses for teachers into T-Groups. So meaningful have been the learnings that in some of these institutions the demand for such groups, involving learning based on direct personal encounter, has grown beyond all expectations.

One elementary-school system in a Western city has made it possible for most of its principals and teachers to have experience in a sensitivity-training group. Likewise, when there is a difficult classroom situation, a member of the guidance department serves as leader of a "problem-solving group" in the classroom, the group including the teacher(s) as well as the pupils involved. Out of these experiences have come much more responsible behavior on the part of pupils, much improved communication in the classroom, and an administrative structure in which faculty-administrator interaction is much more free and real than is ordinarily achieved. In other words, there has been movement toward the establishment of a psychological climate in which pupils, teachers, and administrators can learn, in a self-initiated fashion, in regard to both the interpersonal problems which they face and the factual problems which they face in the world outside.

It appears highly likely that this particular development will become much more widespread in the educational world.

Conclusion

In this chapter, I have tried to present something of what would be involved if a new aim for education were adopted, that of achieving openness to change, and if focus were on that type of learning in which the whole person is involved, a meaningful experience of emotional as well as cognitive learning.

It is clear, I believe, that if this aim were selected, the basic reliance of the teacher would be upon the tendency toward fulfillment, toward actualization, in his students. The teacher would be basing his work on the hypothesis that students who are in real contact with life problems wish to learn, want to grow, seek to discover, endeavor to master, desire to create. The teacher would attempt to develop a quality of climate in the classroom and a quality of personal relationship with his students which would permit these natural tendencies to come to fruition.

The teacher or facilitator of learning who is desirous of creating the conditions for this self-fulfilling type of learning finds that there are a number of new methods already at hand which are congenial to this approach. The conduct-of-inquiry approach in science develops self-initiated learners in that field. The use of simulation techniques makes for responsible learning and decision making. The teaching machine, especially in the form of brief, specific programs, can provide the flexibility which enables the student to learn material when he most needs it. The utilization of sensitivity training for both facilitators and learners not only increases the freedom and depth of communication but also helps the individual to become more independent in his stance toward learning and toward life. These specific approaches suggest, but do not exhaust, the many ways in which the goals of the new education may be implemented.

As for the learner, the result of such self-initiated learning, such development in meeting and mastering new problems, is a more complete openness to all aspects of his experience, both the outer stimuli and his own internal reactions. He would thus be more fully and adaptively present in confronting a new problem. Martin Buber (1955 edition, p. 14) described this situation well: ". . . In spite of all similarities, every living situation has, like a newborn child, a new face that has never been before and will never come again. It demands of you a reaction which cannot be prepared beforehand. It demands nothing of what is past. It demands presence, responsibility; it demands you."

It is in this spirit that the learner would be able to deal creatively with an ever changing world.

References

Barrett-Lennard, G. Dimensions of therapist response as causal factors in therapeutic change. *Psychol. Monogr.*, 1962, 76, No. 43 (Whole No. 562).
———. Personal communication, 1960.

Berlin, J. I., and L. B. Wyckoff. *Relationship improvement programs*. Atlanta, Ga.: Human Developm. Inst., 1963.

Bradford, L., J. Gibb, and K. Benne, eds. *T-Group theory and laboratory method*. New York: Wiley, 1964.

Buber, M. *Between man and man*. New York: Beacon Press, 1955. Works included were first published 1926–1939.

Fry, E. *Teaching machines and programmed instruction*. New York: McGraw Hill, 1963.

Gage, N. L. The educational psychology of American teachers. Paper presented to the advisory council of the Assn. of Organizations for Tchr. Educ., Washington, D.C., Oct. 1963.

Guetzkow, H., et al. *Simulation in international relations: Developments for research and teaching*. Englewood Cliffs, N.J.: Prentice-Hall, 1963.

Lippitt, R. *Teaching behavioral science in the elementary school*. Mimeo report. Ann Arbor: University of Michigan, 1962.

Pressey, S. Teaching machine (and learning theory) crisis. *J. Appl. Psychol.*, 1963, 47, 1–6.

Rogers, C. R. The necessary and sufficient conditions of therapeutic personality change. *J. Consult. Psychol.*, 1957, 21, 95–103.

———, ed. *The therapeutic relationship and its impact: A study of psychotherapy with schizophrenics*. Madison: University of Wisconsin Press, 1967.

Schwab, J. J. Inquiry, the science teacher and the educator. *Sch. Rev.*, 1960, 68, 176–195.

Skinner, B. F. Why we need teaching machines. *Harv. Educ. Rev.*, 1961, 31, 377–398.

Solomon, L. N. Reducing tensions in a test-tube world. *War/Peace Rep.*, July 1963, 3, No. 7, 10–12.

Suchman, J. R. *The elementary school training program in scientific inquiry*. Urbana: University of Illinois, 1962.

———. Inquiry training: Building skills for autonomous discovery. *Merrill-Palmer Quart. Behav. Developm.*, 1961, 7, 147–169.

Wechsler, I. R., and J. Reisel. *Inside a sensitivity training group*. Los Angeles: Inst. of Industr. Relat., UCLA, 1959.

Donna S. Allender and Jerome S. Allender

I Am the Mayor: Inquiry Materials for the Study of City Government

If you were the mayor of a small city in the West, you could say, "I am the Mayor" and you would know what a mayor does. For those of you who are not or never have been a mayor of a small city in the West, this manual should be used for a briefing about the job and its responsibilities.

These materials allow you and your students to be the mayor of a small western city. They were written to teach about city government. But they were also written to do something more. With the inquiry materials, you will be able to teach inquiry skills. The best introduction is for you to pretend you are a mayor. This section will act as your briefing session for being Mayor of Tinker, Colorado, and for being the teacher of other mayors.

So, imagine yourself as a mayor and that you have just received a letter [Figure 1].

You are expected to make some kind of decision about this letter. But you have been asked to support a proposal about which you know nothing. If you accidently made a good decision at this moment, it would have to be a lucky guess. Before you make a decision, you should collect information about the suggestions which come up in Mr. Vale's letter. Before you can collect information you will have to sense embedded problems and formulate questions which will direct you to useful information.

Adapted from The Teacher's Manual for *I Am The Mayor: Inquiry Materials for the Study of City Government*. Philadelphia: Center for the Study of Federalism, Temple University, in press. Reprinted by permission of the Center for the Study of Federalism.

You will of course want then to locate the information that answers your questions.

Look at the letter again and notice that sentences are numbered in the right margin. This numbering system allows you to request sets of questions having to do with problems embedded in the sentences. For example, if you thought there was a problem embedded in the second sentence of the letter, you would turn to page 322 [Figure 2] and find these questions.

One of the information files which you can receive to search for answers to the questions [in Figure 2] is page 599 [Figure 3].

If your particular question wasn't anticipated, you can ask it anyway. You turn to . . . page 300 [Figure 4] the Index of Files, and you can track down the type of information you need.

Suppose you have gathered all the information you need or all that is available. In the broad sense it is necessary for you to come to some kind of decision and in general there are several types of decisions available to you. You can delay action. You can request more information, or you can take action. [See Figure 5.]

Examples of these alternatives are [in Figures 6, 7, and 8].

What a student does as Mayor of Tinker resembles a major part of what he would do as a real mayor. He receives letters, memoranda, and reports to which he can respond; he has files on general information, departments, current business, and correspondence to allow him to make reasonable decisions. Because students are not really mayors, they are not expected to be familiar at first with any of the information and to help them they are provided with sets of ques-

512 South Sun Street
Tinker, Colorado
April   320

The Mayor
City Hall
Tinker, Colorado

Dear Mayor,

     The Business Club of Tinker wants the City to build a new parking lot
in downtown Tinker. We feel the City Council should carefully study Tinker's   321
need for another lot in that part of town. If there were more parking spaces open 322
during the shopping hours, people from towns around Tinker would be more
interested in coming to Tinker to shop. We would be pleased if you would   323
be in favor of the idea when we bring it up at a City Council meeting.   324

Yours truly,

Lee Vale
Tinker Business Club   325

I want to make a decision.   812

Figure 1

322

How many parking lots are there in downtown Tinker? I
would like to see a map of downtown Tinker.   File 4   Page 363

How many parking spaces are available in downtown
Tinker now? I would like to see the Traffic and Parking
Chart.   File 16   Page 599

Are there other letters about the need for more parking in
Tinker? I would like to see the Mayor's letters about parking.   File 20   Page 785

My question is not here. I want to see a list of all my files.   Page 300

Figure 2

599

	1950	1960	Last year
Cars in Tinker	2,000 cars	2,500 cars	3,000 cars
Parking downtown	300 spaces downtown	500 spaces downtown	500 spaces downtown
Stop lights	6 stop lights	10 stop lights	10 stop lights
Time to drive through downtown Tinker	3 minutes	6 minutes	10 minutes

Figure 3. City Growth Chart: Traffic and Parking

300

General Information		Page 301
File 1	Calendars	Page 310
File 2	History	Page 335
File 3	Laws	Page 340
File 4	Maps	Page 360
File 5	Information Bulletins	Page 375
Departments		Page 302
File 6	Electric	Page 405
File 7	Fire	Page 415
File 8	Garbage and Sanitation	Page 425
File 9	Park	Page 435
File 10	Police	Page 450
File 11	Street	Page 490
File 12	Water	Page 505
Current Business		Page 303
File 13	City Budgets and Money	Page 520
File 14	City Committees	Page 540
File 15	City Councils	Page 575
File 16	City Growth Charts	Page 590
File 17	City Plan	Page 605
File 18	Clubs and Committees in Tinker	Page 615
Letters		Page 304
File 19	Mayor's Letters	Page 665
File 20	City Letters	Page 730

Figure 4. Index of Files

	812
I don't want to do anything about this message right now.	903
I need to find out something that is not in my files.	904
I would like to do something about this right away.	905

Figure 5

903

A. Do what you think best with this.
B. Put this where it belongs in my files.
C. Put this with work to be done later today.
D. I want to keep this on my desk for a while.
E. I want to put it somewhere else:

_____

_____

_____

_____

Figure 6

904

A. Ask the Business Club to find out how many parking spaces a city the size of Tinker should have.
B. Call the Police Department and ask for all information they have about parking problems in Tinker.
C. Find out what it costs to build parking lots.
D. I need to know something else:

_____

_____

_____

_____

Figure 7

A. Write Mr. Vale that his group should do what is best for the city.

B. Write Mr. Vale and ask him to find someone to do a study of how many more people could come to Tinker to shop.

C. Write Mr. Vale that I will be in favor of the City building a new parking lot when it is brought up at the Council meeting.

D. I want to do something else:

_____

_____

_____

_____

Figure 8

tions and alternative decisions from which to choose. The purpose of the materials is to enable teachers to realistically involve their students in the process of inquiry.

In the modern world it is difficult for a teacher to decide what body of facts and concepts should be taught in a social studies curriculum. There is no one authoritative source of information. Textbooks and encyclopedias are not always accurate. Concepts without conflicting arguments rarely exist to explain the complex happenings of our daily lives. More and more each person is required to search and sift among a multitude of facts and figures to form knowledge that is meaningful and useful for daily life. No teacher can ever fill a student's mind with enough information — each student must learn how to find and use his own set of data about the world. Moreover, students will not forever remain students and they will not always have a teacher to choose texts and curriculum which decide for them what information they should know, or what conclusions are important. It is important that the students with whom you work have the opportunity to learn to inquire. They should be able to sense problems, formulate questions, and search for information before coming to decisions. *I Am the*

Mayor gives students the opportunity to do this.

Description of *I Am the Mayor*

There are four major sections to *I Am the Mayor*, and they are:

1. The Mayor's Work
2. The Mayor's Questions
3. The Mayor's Files
4. The Mayor's Decisions

Each problem found in "The Mayor's Work" can be followed through with related Mayor's Questions leading to information in the Mayor's Files and finally with the selection of a decision from the Mayor's Decisions.

1. "The Mayor's Work" . . . consists of letters, messages about telephone calls, reports, and a local newspaper. They directly draw the mayor's attention to matters concerning the scouts, school safety, trees, zoning, park development, street repair, a new airport, electric power, and water pressure; the mayor is confronted indirectly with several other local matters. The work can be received and handled in several ways. It does not invite yes and no answers or quick decisions.

2. "The Mayor's Questions" . . . are sets of

questions which follow from each piece of work and are intended to help students formulate problems they sense in the work. There are from six to ten sets of questions for each piece of "The Mayor's Work." Each page of "The Mayor's Questions" has three questions and a direction to go to the main index in the event that a question desired by the student is not included on the page. There are no correct questions on any page. The value of a question can only be evaluated in terms of what the student needs to know and what he or she already knows. There can be several good reasons given for choosing each question. Generally, they are written to include a specific question, a more general one, and a very general question on each page.

3. Each question leads to a piece of information or to a specific file. The information is all contained in the section called "The Mayor's Files". . . . We have tried to construct a filing system for the student mayors which contains information on many aspects of a city and a city government — not only those that pertain to the work. The files include the mayor's calendars, a history, laws of Tinker, maps of the city, general information bulletins, records and reports of city departments, budgets and financial statements, committee information, city council records, city growth charts, the city plan, and letters to both the mayor and the other city officials of various departments. There is ample information available concerning each piece of "The Mayor's Work." Some of the information is relevant to several pieces of work. Some is applicable to only one. An attempt has been made to make the kinds and amount of information available as broad as possible. This allows for the development of various types of inquiry behavior. The information does not offer a definite or correct solution to any problem. A variety of information can be combined and evaluated by the mayor before a decision is reached.

4. There are two parts to the set of decisions. First the mayor must choose a type of decision. . . . The mayor may choose to do nothing now, ask for more information, or take some action. When the mayor has chosen one of these types of decisions, the exact decision must

be specified. . . . Each of these decision pages provides a choice of six prewritten decisions and an opportunity to write an original one, if the student chooses.

There are no correct decisions. It may be possible that any one would be a good decision under certain circumstances. The decisions range from very active to very inactive behavior. The correctness of any particular decision can only be judged against the standards the individual sets. They will be affected by the mayor's philosophy of government, by the amount of data available, by the feelings of the community as he sees them, and by what is legally and financially possible for a mayor or government to do. Some of these standards can be determined somewhat objectively, but others are very subjective.

We have therefore included no correct decision sheets for each problem. It is our hope that each child's decisions will be given full consideration. This is not to imply there can be no criticism or controversy. On the contrary, there will be both. A "good" decision reached by poor methods could be criticized by a teacher or fellow students as only a chance occurrence. A decision which has no rhyme or reason in terms of the information received would need a strong defense by the mayor who made it. We would like to emphasize evaluation which requires all the decisions to be the same for the same problem is not suitable for these inquiry materials.

It is recommended that the materials be used as an individual learning tool rather than for large group instruction. They are most effective when each child can go through his own process of being Mayor from start to decision. Actually, the materials have never been tested in a situation where a whole class plays Mayor together. Perhaps it would be fun sometime for a large group to go through one of the problems together. However, one of the great values of the materials is that they allow the child maximum freedom to act as an individual and work at his own pace. It would be wasteful not to take advantage of this quality when many materials exist which are designed for use with a large group.

There are several arrangements which can be

made for an individual to play Mayor. There is no reason to believe that any one is a great deal better than another. It is more likely that one method will be more suitable for a specific child or group of children. The development and maturity of the children will be a consideration as will the financial situation of the school.

1. A child can use the Mayor materials by himself. He can draw out the file he needs and record his own path through the materials. He would be responsible for refiling the materials as he finishes with them. It is possible that several children could be using the box at one time, especially if they are considering different problems. Multiple copies of important files and the ten problems make it feasible for several children to work on one problem.

2. One child can act as Mayor while another acts as secretary to him. The secretary would give him the pages he asks for, refile the pages, and record the pages he used on the record sheet. This method would free the student from thinking about the clerical aspects of the process. It can also be of value to the secretary, who can closely view another person's inquiry process. (A carrel which simulates a mayor's and secretary's office is available.)

3. A teacher's helper could act as secretary to several children at one time. She could keep records for each Mayor and keep the files in order.

4. A small group could work together using their consensus for making choices. One of them could be chosen as recorder and another as file keeper.

There may be several other arrangements which classes could develop together. This is encouraged. The method which is best suited to the needs of the individual is best for teaching with the Mayor materials.

Ned A. Flanders

Intent, Action and Feedback: A Preparation for Teaching

The Problem

The point is that much of what is learned in education courses is neither conceptualized, qualified, nor taught in a fashion that builds a bridge between theory and practice. Education students are only occasionally part of an exciting, systematic, exploration of the teaching process, most infrequently by the instructor's example. How can we create, in education courses, an active, problem-solving process, a true sense of inquiry, and a systematic search for principles through experimentation? At least one factor favors change and that is the lack of solid evidence that any thing we are now teaching is clearly associated with any index of effective teaching, with the possible exception of practice teaching.

A great many factors resist curriculum change in teacher education. Perhaps the most important is that genuine curriculum innovation, to be distinguished from tinkering with content and sequence, would require that existing faculty members, old and new alike, think differently about their subject matter, act differently while teaching, and relate differently to their students. For some this is probably impossible, for all it would be difficult. Yet changes do occur when enough energy is mobilized and convictions are strongly held.

It is a serious indictment of the profession, however, to hear so many education instructors say that their students will appreciate what they are learning *after* they have had some practical teaching experience. What hurts is the obvious

From *The Journal of Teacher Education*, XLV, 3, (Sept. 1963) pp. 251–60. Reprinted by permission.

hypocrisy of making this statement and then giving a lecture on the importance of presenting material in such a way that the immediate needs and interests of the pupils are taken into consideration. Such instances reveal a misunderstanding of theory and practice. To be understood, concepts in education must be verified by personal field experiences; in turn, field experiences must be efficiently conceptualized to gain insight. With most present practices, the gorge between theory and practice grows deeper and wider, excavated by the very individuals who are pledged to fill it.

One stumbling block is our inability to describe teaching as a series of acts through time and to establish models of behavior which are appropriate to different kinds of teaching situations. This problem has several dimensions. First, in terms of semantics, we must learn how to define our concepts as part of a theory. We also need to organize these concepts into the fewest number of variables necessary to establish principles and make predictions. Too often we try to teach the largest number of variables; in fact, as many as we can think of for which there is some research evidence. Second, in terms of technology we must develop procedures for quantifying the qualitative aspects of teaching acts so that our students will have tools for collecting empirical evidence. Third, in terms of philosophy, we must decide whether our education students are going to be told about teaching in lectures and read about it in books or if they are going to discover these things for themselves. This paper will be devoted to these three issues, in reverse order.

A Philosophy of Inquiry

When Nathaniel Cantor (5) published his nine assumptions of orthodox teaching, there was little evidence to support his criticisms. Must pupils be coerced into working on tasks? In what way is the teacher responsible for pupils' acquiring knowledge? Is education a preparation for later life rather than a present, living experience? Is subject matter the same to the learner as it is to the teacher? The last decade has provided more evidence in support of Cantor's criticism than it has in defense of existing practice.

H. H. Anderson and his colleagues (1, 2, 3, 4) first demonstrated that dominative teacher contacts create more compliance and resistance to compliance, that dominative teacher contacts with pupils spread to the pupil-to-pupil contacts even in the absence of the teacher, and that this pattern of teaching creates situations in which pupils are more easily distracted and more dependent on teacher initiative.

Flanders and Havumaki (8) demonstrated that dominative teacher influence was more persuasive in changing pupil opinions but that such shifts of opinion were not stable since inner resistance was so high.

A research team in Provo, Utah (9) believes that patterns of spontaneous teacher action can be identified and that more effective patterns can be distinguished from less effective patterns. The difference is that more dominative patterns are less effective.

Our own eight-year research program which involved the development of interaction analysis as a tool for quantifying patterns of teacher influence lends further support to Cantor. The generalizations to follow are based on all teachers observed in our different research projects. This total is only 147 teachers, representing all grade levels, six different school districts in two counties; but these teachers came from the extremes of a distribution involving several thousand teachers. The total bits of information collected by interaction analysis are well in excess of 1,250,000.

The present, average domination of teachers is best expressed as the rule of two-thirds. About two-thirds of the time spent in a classroom, someone is talking. The chances are two out of three that this person is the teacher. When the teacher talks, two-thirds of the time is spent by many expressions of opinion and fact, giving some direction and occasionally criticizing the pupils. The fact that teachers are taking too active a part for effective learning is shown by comparing superior with less effective classrooms. A superior classroom scores above average on constructive attitudes toward the teacher and the classwork. It also scores higher on achievement tests of the content to be learned, adjusted for initial ability. In studies (7) of seventh grade social studies and eighth grade mathematics, it was found that the teachers in superior classrooms spoke only slightly less, say 50 to 60 per cent of the time, but the more directive aspects of their verbal influence went down to 40 to 50 per cent. These teachers were much more flexible in the quality of their influence, sometimes very direct, but on more occasions very indirect.

To describe the classrooms which were below average in constructive pupil attitudes and in content achievement (they are positively correlated), just change the rule of two-thirds to the rule of three-fourths plus.

The foregoing evidence shows that no matter what a prospective teacher hears in an education course, he has, on the average, been exposed to living models of what teaching is and can be that are basically quite directive. After fourteen or so years he is likely to be quite dependent, expecting the instructor to tell him what to do, how to do it, when he is finished, and then tell him how well he did it. Now it is in this general context that we turn to the question of how we can develop a spirit of inquiry with regard to teaching.

Thelen (10) has described a model of personal inquiry, as well as other models, and the question is whether teacher education can or should move toward this model. He describes this model as follows (*ibid.*, p. 89):

... (Personal inquiry) is a process of interaction between the student and his natural and societal environment. In this situation the student will be

293

aware of the process of which he is a part; during this process he will be aware of many choices among ways he might behave; he will make decisions among these ways; he will then act and see what happens; he will review the process and study it with the help of books and other people; he will speculate about it, and draw tentative conclusions from it.

Returning to the education course, the student will be aware of the learning process of *that* classroom, he will confront choices, he will make decisions among the choices, he will act and then evaluate his actions, and then he will try to make some sense out of it with the help of books, the instructor, and his peers. This is a tall order, but who knows, it may be the only route to discovery and independence for the prospective teacher.

Occasionally we hear of exciting learning experiences in which education students attain a sort of intellectual spirit of inquiry. A unit on motivation can begin with an assessment of the motivation patterns of the education students. The same assessment procedures can then be used at other grade levels permitting comparisons and generalizations. Principles of child growth and development can be discovered by observation and learned more thoroughly perhaps than is possible with only lecture and reading. But this is not what is meant by inquiry.

Inquiry in teacher education means translating understanding into action as part of the teaching process. It means experimenting with one's own behavior obtaining objective information about one's own behavior, evaluating this information in terms of the teacher's role; in short, attaining self-insight while acting like a teacher.

Procedures for obtaining self-insight have been remarkably improved during the last decade in the field of human relations training. Two characteristics of these training methods seem relevant to this discussion. First, information and insights about behavior must become available in a way that can be accepted and in a form that is understood. Second, opportunities to utilize or act out these insights must be provided. Our ability to accept information about

ourselves is a complex problem, but it helps if we believe the information is objective, valid, and given in an effort to help rather than hurt. Our understanding of this information will depend a great deal on our ability to organize the information conceptually. Freedom to act at least requires freedom from threat or embarrassment.

From all of these things, a spirit of inquiry develops.

The Technique of Interaction Analysis

Interaction analysis is nothing more and nothing less than an observation technique which can be used to obtain a fairly reliable record of spontaneous verbal statements. Most teacher influence is exerted by verbal statements and to determine their quality is to approximate total teacher influence. This technique was first developed as a research tool, but every observer we ever hired testified that the process of learning the system and using it in classrooms was more valuable than anything else he learned in his education courses. Since interaction analysis is only a technique, it probably could be applied to teacher education in a fashion that is consistent or even totally inconsistent with a philosophy of personal inquiry. How it is used in teacher preparation is obviously as important as understanding the procedure itself.

The writing of this manuscript followed the completion of a terminal contract report of a U.S. Office of Education-sponsored, in-service training program based on interaction analysis as a tool for gathering information. How we used interaction analysis is illustrated by the conditions we tried to create for the fifty-five participating teachers, most of whom represented about one-half of the faculties of two junior high schools:[1]

---

[1] Interaction analysis as a research tool has been used ever since R. F. Bales first developed a set of categories for studying groups. Most of our research results can be found in the references at the end of this paper. Its use as a training device is more recent. Projects have taken place in New Jersey, Philadelphia, Chicago and Minneapolis. Systematic evaluation is available in only the Minneapolis project.

1. Teachers developed new (to them) concepts as tools for thinking about their behavior and the consequences of their behavior. These concepts were used to discover principles of teacher influence. Both types of concepts were necessary: those for describing actions and those for describing consequences.

2. Procedures for assessing both types of concepts in practical classroom situations were tried out. These procedures were used to test principles, to modify them, and to determine when they might be appropriately applied.

3. The training activities involved in becoming proficient in the assessment of spontaneous behavior, in and of themselves, increased the sensitivity of teachers to their own behavior and the behavior of others. Most important, teachers could compare their intentions with their actions.

4. By avoiding a discussion of right and wrong ways of teaching and emphasizing the discovery of principles of teacher influence, teachers gradually became more independent and self-directing. Our most successful participants investigated problems of their own choosing, designed their own plans, and arranged collaboration with others when this seemed advantageous.

Five filmstrips and one teacher's manual have been produced and written. These materials would have to be modified before they could be used with undergraduate students. Before asking how interaction analysis might be used in teacher preparation, we turn next to a description of the procedures.

The Procedure of Observation

The observer sits in a classroom in the best position to hear and see the participants. At the end of each three-second period, he decides which category best represents the communication events just completed. He writes this category number down while simultaneously assessing communication in the next period and continues at a rate of 20 to 25 observations per minute, keeping his tempo as steady as possible. His notes are merely a series of numbers written in a column, top to bottom, so that the original sequence of events is preserved. Occasionally marginal notes are used to explain the class formation or any unusual circumstances. When there is a major change in class formation, the communication pattern, or the subject under discussion, a double line is drawn and the time indicated. As soon as the total observation is completed, the observer retires to a nearby room and completes a general description of each separate activity period separated by the double lines, including the nature of the activities, the class formation, and the position of the teacher. The observer also notes any additional facts that seem pertinent to an adequate interpretation and recall of the total visit.

The ten categories that we used for interaction analysis are shown in Table 1.

The numbers that an observer writes down are tabulated in a 10×10 matrix as sequence pairs, that is, a separate tabulation is made for each overlapping pair of numbers. An illustration will serve to explain this procedure.

Teacher: "Class! The bell has rung. May I have your attention please!" [6] During the next three seconds talking and noise diminish. [10]

Teacher: "Jimmy, we are all waiting for you." [7] Pause.

Teacher: "Now today we are going to have a very pleasant surprise, [5] and I think you will find it very exciting and interesting. [1] Have any of you heard anything about what we are going to do?" [4]

Pupil: "I think we are going on a trip in the bus that's out in front." [8]

Teacher: "Oh! You've found out! How did you learn about our trip?" [4]

By now the observer has written down 6, 10, 7, 5, 1, 4, 8, and 4. As the interaction proceeds, the observer will continue to write down numbers. To tabulate these observations in a 10×10 matrix, the first step is to make sure that the entire series begins and ends with the same number. The convention we use is to add

Table 1. Categories for Interaction Analysis

		1.* Accepts Feeling: accepts and clarifies the feeling tone of the students in a non-threatening manner. Feelings may be positive or negative. Predicting or recalling feelings are included.
		2.* Praises or Encourages: praises or encourages student action or behavior. Jokes that release tension, not at the expense of another individual, nodding head or saying, "um hm?" or "go on" are included.
	Indirect Influence	3.* Accepts or Uses Ideas of Student: clarifying, building or developing ideas suggested by a student. As teacher brings more of his own ideas into play, shift to category five.
		4.* Asks Questions: asking a question about content or procedure with the intent that a student answer.
Teacher Talk		
		5.* Lecturing: giving facts or opinions about content or procedures; expressing his own ideas, asking rhetorical questions.
	Direct Influence	6.* Giving Directions: directions, commands, or orders with which a student is expected to comply.
		7.* Criticizing or Justifying Authority: statements intended to change student behavior from nonacceptable to acceptable pattern; bawling someone out; stating why the teacher is doing what he is doing; extreme self-reference.
		8.* Student Talk — Response: talk by students in response to teacher. Teacher initiates the contact or solicits student statement.
Student Talk		9.* Student Talk — Initiation: talk by students which they initiate. If "calling on" student is only to indicate who may talk next, observer must decide whether student wanted to talk. If he did, use this category.
		10.* Silence or Confusion: pauses, short periods of silence and periods of confusion in which communication cannot be understood by the observer.

* There is no scale implied by these numbers. Each number is classificatory; it designates a particular kind of communication event. To write these numbers down during observation is to enumerate, not to judge a position on a scale.

a 10 to the beginning and end of the series unless the 10 is already present. Our series now becomes 10, 6, 10, 7, 5, 1, 4, 8, 4, and 10.

These numbers are tabulated in a matrix, one pair at a time. The column is indicated by the second number, the row is indicated by the first number. The first pair is 10-6; the tally is placed in row ten, column six cell. The second pair is 6-10; tally this in the row six, column ten cell. The third pair is 10-7, the fourth pair is 7-5, and so on. Each pair overlaps with the next, and the total number of observations, "N," always will be tabulated by N-1 tallies in the matrix. In this case we started a series of ten numbers, and the series produced nine tallies in the matrix.

Table 2 shows our completed matrix. Notice that in a correctly tabulated matrix the sums of the corresponding rows and columns are equal.

The problem of reliability is extremely complex, and a more complete discussion can be found in two terminal contract reports (6, 7)

one of which will be published as a research monograph in the 1963 series of the Cooperative Research Program. Education students can learn how to make quick field checks of their reliability and work toward higher reliability under the direction of an instructor.

The Interpretation of Matrices

A matrix should have at least 400 tallies, covering about twenty minutes or more of a homogeneous activity period, before attempting to make an interpretation.

Certain areas within the matrix are particularly useful for describing teacher influence. Some of these areas will now be discussed by making reference to Table 3.

The column totals of a matrix are indicated as Areas "A," "B," "C," and "D." The figures in these areas provide a general picture by answering the following questions: What proportion of the time was someone talking compared with the portion in which confusion or

Table 2

Category	1	2	3	4	5	6	7	8	9	10	Total
1				1							1
2											0
3											0
4								1		1	2
5	1										1
6										1	1
7				1							1
8				1							1
9											0
10						1	1				2
Total	1	0	0	2	1	1	1	1	0	2	9

Table 3. Matrix Analysis

Category	Classification	Category	1	2	3	4	5	6	7	8	9	10	Total
Accepts Feelings	Teacher Talk — Indirect Influence	1	Area E										
Praise		2											
Student Idea		3											
Asks Questions		4				"Content Cross"			Area I				
Lectures	Direct Influence	5											
Gives Directions		6						Area F					
Criticism		7											
Student Response	Student Talk	8	Area G					Area H		Area J			
Student Initiation		9											
Silence		10											
Total			Area A — Indirect Teacher Talk				Area B — Direct Teacher Talk			Area C — Student Talk		Area D		

no talking existed? When someone was talking, what proportion of the time was used by the students? By the teacher? Of the time that the teacher talked, what proportion of his talk involved indirect influence? Direct influence?

The answers to these questions form a necessary backdrop to the interpretation of the other parts of the matrix. If student participation is about 30 or 40 per cent, we would expect to find out why it was so high by studying the matrix. If the teacher is particularly direct or indirect, we would expect certain relationships to exist with student talk and silence.

The next two areas to consider are areas "E" and "F." Evidence that categories 1, 2, and 3 were used for periods longer than three seconds can be found in the diagonal cells, 1-1, 2-2, and 3-3. The other six cells of Area E indicate various types of transitions between these three categories. Sustained praise or clarification of student ideas is especially significant because such elaboration often involves criteria for praise or reasons for accepting ideas and feelings. The elaboration of praise or student ideas must be present if the student's ideas are to be integrated with the content being discussed by the class.

Area F is a four-cell combination of giving directions (category 6) and giving criticisms or self-justification (category 7). The transition cells 6-7 and 7-6 are particularly sensitive to difficulties that the teacher may have with classroom discipline or resistance on the part of students. When criticism follows directions or direction follows criticism this means that the students are not complying satisfactorily. Often there is a high loading on the 6-9 cell under these circumstances. Excessively high frequencies in the 6-6 cell *and* 7-7 cells indicate teacher domination and supervision of the students' activities. A high loading of tallies in the 6-6 cell alone often indicates that the teacher is merely giving lengthy directions to the class.

The next two areas to be considered are Areas G and H. Tallies in these two areas occur at the instant the student stops talking and the teacher starts. Area G indicates those instances in which the teacher responds to the termina-

tion of student talk with indirect influence. Area H indicates those instances in which the teacher responds to the termination of student talk with direct influence. An interesting comparison can be made by contrasting the proportion G to H versus the proportion A to B. If these two proportions are quite different, it indicates that the teacher tends to act differently at the instant a student stops talking compared with his overall average. Often this is a mark of flexible teacher influence.

There are interesting relationships between Area E and Area G and between Area F and Area H. For example, Area G may indicate that a teacher responds indirectly to students at the instant they terminate their talk, but an observer may wish to inspect Area E to see if this indirect response is sustained in any way. The same question with regard to direct influence can be asked of Areas F and H. Areas G and H together usually fascinate teachers. They are often interested in knowing more about their immediate response to student participation.

Area I indicates an answer to the question, What types of teacher statements trigger student participation? Usually there is a high tally loading in cells 4-8 and 4-9. This is expected because students often answer questions posed by the teacher. A high loading on 4-8 and 8-4 cells alone usually indicates classroom drill directed by the teacher. The contrast of tallies in columns 8 and 9 in this area gives a rough indication of the frequency with which students initiate their own ideas versus respond to those of the teacher.

Area I is often considered in combination with Area J. Area J indicates either lengthy student statements or sustained student-to-student communication. An above-average frequency in Area C, but not in Area J, indicates that short answers, usually in response to teacher stimulation, have occurred. One would normally expect to find frequencies in Area E positively correlated with frequencies in Area J.

We turn next to concepts and principles of teacher influence before speculating about how this technique can be applied to teacher education.

Concepts and Principles of Teacher Influence

It may be too early to determine what are the *fewest* number of concepts which, if organized into logically related principles, can be used by a teacher to plan how he will use his authority. Surely he will need concepts that refer to his authority and its use. He will need concepts to describe learning goals and pupil tasks. He will need concepts to classify the responses of students. He may also need concepts to characterize class formations and patterns of classroom communication. These concepts are at least the minimum.

Concepts That Refer to Teacher Behavior

Indirect influence: — Indirect influence is defined as actions taken by the teacher which encourage and support student participation. Accepting, clarifying, praising, and developing the ideas and feelings expressed by the pupils will support student participation. We can define indirect behavior operationally by noting the per cent of teacher statements falling into categories 1, 2, 3, and 4.

Direct influence: — This concept refers to actions taken by teacher which restrict student participation. Expressing one's own views through lecture, giving directions, and criticizing with the expectation of compliance tend to restrict pupil participation. We can define direct behavior operationally by noting the per cent of teacher statements falling into categories 5, 6, and 7.

Other concepts which we do not have the space to discuss include: flexibility of teacher influence, dominance or sustained direct influence, and intervention.

Concepts That Refer to Learning Goals

Clear goals: — Goal perceptions are defined from the point of view of the pupil, not the teacher. "Clear goals" is a state of affairs in which the pupil knows what he is doing, the purpose, and can guess at the first few steps to be taken. It can be measured by paper-and-pencil tests, often administered at different points in a problem-solving sequence.

Ambiguous goals: — "Ambiguous goals" describes a state of affairs in which a pupil is not sure of what he is expected to do, is not sure of the first few steps, or is unable to proceed for one reason or another. It can be measured as above.

Other concepts in this area include: attractive and unattractive clear goals, pupil tasks, task requirements, and similar concepts.

Concepts That Refer to Pupil Responses

Dependent acts: — Acts of dependence occur when a pupil not only complies with teacher influence but solicits such direction. A pupil who asks a teacher to approve of his work in order to make sure that it is satisfactory, before going on to the next logical step, is acting dependently. This type of response can be measured by observation techniques and by paper-and-pencil tests on which he indicates what kind of help he would like from the teacher.

Independent acts: — Acts of independence occur when the pupils react primarily to task requirements and are less directly concerned with teacher approval. The measurement of this concept is the same as for dependent acts.

Other concepts include: dependence proneness — a trait, compliance, conformity, counter-dependence, and similar concepts.

Some Principles That Can Be Discovered

We discovered in our research (7) that, during the first few days of a two-week unit of study in seventh grade social studies and when introducing new materials in eighth grade mathematics, superior teachers are initially more indirect, becoming more direct as goals and associated tasks become clarified. We also suspect that these same teachers are more indirect when helping pupils diagnose difficulties, when trying to motivate pupils by arousing their interest, and in other situations in which the expression of pupil perceptions is helpful. On the other hand, the average or below average teacher did exactly the opposite.

Now the problem in teacher education is not only to create a situation in which education students could verify these relationships but could practice controlling their own behavior so as to become indirect or more direct at will.

One place to begin is to have two, six-man groups work on a task under the direction of a leader. One task is something like an assembly line; it has a clear end product and sharp role differentiation. The other task is much more difficult to describe and does not have clear role differentiation. Now let the class superimpose different patterns of leader influence. Let them interview the role players, collect interaction analysis data by some simplified system of categories, and discuss the results. When undergraduate students first try to classify verbal statements, it sometimes helps to use only two or three categories. In one instance, the issue was the effect of using broad questions versus narrow questions. A broad question was one to which it was hard to predict the type of answer. A narrow question was one to which it was easy to guess at the type of answer. Which type of question was more likely to increase pupil participation? The students role-played this and kept a record of broad questions, narrow questions, and the length of the response. The fact that they verified their prediction correctly for this rather superficial problem was much less important compared with the experience that they gained. They learned how to verify a prediction with empirical evidence, and some had a chance to practice control of their own behavior for professional purposes.

There is no space here to list a complete set of principles that can be investigated by systematic or intuitive data-collecting procedures. The following questions might stimulate useful learning activities. Does dependence always decrease as goals become clear? Is the final level of dependence determined by the pattern of teacher influence when goals are first formulated? Are measures of content achievement related to the pupils' attitudes toward the teacher and the schoolwork? What effects can you expect from excessive and pedantic clarification of pupil ideas and feelings? And many others.

Applications of Interaction Analysis to Teacher Education

Suppose that before education students were given their practice teaching assignment, they had been exposed to a variety of data-collecting techniques for assessing pupil perceptions, measuring achievement, and quantifying spontaneous teacher influence. Suppose, further, that these skills had been taught in a context of personal inquiry as described earlier. What effect would this have on their approach to practice teaching?

One of their suggestions might be that two students should be assigned as a team to the first assignment. While one took over the class the other would be collecting information; the next day or so, the roles could be reversed. Together they would work out a lesson plan, agree on the data to be collected, go over the results with the help of the supervising teacher who might also have the same data-collecting skills. This situation could approach the inquiry model described earlier. The practice teacher might discover that his failure to clarify the pupils' ideas restricted the development of curiosity or that his directions were too short when he was asked for further help; both of these inferences can be made from an interaction matrix with reasonable reliability and objectivity.

Later on a student may wish to take a practice reading assignment by himself and turn to the supervising teacher for aid in feedback. In either case, the requirement is that the learner be able to compare his intentions with feedback information about his actions and analyze this information by using concepts which he found useful in his earlier courses in education.

There are some precautions that can already be stated with regard to the use of interaction analysis in such a situation.

First, no interaction analysis data should be collected unless the person observed is familiar with the entire process and knows its limitations.

Second, the questions to be answered by inspecting the matrix should be developed before the observation takes place.

Third, value judgments about good and bad teaching behavior are to be avoided. Emphasis is given to the problem being investigated so that cause-and-effect relationships can be discovered.

Fourth, a certain amount of defensive behavior is likely to be present at the initial consultation; it is something like listening to a tape recording for the first time.

Fifth, a consultation based on two observations or at least two matrices helps to eliminate value judgments or at least control them. Comparisons between the matrices are more likely to lead to principles.

Just how experiences of the type we have been discussing will fit into the present curricula is difficult to know. If activities of the sort described in this paper are valuable, are they to be superimposed on the present list of courses or is more radical surgery necessary?

Perhaps this is the point to risk a prediction, which is that teacher education will become increasingly concerned with the process of teaching itself during the next few decades. Instead of emphasizing knowledge which *we think* teachers will need in order to teach effectively, as we have in the past, we will turn more and more to an analysis of teaching acts as they occur in spontaneous classroom interaction. We are now at the point in our technology of data collecting at which procedures for analyzing and conceptualizing teaching behavior can be developed. Systems for doing this will become available regardless of whether they are similar or dissimilar to the procedures described in this paper. When this fine day arrives, the role of the education instructor will change, and the dichotomy between field and theory will disappear. The instructor's role will shift from talking about effective teaching to the rigorous challenge of demonstrating effective teaching. The process of inquiry will create problem-solving activities that will produce more independent, self-directing teachers whose first day on the job will be their worst, not their best.

These changes will be successful to the extent that the graduates of teacher education can learn to control their own behavior for the professional purpose of managing effective classroom learning. It will be the responsibility of the education instructor to help prospective teachers discover what their teaching intentions should be and then create training situations in which behavior gradually matches intentions

with practice. Teaching will remain an art, but it will be studied scientifically.

References

1. Anderson, Harold H. "The Measurement of Domination and of Socially Integrative Behavior in Teachers' Contacts with Children." *Child Development* 10: 73–89; June 1939.
2. ———, and Brewer, Helen M. *Studies of Teachers' Classroom Personalities, I: Dominative and Socially Integrative Behavior of Kindergarten Teachers.* Applied Psychology Monographs of the American Psychological Association. No. 6. Stanford, California: Stanford University Press, July 1945.
3. ———, and Brewer, Joseph E. *Studies of Teachers' Classroom Personalities, II: Effects of Teachers' Dominative and Integrative Contacts on Children's Classroom Behavior.* Applied Psychology Monographs of the American Psychological Association. No. 8. Stanford, California: Stanford University Press, June 1946.
4. ———; Brewer, J. E.; and Reed, M. F. *Studies of Teachers' Classroom Personalities, III: Follow-up Studies of the Effects of Dominative and Integrative Contacts on Children's Behavior.* Applied Psychology Monographs of the American Psychological Association. No. 11. Stanford, California: Stanford University Press, December 1946.
5. Cantor, Nathaniel. *The Teaching-Learning Process.* New York: Dryden Press, 1953. pp. 59–72.
6. Flanders, N. A. A terminal contract report on using interaction analysis for the inservice training of teachers. To be submitted to the U.S. Office of Education, N.D.E.A., Title VII. Available from the author, University of Michigan, after April 1963.
7. ———. *Teacher Influence, Pupil Attitudes, and Achievement.* Dittoed manuscript to be published in 1963 as a Research Monograph, Cooperative Research Program, U.S. Office of Education. Available from author, University of Michigan, 1962. 176 pp.
8. ———, and Havumaki, S. "Group Compliance to Dominative Teacher Influence." *Human Relations* 13: 67–82.
9. Romney, G. P.; Hughes, M. M.; and others. *Progress Report of the Merit Study of the Provo City Schools.* Provo, Utah, August 1958. XIX + 226 pp. See also *Patterns of Effective Teaching: Second Progress Report of the Merit Study of the Provo City Schools.* Provo, Utah, June 1961. XII + 93 pp.
10. Thelen, H. A. *Education and the Human Quest.* New York: Harper Brothers, 1960. pp. 74–112.

Additional Resources

Books

Amidon, Edmund J., and Elizabeth Hunter. *Improving Teaching: The Analysis of Classroom Verbal Interaction*. New York: Holt, Rinehart and Winston, 1967.
This book offers various situations in elementary schools and junior high schools and helps the reader to examine how to motivate, plan, lead discussions, discipline, and evaluate students.

Ashton-Warner, Sylvia. *Teacher*. New York: Simon and Schuster, 1963.
This book describes an organic approach to teaching with illustrations of children learning in a Maori school.

Featherstone, Joseph. *Schools Where Children Learn*. New York: Liveright, 1971.
Based on his observations of the British system of primary education, Featherstone makes recommendations for improving American schools.

Holt, John. *What Do I Do Monday?* New York: Dutton, 1970.
Holt gives some specific examples of what teachers can do in various subject areas as well as advice on avoiding some of the traps into which teachers get themselves.

Jackson, Philip W. *Life In Classrooms*. New York: Holt, Rinehart and Winston, 1968.
Chapter 4, "Teacher's Views," discusses how teachers perceive classroom life and includes a useful distinction between the "preactive" and "interactive" phases of teaching.

Kohl, Herbert R. *The Open Classroom*. New York: Random House, 1969.
This practical guide to opening classrooms has some specific ideas about planning, discipline, expectations, and ways of avoiding administrative difficulties.

———. 36 *Children*. New York: New American Library, 1968.
Kohl offers a vivid picture of his experiences in a Harlem classroom and illustrates how a teacher involves children in learning.

Massialas, Byron G., and Jack Zevin. *Creative Encounters in the Classroom: Teaching and Learning Through Discovery*. New York: Wiley, 1967.
This book contains many suggestions for applying discovery methods to various subjects and describes the interaction of teachers with students in this approach.

Oettinger, Anthony G., with Sema Marks. *Run Computer Run*. Cambridge, Mass.: Harvard University Press, 1969.
The authors evaluate how computers can supplement and expand conventional teaching rather than replace it.

Silberman, Charles E. *Crisis in the Classroom*. New York: Random House, 1970.
Of particular interest are Silberman's commentaries on computer-assisted instruction (pp. 186–203) and British primary schools (pp 208–264).

Schmuck, Richard A., and Patricia A. Schmuck. *Group Processes in the Classroom*. Dubuque, Iowa: Brown, 1971.
This book relates group dynamics techniques and studies to the classroom with emphasis on the leadership role of the teacher.

Articles

Allender, Jerome S. "A Study of Inquiry Activity in Elementary School Children." *American Educational Research Journal* 6, (November 1969): 543–558.
This article gives the research findings of a study using the inquiry materials "I Am the Mayor."

Allender, Jerome S. "The Importance of Recorded Communication," *AV Communication Review* 15 (Winter 1967): 399–409.
Allender discusses the need for new forms of instructional materials that meaningfully extend the role of the teacher.

Gleason, Gerald T. "Technological Developments Related to Independent Learning." *The Theory and Nature of Independent Learning*. Scranton, Pa.: International Textbook Co. 1967, pp. 65–78.
Gleason emphasizes the multifaceted types of technology that are available today and the ways one can consider them for assistance.

McDonald, James B., and Bernice J. Wolfson. "A Case Against Behavioral Objectives." *Elementary School Journal* 71 (December 1970): 119–128.
The authors argue against the use of behavioral objectives and as an alternative offer the idea of planned activity from which individuals select their own learning experiences.

Films

An Environment for Student-directed Learning. Time-Life Educational Films, Rockefeller Center, New York, N.Y. 10020.
This film shows a suburban classroom in which children make many decisions and plans.

The Remarkable Schoolhouse. Twenty-first Century Series, Columbia Broadcasting Corporation, McGraw-Hill Publishing Company, 330 W. 42nd St., New York, N.Y. 10036.
Schools using computer-assisted instruction, continuous progress curricula, and other experimental programs in both elementary and high schools are shown.

They Can Do It. Educational Development Center, 39 Chapel Street, Newton, Mass. 02158.
The development over the school year of an open classroom in an urban elementary school is presented.

Resolution Activity

At the beginning of this content area you were confronted with the task of developing ways of approaching teaching that allow for student direction. The materials that have been provided have permitted you to explore the structuring of learning experiences, innovative materials and programs, and styles of interaction with students. With the development of inquiry skills in an open environment in mind, the following simulated problem has been developed to help you resolve your inquiry.

Play the role of a teacher who is planning for the first few weeks of school. Your principal has high expectations for the work you do, and he is open to new and creative ideas if they are carefully thought out. To help you, he has set up a teacher workshop with resources and consultants during the two weeks before school starts. He also has sent all the teachers the following note to help them begin their work:

Dear Faculty:

It is unnecessary to tell you that in a modern world we need a strong commitment to teaching that is not just telling students the information that is in a teacher's head. On the other hand, the idea of teaching children how to think for themselves is a difficult proposition. When we first began to recognize the importance of this idea, a number of ideas were tried. The results were mixed. Here and there, we found exciting things happening in our school, but sometimes students were quite confused. I think one of the central problems was a lack of careful thinking about how a teacher can give guidance while, at the same time, allow for a great deal of student independence. In general, the role of the teacher in helping children develop thinking skills needs to be worked out conceptually and then practically by anyone who is going to structure a class for this kind of goal. I encourage you to experiment, but I would greatly appreciate your sharing with me some of your thinking before you start.

Individually or in a group, do the following:

1. On the basis of your own analysis, ask general questions that you think cover the major considerations in planning how to carry out the suggestions of the note.

2. For each of your questions, identify relevant readings and activities you have experienced and analyze briefly how they are related to the questions.

3. Write a note back to the principal. From the information you have used and the experiences you have had, discuss the principles and concepts that you want to use to guide your planning. Draw implications from your discussion and suggest some concrete ideas if they emerge from your thinking.

Feedback

You may want to use this final feedback to evaluate the materials for the teaching process, as well as all your inquiries taken together. First examine your inquiry into the last content area. Then you may want to compare your reactions now to ways you responded earlier.

Rate the general usefulness of the resources you have used in your inquiry into the teaching process. Leave blank the selections you did not read. Use the following ratings:

1 = not very useful
2 = moderately useful
3 = very useful

_____ Allender, "New Conceptions of the Role of the Teacher"
_____ Biber and Minuchin, "The Changing School"
_____ Wolfson, "Pupil and Teacher Roles in Individualized Instruction"
_____ Kohl, "Excerpt from 36 Children"
_____ Thelen, "Some Classroom Quiddities for People-Oriented Teachers"
_____ Jackson, "Excerpt from The Teacher and the Machine"
_____ Holt, "The Wholeness of Learning"
_____ Rogers, "The Facilitation of Significant Learning"
_____ Allender and Allender, "I Am the Mayor: Inquiry Materials for the Study of City Government"
_____ Flanders, "Intent, Action and Feedback: A Preparation for Teaching"

Rate your interest and involvement in this content area by circling your response. Place a check over your response for the course as a whole.

1	2	3	4	5	6	7	8	9
Low								High

Rate how much you learned during this content area by circling the appropriate number. Place a check above your learnings for the course as a whole.

1	2	3	4	5	6	7	8	9
Little								A lot

Describe any insight you have gained as a result of your inquiries.

Describe any matter about which you are greatly confused.

What aspects of your inquiries do you think you will find helpful in preparing for your own classes in the future?